Thoughts on War

Thoughts on War

Phillip S. Meilinger

UNIVERSITY PRESS OF KENTUCKY

Scholarly publisher for the Commonwealth,
serving Bellarmine University, Berea College, Centre
College of Kentucky, Eastern Kentucky University,
The Filson Historical Society, Georgetown College,
Kentucky Historical Society, Kentucky State University,
Morehead State University, Murray State University,
Northern Kentucky University, Transylvania University,
University of Kentucky, University of Louisville,
and Western Kentucky University.

Editorial and Sales Offices: The University Press of Kentucky
663 South Limestone Street, Lexington, Kentucky 40508–4008

www.kentuckypress.com

Library of Congress Cataloging-in-Publication Data

Names: Meilinger, Phillip S., 1948- author.
Title: Thoughts on war / Phillip S. Meilinger.
Description: Lexington, Kentucky : University Press of Kentucky, [2019] | Includes bibliographical references and index.
Identifiers: LCCN 2019049818 | ISBN 9780813178899 (hardcover) | ISBN 9780813178912 (pdf) | ISBN 9780813178929 (epub)
Subjects: LCSH: War--History. | Military history, Modern. | United States--History, Military. | United States--History, Military--21st century.
Classification: LCC U21.2 .M45 2019 | DDC 355.02--dc23
LC record available at https://lccn.loc.gov/2019049818

This book is printed on acid-free paper meeting
the requirements of the American National Standard
for Permanence in Paper for Printed Library Materials.

Manufactured in the United States of America

Member of the Association
of University Presses

*To Marc, Dianna and Rod, Phil and Monica,
Erin and Samantha, and Rebecca*

Contents

List of Abbreviations viii
Introduction 1

Part I. Theories of War

1. Busting the Icon: Restoring Balance to the Influence of Clausewitz 11
2. Is War an Instrument of Policy? 29
3. The Mutable Nature of War 41
4. Starting with a Blank Sheet: Principles of War for a New Century 49

Part II. War Through the Ages

5. Second Fronts: Success, Failure, and Implications 67
6. Decisive Victories and What They Mean 87
7. Time in War 102
8. Jointness and the Norwegian Campaign, 1940 114

Part III. American Military Experiences

9. American Military Culture and Its Influence on Strategy 127
10. Soldiers and Politics: Exposing a Myth 141
11. Unity of Command in the Pacific during World War II 159
12. Analysis, Intelligence, and Targeting in Strategic Air Operations 167
13. Determining the Effects of the Allied Air Offensive 186
14. Summation: The Emergence of a Paradigm 208

Notes 227
Bibliography 271
Index 291

Abbreviations

AAA	Antiaircraft Artillery
AAF	(US) Army Air Forces
ACTS	Air Corps Tactical School
AFB	Air Force Base
BBSU	British Bombing Survey Unit
C2	Command and Control
CCS	Combined Chiefs of Staff
CENTCOM	(US) Central Command
COA	Committee of Operations Analysts
DRV	Democratic Republic of Vietnam (North)
EOU	Enemy Objectives Unit
GAO	Government Accountability Office
GPS	Global Positioning System
HMSO	His/Her Majesty's Stationery Office
IBC	Iraq Body Count
ISIS	Islamic State of Iraq and Syria
JCS	Joint Chiefs of Staff
JDAM	Joint Direct Attack Munition
MEW	Ministry of Economic Warfare
OEF	Operation Enduring Freedom (Afghanistan)
OIF	Operation Iraqi Freedom
OODA (Loop)	Observe, Orient, Decide, Act
OR	Operations Research
PGM	Precision Guided Munition
RAF	Royal Air Force
SAC	Strategic Air Command
SAM	Surface to Air Missile
SOF	Special Operations Forces

UAV	Unmanned Air Vehicle
USSBS	United States Strategic Bombing Survey
USSTAF	United States Strategic Air Forces
WMD	Weapons of Mass Destruction

Introduction

ALTHOUGH MOST OF MY publications have concerned aviation theory, doctrine, and practice, the bulk of my academic career was spent teaching the broader area of military history. This forced me to see airpower in context over time and place, and also led me to issues I ordinarily might have missed, such as the definition of decisive victories or the nature and purpose of second front operations. I wrote and published a number of essays dealing with war over the centuries. In most cases, time and space constraints limited my ability to fully explore a subject; the papers in this collection therefore tend to be longer, more detailed, and better sourced than accounts formerly published. Other essays have not been printed previously.

Putting these essays together, a pattern became apparent. Starting with the Napoleonic wars, a mind-set took root that such wars and strategies were the harbingers of the future. The Prussian soldier and theorist Carl von Clausewitz participated in those wars and drew from them overarching and, to him, timeless lessons. In my view, the result was unfortunate. Clausewitz emphasized the necessity of decisive and usually bloody battles to defeat an enemy. He wrote mostly of wars he termed "absolute" and, though mentioning lesser types of war, his focus was on major conflicts that utilized the full resources of the state—and it was the state that interested him, not nonstate actors or guerrillas.

Post–World War II, wars involving massive land forces reliant on major battles have become less relevant to our geopolitical situation. The essays that follow dealing with principles of war, decisiveness, the importance of culture on strategy, timing, various campaigns throughout history, and others all convinced me that warfare is fundamentally changing. This should not be surprising. Over the past two millennia warfare has been cyclical in nature—limited wars gave way to more total wars that in turn led back to a cooling-off period of more limited conflict. We in the West are now in a period when our national interests are seldom at stake; instead, we fight to overthrow inhumane dictators, reverse aggression, and, to be honest, to shape the world so that it more clearly represents our ideals and interests.

In a world dominated by wars of choice rather than necessity, it is essential for the United States to maintain popular support both at home and abroad. This in turn requires lowering risks and costs—both monetary and human—to achieve the compassionate goals of our interventions. Experience over the past several decades has shown that a large commitment of conventional land forces involves high risk and high cost, which makes it increasingly difficult to achieve our goals while simultaneously holding the support of the people. The wars in Korea and Vietnam were omens, and the seemingly endless conflicts in the Middle East have shown that another method of using force must be discovered. The old model, stretching back to the sanguinary engagements urged by Clausewitz, is no longer viable.

These essays show that a new paradigm of war has emerged, offering a better chance of achieving political goals, while doing so with less risk and cost. The increasing effectiveness of airpower, both land- and sea-based, combined with special operations forces and *indigenous* ground forces, is a more logical model. Too often the United States has barged into conflicts far from our shores and dominated strategy and tactics to fight the kind of wars with which we were most familiar and not the type of wars that confronted us. We emphasized big forces, big firepower, and big technology. Seldom have such notions worked out well.

A new strategy, more attuned to the cultural situations we encounter on other continents, is now necessary. That is the book's theme that the constituent essays build toward.

* * *

The first part of the collection deals with military theory, focusing on the writings of Carl von Clausewitz. I am leery of his influence on military officers and noticed this predilection while teaching at the Air University, the Naval War College, and the Army War College. One faculty member had spent most of his academic life teaching Clausewitz and would brook no contrary word.

Whatever the occasion, he had a quote from *On War* to bolster his argument. The result was a skewed interpretation of what Clausewitz was attempting to inform, and this tended to push students into a group-think mentality. Some people, in and out of uniform, take their Clausewitz very seriously, so I have tried to restore a balance. I looked at what Clausewitz wrote, but also what military leaders and civilian pundits thought he *meant*. An earlier version was published in *Strategic Studies Quarterly* (September 2007). Comments from colleagues and additional thought led to the result printed here.

I was criticized for giving insufficient coverage to Clausewitz's dictum that "war is an instrument of policy." But when exploring what that famous one-liner actually meant, I received differing replies and eventually decided that Clausewitz's time-honored injunction was flawed—it sounded lofty and sage, but when reduced to its essence it actually said very little to guide civilian or military leaders. Clearly, nations do not always go to war for reasons of policy; rather, sometimes it is waged for cultural reasons, such as pride, honor, fear, revenge, love, hate, or prestige.

The third paper was written after listening to several ground officers and historians argue that the nature of war was unchanging and immutable. One stated that war as experienced by an ancient Greek hoplite was the same as for any soldier today in Iraq or Afghanistan. That statement bears examination. Such attitudes are almost always expressed by those who know only of land warfare—which they equate to war in general. For sailors, aviators, space, or cyber warfare practitioners, the experience of war is fundamentally different, especially today. New methods, but also old ones too often ignored, clearly demonstrate that war is indeed mutable. A version of this piece appeared in the winter 2010 edition of *Air and Space Power Journal*.

This first section concludes by addressing the practice of deducing principles of war. Such principles, and the mental effort to articulate them, are important. During a crisis when time is short and there are many demands on our attention, we must simplify and extract general rules from conflicting data points. Principles of war have been espoused for centuries, but the urge to codify such rules took on added impetus in the twentieth century. Today, such principles are considered invaluable learning tools at military schools. Yet, it is time for an update, because those used today were devised a century ago by a soldier who had little or no insight into warfare at sea or in the air. His precepts have survived, largely intact, until the present day. The result has been a distorted view of war. My intent is to begin anew—not to reshape the earlier principles, but to look at modern war and devise new ones that govern the new environment. This essay began as a lecture to British staff officers.

The second part of the book looks at military operations over the past two millennia. While teaching at the Naval War College, we often discussed what were termed "peripheral operations." I did not like the term because it connoted *secondary* military operations, but some of these campaigns were major actions employing large numbers of troops. Indeed, such maneuvers were often termed "the British way of war." I prefer "second front operations" to describe assaults occurring outside the main theater and note four such campaigns—two were successful and two were not. My intent is to address why such operations were launched, and then to draw lessons to guide future strategists. A version of this essay appeared in the July 2013 issue of *Joint Force Quarterly.*

Decisive victory was another subject that caught my attention while at the Naval War College, where we would ask students to list Napoleon's decisive victories. The term "decisive" is overused. The number of such battles is few—too often we refer to those of only tactical or transient significance. The first step therefore was to define decisive, and the key was to identify victories having long-term significance. This essay was originally published in *Joint Force Quarterly* in the spring of 2011 and won its award as the best Recall Article of the Year.

Years ago I became intrigued by the use of time in war—great commanders understood the critical nature of time on the battlefield. It fits here by reflecting a major factor in war that has long been recognized but seldom achieved. The notion of how to telescope time was a quest for greater speed and of achieving physical and psychological surprise and shock. In modern terms, these were force multipliers. It also appears that conquering time is best suited to the rapidity, flexibility, and omniscience of air and space power, and therefore leads to the future of war. This essay first appeared in *Joint Force Quarterly,* winter 2017.

The final essay in Part II looks at the first major confrontation between Germany and the Allies in World War II. Although poised along the Western Front since September 1939, serious fighting did not break out there; instead, the belligerents first fought in the far north. Germany had sound strategic reasons for conquering Norway, but the Allies attacked them there simply because they did not wish to fight in France. Important lessons were learned in Norway by both sides regarding joint operations, unity of command, and airpower. This essay was first published in *Air and Space Power Journal* in the spring of 2017.

Part III looks at the American military experience. The first essay reviews US military culture and how each service has a different tradition and ethos. These differences affect how soldiers, sailors, and airmen view war, and how they plan to fight. This subject has fascinated me ever since I served in the Pentagon. That was my first close contact with the other services, and I was surprised how often we would disagree on fundamental concepts of military organization, doctrine, and the use of force. These deeply held differences of opinion were shaped by unique service cultures that have had a profound effect on American military strategy. The advent of "jointness" was an attempt to correct the short-sighted parochialism of previous generations. A condensed version of this chapter appeared in *Joint Force Quarterly,* July 2007.

The second essay examines the American military tradition. When discussing this tradition, writers usually state that the US military has always been divorced from political affairs. My research reveals the opposite; the military has often played a major role in domestic politics, and for most of our history that role was considered normal and healthy. Reading into nineteenth-century American affairs, I was surprised to hear of serving generals who dabbled in politics and who actually ran for political office while still in uniform! Yet, such events are passed over lightly by historians, and many still write of an American military tradition stressing the noninvolvement of the military in politics throughout our history. That is a misreading of events, but the situation did change in the aftermath of World War II, especially around the Vietnam War. An earlier version of this essay appeared in the summer 2010 issue of *Parameters.*

The piece on unity of command in the Pacific theater during World War II—or what some would consider its lack—grew out of an inter-service squabble that went too far. Soldiers, sailors, airmen, and marines have strong opinions on how the Pacific War was fought and how victory was achieved over Japan. Too often these views have been shaped by service parochialism dressed up in the guise of war principles. Regarding the issue of unity of command, there was actually more unity in the Pacific theater than there was in Europe. As for strategy, the issue usually breaks into three camps based on the color of one's uniform or their academic specialty: sailors and sea power advocates trumpet the importance of the Central Pacific thrust commanded by Admiral Chester Nimitz—as well as the strangling submarine campaign against Japanese shipping. Soldiers and land warfare historians instead hail General Douglas MacArthur's island-hopping campaign in the Southwest Pacific Area.

Airmen applaud the strategic bombing campaign culminating in the atomic bombs. This argument always left me a bit cold. It was obviously a joint effort by all the services that defeated Japan. An earlier version of this article appeared in *Joint Force Quarterly* in January 2010 and was chosen as the best Recall Article of the Year.

The next two essays deal specifically with airpower. The first recounts the history of Operations Research, intelligence, and their effects on the strategic bombing campaigns of World War II and beyond. Airmen use different weapons employed against different targets to achieve different results than do soldiers or sailors. These necessary differences—the result of the mediums in which they operate—are characterized by airmen's attempts to most effectively and efficiently injure Nazi Germany and Japan. Few situations better illustrate how the services employ different prisms through which to view war, which in turn shapes their strategic thought. Airmen confronted questions on what targets should be struck and how this could be done most effectively. Operations Research was established as a scientific discipline to address these types of questions. Unfortunately, neither the intelligence apparatus nor the technology necessary to measure the effects of air attacks were available, nor was the analytical framework then in place to allow proper measurement. These breakthroughs did not occur until the 1990s.

The next essay deals with the massive report chartered by President Franklin Roosevelt in 1944 to measure the effects of strategic bombing on Germany and Japan—the US Strategic Bombing Survey (USSBS, pronounced *us bus*). Ascertaining the effects of air strikes was critical, and airmen took steps to ensure that data would be amassed and analyzed to determine if the strategic bombing campaign was successful and worth the effort. USSBS went about its detailed examination of the evidence in both Europe and the Pacific, and its answers were fairly clear-cut, as detailed in the statistical findings. I have delved into the survey's finding often over the years and liberally used the facts, quotes, graphs, and tables. This is the first time I closely examined the bulk of the surveys and digested what they actually said. It's a terrific story.

The final chapter is an overview of the entire book, which leads in my opinion to a new paradigm of war. Starting with a past overemphasis on bloody battle inherited from Clausewitz, it then proceeds through discussions of various methods to avoid such battles, to capitalize on speed and surprise, to reflect individual service and national cultures, and to capitalize on new technologies and doctrines. These varied factors suggest alternatives that emphasize the importance of speed, surprise, precision, and the limitation of risk.

A host of people have influenced my views over the years, but I would especially like to thank editor Derik Shelor, Paul Springer, John Andreas Olsen, Bill Eliason, Jack English, Chuck Thomas, Marv Butcher, Andy Petruska, Alan Stephens, Dave Deptula, Seb Cox, Tony Mason, and several anonymous manuscript reviewers. Thank you. Any errors are my own.

I also want to give a special thanks to my son, Phil Meilinger Jr., for creating the map of the World War II theater boundaries, and for reproducing charts from the Strategic Bombing Surveys for chapter 13. He also designed the dramatic cover for this book. He is a master. The sculpture on the cover depicts Menelaus, the King of Sparta and husband to Helen of Troy. He launched the most famous war of antiquity not for reasons of policy, but for motives of revenge, love, hate, and prestige.

Part I
Theories of War

1

Busting the Icon

Restoring Balance to the Influence of Clausewitz

MANY US MILITARY THINKERS and practitioners have embraced a view of war that is out of touch with current circumstances and consequently dangerous. This has a direct effect on the war against Islamic jihadists. There are two main problems: first, too many view war as a bloody clash of arms. For them, battles and occupation of territory are favored strategies, but recent operations have shown this to be ineffective. Second, American military leaders also do not sufficiently take into account the distinct traditions, behaviors, and beliefs of other peoples. The root of this myopia is the infatuation with the ground and Euro-centric ideas of Carl von Clausewitz.

* * *

Carl von Clausewitz was a Prussian general who fought in the Napoleonic wars two centuries ago. Afterward, he was director of the Prussian War Academy, where he wrote a number of historical and theoretical books.[1] He is an icon among military officers, and *On War* is taught in war colleges and service academies worldwide.

Clausewitz stressed the importance of psychological factors in war. He had just witnessed nationalistic wars and an outpouring of passion that had not been seen in Europe for generations. War had become a contest between peoples, not just princes. To help explain this phenomenon he used the metaphor of a trinity—society (passion or "natural force"), the military (chance and probabilities), and a country's government (reason). These three factors were in constant interaction during the course of a war. It was necessary for a state to keep this trinity in equilibrium.[2] Finally, Clausewitz stressed the importance of focusing one's energy. There were many things a commander could do when beginning a campaign, but he first had to think through the process of cause and effect: political objectives led to a military strategy, which in turn led to specific goals/tasks/targets to be affected, struck, or neutralized.

These ideas were not necessarily new, but Clausewitz was seminal because he was the first to examine them at length in his writings. Still, *On War* is a difficult read, partly because it has come down to us as a work in progress. Only the first chapter of the first book (there are 125 chapters comprising eight books) did Clausewitz consider complete.

The unusual style in which he wrote compounds the confusion. Clausewitz began with a paradigm of ideal war that tends to move toward the absolute, what today we term total war. After describing this paradigm, he then uses what has been called a dialectic approach—he contrasts ideal war to that actually occurring in practice. "Real war" is moderated by political goals, resources, chance, and friction that affect war as it unfolds. Yet, the wars shaping Clausewitz's views were those of the Napoleonic era, which were as close to total as Europe had seen in two centuries, and he admitted that warfare "had assumed the absolute state under Bonaparte."[3] In short, during his era "real war" was close to "absolute war"—reality and theory converged. As a result, the historical examples used in *On War* usually relate to those "absolute wars."[4] This is significant because today's wars are far from absolute—at least from our standpoint—so we must question the relevance of some of the Prussian's assertions.

The unusual dialectic approach used in *On War* means that the opening pages must be approached warily. Clausewitz's first chapter contains some of his most pithy and quotable lines: "war is thus an act of force to compel our enemy to do our will," "in war the result is never final," "defense is a stronger form of fighting than attack," and "war is a pulsation of violence." The temptation to seize on these polished and readable pages without absorbing the rest of the book has caused no end of confusion.

Worse, in notes written before his death, Clausewitz confessed that he had come to view his work in a new light. He believed two themes *that he had largely overlooked until then* should now dominate *On War*. The first concerned what has been labeled the "dual nature" of war—some wars are fought "to overthrow the enemy" while others seek a more limited goal. He wanted to distinguish between the near-absolute wars of his own era and the limited wars that had been the norm for the previous two centuries. The second new theme to be stressed was the inherently political nature of war. Clausewitz wrote that he had introduced these two themes in Book I, chapter 1, and had sketched them out in the concluding Book VIII, but *he would need to rewrite virtually everything* (except presumably the first chapter) to explain fully these two new foci.[5] He apparently did not intend to nullify what he had already written, but rather to elaborate on some points.[6] It also appears Clausewitz intended that there be a Book IX—presumably concerning absolute war—which was never written, even in draft.[7]

He died before completing those revisions. Nonetheless, one year later his widow published the unfinished manuscript. Marie von Clausewitz believed her husband's work should be printed, despite its unfinished status. Still, she made changes to ensure a more acceptable reception, and thus "muffled" criticisms of Prussia's King Frederick Wilhelm.[8] That most of *On War* is a rough draft helps explain its contradictions and redundancies—as well as that the two new themes to be stressed are largely missing.[9] The result of these omissions has been for readers to *imagine* what Clausewitz would have written had he been given the chance. Antulio Echevarria warns readers "to resist the temptation to finish it, to rewrite the famous opus according to the values of liberal democracy. At the same time, we must refrain from erasing what revisions its author did make, and allow *On War* to be no less than what it is, even in its unfinished state."[10]

Clausewitz's prose has also made translation difficult. The several English translations of *On War* appearing over the past 150 years read differently. Which captures the real intent? Moreover, there is doubt as to the actual wording of Clausewitz's manuscript. Michael Howard and Peter Paret state that German editors in the 1850s introduced "several hundred alterations of the text" to the 1832 manuscript—which itself was riddled with "obscurities perhaps inevitable in the posthumous publication of so large and complex a work by a devoted but inexpert widow."[11] To resolve these difficulties, Howard and Paret took an approach that should give the reader pause: "We have based our work on the first edition of 1832, supplemented by the annotated German text published by Professor Werner Hahlweg in 1952, except where obscurities in the original edition—which Clausewitz himself never reviewed—made it seem advisable to accept later emendations."[12]

In other words, much of this is not the work of Clausewitz at all! Unfortunately, his handwritten manuscript disappeared long ago, so we cannot compare it with current variants. The result is a degree of confusion as to what it is, precisely, Clausewitz was trying to tell us two centuries ago. There is of course even more debate and confusion regarding what Clausewitz actually *meant*.[13]

Other concerns should trouble us. Nearly half of *On War* is now of little use. Most of Books V, VI, and VII (over half the work) deal with tactical maneuvers and topics such as organization, marches, camps, and defending mountain passes or swamps, subjects of minor importance today.

There are also major gaps in his discussion—his neglect of technology, sea power, and a disdain for intelligence.

The omission of technology is almost understandable, for the Napoleonic wars in which he participated were virtually devoid of technological advances. Armies of his era were little different in their weapons and equipment from those of Frederick the Great fifty years earlier. In fact, the Napoleonic era was unique in that it epitomized a Revolution in Military Affairs (to use the modern term) that did *not* include rapid technological change as one of its components.[14] Even so, Clausewitz was a historian, and he well knew of instances where technology had altered the course of war and strategy in centuries past; he should not have ignored this topic.

Clausewitz's neglect of sea power is even less excusable. The Royal Navy and its dominance of the seas had a major effect on Napoleon's empire and strategy. Clausewitz knew that. More importantly, in his extended study of war strategy it is remarkable he would not discuss a form of war so different from war on land regarding its nature, objectives, and methods. As Julian Corbett wrote in 1911, "The object of naval warfare is the control of communications, and not, as in land warfare, the conquest of territory. The difference is fundamental."[15] During World War II, for example, around 90 percent of the time submarines attacked merchant ships, not warships. In short, navies do not attack an enemy's strong point; they attack its weakest.[16] Clausewitz's focus on land warfare has led to a distorted view of strategy that impacts current military operations.

Clausewitz rejected the importance of military intelligence: "all information and assumptions are open to doubt."[17] This disregard for intelligence is usually passed off as being a simple anachronism that is inconsequential. The role of intelligence in war is most certainly not inconsequential, so this too is a major shortcoming. Even so, there are other criticisms more fundamental.

* * *

In the aftermath of World War I, Basil H. Liddell Hart in Britain was critical of what he saw as Clausewitz's baleful influence and referred to him as the "Mahdi of mass and mutual massacre" whose belief in the necessity of slaughter led to the hecatomb of the Great War.[18] Others agreed with Liddell Hart in that it was standard among historians and theorists to interpret Clausewitz as advocating climactic and bloody battles.[19] It is not hard to see why readers have taken this interpretation. In Book IV ("The Engagement") Clausewitz lists five "unequivocal statements" regarding war:

- Destruction of the enemy forces is the overriding principle of war, and, so far as positive action is concerned, the principal way to achieve our object.
- Such destruction of forces can *usually* [emphasis in original] be accomplished only by fighting.
- Only major engagements involving all forces lead to major success.
- The greatest successes are obtained where all engagements coalesce into one great battle.
- Only in a great battle does the commander-in-chief control operations in person; it is only natural that he should prefer to entrust the direction of the battle to himself.[20]

These are dogmatic, "unequivocal" statements, and the only hint of moderation is the word "usually" in statement two, and note that that statement contradicts number three, which uses the word "only." Moreover, a few paragraphs later, when discussing the unusual situation where victory can be achieved without the destruction of the enemy army, he treats it with disdain. Clausewitz writes that commanders who try to achieve victory without battle are pursuing "nonsense." Rather, "only great victories have paved the way for great results," and he is "not interested in generals who win victories without bloodshed"; rather, he lauds those who "seek to crown their achievements by risking everything in decisive battle." Clausewitz concluded by stressing the "absolute necessity" of fighting a great battle. Also note that in Book I, chapter 1—the only chapter Clausewitz considered finished—he repeats with disgust his warning that "kind-hearted people may think there is some ingenious way to disarm or defeat an enemy without too much bloodshed . . . [but] it is a fallacy that must be exposed."[21] A recent analyst confirms this focus, writing that the Prussian's ideas were "combat centric" and "if we were to remove fighting or violence from Clausewitz's system, it would collapse. Moreover, his other concepts, such as friction, danger, and uncertainty, would lose their significance."[22] This is a telling insight.

Yet, Clausewitz does suggest an interesting idea, that it is possible for some operations to have "direct political repercussions" that may disrupt or paralyze an alliance or favorably affect the political scene.[23] He gives no examples of such operations, however, implying that war is so unpredictable that any manner of unusual things may occur, but when settling down to the serious business of instructing his readers on how to actually *conduct* war, such aberrations are not even worthy of discussion. Clausewitz insisted that policy drove military operations, but although making allusions to such political factors and objectives, he gave no examples; meanwhile, his book is full of historical precedents to support other contentions. Clausewitz did mention capturing territory, a prominent hill, or the enemy capital, but then noted that the intent of such actions was merely to put oneself in a better position to destroy the enemy army. Similarly, the best way to split an alliance was to destroy the army of one member, forcing it out of the war.[24] The focus remained on major battle.

Also understand that Clausewitz held strong views on violence long before writing *On War*. While at the War Academy, he was appointed military instructor to the Prussian crown prince, then fifteen, and in 1812 wrote him a handbook, "The Most Important Principles for the Conduct of War." This overlooked work is not a theoretical treatise. Rather, it is a document prepared specifically for the crown prince as a guide should he need to wage war upon ascending the throne. Clausewitz saw this handbook as a practical guide to be used by his monarch.

We see here the same emphasis on decisive battle that would later permeate *On War*. Clausewitz instructed the future William I that the object of war was to gain a preponderance of physical force at the decisive point. This point was the enemy army: "The most important thing in war will always be the art of defeating our opponent in combat."[25] Audacity and an offensive spirit were crucial: "For great aims we must dare great things." He stressed that concentrating on the enemy army and attacking it decisively were essential. The most important principle of war was "to conquer and destroy the armed power of the enemy."[26] Clausewitz acknowledged the importance of public opinion but argued only two things would sway it: "great victories and the occupation of the enemy's capital." He continued that "battle decides everything" and once again advised his prince to be audacious and cunning, firm and persevering, and "a shining glory" will "crown his youthful brow."[27] It must be reemphasized that this work was not written as a theoretical think-piece but as a practical guide for his future sovereign regarding how he should wage war.

Although Clausewitz apparently intended to emphasize the "dual nature" of war in a revision of *On War*, he seemed to be referring to objectives. In other words, some wars are fought for limited goals, such as Frederick II's First Silesian War of 1740. As for the means used, limited wars might involve a lesser degree of resources, but they should still be directed toward a single purpose: to engage and destroy the enemy army. The more total and bloody the climactic battle would be, the quicker the war would be over, the easier would be the resulting occupation of enemy territory, and the more decisive would be the result. Battle must be "a fight to the finish." As Clausewitz phrased it: "Our discussion has shown that while in war many different roads can lead to the goal, to the attainment of the political objective, fighting is the only possible means. Everything is governed by a supreme law, the *decision by force of arms*."[28]

Perhaps Clausewitz would have introduced a degree of moderation in later revisions, but the version of *On War* we now possess shows no such ambiguity.

Noted below are twenty statements in *On War* regarding the necessity of decisive and violent battle. (The emphasis is in the original in all cases, and the page numbers are from the Howard and Paret translation.)

- "It follows, then, that to overcome the enemy, or disarm him—call it what you will—must always be the aim of warfare" (77).
- "The fighting forces must be *destroyed*: that is, they must be *put in such a condition that they can no longer carry on the fight*" (90).
- "If we wish to gain total victory, then the destruction of his armed forces is the most appropriate action and the occupation of his territory only a consequence" (92).
- "Since in the engagement everything is concentrated on the destruction of the enemy, or rather of *his armed forces*, which is inherent in its very concept, it follows that the destruction of the enemy's forces is always the means by which the purpose of the engagement is achieved" (95).
- "It follows that the destruction of the enemy's force underlies all military actions; all plans are ultimately based on it, resting on it like an arch on its abutment" (97).
- "Thus it is evident that destruction of the enemy forces is always the superior, more effective means, with which others cannot compete" (97).
- "To sum up: of all the possible aims in war, the destruction of the enemy's armed forces always appears as the highest" (99).

- "What do we mean by the defeat of the enemy? Simply the destruction of his forces, whether by death, injury, or any other means—either completely or enough to make him stop fighting" (227).
- "We do claim, however, that direct annihilation of the enemy's forces must always be the *dominant consideration*. We simply want to establish this dominance of the destructive principle" (228).
- "Later, we will show how we shall apply the principle that the destruction of enemy forces must be regarded as the main objective; not just in the war generally, but in each individual engagement and within all the different conditions necessitated by the circumstances out of which the war has arisen" (229).
- "In the previous chapter we defined the purpose of the engagement as being the destruction of the enemy. We have tried to prove this to be true in the majority of cases and in major actions, since the destruction of the enemy's forces must always be the dominant consideration in war" (230).
- "The destruction of the enemy's forces is admittedly the purpose of all engagements" (236).
- "But since the essence of war is fighting, and since the battle is the fight of the main force, the battle must always be considered as the true center of gravity of the war. All in all, therefore, its distinguishing feature is that, more than any other type of action, battle exists for its own sake alone" (248).
- "The major battle is therefore to be regarded as concentrated war, as the center of gravity of the entire conflict or campaign" (258).
- "Battle is the bloodiest solution . . . it is always true that the character of battle, like its name, is slaughter [schlact], and its price is blood" (259).
- "Even if a battle were not the primary, the most common, the most effective means of reaching a decision (as we think we have already shown more than once) the mere fact that it is one of the means of obtaining a decision should be enough to call for the *utmost possible concentration of strength* permissible under the circumstances" (489).
- "In war, the subjugation of the enemy is the end, and the destruction of his fighting forces the means. That applies to attack and defense alike" (526).
- "We ended up with the conclusion that the grand objective of all mil-

itary action is to overthrow the enemy—which means destroying his armed forces" (577).

- "Basing our comments on general experience, the acts we consider most important for the defeat of the enemy are the following: 1. Destruction of his army, if it is at all significant" (596).
- "Whatever the final act may turn on in any given case, the beginning is invariably the same—annihilation of the enemy's armed forces, which implies a major victory and their actual destruction. The earlier this victory can be sought—that is, the nearer to our frontiers—the *easier* it will be" (624).

Given the relentless hammering of this point throughout *On War,* it is small wonder that generals like Ferdinand Foch and Erich Ludendorff—who professed to be disciples of Clausewitz—took their intellectual mentor at his word and during the Great War strove to achieve the "slaughter" he thought essential, and that "the name of Clausewitz became associated in the popular mind with battle and blood."[29] Liddell Hart's antipathy toward Clausewitz thus becomes understandable. Today it is common to dismiss the British thinker as having been so overcome by the horrors of World War I that he simply misunderstood the true meaning of Clausewitz.[30] That is possible, as it is also possible Foch and Ludendorff similarly misunderstood him.

Indeed, commentators have listed a host of individuals who allegedly misread or misunderstood Clausewitz. German military historian Hans Delbrück argued that virtually the entire German General Staff from von Moltke through World War I had tragically misinterpreted Clausewitz regarding the necessity of a bloody and violent battle.[31] Others have echoed Delbrück's verdict regarding the German officer corps as well as condemning others, such as Antoine-Henri Jomini, Douglas Haig, Ludwick Beck, Hans von Seeckt, Klaus Reinhardt, Douglas MacArthur, Dwight Eisenhower, Maxwell Taylor, and William Westmoreland—as well as military thinkers and historians like G.F.R. Henderson, V. I. Lenin, T. E. Lawrence, J.F.C. Fuller, B. H. Liddell Hart, Hoffman Nickerson, Edward Luttwak, Raymond Aron, Peter Paret, Russell Weigley, Martin Van Creveld, John Keegan, Michael Handel, Stephen Cimbala, Christopher Coker, G. F. Freudenberg, and Joseph I. Greene.[32] One analyst bluntly dismisses all those who disagree with his interpretation of Clausewitz as "second-rate soldiers and third-rate intellectuals."[33] However, another scholar admits that *On War* is "virtually impossible" to comprehend because of faulty preconceptions, ignorance of historical context, the sophistication of Clausewitz's philosophical reasoning, and the complexity and difficulty of his exposition. The author then offers to "decode" *On War,* enabling him "to clarify much that has mystified general readers, military professionals, and even expert scholars." He argues that "accurate comprehension of Clausewitz's treatise has . . . escaped all authoritative commentators"—until now.[34] Others have used Clausewitz to explain mistakes in war.

Colonel Harry Summers—then on staff at the Army War College—viewed the Vietnam War through a Clausewitzian perspective and argued that President Lyndon Johnson, Congress, and military leaders were at fault for not recognizing the true nature of the war. To Summers, it was a conventional war; the misinformed thought it was about guerrillas and counterinsurgency—the "fashionable" notion among the elites at the time. To Summers, the insurgency was merely a "smokescreen"; the *cause* of the problem resided in Hanoi. He contended that the United States should have focused on the source and fought a conventional war against the North Vietnamese—invade Laos, Cambodia, and North Vietnam—and fight the decisive Clausewitzian battle prescribed in *On War.* As for the Chinese, Summers argued they were never a threat; rather, we were "bluffed by the Chinese throughout most of the war" into thinking they would intervene (as in Korea) if we moved north.[35] He also argued the United States should have declared war on North Vietnam and mobilized the reserves so as to energize the American population. Without such moves, the "passion" required to balance the Clausewitzian trinity was missing.[36] Johnson, his civilian whiz kid advisers, Congress, Westmoreland, and the joint chiefs had not read their Clausewitz.

Taken together, these accusations seem hubristic. We are to believe that generations of men, many with a lifetime of military experience who had commanded great armies in great battles—often successfully—all misinterpreted Clausewitz. Is it credible to assert they were all intellectually incapable of understanding him? Is it even more presumptuous to believe that academics and military officers today have succeeded in solving his mysteries when so many others before them have allegedly failed?[37]

Another interpretation is that Clausewitz meant what he said regarding the primacy of slaughter in war, so von Moltke, Foch, Ludendorff, Liddell Hart, Westmoreland, and dozens of others interpreted Clausewitz correctly, and it is modern theorists who misunderstand. To Clausewitz decisive battles were the crux of war. He had lived through the Napoleonic wars and written of them at length. Fighting major battles made that era different from what had preceded it, which is why Clausewitz emphasized it. In his introduction to *On War,* Michael Howard summed up the issue: "no one who experienced Napoleonic warfare could have quarreled with his [Clausewitz] statement 'the character of battle is slaughter.'"[38] Another observer concluded: "The emphasis on decisive battles continued to characterize not only the German way of war, but also that of the West overall, well into the twentieth century."[39]

But now one must seriously question whether it is necessary or desirable to fight such battles. They are not only dangerous and potentially bloody, but Western societies now require that war be less sanguinary. We must minimize casualties in conflict. General Wesley Clark was told by his political masters that limiting NATO casualties was a major concern during the war against Serbia in 1999—the alliance would not hold if casualties were too high.[40] An increasing US death toll in Iraq corresponded to the fall in popular support among the American people.[41] As for collateral damage, the news media are ever-present where our forces fight, and it will highlight every bomb or artillery shell that falls short and every rifle bullet that kills an innocent bystander—to say nothing of blunders like the prison depredations at Abu Ghraib and the Haditha massacre. Such events can undermine US foreign policy; hence, the emphasis is now placed on limiting collateral damage in our military operations.

* * *

I fear the average American ground officer still believes that the key to war is a major battle, and that such engagements are both necessary and desirable. This bias may cause commanders to reject or overlook strategies not dependent on coming to grips with enemy ground forces in a major fight—was the failed Operation ANACONDA in Afghanistan really necessary? As noted, sailors, marines, and airmen have differing views on how best to defeat an enemy. These service-specific cultural views on war and strategy shape how commanders approach the crucial issue of campaign planning.

Martin Blumenson, a US Army historian of World War II, stated: "According to Clausewitz and common sense, an army in wartime succeeds by defeating the enemy army." Rejecting the "soft underbelly" argument (the "Mediterranean Strategy" advocated by Churchill and his generals), he scored Allied leadership for prolonging the war with diversionary attacks in North Africa, Sicily, and Italy; it should have "gone for the throat" and landed in

France to destroy the main German army.[42] After DESERT STORM the US Army chief of staff stated peremptorily: "Achieving victory against an information-based state will entail destroying that country's armed forces, as well as its war-making capability."[43] The following year he was even more emphatic: "Death and destruction remain the coins of war's realm, and no amount of technology or euphemistic labels will alter their weight. As much as one would like to think that simple solutions are possible, the reality is that wars are messy."[44]

Have these types of pronouncements, inherited from Clausewitz, become dogma? One historian has studied the intellectual development of the US Army following the Civil War and concluded that army leaders were "naturally Clausewitzian," and that after World War II they became "just plain Clausewitzian."[45]

Yet, what if the enemy's center of gravity is defined not as his strength—the army—but as his weakness or vulnerability? What if, as sailors and airmen believe, a country's industrial infrastructure, or economy, or transportation network, or leadership is the key center of gravity? It is quite possible that a soldier, sailor, or airman could look at the same country and disagree on the identity of the main strategic focus—their conclusions drawn as a result of unique service cultures that view war through different prisms.[46] The designation of a different focus would thus shape a campaign's strategy, weapons, force structure, targets, logistics preparations, and even tactics.

For example, US Army Field Manual 1 states boldly: "Offensive operations carry the fight to the enemy by closing with and destroying enemy forces, seizing territory and vital resources, and imposing the commander's will on the enemy. They focus on seizing, retaining, and exploiting the initiative. This active imposition of landpower makes the offense the decisive type of military operation, whether undertaken against irregular forces or the armed forces of a nation state. In addition, the physical presence of land forces and their credible ability to conduct offensive operations enable the unimpeded conduct of stability and reconstruction operations."[47]

This appears much like a paraphrase from *On War* without the now politically incorrect references to violence and slaughter. In US Army Field Manual 3-0, titled "Operations," this belief in the necessity and desirability of close combat is reiterated: "Land combat continues to be the salient feature of conflict. It usually involves destroying or defeating enemy forces or taking land objectives that reduce the enemy's effectiveness or will to fight."[48]

The Marines have a similar view of war. In Fleet Marine Field Manual 1, "Warfighting," they too paraphrase *On War* to educate their troops on the nature of conflict: "The means of war is force, applied in the form of organized violence. It is through the use of violence—or the credible threat of violence, which requires the apparent willingness to use it—that we compel our enemy to do our will. In either event, violence is an essential element of war, and its immediate result is bloodshed, destruction and suffering. While the magnitude of violence may vary with the object and means of war, the violent essence of war will never change. Any study of war that neglects this characteristic is misleading and incomplete."[49]

Such thoughts have been internalized by soldiers and marines. One retired Army officer wrote in an essay titled "In Praise of Attrition" that there should have been more killing in Iraq. Echoing Clausewitz, he too wants to hear nothing of generals who would make war without bloodshed. Instead, he states that the object of war is killing: "There is no substitute for shedding the enemy's blood." He advises commanders to "Focus on killing the enemy. With fires. With maneuver. With sticks and stones and polyunsaturated fats."[50] How many other soldiers similarly desire such bloodshed?

In Korea, Vietnam, DESERT STORM, Bosnia, Kosovo, Afghanistan, and Iraq the theater commanders were almost all ground officers. Was their strategic vision shaped by a dogmatic belief in the necessity for close combat and occupation—a belief inherited from Clausewitz that was expounded in official doctrine, preached in their schools, and echoed in their professional journals?[51] Did Westmoreland, for example, become so intent on destroying the Viet Cong and North Vietnamese Army—to the detriment of using political and economic tools to help win the hearts and minds of the populace—that he shaped his plans to that end, with disastrous results? Army lieutenant colonel Andrew Krepinevich thought so and criticized his superiors for not being more attuned to the political aspects of war that emphasized civil-action programs, which might have achieved objectives without the "body counts" advocated by Westmoreland.[52] Another Army officer has argued that Westmoreland's strategy for the war was actually quite comprehensive and was, in fact, a good strategy. Unfortunately, he concludes, the "grand strategy" of President Johnson and his advisors was fatally flawed, making it impossible for Westmoreland to be successful. He concludes that Westmoreland was "not a bad general, but rather a good general fighting a bad war."[53] The debate continues.

It is significant that in several recent conflicts—Bosnia, Kosovo, Afghanistan, the operations in northern Iraq during 2003, Libya, and Syria—diplomatic considerations forestalled strategies calling for the introduction of sizable numbers of conventional US ground troops. Those in command were therefore forced to improvise. The result was a series of operations proving unusually successful—providing politically desirable results with a remarkably low casualty toll.[54] These campaigns relied primarily on land- and sea-based airpower combined with special operations forces and indigenous ground troops, such as the Northern Alliance in Afghanistan, to achieve success.[55] In the modern era of standoff precision weapons, near-real time command and control, pervasive sensor systems, and dominance in air, sea, and space, alternative strategies are possible and desirable.[56] Conversely, the turmoil and bloodshed in Iraq stability operations after 2003 highlighted the dangers inherent in occupation. In such a situation, the words of another noted strategic thinker, Niccolò Machiavelli, are eerily apposite: "The enmity of a defeated population in its home is more dangerous than its hostility on the battlefront."[57]

It is said that General Eric Shinseki was relieved as Army chief of staff in 2003 because he advocated for more ground troops in Iraq, which was contrary to the Bush administration's views.[58] Afterward, Shinseki supporters lamented that not enough ground troops were in place. Similarly, several retired Army and Marine Corps generals complained that their civilian superiors had not sent in more ground troops—they called for the firing of the "incompetent" secretary of defense.[59] Others have wondered if the opposite was the case.[60] Echoing the words of Machiavelli, they asked if the US presence in Iraq was too large and provocative—and was so from the beginning. Was there a better way to remove Saddam Hussein, disarm the country, and avoid prolonged guerrilla operations than to send in tens of thousands of conventional ground troops?[61] Did a Clausewitzian focus on battle and occupation of territory so permeate the thinking of military leaders that they viewed such strategies as the first choice rather than as a last resort?[62] If so, we have paid a heavy price for such target fixation. Over seventeen years of continuous fighting in the Middle East has taught us that destroying an army and occupying territory do not equal victory and are not the primary objectives of war. This seems especially the case in Islamic countries that resent more than most the presence of foreigners and infidels on their soil.

The conflicts that America has experienced for much of the post–World War II era have involved wars of counterinsurgency not anticipated by Clausewitz. Although he devotes a chapter to "the people in arms," he gives no examples from the most important insurgency of the Napoleonic era—that in Iberia.[63] This is a damning oversight. Such wars are fundamentally different than those which form the focus of his work. In fact, it is clear from his scanty coverage that he viewed such operations with skepticism. He stated that resistance movements must be employed in conjunction with the main army in order to achieve useful results: "*Insurgent actions* are similar in character to all others fought by second-rate troops: they start out full of vigor and enthusiasm, but there is little level-headedness and tenacity in the long run."[64] Obviously, this disdainful description hardly reflects the reality of the Spanish and Portuguese forces or Cossacks that stymied the French, or of the Viet Cong, Taliban, al Qaeda, and ISIS in modern times.[65]

And yet, modern-day students of Clausewitz insist that *On War* teaches us about such wars. In truth, any lessons derived from *On War* regarding revolutionary warfare are largely imagined by hopeful readers.[66]

* * *

Let us also visit Clausewitz's most noted principle: that war is a continuation of politics/policy. Although this issue is examined more thoroughly in the next chapter, it should be noted here that not all cultures agree with this premise.

In *A History of Warfare*, John Keegan argues that, given Clausewitz's experiences in the Napoleonic wars and his Euro-centric world view, he must have intended a narrower definition of "policy"; namely, that war was an affair of states, and that the decision to wage it was based on rational decisions regarding political issues and major state interests.[67] Using this interpretation, Keegan states flatly that Clausewitz was wrong: there were other reasons for war causation, specifically the cultural background and tradition of the belligerents.[68]

Clausewitz argued: "War is no pastime; it is no mere joy in daring and winning, no place for irresponsible enthusiasts."[69] Keegan thought otherwise, noting that numerous peoples in modern times—Cossacks, Samurai, Vikings, American Indians, Janissaries, and Mamlukes—have made war for cultural reasons that to Westerners sound primitive or nonsensical. In such societies war was virtually constant, without beginning or end, it simply continued: war was a way of life. Although Clausewitz correctly recognized that war is the province of passion and emotion, Keegan argued these passions occurred before conflict, and are often the reasons for the war itself and the specific way in which it is conducted.

If we accept Keegan's argument, then Clausewitz's formulation of war being an instrument of policy appears peculiarly "post-Westphalian" and Western European in focus, a focus that usually did not include such motivations as religion, ideology, or culture.[70] Another student of war over the centuries similarly argues that "some societies indulge in warfare for 'autotelic' reasons, that is to say they find it—or certain aspects of it—exciting and pleasurable *in itself*. For them, war is a kind of ritualized game, a pastime, an interesting diversion."[71] In other words, Eric Carlton disagrees fundamentally with the Clausewitzian premise that "war is no pastime."

Many of America's adversaries have been motivated by precisely these types of impulses. To give an example of how this can cause difficulties: In April 2001 a Chinese F-8 jet fighter collided with a US Navy EP-3 patrol plane flying off the Chinese coast in international airspace. The fighter went down and its pilot was killed. The damaged EP-3 landed on the island of Hainan and its crew was imprisoned. The Chinese reacted vociferously, accusing the United States of spying and provocative acts; it stated that the EP-3 deliberately rammed its fighter.[72] The US reaction was shock: the American ambassador labeled the Chinese response "inexplicable and unacceptable." Why was China making an issue of what obviously was an accident prompted by an over-zealous and not very capable Chinese fighter pilot?[73]

It was expected that Chinese politicians would want to avoid confrontation with the United States: they had no desire to disrupt trade relations, to jeopardize their bid to host the 2008 Olympics, or to inflame the Taiwan situation. The military, apparently, had other ideas. The military traditionally wields enormous influence in Chinese affairs, a situation that predates the communist regime. Until recently, the military even played a major role in the country's domestic economy. But the military had been losing ground, and it may have seen the collision as an opportunity to reassert its influence. Was all of this merely about trying to realign the political balance of power within the Chinese hierarchy? Were the generals calling the shots because they were in an internal power struggle with Chinese civilian leaders? If so, how could their actions—risking military confrontation with the United States over a trifle—be considered a rational act of policy?[74] It is not surprising we were confused by the "inexplicable" behavior of Chinese leaders.

There is a cautionary tale here. Not only do other cultures have differing views on what constitutes rational acts of policy, but the role of the military in their societies and the balance between civil and military affairs may be far different than our own—their "trinity" (if it exists at all) operates under laws and formulae we do not understand. We assume the military will be subordinated—physically, ideologically, and legally—to civilian officials. That is how we in the West now do things—to ensure the militarists do not drive the ship of state. Much of the world rejects such a hierarchy.

The problem indicated by the above examples: American leaders have attempted to impose a Clausewitzian framework of a rational, policy-driven strategy on the wars they have fought, but their adversaries have not read the same book. They often have other reasons for waging war—reasons that to us are illogical, unworthy, or inexplicable.[75] As a result, we continually mirror-image. We view war—how and why it occurs and how it should be fought—in ways often having little to do with what our enemies are thinking. We are repeatedly caught by surprise by the "irrational policy decisions" of others. It is little wonder we have been so often stunned by the actions of our enemies, whether they were Japanese, Korean, Chinese, Vietnamese, or jihadists.

* * *

I am not advocating we cease the study of *On War.* When one gets past the excess verbiage, Clausewitz is an intelligent, thoughtful, and insightful writer; more importantly, he is provocative—in that he provokes the mind to think and challenge. For any officer or civilian leader who seeks to understand military operations, that is a valuable attribute. Yet, it is fruitless to seek answers in Clausewitz or to compare others, always unfavorably, to his ideas. Clausewitz should be seen as an intellectual exercise to train the mind and provide insights into the military profession. His discussions of fog and friction, the importance of defining objectives, the need to focus efforts, and the realization that war is primarily a test of wills, are valuable insights. It must always be remembered, however, that *On War,* more so than other books because of the redundancies, omissions, and inconsistencies noted, should never be approached looking for answers. This is not a book of answers; it is a book of questions.

The problem centers on Clausewitz's expounding bloody battle as the essential feature of war, but, somewhat paradoxically, also arguing that the use of force must conform to the rational policy decisions of state leaders. Such interpretations are now inadequate. In fact, it is one of the many contradictions and confusions of Clausewitz that these two ideas are in opposition. After all, can a decision for slaughter ever be construed as a rational act of policy? Which of these two key principles are we to take most seriously?

Mistakes were made in Iraq and Afghanistan, and thus far (in 2019) nearly 7,000 Americans have died for those mistakes, as well as hundreds of thousands of natives. The future has yet to be written, and we have an opportunity to move beyond the narrow vision of war preached by Clausewitz. We must not allow our strategies to be dominated by beliefs regarding the necessity of bloodshed. We cannot afford a war of attrition with terrorists, either physically or morally. We must find another way. It is not coincidental that the use of drones has assumed such great importance over the past several years—they greatly reduce our risk. Just as importantly, we must open our minds to the world around us and cease mirror-imaging and expecting all cultures to think, act, and react as we do—as rational policy makers who see a resort to force as a calculated political decision. If we train our military forces merely to seek and fight bloody battles, we are not training them to solve the problems confronting us. We must broaden our vision of war. Busting the Clausewitzian icon that dominates our strategic thinking would be a good place to start.

2

Is War an Instrument of Policy?

THE HEADLINE READ, "RAGE over Cartoons Perplexes Denmark." It was the latest flare-up between the Islamic world and the West.[1] The cartoons depicting the Prophet Mohammed published in a Danish newspaper and the resulting outrage of Muslims was mystifying to most of the West.

This incident was symptomatic: we are reading from a different text and do not understand each other's basic principles and motivations. To appreciate this dichotomy, simply contrast Muslim reaction to the cartoons—which to Westerners were not offensive—to the assault on Catholic theology engendered in books/movies like *The Da Vinci Code* and its sequels that elicited scarcely a protest from Catholics around the world.[2] After all, freedom of speech is a basic human right—for Westerners. To Muslims, there are beliefs of higher priority.[3]

Despite admonitions to know our enemy, we seldom bother to do so except in a narrow military sense. Intelligence analysts can tell us the numbers and capabilities of the equipment and force structure of adversaries we may have to face, but we have been less effective in understanding the social values, traditions, and beliefs of those peoples. What were the Japanese thinking in December 1941? Didn't they realize a sneak attack would rouse the sleeping giant? How could the North Vietnamese not understand the simple and elegant logic of gradual escalation and respond to it accordingly? And of course, the entire concept of suicide bombers—either Kamikazes or jihadists—is alien to our mind-set.[4]

I attribute the myopia of America's leaders regarding the importance of foreign culture and its influence on war and strategy in no small part to an over-reliance on Carl von Clausewitz. The nut of the problem focuses on his most famous sentence.

In Book I, chapter 1, Clausewitz wrote: "War is merely the continuation of . . ." Of what? What specifically was it war was a continuation of? Clausewitz used the word *politik* in a subtitle in chapter 1. When explaining that line in the following paragraph, his sentences in German read: "*Der Krieg ist eine blosse Fortsetzung der Politik mit andern Mittel. So sehen wir also, das der Krieg nicht bloss ein politischer Akt, sondern ein wahres politisches Instrument ist, eine Forsetzung des politischen Verkehrs, ein Durchfuhren desselben mit anderen Mitteln.*" That second explanatory sentence has been translated in a number of ways (emphasis added below).[5]

> "War is . . . a continuation of *political commerce* . . . by other means"
> —Graham translation (23); Rapoport (119)
>
> "War is . . . a continuation of *political intercourse* . . . by other means"
> —Jolles translation (16)
>
> "War is . . . a continuation of *political activity* . . . by other means"
> —Paret translation (87)
>
> "War is . . . a continuation of *politics* by other means"
> —Paret introduction (7)
>
> "War is . . . a continuation of *policy* by other means"
> —Pilcher translation (13)
>
> "War is . . . only a continuation of *political methods with* an intermixture of other means"
> —Maguire translation (155)
>
> "War is a continuation of *diplomacy* intermingled *with* other means"
> —Craig translation (180)

Words are important. They can mean different things to different people in different circumstances. In English, the words "policy," "politics," and "diplomacy" all have varying definitions and usages. "Policy," for example, often has a negative, bureaucratic connotation ("sorry, it's company policy"); while "politics" often carries with it the baggage of unsavory backroom deals ("it's all just politics"). "Diplomacy" is the stuff of the State Department and foreign, not domestic, affairs. Which of these connotations—or perhaps others not mentioned—did Clausewitz have in mind when he wrote two centuries ago that war was an extension of *politik*? And of course there are also differing meanings for the terms "commerce," "intercourse," and "activity."

It is one thing to quote Clausewitz's most famous sentence; it is another to use it as a basis for national strategy. Yet, some would have us do so, even though we may have only the vaguest idea of what the Prussian meant by it.

* * *

Those who criticize Clausewitz's skeptics generally argue they have taken too literally his comments regarding the necessity of bloody battle—despite the dozens of occasions he iterates that idea—while not taking literally enough his advice that combat was merely one instrument of policy at a commander's disposal. Unfortunately, Clausewitz himself gave few alternatives to battle or its threat.

Nonetheless, his dictum has been used repeatedly to explain foreign policy failures. In fact, Clausewitz underwent a renaissance during the Vietnam War as disgruntled observers sought to explain the errors of Lyndon Johnson and his generals as a failure to heed the Prussian's advice. This trend continues, and military operations in Iraq and Afghanistan have been criticized as lacking an appropriate Clausewitzian focus.[6] Such arguments are unfounded. It has been a too-eager willingness to view world problems through his Western European prism that has caused us trouble.

Let us assume that Clausewitz was actually arguing that war *should* be an instrument of policy, but too often political and military leaders fail to view it as such. Even so, the adage needs further elaboration. What is meant by policy, and, more to the point, what did Clausewitz mean by that term? Christopher Bassford argues that to Clausewitz it meant: "rational action undertaken by an individual or group which already has power in order to use, maintain, and extend that power."[7] This definition is far too broad, and note that guerrillas, who are not already in power, are excluded. Also, this interpretation means that virtually any motive could be forced inside it: greed, economics, religion, irredentism, revenge, honor, fear, domestic politics, *realpolitk,* or resource deprivation to name but some. Is Clausewitz saying, merely, that one should have *a reason* for going to war? If so, that is hardly a useful insight.

Rather, I would argue that given Clausewitz's background and experiences the dictum has a few unstated sub-correlates that give it greater depth and meaning.

- War should be an act of *state* policy devised by recognized leaders and not left to those interested in personal gain. The good of the state should be at issue.
- Decision-making should be part of a rational, established process. Leaders should perform a rigorous net assessment and not act on trivialities or whims.
- This decision-making process should include a calculus of expected results, and a country ought to not go to war unless it intends to achieve its goals.
- Motives ought to be grounded in a sense of legitimacy. The war should be portrayed as just, legal, or righteous—not simply "an act of aggression."
- Decision makers should prepare the people mentally and physically for war and its sacrifices. The war should enjoy a large measure of popular support.

These five caveats—and note they are my own devices and not stated by Clausewitz—make the dictum more practicable for those contemplating war. In actuality, even these caveats and criterion soon devolve into nonsense.

* * *

Over the past two centuries there has been seldom an instance when belligerents did not believe that when going to war they were following the Clausewitzian dictum as expanded above. Pick a war—Napoleonic, the American Civil War, Franco-Prussian, Spanish-American, the European colonial wars in Africa and Asia, the Russo-Japanese War, both World Wars, Korea, Vietnam, Afghanistan, and Iraq—and pick any side in those wars. Any and all of the belligerents thought they fulfilled Clausewitz's requirements. To give some examples:

- In 1898 the US battleship *Maine* blew up in Havana harbor, ostensibly at the hands of Spanish colonial officials. President William McKinley used this event, along with other alleged depredations by the Spaniards, to obtain a declaration of war from Congress. The nation responded enthusiastically. The empire of sorts that followed was seen as a natural extension of America's "manifest destiny." Spain, who believed itself unjustly accused of wrongdoing, responded vigorously to defend itself.
- All sides marched off to war in 1914 believing in the righteousness of

their cause to battle—pick one—the Hun, the Slav, Perfidious Albion, or Gallic militarism. Colonialism, arms races, and threatening alliances helped justify the decision for war. The United States joined three years later as a result of the "immoral and illegal" German policy of unrestricted submarine warfare. A stated US goal was "to make the world safe for democracy."

- Chancellor Adolf Hitler tapped into German resentment to redress what were viewed as unfair provisions of the Versailles Treaty, to reacquire "stolen" German territory, and to cleanse itself of dangerous internal elements—Jews, gypsies, and Slavs. Those fighting against Germany considered it their duty to defend themselves against Nazi aggression and halt Hitler's genocide.
- Three US presidents conducted a war in Southeast Asia to defend a helpless people from outside aggression and to counter the designs of Moscow and Beijing—viewed as part of a monolithic Communist movement bent on world domination. For their part, the North Vietnamese and Viet Cong were striving for freedom from colonial masters and their "puppets," who were attempting to impose on them an alien form of government.
- The invasion of Iraq in 2003 enjoyed great support among the US population and Congress, and worldwide sympathy. The rationales for war: a response to the terrorist attacks of 9/11 and to depose a dictator who murdered thousands of his own people and threatened his neighbors with weapons of mass destruction. This US-led invasion in turn resulted in thousands of Islamic warriors pouring in from neighboring countries and an uprising within Iraq itself to throw out the infidel invaders.

The point: all of the belligerents mentioned above, plus dozens of others during the past two centuries—could be deemed to have followed, even if unconsciously, the five precepts that comprise the Clausewitzian dictum that war is (should be) an act of policy.

Unfortunately, the decision for war often looks bad in hindsight. Usually, it is the losers who realize their motives were neither as pure nor as rational as first supposed. The populace came to believe the leaders who took the nation into war (Napoleon III, Czar Nicholas II, Mussolini, LBJ, George W. Bush, etc.) were either illogical or incompetent. Often, the population, news media, and opposing politicians claim they were deliberately misled regarding motives and possibilities of success. But such complaints and reservations were seldom heard at the war's beginning. It is generally only the defeated who later harbor such regrets. Would the Russian populace in 1917, the Italian in 1945, the American in 1968, or the Israeli in 2006 have been as vocal (and in some cases violent) regarding a war's policy if that conflict had been a success?

If it is possible for nations and peoples in such widely diverse places, times, and circumstances to claim they went to war only after fulfilling certain preconditions regarding rationality, legality, practicality, consequences, and domestic support, then the criteria demanded by Clausewitz are useless. If virtually anything can fall under the rubric of "an act of policy," then the dictum loses all utility as a guide to decision makers.

* * *

The second major problem with Clausewitz's aphorism is that it simply does not correspond to the mind-set of many nations. Clausewitz was a nineteenth-century European soldier who witnessed war between Europeans. He thus viewed war through a constricted lens. Although "partisan warfare" occurred during his lifetime—in America, Iberia, and Russia—Clausewitz largely ignored it so as to focus on the major, conventional battles fought by his contemporaries.[8] That myopia courses throughout *On War,* and the problems such a limited purview entails are with us today.

For much of the world and for much of its history, "policy"—however one defines it—was not the prime motive for going to war. To most humans over the past 3,000 years, war has been a distinctly biological or cultural phenomenon.

To understand this, we must first look at our closest cousins—the great apes, who share 98 percent of our DNA. It is only during the past several decades that in-depth research has been conducted on orangutans, gorillas, and chimpanzees in the wild, and the results have been startling. It was long held, for example, that only man had "evolved" to the point he would routinely rape or kill his own kind. We now know differently. Beginning with the ground-breaking work of primatologists Dian Fossey and Jane Goodall, we now realize that perhaps half of all "couplings" occurring between orangutans are forcible and brutal—they are rape. Worse, in a bizarre logic, a male gorilla without a mate will often entice a female to join him by killing her child. The mother will then often go with the murderer, seemingly deciding that her previous mate was unable to protect her offspring: perhaps she'll have better luck with this obviously aggressive male. It is estimated that female gorillas will experience at least one infanticide of their offspring during their lifetime.[9]

Chimpanzees are the cute primates most like humans genetically who are the subject of humorous films and television commercials, and who we enjoy dressing up in silly costumes. Primatologists have discovered that chimps in the wild are extremely violent and aggressive. Small groups of males will periodically venture outside their territory looking for other chimps. If they find a single male, they will surround him; some will then hold him down while the others bite and beat him, usually to death. If a female is sighted, they will generally gang-rape her, and then either leave her for dead or bring her back with them as a concubine.[10]

Why? There seems no rational reason: they are not threatened; it is not a question of food; there is no contest over hunting grounds; and there are plenty of females in their own group to ensure propagation. It appears such behavior stems from the nature of the male-dominated chimpanzee society in which great importance is placed on pride. Chimps raid, fight, rape, and murder to display their male-hood. They do it in response to slights or a lack of respect from others; they do it to be recognized as dominant. The implication of this premise is apparent: if man's nearest relative kills and rapes over matters of prestige, then perhaps we have inherited that same affliction. We may make war not for rational reasons of policy, but out of the dictates of biology.

A related interpretation of how biological factors affect war comes from Stephen Peter Rosen in *War and Human Progress*. Rosen examines psychological and physiological responses to various stimuli. He argues that *status* is a key element in group and individual human relations. Thus, status plays a key role in foreign policy, as some countries and their leaders place much emphasis on perceived slights, snubs, or inequalities. In some cultures this is referred to as "losing face."

Rosen discusses the role of testosterone, which is present in all humans, although its level varies greatly depending on age, sex, situational factors, environment, and culture. Basically, testosterone equals aggressiveness and "dominant behavior," and Rosen argues that states and their leaders can be driven by it. Some societies cater to their more aggressive "macho" elements, and it is these groups and individuals who rise to the top. As he phrases it: "In plain language, some people, under specified conditions, are more likely to fight when challenged. Subjectively, they get satisfaction from subduing challengers apart from the rewards that others give to them. . . . Such people will tend to be high-testosterone men who are members of groups of high-testosterone men existing in unstable status hierarchies."[11] Such societies tend to rely on tyrants who remove perceived challengers, are unwilling to coexist with rivals, rule by fear, and whose behavior fosters the growth of "yes men" unwilling to tell them the truth. These leaders are generally more interested in short-term gains and prestige than they are in long-term calculations.[12] This indeed sounds much like Adolf Hitler, Benito Mussolini, Saddam Hussein, Muammar Gaddafi, and other dictators.

Rosen also contends that such testosterone-prone societies and individuals react quickly, forcefully, and automatically to *perceived* slights and challenges. Consider Rosen's assertion in light of combat operations in Iraq. A critique of US military operations was presented by Pulitzer Prize winner Thomas Ricks in his book *Fiasco.* Ricks provides examples of US troops going into native areas, breaking down doors in the middle of the night, and then arresting and humiliating husbands and fathers in front of their families. In what Rosen would argue were testosterone-induced tactics, soldiers and marines were attempting to overawe the populace and demonstrate American might and hence Iraqi impotence in order to ensure passivity and compliance. The actual result was different. Ricks cited one sheikh complaining that although he wanted to support US efforts, "Many of the arrests were done with a boot on the head, in front of the women. You've created a blood debt when you do that."[13] In Ricks's assessment, the Americans' aggressive conduct actually *created and fueled* the insurgency. They did not understand the cultural implications of their actions. In other words, because of cultural and biological conditioning, Iraqi men, more than most, are outraged by such treatment, and their natural response is to seek revenge regardless of logic or consequences. The result was a vicious and escalating circle of violence by both sides.

Examining national culture, Amy Chua at Yale argues that Americans are in a unique position.[14] Although a nation of great diversity, the US has assimilated immigrants so successfully that after only a single generation, newcomers usually consider themselves Americans. That is not often the case elsewhere. In some instances, as in Japan, the population is extremely homogeneous and does not welcome foreigners who come to settle. Other nations—including most Middle East countries—are tribal and ethnically diverse; yet, they do not assimilate. Americans are not accustomed to this societal model, and so we are surprised by the level of animosity and alienation between different tribes or ethnic groups; our consequent actions are thus often seen by these factions as inappropriate, biased, or divisive.

This situation was evident in Vietnam. For over a thousand years the Vietnamese were at war with the Chinese, for whom they hold great antipathy. They were thus derisively amused by Americans who saw Ho Chi Minh as a pawn of communist Beijing. The history of Vietnam and the fact that Ho had spent over a year in a Chinese prison were unknown to most Americans who served in Vietnam, either in or out of uniform. Thus we did not realize the implications of the fact that although ethnic Chinese made up only 1 percent of the South Vietnamese population, that small minority controlled over 70 percent of the commercial wealth and held many key government positions.[15] Most of the remaining top slots were filled by ethnic Vietnamese who were Catholics, a group associated with French colonialism. How could the vast majority of the population, Animist and Buddhist peasants, relate to these power groups? This was a huge cultural factor of which we were largely unaware. It is likely that when China invaded Vietnam in February 1979, the only ones surprised were the Americans.

The result of this ignorance was that America made political and economic decisions in South Vietnam that contributed to the wealth and power of the Chinese and Frenchified elites, but to the detriment of the peasants who comprised the vast majority of the population. This majority therefore equated our attempts at instilling democracy and capitalism with the hated Chinese minority or the French colonials, and this was a powerful propaganda tool in the hands of Ho Chi Minh. In sum, Chua argues: "From a tribal politics perspective, virtually every step we took in Vietnam was guaranteed to turn the Vietnamese against us. The regimes we supported, the policies we promoted, the money we spent, and the attitudes we brought made the Vietnamese hate us, hate capitalism, and only enhanced the appeal and status of the charismatic Ho Chi Minh."[16]

Misunderstanding the nature of the people and countries we were dealing with was evident in Afghanistan and Iraq as well. Chua begins with the sobering comment: "As in Vietnam, the core reason for America's failure in Afghanistan is that we were oblivious to the most important group identities in the region, which do not fall along national lines, but instead are ethnic, tribal, and clan based."[17] Her story is one of well-intentioned American politicians and soldiers blundering into a situation they did not understand.

We were unaware that most Taliban leaders were Pashtuns, and our cooperation with the Northern Alliance, composed largely of Tajiks and Uzbeks, bore the seeds of continuing conflict. In addition, such tribes seldom honor international boundaries, so the Pashtuns of western Pakistan move back and forth across the border with impunity. We thought the war concerned various Islamic sects and political ideologies, but to the dozens of Afghan tribes and clans it was something far different. We were equally unaware fully of the sharp divisiveness between the Sunnis and Shias in Iraq and how our policies there aggravated conflict.

* * *

Anthropologists and military historians have picked up on these various themes. Rejecting a Rousseauite dream of peaceful primitive man, writers like Lawrence Keeley, Steven LeBlanc, John Keegan, Keith Otterbein, and Azar Gat have argued that "the state of nature" is a hellish place marked by violence and death. The archeological record is increasingly showing that primitive people fought more frequently, involved a higher percentage of their male population in warfare, employed particularly deadly weapons (arrows and spears tipped with poison so that even a scratch might cause death), were especially brutal to women and children, and generated higher casualty percentages than do the vast majority of "civilized" wars. These experts estimate that death rates due to violence in these societies routinely approached 20 percent—an astonishing figure.[18]

What were the reasons for this level of violence? It seems primitive peoples often went to war in retaliation for previous acts of violence or disrespect, which led to a vicious cycle in which tribes warred against each other for generations, with the original *casus belli* long forgotten. War became ingrained in their culture, and thus the raiding parties by the present-day Yanomamö tribesmen of Venezuela are remarkably similar in size, duration, motivation, and results to the chimpanzee raids described earlier.[19] The dominant motivations of revenge, honor, and respect are similarly familiar.

In warrior societies—Cossacks, Samurai, Vikings, and Plains Indians to name some—war was a virtual constant that continued from generation to generation.[20] Thus, the Clausewitzian aphorism regarding war being a political instrument is a modern, Western phenomenon that is out of place in many societies.[21] The significance of this is not that some peoples, tribes, and ethnic groups engage in violence for reasons we might consider quaint; rather, if such primal motives are present in those peoples, they are likewise present in all of us—much like the testosterone imperatives noted by Rosen. Even if we are able to put such dark urgings behind us, it is probable we will someday be engaged with societies who have not. They will not have read Clausewitz and will not realize that war can only be a rational act of state policy.

Of course, that "someday" came in 1941 when Samurai-influenced Japanese leaders took the seemingly insane step of attacking Pearl Harbor to challenge the United States, a country far more powerful in virtually every category—while they were already engaged in a land war in China. For their part, Americans did not understand the fanaticism of the Japanese that saw 95 percent of their soldiers fight to the death rather than surrender. Americans did not understand the culture that produced suicide bombers—kamikazes—who sacrificed their lives in hopeless attacks.

The "someday" came again in Vietnam when a small, technologically backward people dared to make war against the greatest military power in the world. Americans did not understand what motivated men and women to fight against impossible odds for decades, seemingly with little hope of victory, for the goal of simply being left alone to form a government that *limited* what to us were the basic human rights of its populace.

And the "someday" occurred on September 11, 2001, when modern-day kamikazes flew airplanes into the World Trade Center and the Pentagon for reasons that we will probably never fully comprehend. Americans, Europeans, and Israelis continue to puzzle over the motivations that drive men—and increasingly women and children—to sacrifice their lives as suicide bombers, doing so with shouts of encouragement from family and friends. We also are willing to die for a cause—and have done so in great numbers in our nation's wars—but the culture that now confronts us is beyond our ken.

We must view war as an extremely serious undertaking, and we must approach it with a clear purpose and use it only as a last resort. Even so, we must also realize that despite precautions and due deliberations, we may still be making a huge mistake.

The most recent example of such an error was the decision to invade Iraq in 2003. The national security team assembled by President George W. Bush was top-notch, including two former secretaries of defense, a former chairman of the Joint Chiefs of Staff, seasoned diplomats, noted academics, and the serving military chiefs. And yet, we now realize that team moved slowly, deliberately, and inexorably toward a bad decision. The team did its homework:

it studied, debated, and pursued a solution through the United Nations for months and then secured the support of the American people. At the same time it delved deeply into various intelligence sources to divine the situation in Iraq and the mind of its leaders. Clearly, the Bush administration believed that its war was an extension of a policy logically arrived at. Yet, if we could go back to March 2003, we would not do it again.

A large part of this failure was that American leaders did not understand that the warriors of al Qaeda, Hezbollah, Hamas, the Taliban, ISIS, and other sects that fight us do not view war as an instrument of policy. There are other cultural, biological, and religious factors that motivate them. They are not following the script of *On War.* They are not Clausewitzians. We need to understand what motivates *them* and not rely on an outdated dictum for policy-making that belongs to another place and another time. We must cease mirror-imaging, expecting all cultures to think, act, and react as we do ourselves—as rational policy makers who see a resort to force as a calculated political decision, generally made as a last resort. If we do not broaden our view of war and its causes, we will continue to be caught by surprise at the hands of cultures we do not understand. We will relive the agonies we have experienced in the seemingly endless conflicts in Vietnam, Iraq, and Afghanistan.

3

The Mutable Nature of War

CARL VON CLAUSEWITZ DISCUSSED the nature of war—which he also referred to as the "essence," "culture," or "atmosphere of war." To him, this nature was timeless and immutable. He repeatedly referred to war as combat, fighting, and bloodshed. There were no easy paths to success in war, and he continually emphasized that combat and violence were the nature of war and for the individual soldier war was hell:

> War is an act of force, and there is no logical limit to the application of that force. . . . War is a pulsation of violence. . . . It is inherent in the very concept of war that everything that occurs *must originally derive from combat*. . . . War is the realm of physical exertion and suffering. . . . Danger, physical exertion, intelligence, and friction [are] the elements that coalesce to form the atmosphere of war. . . . Every engagement is a bloody and destructive test of physical and moral strength. . . . It is always true that the character of battle, like its name, is slaughter (*schlact*), and its price is blood.[1]

His work is a relentless hammering of these ideas, and he belittled those who believed war could be won without bloodshed. Clausewitz focused on morale and fighting spirit: such a thesis implies a fundamental reliance on soldiers and a devaluation of technology.

Clausewitz's beliefs have influenced military historians, theorists, soldiers, and marines. John Lynn cautions his readers not to forget that "the ultimate fact of military history is combat, actually fighting, with all its danger and its heavy costs."[2] Victor Davis Hanson echoes this view: "military history must never stray from the tragic story of killing, which is ultimately found only in battle. . . wars are the sum of battles."[3] Martin Van Creveld said much the same thing, noting war's timelessness and immutable character: "in many ways it has remained essentially the same at all times and in [all] places." To Van Creveld, the essence of war involved danger, risk, destructiveness, selflessness, hardship, and even exhilaration.[4] Not everyone has agreed with the Prussian theorist or the others noted above. Basil H. Liddell Hart, a lifelong skeptic of Clausewitz, wrote that "the spirit cannot win battles when the body has been killed through failure to provide it with up-to-date weapons."[5]

The US Army supports the Clausewitzian view of war. One study states that the Army's self-image views "the primary instrument for combat" as "a soldier armed with an individual weapon" and that "the principal mission of the Army" is to "fight the nation's wars by closing with the enemy and destroying his main Army in battle." Adrian Lewis concludes that to the Army, "man is the dominant instrument on the battlefield."[6] Although Army doctrine noted the move toward more capable technology, it quickly dismissed such trends: "warfare remains a test of the soldier's will, courage, endurance and skill. Freezing rain, muddied foxholes, blistering heat, physical exertion, and imminent danger will remain the domain of the soldier."[7] The field manual dealing with counterinsurgency echoes this view, stating that war in the twenty-first century "retains many of the characteristics it has exhibited since ancient times." It contends these characteristics include war being "a violent clash of interests," and it posits the need "to generate enough violence" to achieve objectives.[8] America's other army takes a similar view.

The US Marine Corps' basic doctrine manual, Fleet Marine Field Manual 1, "Warfighting," states that "the basic nature of war is constant." It defines this nature as "a violent clash between two hostile, independent, and irreconcilable wills, each trying to impose itself on the other." It continues that war is "organized violence," and it cautions against those who would try to trick us into believing otherwise. Don't be deceived: "the violent essence of war will never change. Any study of war that neglects this characteristic is misleading and incomplete."[9]

Many senior officers have been inculcated in this belief. A retired lieutenant general argues that "the fundamental nature of war hasn't changed, won't change, and, in fact, can't change. . . . Nothing has happened that's going to change the fundamental elements of war. The nature of war is immutable." He is dismissive of technology that some argue has altered the nature of war.

Says the marine: "My experience has been that those who focus on the technology, the science, tend towards sloganeering." To him, new ideas and revolutionary doctrines such as network-centric warfare or information dominance are mere semantic sleight-of-hand: "you could fill a book with all those slogans." The general insists that war is a "terrible, uncertain, chaotic, bloody business" and anyone who attempts to devise methods that will reduce or eliminate such calamities are "very shallow" and "fundamentally flawed." Boots on the ground are what war is all about, and he argues that if there had been more of them in Iraq at the beginning "you might have convinced a lot of people that the war was over at that time."[10] He is not the only general to feel strongly about throwing more human beings at problems instead of machines. A former head of US Central Command stated: "There comes a point when a country puts young folks at risk because it becomes important for them to defend a certain way of life. . . . From a Marine point of view, we can't lose our honor by failing to put our own skin on the line."[11]

Where the above generals and historians most seriously err is in equating land warfare, and specifically conventional battle as it once was practiced, with war. This reflects both institutional bias as well as downplaying the role of technology.

* * *

One of the most effective and ancient aspects of naval warfare is the blockade. A form of economic warfare not dependent on a bloody clash of armed men, the blockade is a traditional weapon that attempts to disrupt and strangle an enemy's commerce. All countries—and today nonstate actors as well—require money and resources with which to wage war. The object of a blockade—and its cousin the sanction—is to control sea lines of communication so as to reduce the resources available to an adversary so he can no longer prosecute the war effectively. In some cases, blockades are deliberately meant to starve a population into submission.

Naval blockades are often the preferred weapon of nations that possess a sizable fleet but only a small army.[12] In World War I, for example, Britain established a starvation blockade against the Central Powers—Germany and Austria-Hungary. According to the British official history, more than 800,000 German civilians died as a result of this blockade.[13] Such odious results also occurred in Iraq during the 1990s as a result of sanctions imposed by the United Nations, instituted to pressure Saddam Hussein into submission. These sanctions killed over 1 million Iraqi civilians—the majority of whom were women and children.[14] The sanctions imposed on Haiti between 1991 and 1993 in an attempt to topple the military junta in power were similarly horrific. During those two years the Haitian economy was devastated: unemployment soared to 70 percent, inflation doubled, GDP dropped 15 percent, and 1,000 children died each month as a result of the legally levied sanctions.[15] Small wonder two observers wrote a cynical article on the matter titled "Sanctions of Mass Destruction."[16]

This was war, and it was extremely deadly, but there were few battles or violent clashes of arms. If violence occurs during a blockade or the enforcement of sanctions, it generally happens far out at sea or at a roadblock: the civilians who are the real targets die quietly and bloodlessly. Indeed, in some cases, as in Iraq and Haiti, the targeted countries did not and could not respond to the blockade and sanctions—there was no violence at all. Just death. Cynically, it could be argued these civilians being slaughtered do indeed have much in common with their unfortunate ancestors. But Clausewitz and others were not arguing that the nature of war was immutable for the *victims,* but rather for the *practitioners* of war.

A similarly bloodless yet potentially devastating new method of war involves cyberspace. Adversaries can hack into computers, implant viruses, shut down systems, or order bogus actions. In May 2007 Estonia was attacked, presumably by Russia, and experienced problems with computers in businesses, banks, telecommunications, the media, and government. To stop the attack, the government and banks were forced to shut down access to the Internet for several days. In August 2008 cyber attacks were launched against Georgia, again probably by Russia. They concentrated primarily on Georgia's ability to access the Internet and media to tell its side of the story in the dispute.[17] In November 2008 Pentagon computers were attacked. The goal was to "remotely take control of computers and rifle their files." In July 2009 the Republic of South Korea was barraged—tens of thousands of government and military computers were shut down. It is believed North Korea was the attacker.[18] In 2018 Taiwan revealed it has been the victim of over 40 million cyber attacks originating from China that targeted civil, military, and research departments. Although most attacks were minor, several infiltrated government agencies and "might have compromised sensitive and classified data."[19]

The most serious cyber attack was against the Iranian nuclear research program, probably by Israel. In 2009 a program called Stuxnet was introduced into computers controlling 1,000 centrifuges, of around 10,000 being used. (Centrifuges are used to separate Uranium 235 from Uranium 238—only the former is useful in making nuclear weapons.) The virus instructed the centrifuges to speed up and slow down at dramatic rates, and it also infected the machines' monitoring program so they indicated all was working properly. The result, over a period of weeks the centrifuges self-destructed, and the Iranians never even detected the problem until the breakdowns occurred. It was suggested these attacks set back the Iranian nuclear program by several years. This was the first time a cyber attack actually "broke something."[20]

The Congressional Research Service (CRS) and Government Accountability Office have studied the issue and posted repeated warnings that the US government is ill-prepared to defend against a robust cyber attack. They noted that the number of reported cyber incidents against the United States has more than tripled in recent years. The reports continued that hitherto unsophisticated terrorist attempts may lead to complacency, leaving the United States unprepared for serious assaults. Both agencies are especially concerned about the danger posed by China and Iran.[21] In 2018 the CRS warned that the nation's electrical power grid was particularly vulnerable to cyber attack.[22] Another report foresees China using coordinated cyber and kinetic strikes against a foe's networked information systems. The Chinese have adopted a formal strategy for this offensive system termed "Integrated Network Electronic Warfare."[23] As a way of testing this new capability, it is alleged that in 2014 China stole more than 20 million personnel files from the US Office of Personnel Management, which included security background information.[24] In July 2018 the director of national intelligence warned that indicators were "blinking red" regarding an eminent cyber attack. Dan Coats stated that Russia has been the most aggressive foreign actor, but cyber threats are also coming from China, Iran, and North Korea as well as criminal networks and individual hackers. The last time warnings were this insistent was before 9/11.[25]

Although a cyber attack has not yet killed anyone, the above incidents reveal a probing approach and learning curve that bodes ill for the future. Stuxnet was a serious wakeup call. Nightmare scenarios abound, and it is not difficult to imagine a situation in the near future when cyber attacks occur simultaneously with kinetic strikes in a major assault. The nature of such cyber offensives could include degradation of everyday services, such as ATMs, traffic lights, and power grids, but also more serious assaults on the banking and financial systems, hospitals, nuclear power plants, the stock market, and air traffic control radars. It must be assumed that military facilities, such as air defense systems and command and control networks, would also be targeted.

These cyber attacks would be carried out by individuals in shirt sleeves, perhaps civilians, sitting at computer terminals thousands of miles from where the effects of their operations would be felt. The offensives would involve minor risk, and there would be little bloodshed; yet, they could wreck havoc on a nation's economy, way of life, and even its military forces.

The notion that battle is the province of fear, anxiety, and exhaustion is outdated, because technology has dramatically altered this archaic situation. Modern air warfare has proven to be remarkably bloodless for American airmen. Since the Vietnam War ended over four decades ago the US Air Force has flown hundreds of thousands of combat sorties all over the world; yet, losses have been thankfully slight. Since 1975 the service has lost a total of eighteen manned aircraft in combat (costing the lives of twenty crewmembers, fourteen in one crash), an astoundingly low loss rate.[26] In most cases modern air warfare as practiced by the United States and its allies is not the realm of death, exhaustion, blood, and fear—at least not to the degree inherent in land warfare.

Then there are the drones. Unmanned air vehicles were tested in the First World War, used in the Second and Vietnam, but came into their own during DESERT STORM in 1991. In most cases, drones were used for reconnaissance and intelligence gathering. The Predator first flew in the Balkans in 1995. After the terrorist attacks of September 11, 2001, the drone was armed, and its first attack was against al Qaeda targets in Afghanistan the following month. Since then, the Predator and its updated brother the Reaper have flown tens of thousands of sorties in the Middle East and elsewhere, with stunning success.[27] Predators and Reapers launching guided missiles and precision bombs flew over 5,800 strike sorties between 2002 and 2018.[28]

Drone strikes are flown by pilots sitting as far distant from the battlespace as Creech Air Force Base in Nevada.[29] Such missions have become commonplace for the operators. Military pilots report for work and during a typical shift fly drone combat sorties halfway around the world. On many occasions the sensors locate, identify, and track terrorists and enemy combatants. Sometimes the drones fire missiles at those targets in order to destroy them; at other times they simply "follow" certain people to determine their activities and contacts. This is world war in real time. After a normal shift, the drone pilots return home to their families. There is no personal danger involved; there is no risk, no fear, and no physical exertion. There is no overwhelming thirst, hunger, and exhaustion. And the drones themselves can be very courageous.

I am *not* in any way denigrating the efforts or courage of our valiant combat aircrew members or the drone pilots. It is a very *good thing* they are able to wage war while severely limiting their exposure to death and casualties. That is as it should be. As one fighter pilot colleague phrased it to me: "if you're in a fair fight you didn't plan it properly." It should be the role and *duty* of military planners and commanders, from any service, to do all in their power to plan operations that limit the exposure of American forces to danger. Deliberately and unnecessarily risking the lives of America's sons and daughters is not honorable as some desk generals would argue, it is criminal.

The nature of war is mutable. Modern warfare is still deadly and destructive, but it need not be bloody. The fundamental aspect of war in centuries past may have been the sanguinary battles between infantrymen, but that is no longer necessarily the case. Traditional sea warfare, but also present-day cyber operations, can be enormously deadly and destructive, although neither violent nor bloody. Technology has also helped to ensure that modern air warfare has become remarkably effective, but also efficient. Loss of aircraft and the lives of crewmembers have dropped dramatically over the past several decades. Moreover, this decline in casualties has been the rule not only for the United States, but for those on the receiving end of our airstrikes.

The civilian casualty toll in DESERT STORM, Bosnia, Kosovo/Serbia, Afghanistan, and Iraq due to air attack has been remarkably small given the weight of bomb tonnage dropped. As Marc Garlasco from Human Rights Watch has stated, airpower is "probably the most discriminate weapon that exists."[30] One report by that organization regarding initial operations in Iraq states that "the ground war caused the vast majority of deaths," noting that at al-Hilla ground-launched cluster bomb munitions caused 90 percent of all civilian casualties.[31] Another expert is even more effusive in her praise of airpower. Sarah B. Sewall was the deputy assistant secretary for peacekeeping in the Defense Department, and also ran the Carr Center for Human Rights Policy at Harvard. In her seminal work on the subject of efforts to reduce civilian casualties in war, she begins by stating categorically: "The United States Air Force has led the way within the US armed forces and globally in its efforts to minimize harm to civilians."[32] She argues that airmen recognized the crucial importance of limiting casualties more than a decade earlier than the other services, and took deliberate steps to implement policies to limit collateral damage. Airmen recognized that reducing the loss of life while employing force was essential to maintain legitimacy in the eyes of the world. Keeping destruction and death to a minimum were also a natural goal to ensure military effectiveness and efficiency. The result of the Air Force's recognizing this new reality was a determined effort to improve weapons, tactics, and decision-making to ensure such a discrete and limited use of force were institutionalized.

An account of civilian casualties in Iraq is provided by Iraq Body Count (IBC), which determined that up to 189,808 Iraqi civilians died as a result of the war through February 2017. (Preliminary data adds another 13,817 after that date through May 2018.) Of the confirmed total, 7,999 were killed in Coalition air strikes, or 4.2 percent. In contrast, IBC states that ISIS was responsible for 26,745 civilian deaths, more than the entire Coalition total from all causes (24,676.)[33] In Afghanistan, the statistics are comparable. According to a United Nations study, civilian deaths between 2009 and 2017 totaled 28,291, of which 20,280 (71.6 percent) were caused by "anti-government forces" and 6.6 percent were due to air strikes.[34]

Regrettably, airpower is often depicted as being violent and graphic, whereas a blockade is seen as nonviolent and bloodless despite the number of people who die as a result. A RAND study refers to airpower, and especially any collateral damage caused by it, as being "mediagenic." It notes that collateral damage incidents are four times more likely to be reported via the more graphic-oriented television media than in print.[35] This circumstance distorts the true discrimination and accuracy of modern air warfare.

Can we always expect such dramatic effectiveness at such low cost? No. But it should be the *entering premise* in crises we face that such results should be the goal. We are not condemned to suffer horrendous death, destruction, and "*schlact*" in our military operations. Technology, especially as exemplified by modern air warfare, shows that we can aspire to a higher goal. The old canard that the nature of war is immutable, that its nature was the same for one of Alexander's hoplites as it is for a grunt in Iraq, is simply not true. War has changed, and so has its nature. We should plan future military operations with these changes in mind.

4

Starting with a Blank Sheet

Principles of War for a New Century

THE WORLD HAS CHANGED over the past several decades, and basic questions need to be addressed. What, precisely, is the nature of the new geopolitical situation confronting us? How can we meet this challenge most effectively and efficiently—how can we defend ourselves and our interests with the least cost in blood and treasure? Appropriate responses demand that we start fresh, with a blank sheet of paper, to explain the nature of the present environment and how our military should operate within it.

Just as important, we must then revise our thinking and doctrine to reflect new conditions and teach the resulting ideas to soldiers, sailors, marines, and airmen so they can internalize them before a crisis occurs. Such an educational rebirth involves an understanding of what are termed the Principles of War. Unfortunately, these Principles, articulated a century ago and enshrined in British Army doctrine following the Great War, in US Army doctrine soon after, and in US Air Force doctrine after World War II, are outdated, insufficient, and misleading in a modern era dominated by air and space assets, near real-time intelligence, speed-of-light command and control systems, and ubiquitous multimedia news sources. Simply put: the old Principles of War no longer fit in a transformational age that calls for new ways of fighting, not just more efficient ways of fighting the old way. Reliance on the old Principles of War will have us looking backward and fighting the last war, rather than looking forward to fight the next.

* * *

The Gulf War of 1991 was a watershed. Iraq had a large military force stocked with Soviet- and French-built equipment and had been hardened during an eight-year war against Iran.[1] But when the Coalition struck in January 1991, Iraqi forces were doomed. Coalition commander General Norman Schwarzkopf directed his air component commander that he wanted airpower to reduce all forty-eight frontline Iraqi divisions by at least 50 percent *before* major offensive ground operations began. This in fact occurred.[2] The short and sharp land offensive that followed the five-week air campaign sealed the outcome. It soon became apparent, however, that the victory was incomplete. For sound political reasons the Coalition did not move north to Baghdad. For *un*sound military reasons the bulk of Iraq's Republican Guard divisions that had been positioned behind the front lines escaped. The failure to neutralize these elite divisions assured Saddam Hussein of a Praetorian Guard for suppressing dissident elements within Iraq, giving him another decade in power, and serving as a nucleus for a rebuilt military.

DESERT STORM was a precursor of a new type of war and, paradoxically, the last of the old wars. A ground force of over 500,000 troops supplied by the United States, Britain, Egypt, Saudi Arabia, France, and other countries served as a blocking and pinning force to ensure Hussein's ground forces remained anchored in place along the Saudi border. Robbed of mobility, the Iraqis were easy prey for around-the-clock Coalition air strikes that rendered them "combat ineffective." When the Iraqis attempted to move, as at Khafji in late January 1991, airpower simply killed them more quickly. Over a two-day period the Iraqi III Corps and over 300 armored vehicles were destroyed from the air.[3] Khafji was Iraq's only attempt to take the initiative. When the Coalition ground assault began, it faced a broken army primed for a massive retreat. The US Air Force chief of staff stated bluntly it was the first time in history that an army had been defeated by airpower.[4]

There was a revolution taking place. The combination of precision weapons, stealth, and ubiquitous intelligence sensors and disseminators made airpower dramatically more effective than previously. A metric once used by air planners was "how many aircraft are necessary to neutralize a given target?" In World War II the answer would have been hundreds. That number steadily dropped with the introduction of laser-guided bombs used in Vietnam.[5] By 1991, with the development of increasingly sophisticated and accurate laser bombs and radar guidance systems, air planners had a new metric: "how many targets can one aircraft neutralize on a single sortie?"[6]

The issue of collateral damage and civilian casualties is another reason precision-guided munitions (PGMs) have become crucial to the way the United States fights. Western societies now require that war be largely bloodless, not only to ourselves but also to our enemies. We must minimize casualties to both sides. Collateral damage can seriously undermine US foreign policy, so great emphasis is now placed on limiting such damage in military operations. PGMs have become essential. Even though such weapons are not required by international law, the US is now *expected* to use them.

Conflicts following DESERT STORM buttressed claims of a new paradigm. In Bosnia, Kosovo, Libya, Syria, and the initial takedowns in Afghanistan and Iraq, diplomatic constraints shaped operations that provided politically desirable results with a remarkably low casualty toll. These notable campaigns were alike in relying primarily on airpower—both land- and sea-based, manned and unmanned—combined with special operations forces (SOF), indigenous ground troops such as the Northern Alliance in Afghanistan and the Kurds in northern Iraq, and robust intelligence and command and control (C2) systems that were linked together in a global array.

In sum, the new environment in the aftermath of the Soviet collapse in 1989 was dominated by countries and nonstate actors who learned that taking on the West in a conventional war was folly—asymmetrical warfare and terrorism were to become the weapons of choice. Fortunately, we reacted with gratifying quickness and cleverness with our own asymmetrical advantages.

It is now time to posit a new set of Principles of War that reflect the new realities and this new revolutionary method of war.

* * *

The age-old desire to impose order on the chaos of war has led generations of military thinkers and generals to posit rules, laws, maxims, and principles that govern its conduct. This was highly practical—the human brain needs to limit complexity, especially in a crisis when time is short. It does this by categorizing. For soldiers, sailors, and airmen this means reducing their job to certain basics. Some of these ideas have assumed the character of adages: take the high ground or, for the airman, check six.

Over two millennia ago Sun Tzu wrote a classic work of strategy and was perhaps the first to compile a group of statements that he termed "considerations." These were fairly simplistic, including questions such as "which of the two generals has the most ability?" and "which army is the stronger and most highly trained?"[7]

Many generals, and others wishing they could be, continued to propose rules regarding warfare: Machiavelli, Henry Lloyd, Maurice de Saxe, Carl von Clausewitz, and Antoine-Henri Jomini.[8] These last two, participants and observers of Napoleonic warfare, have had a great influence on modern military thought.

Clausewitz has had a greater impact on Western military leaders than anyone else over the past two centuries, and I have dealt with him in earlier chapters. Jomini has also been influential in officer training and education. Jomini wrote what he believed were practical guidelines for the conduct of war. To many, this smacked of trying to make war a science rather than an art, and they have seen these guidelines as overly facile; yet, the enduring drive to simplify the practice of war with "principles" testifies to the need for just such formulations. In 1807 Jomini listed ten maxims, paraphrased here:

- Take the initiative.
- Attack the enemy's weakest point.
- Attack the extremities of the enemy's position.
- Concentrate for ease and rapidity of movement.
- Force the enemy to commit errors.
- Know the enemy's position and intentions.
- Mass for effectiveness at the decisive point.
- Pursue the beaten foe.
- Emphasize morale.
- Summarizing the above: a general should occupy favorable positions, move quickly, and hit hard with a concentrated force.[9]

It has been argued that because of Jomini's long life, his straightforward and uncluttered prose, and his writing in French—then the lingua franca for the militaries of the West—his influence was great. In contrast, Clausewitz died relatively young, wrote in a confusing, redundant, and contradictory fashion, and published in German. In other words, Jomini beat him on all three counts. Some contend it was Jomini's *Précis* that accompanied Union and Confederate generals to battle in the American Civil War.[10]

The nineteenth century was a rich period for military thought. Staff and war colleges, along with various branch schools—infantry, cavalry, artillery, etc.—were founded in most European countries as well as the United States. Partly this was the result of a drive to rationalize war—as well as other aspects of life. This was the age of managerial and administrative revolutions that attempted to treat the complex processes of society as scientific problems to be overcome with rationality, organization, and technology. Not coincidentally, it was also when general staffs were formed in most major armies.[11] The era also gave birth to a number of theorists who continued to refine ideas for warfare, including Ferdinand Foch, Colmar von der Goltz, Ardant du Picq, G.F.R. Henderson, and, significantly, naval theorists Alfred Thayer Mahan and Julian Corbett.

Unfortunately, all of this failed to avert the catastrophe of World War I. If schools and staffs were intended to minimize mistakes by commanders, they failed. Alan Clark evocatively referred to Great War generals as "the donkeys" who seemed unable to think beyond Clausewitz's prime directive: find and destroy the enemy army.[12]

Hope springs eternal. Despite the carnage and muddle-headed thinking of the war, one officer stepped forward with an idea. J.F.C. Fuller was a British soldier with a brilliant mind—a condition not always welcomed by his colleagues. He later wrote: "When, in 1898, I joined the Army, though a normally indifferently educated young Englishman, I was appalled by the ignorance which surrounded me and the immense military value attached to it."[13] He was not deterred. In 1916 he compiled a list of "strategic principles" imbued with a logic and pithiness that have stood the test of time:

- Objective
- Offensive
- Mass
- Economy of force
- Movement
- Surprise
- Security
- Cooperation[14]

In 1920 they entered British Army Field Service Regulations. The following year the US Army adopted Fuller's principles while adding a ninth—*simplicity.*[15]

Over the next several decades these principles remained largely intact. One notable addition was made in 1945 when Field Marshal Bernard Montgomery listed "Air power" as the first principle of modern war.[16] The newly independent US Air Force came up with its own "Basic Principles of War" in 1949:

- The will to win rapidly
- Singleness of purpose
- Coordination of ends and means
- The principle of indirect approach
- Surprise—alternative objectives
- Intelligence
- Air Supremacy[17]

There were some interesting ideas here, and, in fact, Air University exclaimed proudly and a bit self-consciously: "The principles of Air Warfare stem from Mitchell, Arnold, and Knerr, more notably than from Frederick or Napoleon, and Air Force thinking needs no Old Testament text for justification."[18] Despite the bold talk, the Air Force failed to follow up. The first official Basic Doctrine Manual of 1953 listed the same principles then being used in Army doctrine manuals. Today, US Air Force doctrine still lists the original principles, while also adding *restraint, perseverance,* and *legitimacy.*[19] Airmen copying these land warfare principles labored to make them into something useful for the Air Force—not always successfully. The discussion of mass, for example, makes little sense in an age of precision-guided munitions.

It is time to start over. War has changed so dramatically since 1916, when Fuller first wrote, that the continual attempts to shape and sand these square pegs to fit into round holes is becoming useless.

* * *

To the extent that Principles of War are useful to modern military and civilian planners, then, the new environment coupled with the revolutionary transformation in the conduct of war demands a fresh start, and here is my proposed list. Note, these principles reflect the way that the United States and its closest allies now fight, not necessarily the methods or strategies of potential adversaries.

1. Air, space, cyberspace, and naval supremacy. The United States and its closest allies have come to assume this dominance and do so for good reason. The US Army has not had to fight without air superiority since the Kasserine Pass in 1943. It has not lost a soldier to enemy air attack since 1953 during the Korean War. It has never fired a surface-to-air missile at an enemy aircraft, as they have never gotten that close.

US and allied sea superiority has been equally impressive. Since the 1943 victory in the Battle of the Atlantic, our dominance at sea has been unquestioned, and we have been able to deploy forces worldwide, by air and sea, for over seven decades with virtually no losses. Once those forces have been established in theater, they have been resupplied largely unopposed.[20] Given that virtually all US military operations occur abroad, this is significant. In the battle space itself, air superiority means that other air missions so essential to the joint force—deep strike, interdiction, close air support, reconnaissance, battle management, airlift, and air refueling—have gone largely unimpeded since the Vietnam War ended.

Cyberspace is a new environment that is rapidly becoming a crucial front in modern war, but there is danger here. Western strength in air, space, and sea power is so profound that it is unlikely an enemy will be able to seriously challenge us there in the foreseeable future—barring some unanticipated technological breakthrough. Cyberspace is another matter. Because it is such a new field, dependent on brain power rather than industrial might, it is a prime area for potential adversaries to seek an asymmetric advantage. According to one expert, China and Iran are pursuing this technology assiduously, seeing it as a force multiplier over Western strengths.[21] Russia is viewed as a serious threat as well, and the United States and United Kingdom issued a joint communiqué in 2018 stating their fears that "Russia is actively preparing for a future cyberwar against the West." The report went on to note that most to be feared were attacks on network infrastructure devices, such as routers, switches, and firewalls. Compromised routers would help Russia "support espionage, extract intellectual property, maintain persistent access to victim networks, and potentially lay a foundation for future offensive operations."[22]

US Cyber Command has now been upgraded to a Combatant Command at the four-star level, thus signaling the importance with which this new medium is viewed by political and military leaders and the threats it poses.

2. Homeland Security. The terrorist attacks of 9/11 were among the worst assaults on the US mainland in history. Airpower, in the form of commandeered civilian airliners, killed over 3,000 civilians in the attacks on New York City, the Pentagon, and the abortive attack ending in a Pennsylvania field. The devastating terrorist attacks on the Madrid and London subway systems in 2004 and 2005 were no less horrific. One result has been the establishment of the Department of Homeland Security, which is responsible for thwarting future attacks. Certainly, home defense has always been a major component of US policy—and of every other country for that matter—but new terrorist threats demand a different response. Police forces, border patrols, and intelligence agencies like the FBI are no longer adequate to defend against worldwide and networked terrorist forces. Entirely new technologies like unmanned air vehicles, information warfare, and computer self-defense systems have been built to conduct this new fight.

A listing of the organizations and agencies comprising this new cabinet-level department is informative: US Customs Service, Immigration and Naturalization Service, Border Patrol, Transportation Security Administration, Animal and Plant Health Inspection Service, Federal Emergency Management Agency, Nuclear Incident Response Team, Plum Island Animal Disease Center, Federal Computer Incident Response Center, National Communications System, Secret Service, and the Coast Guard—among others. This diverse grouping illustrates the wide range of threats now on the radar scope. These threats and the groups listed are not necessarily new; what is different is the requirement to tie them together in order to more quickly and effectively counter terrorist threats and to do so on US territory—a concern we have seldom worried about in the past.

It is likely that military forces will be needed in future crises to combat terrorists, provide logistical or medical support, or to enforce laws and keep the peace when civilian institutions are unable to do so. The military has been used for all of these roles throughout American history, and may be required to do so again.[23]

The US Air Force has resurrected an old weapon of defense to address this new threat. For decades during the Cold War the USAF had an Air Defense Command consisting of over 2,000 interceptor aircraft designed to meet a Soviet bomber attack. Over time this force dwindled to a few squadrons. It is now reestablished in a smaller form to protect against further 9/11-type airliner attacks by terrorists.

3. *Unity of Command.* This is an old concept, but in the past it generally meant the control over similar forces in a given theater. In World War I, for example, it led to a single commander on the Western Front who controlled British, French, and American ground forces. In the past, commanders of national contingents were more responsive to politicians in their capitals than they were to the needs of the alliance as it confronted an enemy. The coalitions that fought Napoleon were unsuccessful for this very reason: the differing concerns

of Austria, Prussia, Russia, and Britain meant that a unified front seldom presented itself against Napoleon. For two decades he played upon these divisions, splitting the coalitions and defeating members piecemeal. It was only in 1814 that Europe united against France, appointed a single field commander (Austria's Prince Karl Philip Schwarzenberg), and temporarily put aside individual concerns to defeat the common foe.[24] The epitome of this new attitude was at Waterloo, when Prussia's seemingly defeated Marshal Gebhard von Blücher returned to the battlefield to combine with Wellington's forces to defeat the French—an event that Napoleon did not expect simply because such a spirit of unity against him had not existed previously.

The demands of theater-wide warfare necessitate unity of command due to the increasingly long ranges and the responsiveness of the weapons at a commander's disposal. Aircraft can travel hundreds of miles in minutes to deliver ordnance, and space assets can survey an entire theater during a single pass. When such systems can see or shoot at continental distances, there must be a guiding hand to ensure those systems are operating in a coordinated and seamless fashion to achieve a specific purpose.

Moreover, today's demands require that unity of command be taken to a new level. Unifying and focusing the efforts of several military services—from several different countries in the case of a coalition—while at the same time controlling and coordinating the efforts of nonmilitary agencies so as to ensure a holistic strategy and policy, demands that a single individual be in charge. Although this will not ensure that the resulting policy or strategy is the correct one—witness the events in Iraq after 2003—such unity of command is a necessary if insufficient condition for success.[25]

4. Integration. This is the coordinated use of all instruments/levers of power—military, political, economic, psychological, and cultural. Asymmetric actors and challenges necessitate a combination of these levers of power.

During the 2006 Quadrennial Defense Review, Defense Secretary Donald Rumsfeld pushed a concept of four major challenges to the United States and its interests: *traditional* (regional competitors posing conventional threats), *disruptive* (adversaries negating US advantages with asymmetrical technology), *irregular* (terrorist attacks by nonstate actors), and *catastrophic* (a major attack on the United States involving weapons of mass destruction).[26] It was his belief that the threats facing the United States were shifting away from the traditional threat—although it did not disappear—and toward the other three.

These "other three" required fundamentally different types of forces, doctrines, and organizations to combat them effectively. More importantly, these threats required an integrated effort that crossed cabinet departments and agencies: the Department of Defense could not handle these problems alone. Although these notions were introduced over a decade ago, they still hold true today even if the terminology may have changed.

An example of when integration was not present and led to difficulties was the conclusion of the Gulf War. After military hostilities ended, General Schwarzkopf met with the defeated Iraqi commander at Safwan to negotiate a cease fire. Schwarzkopf received little guidance from the US State Department for this critical meeting. Another participant, Lieutenant General Charles Horner, remembers sitting down with other senior officers the evening before the meeting to discuss their agenda. They were not prepared. Horner pulled out a writing pad and after some initial discussion wrote "prisoners of war" at the top—all those present remembered the fate of their comrades at the hands of the North Vietnamese and were determined to receive a full accounting this time. Further discussions were equally unfocused and haphazard.[27] War *and its aftermath* must be addressed by a coalition of agencies, not simply the military. Today, a concerted effort emphasizing expertise from Defense, State, Treasury, Homeland Security, Intelligence, and nongovernmental agencies will be needed to confront the varied challenges facing us.

5. *Jointness.* For centuries, the need for cooperation between the services was considered a sometimes desirable but seldom necessary occurrence. An exception was often seen in England, where the British Way of War, as characterized by Basil H. Liddell Hart, was an indirect approach that relied on second front operations.[28] When the enemy—usually France—was too strong to confront head-on, amphibious operations in a different theater—the Americas, Middle East, Iberia—were conducted instead. In Lord Grey's phrase: the British Army was a projectile fired by the Royal Navy.[29]

In the United States, such cooperation was less evident. An Army-Navy Board existed to coordinate the efforts of soldiers and sailors, but the two services seldom actually worked together. That changed during World War II for two major reasons. First, global war against major powers *demanded* close cooperation to achieve victory. Second, airpower introduced a new dimension to war that required integration between the Army and Navy. When the mediums of the sea and land were clearly demarcated, sailors and soldiers could often ignore each other with few ill effects. When airpower spanned both domains, arguments regarding priorities, targets, command and control, basing, and allocation of resources had to be solved using a joint approach.

Even so, the services resisted. A main problem leading to defeat in Vietnam was the parochialism and sometimes childish rivalry that existed between the Air Force and Navy, and between the Army and Marine Corps. It was the botched Iranian hostage rescue and issues that arose during the invasion of Grenada that forced reform. The result was the landmark Goldwater-Nichols legislation of 1986.[30] Today it is difficult to see what the problem was all those years. Jointness works.

6. *Intelligence*. Intelligence is the key to airpower. The nature of global strike capability means all aspects of an enemy nation are vulnerable to attack. Before airpower, that was not the case: a nation's vital centers were protected by armies, fortresses, and geography. If the French wished to strike Berlin, for example, they had to first get close enough to do so—and that might take years and countless lives. Airpower changed that. At the same time, just because all targets were now vulnerable did not mean they were of equal value or promised the same return if neutralized. Intelligence of a new type focusing on economic and industrial data was needed to effectively and efficiently target an enemy's vital centers.

Today, intelligence is in greater demand while also more difficult to obtain in some ways. As our intelligence-gathering sensors and techniques have improved, so too have adversaries learned new tricks at hiding or camouflaging the objects we try to examine. This can lead to disaster—as with "The Case of the Missing WMD" in Iraq—and means the *type* of intelligence has metamorphosed. Just as airpower demanded a new type of economic intelligence, so now does the asymmetrical warfare of insurgency and terrorism require cultural intelligence that our present system is not always equipped to collect. We simply do not know or understand the motivations of many who seek to destroy us. The psyche of al Qaeda, Taliban, and ISIS leaders mystifies us.

In addition, although we now have sensors—based in space, in the air, on land, and at sea—that can detect objects, both moving and stationary, as well as intercept all types of electronic emissions, there are certain targets that still confound us. We need to discern the presence of all types of weapons of mass destruction—where they are made, stored, and transported.[31] Until we can do so, accurately and continuously, we will be unable to coerce rogue states like North

Korea or Iran. Given our failure to locate such weapons and facilities in Iraq—a country subjected to intelligence over-flights and UN inspectors prowling the ground for a decade—we can hardly claim our intelligence tells us where such targets exist in closed societies we can monitor only from a distance.

7. Netcentricity. This refers to the necessity of linking together in real time the intelligence-gathering sensors and C2 links deployed around the world. The connection of aircraft with air- and space-based sensors and other C2 assets, virtually instantaneously, using machine-to-machine interfaces, has happened. In the Middle East, for example, drones are flown by pilots from airbases in the United States.

One of the dominant themes of modern war is speed. Everything happens faster than even a decade ago. The greatest venue for this revolution in speed takes place in air, space, and cyberspace. "Near-real time" is a phrase used in air operations centers to denote the requirement for intelligence and communications as soon as an incident occurs. Such a capability is not a pipe dream: operations in Afghanistan, Iraq, Libya, and Syria have shown an increasing ability to employ force with tremendous speed. Indeed, one of the early problems in Afghanistan was that sensors and aircrews were not usually the limiting factor in putting weapons on target. Rather, the reason for delay in the kill cycle was often human—the time necessary to make a decision based on a deluge of intelligence data. The problem was not a dearth of information—a difficulty in times past—but the need for commanders to sift through an *abundance* of information and rapidly determine an appropriate decision.[32] A major factor was the necessity to ensure the target struck was the correct one and that minimal collateral damage would occur when it was hit—concerns that will be discussed in more detail below.

The demand for speed has in turn necessitated that sensors from all services, sources, venues, and mediums be linked together and disseminated to the appropriate users at all levels virtually instantaneously. Arthur Cebrowski, a retired admiral who ran the Office of Transformation in the US Defense Department until his death in 2005, was the individual who coined the term "netcentricity." He saw it as a revolution, and like other revolutionary turns in military affairs, it grew out of fundamental changes in American society. In his words: "These changes have been dominated by the co-evolution of economics, information technology, and business processes and organizations, and they are linked by three themes: 1) The shift in focus from the platform to the network; 2) The shift from viewing actors as independent to viewing them as part of a continuously adapting ecosystem; and 3) The importance of making strategic choices to adapt or even survive in such changing ecosystems."[33] He foresaw global links and networks that could communicate instantaneously, providing needed information to warfighters at all levels. We are moving toward this vision.

There is an intrinsic tension between the principles of netcentricity and unity of command. The latter can be seen as fostering a centralized view of command and control; whereas, netcentricity can often be viewed as an attempt to decentralize—to flow information downward to the tactical level, allowing commanders on the scene to make more timely decisions. This seeming paradox is not insoluble. One could argue that the key to sound decision making—or judgment—at all levels is the accurate information provided by a network-centric C2 system. Information does not ensure sound judgment, but is becoming a necessary ingredient for that result.

8. *Mobility.* In the aftermath of the Cold War, two-thirds of all US military bases overseas were closed. This did not, however, signal a turn toward "Fortress America." The United States continued to believe its interests were best defended as far from her shores as possible. Power projection became ever more important.

Looking at the quantity and composition of air forces worldwide reveals interesting statistics. First, with over 13,000 military aircraft, the United States is by far the largest Aerospace Nation. Russia and China are next in line, with each barely fielding a third of that total. Significantly, although the US Air Force with its 5,000-plus aircraft is the largest air arm in the world, the US Army and the US Navy are each in the top five, and the US Marine Corps is not far behind.[34] But the statistics are even starker, as evidenced by the dominance the United States enjoys in power-projection forces. The Air Force has over 600 airlifters and another 350 tankers. This air mobility fleet allows the United States and its allies to project power anywhere in the world, rapidly, and to *sustain* those forces for extended periods of time. And of course the US Navy has its own brand of global power projection forces.

Airpower projection has been demonstrated on a number of occasions over the past few decades. The Gulf War of 1991 saw mountains of materiel and hundreds of thousands of personnel deployed to the Middle East. US airlifters—enabled by tankers—hauled 500,000 people and 540,000 tons of cargo into the theater, making it the most massive airlift in history.[35] During DESERT STORM itself, the tankers flew 16,868 sorties to offload over 800 million pounds of fuel in 51,696 hook-ups. On any given day tankers accounted for 20 percent of all Coalition sorties flown, and nearly one-third of the aircraft refueled were from the US Navy, the US Marine Corps, and Coalition countries.[36]

Since DESERT STORM, the United States and its allies have flown in NORTHERN and SOUTHERN WATCH over Iraq and in operations in the Balkans and Middle East (Afghanistan, Iraq, and Syria), as well as Libya. During all of those operations airlift and air refueling were essential. Tankers refueled deploying fighters from all the services and allies to bases in the crisis regions; they then refueled the airlifters maintaining the air bridge between the theaters and the United States; and they also refueled US and Coalition aircraft throughout the combat operations themselves. These conditions are likely to remain in effect.

9. *Precision.* The development of precision-guided munitions (PGMs) is one of the military revolutions of our age. These weapons, which continue to evolve, have generated fundamental revisions in the way we plan military campaigns.[37]

Although used in World War II and Vietnam, PGMs came to the fore during the Gulf War of 1991. Television showed cockpit videos detailing the accuracy of these weapons so frequently that they became one of the defining images of that war: the public saw bombs going down chimneys, through doors, and into specific windows. "Air-shaft accuracy" had become routine. When American aircraft struck Serbian targets in Bosnia in 1995, Serbia/Kosovo in 1999, and targets in Afghanistan, Iraq, Libya, and Syria since then, they used PGMs almost exclusively in populated areas. Once again, the accuracy of these weapons was extraordinary.

PGMs have reduced by orders of magnitude the number of sorties required to neutralize a given target. This reduction has a direct relation on the logistics tail required for an air campaign: fewer weapons mean fewer sorties, which in turn mean fewer aircrew and maintenance personnel, less fuel, less ordnance, and fewer spare parts. Rather than mass, *density* (mass per unit of volume) has become the operative term. These reductions cause a cascading effect on the number of support personnel required in-theater to supply and maintain these fewer numbers of aircraft. Because many of these personnel and much of the materiel must come from the United States, their reduction puts a correspondingly lighter load on the mobility forces that deploy and sustain these assets.

Finally, and perhaps most importantly, PGMs ensure fewer casualties to both sides. These new weapons have a high probability of success, so generally only a single aircraft is needed to neutralize a given target.[38] Compare this to the thousands of aircrew members who flew into harm's way in times past. In addition, PGMs mean dramatically less collateral damage and fewer civilian casualties, as was demonstrated in the conflicts from the 1991 Gulf War to the present.

Significantly, precision weapons are not limited to airpower: sea- and land-based weapons systems are increasingly moving into this vital realm as well.

10. Media Awareness and Initiative. I *am not* advocating that the military devise ways to manipulate or deceive the news media. Rather, global communications make it inevitable that virtually everything we do will now be scrutinized by a skeptical news media over which we have no control.

Every bomb, missile, or bullet fired by an American airman, soldier, marine, or sailor is a political act. When a bomb hits a residential area, when a Tomahawk missile crashes into a hotel lobby, or an edgy soldier on patrol kills a civilian at a roadblock, US *foreign* policy suffers a setback. We can no longer afford to miss. Moreover, even when we hit the target, we have to do so almost softly and with minimal impact.

Photographic images often shape our memory of the past. When one remembers the Vietnam War, most of us recall three images in particular: a Viet Cong terrorist being executed with a shot to the head by a South Vietnamese general on a Saigon street; a young girl, naked, running away in terror from a napalm strike; and an American soldier using his lighter to set fire to a Vietnamese hooch. These are not images our military would have chosen to depict its decade-long agony in Vietnam, but it did not have a vote. Similarly, it is likely the war in Iraq will be forever linked with the photographs of prisoner abuse at Abu Ghraib and the image of a US marine firing his rifle into a helpless Iraqi at his feet. These photos, which spread throughout the Islamic world, have become a metaphor for our attempts to democratize Iraq.

In short, the days when we could control news reporting from the front lines are gone. Anyone with a camera, cell phone, or satellite uplink can monitor the military's actions and beam their images, instantaneously, worldwide.

Commanders must be aware of this and take it into account. They must also be proactive and not reactive, because, as the adage goes, bad news never gets better with age.

The issue of media awareness takes on increasing significance in this era of "information warfare." This is a huge topic, but its importance can be summed by noting that the war against Islamic radicals is largely an information war occurring within Islam itself between the radicals and the moderates. The emergence of ISIS clearly demonstrates this civil war between, among others, Sunnis and Shias. This internal battle is the true center of gravity of this war, and our primary task should be to devise ways to aid the moderates in their struggle. In this vision, the information war should be the "supported campaign," and our military actions should have the goals of the overarching information war always in the forefront. Thus, all we do in the Middle East should be with the aim of aiding the Islamic moderates in their struggle to police the radicals who are hijacking their religion.

* * *

These Principles of War reflect the new conditions, new enemies, and new technologies that now dominate warfare. Admittedly, they largely apply to the United States and its closest allies, so they are not universal. But they do reflect how the West now fights. Warfare has changed dramatically over the past few decades. The current list of principles, now a century old and formulated almost exclusively for land warfare, belongs to a bygone era that is obsolete and increasing unlikely to reoccur. We need new ideas for this new environment and must broaden our horizons to understand and interpret how warfare has changed in the past few decades, what it means, and how we should adapt to it.

Part II
War Through the Ages

5

Second Fronts

Success, Failure, and Implications

SOME ARGUE THE BEST way to confront an enemy is to face him head on. At times, however, a belligerent realizes it cannot do so because it is not strong enough, it involves unacceptable risks, or it believes greater gains can be made by opening a "second front."

The purpose of a second front may be to strike a powerful blow, gain resources or deny them to the enemy, split an alliance by knocking out a member, assist an ally by diverting the enemy, or influence a third party—perhaps to deter it from entering the war.

Below are four examples of such maneuvers: two of them succeeded and two others failed.[1] These operations have implications for the way America will fight for the foreseeable future, because our wars are now ones of choice, and the motives and constraints driving such conflicts are comparable to those leading to second fronts throughout history.

The Sicilian Expedition during the Peloponnesian War

The Peloponnesian War between Athens and Sparta was in its sixteenth year when Athens decided to invade Sicily. It proved to be a disastrous decision.

The motives for the Athenian invasion now appear trivial, but the proximate cause occurred in 416 BC, when envoys reached Athens from Egesta, a city in Sicily, seeking aid. Egesta was a member of the Athenian alliance and was being harried by Selinus, a nearby city. The Egestaeans asked the Athenian Assembly to honor its treaty commitments and lend assistance. The Egestaeans also warned of Syracuse, an ally of Selinus and the most powerful city on Sicily. Syracuse, the envoys claimed, was bent on dominating the entire island. Worse, they were friendly toward Sparta, so if Syracuse were to enter the war, Sparta would have access to huge resources in grain, men, and ships that could be used to destroy Athens.

Such catastrophizing on what might occur if several other events took place was an inadequate justification for war. Nonetheless, the Athenians, swayed by the gifted orator Alcibiades, pushed for an invasion of Sicily to defeat Syracuse and conquer the island.[2]

A fact-finding team sent to Egesta returned with favorable views. The Egestaeans would recompense Athens while also providing men and horses. The Assembly voted to send aid, and Nicias was chosen for command, but he attempted to dissuade the Assembly, asking for more debate and another vote. In his oration, Nicias warned that the expedition made little sense. It would anger Sparta—which was then in an uneasy truce with Athens—and involve war with Syracuse. The attack would involve great risk but offer little gain. In a prescient comment, Nicias allegedly stated: "I affirm, then, that you leave many enemies behind you here [the Spartans and their Corinthian allies] to go there far away and bring more back with you." He concluded that even if the invasion was a success and Syracuse defeated, there would be no clear gain: "the Sicilians, even if conquered, are too far off and too numerous to be ruled without difficulty. Now it is folly to go against men who could not be kept under even if conquered, while failure would leave us in a very different position from that which we occupied before the enterprise."[3] Nicias advised his fellow citizens to focus on the main threat, Sparta.

Alcibiades argued instead that Sicily would be an easy conquest, would heap glory on Athens, and would intimidate Sparta. He believed the conquest of Sicily would lead to the overthrow of Carthage and then Libya: "All should be set in the diadem of Athens, and it should be he, Alcibiades, who gave her an Empire, so infinitely greater than was hers now."[4] Alcibiades was persuasive, causing Thucydides to remark caustically that "Everyone fell in love with the enterprise."[5] To his chagrin, the Assembly again voted to put Nicias in charge along with Alcibiades and Lamachus.

The invasion sailed in the summer of 415 BC with 136 warships and 5,100 hoplites—but only thirty horses.[6] Soon after landing in Sicily, Alcibiades was summoned back to Athens to stand trial on charges of impiety and blasphemy.[7] Fearing he would be found guilty, Alcibiades fled to Sparta, where he offered his services against his home city.

Most historians argue that had the Athenians moved quickly, they would have overcome Syracusan resistance. Instead, the Athenians dallied, partly because of Alcibiades's recall, and partly due to the inherent caution of Nicias. Things turned sour. Egesta had not the money, men, or horses promised, and the Sicilians did not welcome their liberators: "The arrival of the Athenian armada had united Sicily as nothing else could have done."[8] The Syracusans also proved to be tough adversaries. Although the Athenians won a few skirmishes, they were unable to reduce the city. Sparta, influenced by its new friend Alcibiades, sent General Gylippus to assist the Syracusans along with a contingent of Corinthian soldiers. In addition, Sparta invaded Attica—the area surrounding the city of Athens—and laid it to waste. As Nicias had predicted, Athens was now fighting a two-front war against formidable opponents.

In 415 the Spartans built a fort at Decelea, ten miles from Athens (on the advice of Alcibiades), from which to disrupt Athenian agriculture. The effort's main effect was psychological: the Athenians sat behind the walls and watched their farms being destroyed. The Spartans hoped this would induce them to come out and fight, but other than small cavalry raids the Athenians remained within the city.[9] Morale plummeted and was hurt further when plague hit the city. It was disaster. This pestilence killed 4,400 hoplites and 300 cavalrymen (around a third of her military forces) and tens of thousands of citizens, including Pericles.[10]

For the army in Sicily, it was a question of time. Nicias, commander after the departure of Alcibiades and the death of Lamachus in battle, pleaded for either reinforcements or evacuation. He was sent another army, but it made no difference. In the summer of 413 Gylippus defeated the Athenians in a series of battles. Nicias was killed and 7,000 Athenians were captured. By the end of the Sicilian disaster the number of Athenian hoplites had fallen from 29,000 to 9,000; it lost 160 triremes and most of their crews; and it did not have the funds to build anew.[11] Hans Delbrück states that when all hoplites, sailors, and slaves working as rowers and supply carriers are counted, Athens lost 60,000 men.[12]

Observations

- The motive behind the Sicilian expedition was dubious. The fifty-year Peace of Nicias between Athens and Sparta had been signed in 421 BC, but seven years into it the Athenians invaded Sicily. Although Syracuse was a powerful city-state, there was no indication it was planning war against Athens. Sending an army to Sicily denuded Athens itself of an adequate defense, leaving it prey to a Spartan attack.

- There were no Spartans in Sicily when Athens invaded, but then Gylippus and a Corinthian contingent brought aid to Syracuse. As a result, Spartan resources were not depleted during the two-year campaign, while those of Athens were.
- The Athenian net assessment was faulty. Athens did not encounter a friendly population, nor the horses, troops, and money promised.[13] The lack of financial support was a setback, but the lack of horses was serious: chronically short of cavalry, the Athenians were often outflanked or rendered immobile by the Syracusan mounted arm.[14]
- Nicias was a poor choice to command. As the architect of the peace treaty with Sparta, he was reluctant to wage war over a weak pretext. Alcibiades was a born leader and successful general despite his character flaws. Had he not been summoned back to Athens, it is likely the Athenians would have aggressively attacked. Lamachus was a fine soldier but was killed early in the campaign. Nicias, with no counterbalance, became increasingly passive and was out-generaled by Gylippus. By the time reinforcements arrived, the die had already been cast.
- Athens had command of the sea but did not exploit it. One historian argues that Athenian naval supremacy was untested and had gained a reputation by default and tradition rather than by combat.[15] Supply lines were open to Athens, but the fleet was unable to blockade Syracuse and thus could not prevent its resupply and reinforcement from Sparta and Corinth. As time wore on the Athenian fleet deteriorated, and in 413 the Syracusan navy destroyed it.[16] The army was then trapped and quickly surrendered.

This was seen by Athens as a preventive war to abort the presumed union of Sicily and Sparta, but there was little indication such an alliance would have occurred. Indeed, it was the expedition itself that drove Syracuse into the arms of Sparta. One historian claimed Athens embarked on the adventure purely to satisfy ambitions of empire.[17]

The expedition to Sicily was a huge defeat for Athens. It made a brief recovery when the Athenians, astonishingly, recalled Alcibiades and made him supreme commander in 407. After some initial successes, his arrogance and ambition resulted in exile. Soon after, Sparta was victorious in 404.[18]

Wellington in the Peninsula

In 1807 Napoleon controlled most of Europe. Britain still held out, and after Admiral Horatio Nelson's victory at Trafalgar in 1805, Napoleon realized he could not launch an invasion. He therefore instituted the Continental System to break her economy. He then ordered Europe not to trade with Britain. Portugal had long been a British ally and refused to obey. To teach them a lesson, the emperor marched 30,000 men through Spain and conquered Portugal.

In order to better secure the Iberian Peninsula and ensure there would be no leaks in his embargo, Napoleon then made a serious mistake. The Spanish government was corrupt and ineffectual, so Napoleon installed his brother Joseph on the throne, hoping this would give him a solid ally to the south and improve Spanish governance. To his surprise, the Spanish population rose up against Joseph, and this resistance movement, one of the bloodiest and most effective guerrilla wars in centuries, proved an endless drain on French resources.[19]

The French army was 120,000 strong, battle tested, and led by senior commanders. Spanish resistance was initially inchoate and disorganized, but still gave the French fits. In July an army of 18,000 men under General Pierre Dupont surrendered to the Spanish at Bailen. Napoleon was furious and headed south personally: "I realize that I must go there myself to get the machine working again."[20] By October 1808 he had 270,000 men in the peninsula.

Britain sent an army to Portugal to assist the rebels, but this effort, under the command of Lieutenant General John Moore, was unsuccessful.[21] After smashing the Spanish armies, Napoleon moved against Moore, driving him back to the coast. Moore evacuated his army, but the following year Lieutenant General Arthur Wellesley returned with another force.[22]

Wellesley believed he could defend Portugal and take the war into Spain if able to maintain his sea lines of communication, if the Portuguese and Spanish assisted him, and if the French were never able to concentrate 100,000 men against him.[23] Wellesley proved correct. For three years he defended Lisbon and drove back French armies. He was greatly aided by the tenacity of the Spanish, who struck continually at the French supply lines stretching back to France. Spain's rebel army was not well equipped or trained, but it possessed spirit and toughness. The bloody but ferocious defense at Saragossa in early 1809 served as a rallying point to give the Spanish population courage and hope.[24] Indeed, 70 percent of French battle casualties sustained during the war were inflicted by the Spanish Army and the guerrillas.[25]

Throughout 1810 and 1811, Wellesley, now Viscount Wellington and soon to be a duke, coordinated with the Spanish to pressure French forces throughout the peninsula. Battles were fought at Bussaco, Fuentes d'Oñoro, Albuera, Caia, and Upper Côa, all French defeats. It was a hard-fought war, but in 1812 everything changed.

Napoleon invaded Russia with 500,000 men, and Iberia became a sideshow. Wellington assaulted Spain and over the next year bested a number of French generals, winning battles at Ciudad Rodrigo, Badajoz, and Salamanca. In August he liberated Madrid, and the following year he crossed the mountains to invade France.

Observations

- Napoleon overestimated Spain's value, hoping it would be a productive puppet, but the army was weak and the navy had been virtually destroyed at Trafalgar.[26] The emperor also believed Spain was fabulously wealthy, but the richness of the Spanish empire and the gold extracted from the Americas had long since dried up; Madrid was nearly bankrupt when Napoleon invaded. Moreover, putting Joseph on the throne was an error. King Ferdinand may have been incompetent and an autocrat, but he was Spanish.[27]
- Spain was virtually a desert, and French supply over the Pyrenees proved a huge problem. It is surprising the French survived. Even Wellington commented that "with all our money and having in our favour the good inclinations of the country, I assure you that I could not maintain one division in the district in which they have maintained not less than 60,000 men and 20,000 animals for more than two months."[28]
- France had imposed occupation governments in several locales with little reaction from the populace. Spain was different, and fanatical resistance opposed the French. In addition, the Napoleonic practice of living off the land—confiscating the food and livestock needed from the local peasantry—greatly irked the people forced to provide.[29] Wellington learned from this error and forbade its practice.
- Leadership was crucial. French generals had never encountered the bleak terrain of Iberia nor endured such relentless guerrilla warfare. Most could not adapt. To be clear, these were not second-string generals sent to Spain: most of France's marshals endured tours there, and they could not adjust.[30] In contrast, Wellington was an excellent general

who maintained a well-equipped and -trained force that cooperated effectively with the Spanish and Portuguese.[31] In addition, Wellington did not have to face the best French commander—Napoleon himself. When the emperor entered Spain in October 1808 he quickly crushed resistance but then departed and left his marshals to mop up.[32] His absence was dearly felt. Wellington himself noted after one hard-fought victory that "If Boney had been there we should have been defeated."[33]

- Napoleon named Joseph head of the French armies in Spain, but he had little military experience and none of his brother's brilliance. The marshals ignored him, and the emperor sent orders directly to his commanders, bypassing his brother. In addition, the marshals were vain, ambitious, and egotistical. They schemed against each other and often refused to cooperate, despite the costs of such intransigence. As one historian describes the feuding: "Junot, mindful of his own failure in Portugal, resented him [Massena] and wished him ill; Reynier disliked him, and Ney, never an easy officer to control, became utterly recalcitrant."[34]
- Wellington enjoyed excellent intelligence because the Portuguese and Spanish kept him well informed, whereas it was extremely difficult for the French to communicate with Paris. Wellington commented: "The French armies have no communications and one army has no knowledge of the position or of the circumstances in which the others are placed, whereas I have knowledge of all that passes on all sides."[35] One historian argues that Wellington's intelligence was the "most sophisticated" of the nineteenth century.[36]
- The Royal Navy's control of the sea was crucial. The fleet supplied the British with food, ammunition, and reinforcements on a constant basis—over 13,000 ships landed in Iberia during the war and brought 348 cannon, 336,000 muskets, and over 60 million rounds of ammunition.[37] This constant resupply was a huge advantage, but the Royal Navy did more. It provided fire support to army units ashore; transported millions of pounds of sterling and bullion to the Portuguese and Spanish to maintain their financial viability; swept the seas of French vessels; resupplied Allied coastal fortresses under siege while blockading those held by the French; and served as a transportation service for Wellington's troops.[38] The fleet landed and embarked British units all around the 1,500 miles of Iberian coastline, usually catching the French by surprise. The navy was especially valuable in moving British artillery

around the periphery of the peninsula—an important advantage given the miserable nature of Spanish roads.

Gallipoli, 1915

The Great War had deteriorated into a bloodbath within five months of its outbreak in July 1914. A line of trenches stretching from the North Sea to Switzerland separated the opposing sides, and stalemate would remain on the Western Front for most of the war.[39] Various solutions were attempted to break the impasse, including a massive use of artillery, poison gas, flame throwers, and infantry penetration tactics. Eventually, tactical mobility was restored by a combination of tanks, aircraft, improved tactics, and fresh troops.

Strategically, there were other ideas. Allies were courted to outflank the enemy: the Ottoman Empire, Italy, Bulgaria, Romania, and the United States all joined the war. Another idea was to open a second front. Britain was keen on this notion because such operations were the "British Way of War."

The First Lord of the Admiralty in 1915 was Winston Churchill and the First Sea Lord was Admiral "Jackie" Fisher.[40] Both were noted for creative thinking. Churchill was appalled by the slaughter on the Western Front and asked plaintively "are there not alternatives than sending our armies to chew barbed wire in Flanders?"[41] The plan offering the greatest reward for the least risk involved opening a second front at the Dardanelles Strait, the waterway separating the Mediterranean Sea from the Black Sea. Constantinople (modern-day Istanbul) was located along this waterway. Churchill opined that a naval move up the strait would cow the Turks and push them out of the war, in turn opening a supply line to Russia. The country could then be used as a base from which to strike Austria-Hungary from the rear. Conveniently, in January 1915 Grand Duke Nicholas, commander in chief of the Russian armies, asked his allies for a diversion to relieve pressure on his forces battling the Turks in the Caucasus.[42]

Churchill and the admirals believed a navy-only operation would suffice to force the strait.[43] This passage was flanked on the north (the European side) by the Gallipoli Peninsula and on the south (the Asian side) by the Anatolian mainland; both coastlines were littered with forts and artillery positions.[44] Nonetheless, the seamen thought that battleship guns could silence the enemy cannon. The strait was also mined, but the armada would include minesweepers to clear the way for the battleships to pass through (after they had silenced the enemy guns), confront Constantinople, shell it if necessary, and then accept the Ottoman surrender.

On January 13, 1915, the British War Council approved the plan. Field Marshal Horatio Kitchener agreed only because Churchill assured him British soldiers were not necessary—Kitchener was determined to save his infantry for the Western Front. A British and French fleet arrived off Gallipoli in January 1915 consisting of eighty-two ships, including eighteen battleships.[45]

On February 19, 1915, ten battleships under the command of Vice Admiral Sackville Carden entered the strait and began shelling the forts. It was expected the enemy guns would be silenced by naval gunfire within a month. That first day, however, *no* enemy guns were destroyed despite a barrage lasting seven hours.[46] Over the next three weeks several more forays into the strait were launched, with meager results. It was clear that using naval gunfire to knock out coastal forts was a difficult if not impossible job.

On March 18 the ships went in again, but this time they hit the mines. Three battleships were sunk and three others heavily damaged, putting a third of the Allies' capital ships out of commission in one day. Vice Admiral John de Robeck, who had replaced an ill Carden, ordered his ships out of the strait and would not send them back. Attempts to remove the mines at night were unsuccessful. The Turks used searchlights to illuminate the trawlers being used as minesweepers, and shore-based guns sent up a hail of fire that drove the ships back.[47]

It was obvious a naval-only operation was impossible. Churchill went back to the War Council and requested an invasion force to capture the Gallipoli Peninsula and overrun the forts from the land side. Once secured, the fleet could then move through the strait to Constantinople. Fisher agreed, arguing the British effort must be *totus porkus* (whole hog).[48] Surprisingly, the War Council agreed. The high gain/low risk navy-only operation had now become a high-risk joint operation.

In April 1915, a force of 62,000 Allied soldiers landed at Gallipoli.[49] They were met by rugged terrain, entrenched positions, and well-led Turkish forces. For the next eight months the opposing sides hammered away at each other. Trenches were dug, barbed wire was strung, and the Gallipoli battlefield quickly resembled the Western Front that the entire operation was intended to bypass. Five more Allied divisions were sent, to no avail.

As casualties mounted, the War Council debated what to do. General Ian

Hamilton, the Gallipoli commander, asked for more divisions and was promptly sacked; his place was taken by General Charles Munro. Upon arrival, Munro decided further efforts were useless and recommended evacuation, prompting the acerbic comment by Churchill: “He came, he saw, he capitulated.”[50] Kitchener was shocked by this suggestion and sailed out to look things over himself. He was stunned by the terrain and the formidability of the Turkish defenses. Returning to London, he told the War Council that Munro was correct: evacuation was essential. A withdrawal began on December 7, and the last soldier left Gallipoli in January 1916.

The Gallipoli operation was an Allied disaster, costing nearly 400,000 casualties and gaining nothing. The Ottoman Empire remained in the war; Russia was still largely cut off from her allies, and the Western Front was stagnant.

Observations

- The strategic concept articulated by Churchill in 1914 appeared reasonable. The navy-only option was low-risk, yet the gains seemed large: Ottoman surrender, the opening of a supply route to Russia, and a venue from which to strike Austria-Hungary. One historian concludes that if the operation had been a success, it would have shortened the war by two years.[51] Unfortunately, the orders given Admiral Carden were vague: he was to force the strait and take Constantinople. It was not clear how a naval force could “take” a well-defended fortress without troops. Horatio Nelson had once commented that “A ship’s a fool to fight a fort,” but Churchill and Fischer persisted.[52] Most historians now believe the navy-only option could never have worked.[53]
- The British net assessment was poor. They underestimated the strength of the Turkish forts, the number of artillery batteries along the strait, the difficulty in knocking out those cannon with low-trajectory naval guns, the impossibility of using civilian trawlers to sweep mines in the narrow waters with hundreds of enemy guns on either coast, the horrendous terrain, and the determination of the defenders.[54]
- British leadership and staffing were deficient. Admiral Fisher went along with Churchill despite what he later claimed was his better judgment. Admiral Carden and General Hamilton lacked aggressiveness. In February 1915 there were only two Turkish divisions deployed along

the strait; that number doubled by the time the naval assault began. There were still only six divisions at the time of Hamilton's landings. Unfortunately, this dilatory Turkish reaction was matched by the Allies. Basil Liddell Hart, an advocate of the operation, railed against the piecemeal application of force: "If the British had used at the outset even a fair proportion of the forces they ultimately expended in driblets, it is clear from Turkish accounts that victory would have crowned the undertaking."[55] In addition, the Admiralty staff in London offered no plans for reducing the forts or overcoming the mines. One observer commented: "as products from the senior staff of the largest navy in the world, they [the plans] represented a lamentable failure to get to grips with most of the important issues confronting Carden."[56]

- Intelligence on Turkish dispositions was inadequate. Hamilton, who had no knowledge of the area, received two days' notice before leaving for Gallipoli and was forced to rely on prewar reports and outdated maps.[57] In addition, the nature and challenges of large-scale amphibious operations were not yet understood. When supply ships reached Gallipoli it was discovered they had been improperly loaded—virtually everything needed immediately was located in the bottom of the hold, while those things not essential were stored on top. The ships were sent back to Egypt, where they were unloaded and then repacked in the proper order, resulting in a two-week delay.[58]
- Command of the sea was seemingly assured, but that was not the case. There are two aspects to sea control: the enemy is prevented from using the sea either to resupply himself or to attack. The Royal Navy fulfilled this requirement. The second aspect is often overlooked: the enemy is unable to halt the actions of the attacker. This second aspect is just as important as the first. Defeating the enemy's fleet is not an end in itself: control of the sea must then be exploited. This was impossible at Gallipoli because Turkish land-based defenses and mines prevented the Royal Navy from forcing the strait and achieving victory.

Gallipoli was the only major victory of the war for Ottoman forces. Admiral Fisher resigned and Churchill was fired soon after the evacuation. The second front strategy was discredited and advocates of a Western Front approach gained ascendancy in the Allied camp.

North Africa, Operation TORCH, 1942

When the United States entered the war against Germany in December 1941 the alliance was at low ebb. Most of continental Europe had fallen, the Soviet Union was reeling, German submarines were playing havoc with Allied shipping, and Erwin Rommel was running loose in North Africa. In the Pacific, Singapore was about to fall to the Japanese, as were the Philippine Islands and the Dutch East Indies. The Allies needed victories.

The American and British Combined Chiefs of Staff met to discuss where and when to strike. A "Europe First" strategy was affirmed in late December 1941: "Germany was the predominant member of the Axis Powers, and consequently the Atlantic and European area was considered to be the decisive theater. . . . Only the minimum of force necessary for the safeguarding of vital interests in other theaters should be diverted from operations against Germany."[59] The question in early 1942 was where to attack the Nazis.

General George Marshall, the US Army chief of staff, argued for a landing in France that year.[60] The British were aghast. They had already evacuated at Narvik (Norway), Dunkirk (France), and Greece and had no wish to do so again. The German forces in France were too strong to meet with a paltry six to ten Allied divisions; a frontal assault in 1942 would be suicidal. Although the Soviets wanted a second front, it would do them no good if a landing in France was thrown back into the sea.[61] The British argued instead for an invasion of North Africa. It would be easier, allow the green American troops (and their commanders) to gain combat experience, secure the Mediterranean for Allied shipping, protect Middle East oil supplies, and ensure the safety of the Suez Canal.[62] The chiefs dickered until Prime Minister Churchill and President Franklin Roosevelt stepped in and ordered a landing in North Africa.[63]

This decision solved one problem, but there were others. Where in North Africa should landings occur, what mix of troops would be used, and who would command? The last point was easy to resolve: Lieutenant General Dwight Eisenhower was chosen to command largely because American troops would supply the bulk of the invasion force and, for reasons discussed below, it was deemed prudent for the British to take a less prominent role in the operation.

Eisenhower wanted landings at Casablanca and Oran. The British disagreed, believing that once the Nazis saw the invasion they would rush troops into Tunisia and block the Allies from linking up with General Bernard Montgomery's forces in Libya. The British wanted additional landings at

Algiers, Bone, and Philippeville in Algeria. This would put the Allies close to Tunisia, allowing them to move in quickly and forestall a Nazi advance. Eisenhower demurred: he had neither the troops nor landing craft for all five locations. A compromise was reached: the Allies would land at Casablanca, Oran, and Algiers—500 miles from Tunis.[64]

North Africa was under the control of Vichy France and defended by 120,000 troops plus tanks and heavy artillery, 500 aircraft, and numerous combat ships.[65] However, the French distrusted the British, feeling they had been left in the lurch during the battle for France. Eisenhower therefore decided that British troops would not be in the vanguard of the attacks, lest they spur a spirited defense. It was hoped using American troops would mute the French response.

The invasion took place on November 8, 1942, and resistance was short-lived: within three days Morocco and Algeria were under control.[66] Unfortunately, the decision not to land farther east proved a problem. While the Allies were securing the landing areas, the Germans flooded into Tunisia. At the time of the Allied landings there were 11,000 Axis troops in Tunisia: six weeks later there were over 47,000.[67] A bitter battle would be required to drive them back out. One historian concluded that "The Axis build-up was much quicker and more powerful than had been predicted, but the Allied reaction to it was culpably slow."[68]

Tunisia finally fell on May 13, 1943. The North African campaign was over. The Allies had suffered 75,000 casualties, but the Axis took over five times that number.[69]

Observations

- The turmoil over the invasion was serious. Nonetheless, the combined chiefs, with the hands-on leadership of Roosevelt and Churchill, eventually produced an effective plan. A frontal assault against France was rejected with good reason. Such an attack with inexperienced commanders, green troops, and insufficient logistical support would have been a disaster. Sufficient forces simply were not available; moreover, air superiority over France could not be attained in 1942. (In fact, it would not be achieved until spring 1944.) As a result of these implacable facts, cooler heads prevailed.
- The Allied net assessment was unusually accurate: the Allies knew where Axis troops were located and how well they were equipped. They also

possessed insight into the Vichy forces in Africa.[70] This was a thorny issue. The French were forced to walk a treacherous line between wanting to throw off the German yoke but not giving the Nazis a pretext for occupying all of France and ending Vichy's autonomy. Ensuring a largely unopposed landing was a challenge, but the Allies were successful. Overall, the Allies suffered around 1,900 casualties and the French about 1,350.[71]

- It would be tempting to hail the brilliance of Allied leadership during this campaign and see victory as inevitable, but that would be hindsight. The commanders who would go on to become household names in the United States and Britain—Eisenhower, Montgomery, Spaatz, Patton, Tedder, et al.—did not begin brilliantly. American commanders were either untested or prone to mistakes. Eisenhower had no combat experience, and although a consummate planner, even he showed a lack of vision. His original intent of landing at Oran and Casablanca was insufficient, and after the landings he procrastinated in his move toward Tunis.[72] Delay prolonged the campaign for four months and cost thousands of casualties.[73] To a great extent, the lengthy Tunisian campaign determined Allied strategy for all of 1943, pushing the invasion of France back until the summer of 1944.
- This was an excellent example of allies working together to plan, organize, and conduct a major amphibious operation. Eisenhower proved adept at working with allies, but it was not an easy road. The British thought the Americans to be upstarts with little experience in war; the Americans believed the British were only good at successful evacuations.[74] And then there were the French factions. It took all of Eisenhower's charm and persuasiveness, along with determined good will at all levels, to make TORCH a success.
- Intelligence played a key role throughout the campaign, and the Allies had an excellent overview of the Axis and Vichy situations.[75] In addition, the deception campaign carried out before the invasion was flawless. Although the Germans knew something was afoot, they expected reinforcements at Malta, landings in Sicily, or an attack in the eastern Mediterranean. They were caught by surprise in North Africa.[76]
- Command of the sea and air were crucial. It was not coincidental that a key objective on November 8 was to secure airfields. This was done,

> and although Allied airpower outnumbered the French, the same was not true regarding the Germans. Initially, Luftwaffe aircraft based in Sardinia, Sicily, and Libya caused serious problems with Allied sea transport operations.[77] In addition, land operations for all sides were becoming increasingly dependent on airpower. The Luftwaffe was more numerous as well as more effective at providing air support for its troops at this stage of the war. Allied air operations were also hindered by lack of aircraft, logistical difficulties, ineffective peacetime doctrine, and confused command and control relationships. Fortunately, the airmen learned quickly. Air superiority was gained by March 1943 and not relinquished.

The invasion of North Africa was an extremely successful second front operation. Allied goals were fulfilled: the Axis suffered defeat and was thrown out of Africa with heavy losses, while Mediterranean sea lanes were secured for Allied use. Troops, planners, and commanders gained invaluable experience that would be much needed for the operations to come.

Overall Observations

The dominant reason for opening a second front is to avoid enemy strength. If the enemy defends vigorously at the new venue, it often requires him to disperse forces. Gaining an economic advantage can also be a major motive, and this was a partial explanation for the Sicilian expedition. Similarly, Britain saw Iberia as a major trade market after Napoleon shut down most of Europe to her merchant fleet.

Another motive for a second front is to split an alliance. This was a goal of the British and French at Gallipoli in 1915 when they hoped to force the Ottoman Empire out of the war.

Other operations, such as TORCH in 1942, were a combination of several motives: driving Axis forces out of North Africa, securing the Mediterranean and Suez Canal, and providing experience for American troops and commanders. Below are some overall observations regarding factors that helped lead to either success or failure.

Logical and Achievable Strategic Plan

The most important determinant of a second front's success is its logic and achievability. In some cases, goals are well-thought out—the decision to launch TORCH in 1942, or Wellington's peninsular campaign. Other goals make less sense. It was not obvious how the Sicilian expedition would weaken Sparta; instead, it split Athenian forces and left Athens open to attacks in Attica. Even had the invasion been successful, it is not clear what gains would have accrued to Athens in her war with Sparta.

In some instances the objectives sought appear worthwhile but their achievability is questionable. Gallipoli looked reasonable at first glance, but it had glaring flaws. It is difficult for ships to compel the surrender of a defended fortress—much less an entire nation—but Royal Navy leaders persisted. Reinforcing failure, the Allies committed several divisions of ground troops in a futile attempt to correct earlier misjudgments. The result was an even greater failure.

Accurate Net Assessment

A net assessment should contain a weighing of goals balanced against expected costs. The Athenian assessment was faulty. It did not encounter a friendly population, and the horses, troops, and money promised were not forthcoming. The Athenians also overestimated the willingness of Sicilian city states to support an attack on Syracuse.

Napoleon overestimated Spain's economic and military value. Moreover, establishing Joseph on the throne was a huge error. The Spanish people displayed a surprising affection for King Ferdinand and fought ferociously against the French invaders. In addition, Spain was incapable of supporting a large army that intended to live off the land. This was soon recognized in Paris, but supplying an army over the Pyrenees Mountains proved a monumental problem.[78]

The net assessment conducted by the British at the Dardanelles in 1915 was poor. They underestimated the strength of the Turkish forts, the difficulty in knocking out coastal fortifications with naval guns, the impossibility of using trawlers to sweep mines in the narrow waters with hundreds of enemy guns on either coast, the terrain to be encountered on Gallipoli, and the determination of the Turkish defenders.[79]

The Allies' assessment was unusually accurate for TORCH; the Allies knew where Axis troops were located and how well they were equipped. More importantly, they possessed insight into Vichy forces and leaders in North Africa, and this was crucial for the landings' success.[80]

Leadership

Leadership at all levels was crucial. In Sicily, once Alcibiades fled and Lamachus was killed, Nicias was too hesitant and pessimistic. He had not supported the expedition in the first place, and his penchant for delay meant his forces were ever on the defensive.

French generals in the peninsula were unprepared for the austere conditions they encountered and were surprised by the vicious guerrilla war waged against them. On the other hand, Wellington was adept at working effectively with his allies.

Allied leadership at Gallipoli was mediocre. Royal Navy planning was poor, and commanders and staffs were unable to devise solutions to the problems of the defensive guns and mines. The Allied generals were too ready to fall into the bad habits of the Western Front and simply dig in and hope they would win a battle of attrition.

Victory was not inevitable in North Africa. American commanders were untested and prone to mistakes. Eisenhower's original plan to land only at Oran and Casablanca was insufficient. After the success of the landings at Algiers he procrastinated in his move toward Tunis, and this delay prolonged the campaign and cost thousands of casualties.

Intelligence

The Athenians had little intelligence upon landing in Sicily. The populace saw them as invaders and instead channeled information to Syracuse. Similarly, the French in the peninsula were denied information on the dispositions and intentions of the British, Spanish, and Portuguese. The population hated the French and not only served as guerrillas to harry their supply lines, but was ruthless in tracking down and killing French spies and couriers.[81]

In World War II the Allies broke the top secret German codes early in the war, and this was fundamental in staying ahead of the Germans.[82] Good military commanders appreciate the importance of intelligence to success, but great commanders ensure they actually have timely and accurate intelligence. Intelligence is always a key to victory, and the commander's attitude and personal involvement in the intelligence process are crucial.

Friendly Population

It is difficult for an invader to attack a defended shore, and once there he must ensure the enemy is unable to counterattack effectively. Even if landings are unopposed, an attacker must establish a firm base for resupply. Wellington enjoyed such a base in Portugal, which allowed him to operate in Spain and eventually France itself. The opposite was the case for France. The French could not ignore the Spanish army that constantly appeared in their rear and along their lines of supply, making it impossible to marshal their full strength against Wellington.[83]

It was not necessary to win over the population and make them allies—although this occurred in Iberia and was a major factor in British success. The Arab populace in North Africa was indifferent to whoever occupied the country in 1942, and the French were easily won over, thus making Allied operations significantly easier.

Force Size

It is an aphorism that attacking an enemy in a defended position requires superiority, but at Gallipoli the Allies fed in twelve divisions piecemeal. This slow buildup allowed the Turks to counter, with the result that the Allies were never able to establish superiority.

During the North African invasion there was concern over the resistance that would be offered by the French defenders, but Allied intelligence placed it at an acceptable level. Moreover, the 200,000 Allied troops hitting the beaches in Morocco and Algeria were sufficient to overawe the French defenders into but a token fight. The argument over the venue for the second front—France versus North Africa—was an important one for this reason. France was defended by German troops, and that presented an entirely different level of risk.

Command of the Sea

Command of the sea was a significant factor in success. Due to poor Spanish roads, the British fleet supplied food, ammunition, and reinforcements on a constant basis. The Royal Navy also provided fire support, resupplied coastal fortresses under siege while blockading those held by the French, and served as a rapid and efficient transportation service for Wellington's troops. Likewise, Allied naval superiority in the Mediterranean was crucial to success in 1942.

Sea supremacy was not enough to guarantee victory. The Athenians had the greatest fleet in Greece during the Peloponnesian War; yet it did not provide victory in Sicily because it was not exploited. The fleet could not effectively blockade Syracuse and thus did not prevent its resupply and reinforcement from Sparta and Corinth.

Similarly, command of the sea was seemingly assured at Gallipoli, but that was not the case, because Turkish defenses were able to thwart the plans of the Allies and render their sea power useless. In sum, naval superiority was an essential but insufficient factor in success.

Implications

The decision to open a second front against an enemy is a time-tested strategy that offers a less risky option when fighting a powerful opponent while at the same time offering a chance for surprise and initiative. Some of these operations have been successful while others have not.

Since World War II, the United States has fought wars of choice, not necessity. Korea, Vietnam, the Balkans, Afghanistan, Iraq, Libya, and Syria were fought as responses to aggression against the United States or its allies or to aid nations it chose to protect. These actions were similar to second front operations based on the motives and constraints involved: a deliberate decision to limit American commitment and avoid a major war.

The terrorist attacks of September 2001 necessitated a strong response. Even so, faulty intelligence pushed the United States into an invasion of Iraq in 2003. That war, plus Afghanistan, employed substantial resources in men and material, but any results gained were dearly bought over an unusually lengthy period of time.

Our experience in the Middle East over the two decades is in contrast to the wisdom and economy of second front operations and their restraint. The American use of force should now be characterized by limited liability and an effort to avoid casualties, not just to ourselves but to the enemy as well. Because the United States is attempting to shape events in foreign countries, it is imperative that we not employ so much force that the populace is turned against us.

These unusual objectives and limitations push us toward military responses similar to those that dictated second front operations of the past. We wish to avoid taking on an enemy too directly; continued presence should be avoided; risk must be minimized; casualties, especially to the civilian populace, must be strictly limited.

As in second front operations, the keys to success are seemingly timeless: the necessity of a clear and achievable strategic goal; a sound net assessment; accurate and detailed intelligence before and during the operation; capable if not exceptional leadership at all levels; a sound base and friendly populace; and both sea and air control.

The US must have a capability to project power, worldwide, quickly and sustainably. Sea and air control and intelligence assets are essential to protect those lines of communication. In addition, airpower's flexibility allows rapid and long-range employment combined with accurate and tunable force application. The 2011 action in Libya, sanctioned by the United Nations, was intended to remove a brutish dictator and give the populace a chance for democracy, but like Kosovo in 1999, it did not involve the use of NATO ground troops.

Given the troubles in Afghanistan and Iraq, America should ponder the decision to inject conventional troops into a hot area—the costs and risk may be too high. Instead, we should take a page from the successful second front operations of the past: we should maximize the attributes of our sea and air forces that can project enormous but discrete power over great distances while doing so at relatively low cost and considerably less risk.

6

Decisive Victories and What They Mean

DECISIVE VICTORY HAS BEEN sought by military commanders for millennia because such victories end the war more quickly, reducing the cost. But the list of decisive victories is a short one. My purpose is to define the meaning of decisive victory and list history's most important.

Wars are fought for specific purposes that meet several criteria: They should be launched only after considerable thought by a nation's leaders. Motives should concern weighty issues of state—not matters of whim or personality—and the goals should be achievable. Finally, the leaders should prepare the nation for war, both materially and psychologically. These criteria appear to be straightforward common sense, and most countries entering a war believe they have fulfilled them. It is only later, when a nation begins to taste defeat, that it realizes the criteria were not followed after all. It is then usually too late.

Therefore, the first requirement of decisive victory is that it achieves one's goals, and that goal must be of importance—the destruction of a dangerous enemy, for example.[1] Great victories are often of a negative variety: rather than defeating an enemy, the result is the assurance that the enemy cannot win—the victor therefore ensures his survival.

There is a time element involved. A smashing victory, regardless of the death toll, is not decisive if the enemy is able to raise another army and continue the war. A victory should not be reversible except in the long term. Thus, the iconic battle of Cannae in 216 BC where Hannibal annihilated sixteen Roman legions in one day was a brilliant tactical victory, but the strategic results were minimal. Rome formed more legions, the war lurched on for a further fourteen years, and Carthage eventually lost. Similarly, Chancellorsville was one of Robert E. Lee's masterpieces. Heavily outnumbered by Federal forces, Lee won a crushing victory—but the war continued and went badly for the South. Chancellorsville was a transient tactical advantage for the Confederates, nothing more.

Smashing victories often lead to surrender and war's end—they are the "last battle." However, the time element again comes into play: if the defeated party rebuilds its forces and resumes the war, the battle was not decisive at all. Most of Napoleon's victories merely ended hostilities temporarily while both sides regrouped before going at each other again. The triumphs over the Austrians at Ulm and Austerlitz in 1805 broke the Third Coalition, but Austria attacked again in 1809. After Napoleon's victory at Wagram, Austria once again sued for peace—only to restart hostilities in 1813. Similar Napoleonic battles that led to truces, not lasting peace, included Jena-Auerstadt over the Prussians in 1806 that shattered the Fourth Coalition, and the bloody decision over the Russians at Friedland leading to Tilsit in 1807.[2]

Although one generally refers to decisive *battles,* sometimes it is *wars* that are decisive. Some wars are attritional slugfests that kill thousands yet fail to yield conclusive battlefield decisions. The American Civil War was the bloodiest in US history and witness to several tactical gems—such as the Chancellorsville battle already noted, but also the Shenandoah Valley campaign of Thomas Jackson and the persistent industriousness of U. S. Grant at Vicksburg—but conflict ended in June 1865 with a whimper, not a bang. The exhausted armies of Lee, Joseph Johnston, and Kirby Smith simply gave up. Yet, the war was decisive: the Confederacy would not rise again. Similarly, World War II contained many battles, but the decisive defeat of Germany was due to grinding pressure on multiple fronts—massive land armies east, west, and south, strategic bombing, and a strangling naval blockade.

The enemy must acknowledge defeat, and battlefield success may or may not have a role in that decision. In 1870 the French were crushed by the Prussians at Sedan and Metz, and Paris was then surrounded. Yet, the French refused to admit defeat, and the war continued for five more months. Similarly, Germany was never reconciled to its defeat in 1918. Almost immediately following the Armistice it began secretly preparing for a rematch. On the other hand, the United States suffered less than two dozen dead in the 1993 battle of Mogadishu, but the deaths of those relatively few soldiers broke the will of American leaders—the United States pulled out and abandoned Somalia. In sum: an enemy's will may be broken without breaking his military forces, and forces can be crushed without shattering the nation's will.

The likelihood of achieving decisive battles has decreased over the past two centuries. Russell Weigley argues this is due to the emergence of the nation in arms. Not only are armies substantially larger than in the past—thereby making them more difficult to destroy all at once—but warfare has become increasingly total. Greater numbers of personnel, resources, and funds were devoted to war, and a knockout blow was almost impossible. A nation could lose hundreds of thousands of men on the Western Front but still draft millions more to continue the fight.[3] In the aftermath of World War II, nations grew less inclined to risk their survival; yet, decisive wars may still occur—for example, the triumph of North Vietnam. On the other hand, the overwhelming military victory by the Coalition over Iraq in 1991 did not lead to a sound peace. As always, the purpose of war is a better condition in its aftermath, and destroying armies may have little or nothing to do with achieving a better peace.

Combining these considerations leads to my definition of "Decisive Victory": *Achieving major, long-term political results in war that include attaining grand strategic objectives or causing a fundamental change in strategy by the enemy. These results can be negative: the enemy is prevented from achieving his objectives as a result of losing a key engagement, or a victor ensures he will not lose the war.*

It is useful to differentiate between a decisive victory and a turning point—a battle that changes the momentum in war. Usually identified in retrospect, it is an engagement when one side, which had been losing, sees its fortunes reversed and then moves with increasing momentum to victory. In modern history, such turnings points were Saratoga (1777), where American colonial forces defeated a British army, thus securing French support; Gettysburg (1863), whose aftermath saw the South in constant retreat; Midway (1942), the battle that broke the back of the Japanese carrier fleet and began its long withdrawal to the Home Islands; Stalingrad (1943), where Soviet troops destroyed the chances of German victory in the east; and Tet (1968), when the Viet Cong broke the will of the American people and their political leaders, leading to a slow but steady retreat.

What I consider the eleven decisive victories with the greatest impact in history are listed below. In truth, I shudder to make such a list; invariably, more knowledgeable military historians will cry that this battle should have been included, while that battle should not.

Decisive Victories in History

Salamis/Plataea (480/479 BC)

The Persians under Darius invaded Greece in 490 BC. The army landed on the beach at Marathon, about twenty miles from Athens, and was met by a Greek force and defeated. The Persians returned to Asia, but came back ten years later, now led by Xerxes. Checked momentarily at Thermopylae, they went on to occupy most of northern Greece, including Athens, which they burned to the ground.

The Greeks did not surrender. They gathered a fleet of 350 ships (60,000 men) under the command of Themistocles and based them near the island of Salamis, directly opposite Athens. In late September 480 BC, the 700-ship Persian fleet was confident of victory, and Xerxes set his golden throne atop a hill to watch the battle that would give him mastery of Greece.

Themistocles chose to fight in the narrow channel between the mainland and Salamis. Greek ships were heavier than Persian vessels, which were more maneuverable. The purpose of trireme warfare was to ram the enemy ship and then back out quickly while the victim foundered. In confined waters the agility of the Persians was of no avail; instead, the heaviness of the Greek boats made them superior rammers.

The Greeks attacked at seven in the morning, and the battle lasted twelve hours. The Persians, who had rowed all night to arrive at Salamis, were thus at a disadvantage from the outset. Eventually, the heavier Greek ships battered the Persians to such an extent that as evening fell they broke and fled. Many were then caught from behind and sunk. Overall, the Persians lost over 200 ships and 20,000 dead.[4]

The Persian fleet destroyed, Xerxes returned home disgusted, but left behind an army of 70,000 to mop up the Greek armies. Without fleet support, however, the Persians were in peril so far from home. In July 479 a Greek army of 40,000 men under Pausanias met the Persians at Plataea. The Persians attacked the Greek phalanx and were initially successful, but the stoutness of the Greeks, especially the Spartan contingent, turned the tide. By the end of the day the Persians, driven back against a stream, were slaughtered.[5]

Salamis and Plataea meant the end of Persian plans for the subjugation of Greece. These battles did not break up the Persian Empire, but they ensured Greece would remain Greek.

Arbela (331 BC)

A century after Xerxes gave up his attempt to conquer Greece, a Greek marched on Persia. Macedon was a mountainous area of northern Greece that produced a race of excellent warriors. In the fourth century BC, King Philip II of Macedon built a mighty army, moved south, and defeated the Greek city states. Upon his death in 336, his son Alexander took the throne. The young king, only twenty, consolidated his power in Greece, putting down rebellions fostered by Persia. He then decided to move southeast. After crossing the Hellespont (present-day Dardanelles), Alexander's army defeated the Persians at Granicus and Issus, but Darius III refused to surrender. The armies met again at Arbela (also called Guagamela, near modern Mosul) in October 331. Alexander's army numbered around 50,000 and was opposed by a significantly larger Persian force.

The Macedonians began the battle by marching toward the Persian formation but also edging to their right while doing so. When the Persians attempted to match this maneuver by shifting their own forces so as not to be outflanked, their less flexible formations became disconnected—gaps appeared in their front. Upon spying this, Alexander attacked through one of these gaps with his heavy cavalry and charged straight at Darius.[6]

The Persian front split asunder. The king escaped, but his army was destroyed. A few months later Darius was murdered by his generals, who then sued for peace. The mighty empire of Persia was turned over in its entirety to Alexander.

Although Alexander died in Babylon in 323 at the age of thirty-two, Egypt and most of the Middle East would remain under Greek cultural influence for centuries thereafter.

Zama (202 BC)

In the aftermath of Alexander's death, his kingdom was split between his generals. Over the next century these kingdoms fell into decline as two new powers rose on the scene, Rome and Carthage. Both empires fronted the Mediterranean Sea and both viewed it with proprietary eyes, thus bringing them into conflict.

The First Punic War lasted from 264–241 BC and saw Rome victorious. Tensions remained, however, and in 218 the Carthaginians renewed hostilities. With an army of 90,000 men, Hannibal secured Spain and then crossed the Alps into Italy. Over the next decade he shattered Roman armies at Trebia, Lake Trasimene, and Cannae. But Rome would not surrender, and Hannibal was never strong enough to besiege the Eternal City.

Publius Cornelius Scipio then restructured and retrained his Roman legions and took the war to the enemy. He crossed the Mediterranean and moved on Carthage itself. Hannibal was forced to return to Africa and defend his capital. In March 202 the Romans under Scipio with approximately 35,000 men met Hannibal's slightly larger army near Zama, south of Carthage. Although Hannibal's army was slightly larger, it contained more raw recruits and foreigners than he wished, and his cavalry was heavily outnumbered by the Romans. The Carthaginians also had eighty war elephants.

Hannibal attacked first, launching his elephants in the hope of disrupting the Roman formation, but the flexible maniples instituted by Scipio simply parted to allow the animals to pass to the rear. The Roman cavalry charged next, sweeping Hannibal's horsemen from the field. The two infantry contingents then clashed and fought desperately for the next several hours. When it appeared the Carthaginians were gaining the upper hand, the Roman cavalry returned on the scene and struck them from the rear. Surrounded, most of Hannibal's army was destroyed or captured, although he himself escaped. The war was over. Henceforth, Scipio would be known as "Africanus."[7]

Zama ended Carthage as a military factor, while at the same time elevating Rome to a world power—a status she held for the next six centuries.

Tours (732 AD)

The western portion of the Roman Empire was overrun in the fifth century AD. Ostrogoths, Visigoths, Vandals, and Huns all contributed to the demise, plunging Europe into darkness and confusion. During the seventh century another force arose to challenge both Europe and the Eastern Empire at Byzantium. This force was the militaristic and expansionist religion of Islam. Over the next several centuries Islam would conquer much of Africa and the Middle East. One Islamic ethnic sect, the Moors, crossed into Spain, displacing the Visigoth kingdom there, and began moving north toward the land of the Franks.

By the early eighth century the Franks watched the advancing Moors with growing concern. In 717 the Moors crossed the Pyrenees and moved into Aquitaine; in 732 an army of perhaps 50,000 under the command of Abd-ar-Rahman marched on Poitiers and Tours. The Franks, led by Charles Martel, hurried to meet the invaders. Charles had fought the Moors and their light cavalry before and knew they were more maneuverable and agile than his own mounted forces, but they offered little shock value. He therefore dismounted his men to meet the attack. As he expected, the Moors were unable to penetrate his formation despite repeated and frenzied charges. As one chronicler phrased it, the Franks stood motionless, "like a wall of ice." During the day-long struggle Abd-ar-Rahman was killed, and his army panicked, fleeing south.[8] Martel elected not to pursue—the Moors were adept at feigning retreat and then turning on a pursuing foe. Pursuit was unnecessary.

The victory of Charles Martel at Tours saved the Christian kingdom of the Franks. Over the next several decades the Moors were driven back over the Pyrenees, never to return. The grandson of Martel, Charles, would use the subsequent peace on his southern flank to consolidate power. On Christmas day, 800, Charles was crowned the first Holy Roman Emperor—he would now be called Charlemagne. Although his vast empire would shrink after his death, Charlemagne's efforts would eventually lead to a united France.

Constantinople (1204)

After the fall of Rome, Byzantium remained the bulwark of Christendom against Islam. Yet, for reasons of greed and power Constantinople was coveted by many in Europe. The Crusades, ostensibly launched to recover the Holy Land from the Muslims, provided an opportunity to conquer the city.

The Fourth Crusade, launched in 1199, was led by Count Boniface of Montferrat. The land path to the Holy Land was long and dangerous, so Boniface elected to purchase sea transport from Venice. He sat down with the Doge, Enrico Dandolo, and worked out a deal: transport to the Holy Land for a cost of 85,000 silver marks. This was a huge sum, and both knew such an amount could not be gained from the recapture of Jerusalem. Twisted politics involving the rulers of Constantinople then intervened, and in order to raise money the Crusaders agreed to take Zara, a Christian city on the Adriatic coast, and then Constantinople. When Pope Innocent III heard of this nefarious deal he threatened to excommunicate any Christian who took the life of a fellow Christian while on Crusade. He was ignored.

In June 1203 the forces of Boniface camped outside Constantinople while the Venetian fleet blockaded the fortress from the sea. The Golden Horn, the city's harbor, was protected by a huge chain drawn across its width and secured by forts on either side. The army captured one of the forts and removed the chain, allowing the Venetian boats to sail close to the city walls. The Byzantines fought valiantly and resisted the attackers for nine months. Eventually, fires started by Venetian missiles catapulted into the city, combined with starvation among the populace and dissent among Byzantine leaders themselves, led to fatal weakness. On April 12, 1204, the "Crusaders" broke through the defenses and began a rampage of looting, plunder, and rape.[9]

After more than a thousand years Byzantium, heir to the Roman Empire, fell. Sadly, she did not succumb to the Muslim armies that had assailed her so often in the past, but to fellow Christians. More tragically, the collections of art, books, and sculpture—a culture that had survived for centuries—was scattered or destroyed. There were brief revivals in Byzantine fortunes over the next two centuries, but the great empire never recovered. In 1453 the city was sacked again, by the Ottoman Turks, who remained in power until the advent of modern Turkey.

Spanish Armada (1588)

Spain was a great European power of the sixteenth century. Its galleons had circled the globe and returned with untold wealth. England would challenge that supremacy. Religion was an issue between the two nations. Henry VIII had overturned Catholicism in England, and this was seen as heresy in Spain. After Henry's death and that of his young son, his daughter Mary took the throne. A Catholic because of her mother, Catherine of Aragon (Henry's first wife), she married Prince Philip of Spain, who then became coregent. Upon the death of his father two years later, Philip also became king of Spain. When Mary died childless in 1558, her half-sister Elizabeth took the throne in England. Even though his wife was gone, Philip still felt a proprietary interest in English matters.[10] He was concerned by Elizabeth's intention of strengthening Protestantism and persecuting Catholics. His ire increased when she aided the Dutch Netherlands in their rebellion against Spain. Worse, Elizabeth allowed her "sea dogs" to prey upon Spanish galleons returning from the Americas laden with bullion. King Philip II decided that England needed to be punished.

He assembled a fleet to meet the English at sea and destroy them by boarding them and allowing his soldiers to decide the matter. Once the English Channel was clear, an army would be ferried over, sweep away English resistance, depose Elizabeth, and install a Spanish princess as queen. The admiral of the fleet, numbering over 130 ships and 30,000 men, was the Duke of Medina Sidonia—a competent soldier but with no naval experience.

In May 1588 the Spanish Armada set sail. Sidonia arrived off Plymouth on July 25, but the rival fleets had difficulty in engaging. The English had no intention of grappling with the Spanish: rather, they kept their distance and used their superior gunnery. An examination of Armada wrecks showed that the Spanish guns were large affairs built for siege warfare on land. That made them difficult to load and maneuver on board the ships. In addition, over 2,000 cannon balls were found in one wreck, but none of them were of the correct caliber for the guns on deck! As a result, the English outshot the Spanish by three to one.[11] Finally, on July 29 the fleets fought off Gravelines, north of Calais. Although the battle hardly seemed decisive—the Spanish lost less than ten ships—Sidonia decided all was lost and ordered his fleet to return to Spain. Because the route south was blocked by the English fleet, the Armada headed north—to sail *around* the British Isles. It was a fateful decision because a series of major storms then struck that raged for weeks. The Armada was ravaged. By the time it finally arrived back in Spain it had lost half its ships and three-quarters of its men.[12]

The "Protestant Wind," as the fortuitous storms were dubbed in England, removed all possibility of a Spanish invasion. England was saved. From this point on the English fleet grew in size and competence: it would rule the seas for three centuries.

Hansando (1592)

In 1591 the Samurai chieftain Toyotomi Hideyoshi took over Japan. He immediately planned expansion with a goal of conquering China, and he would do this by first overrunning Korea as a base and then moving north.[13]

On May 23, 1592, a Japanese army of 143,000—the greatest military force in Japanese history to that point—landed at Pusan. The citadel fell quickly, and the invaders moved north. Korean resistance was sparse, usually fleeing at sight of the samurai army. Seoul fell without a fight, as did Pyongyang a month later. It appeared the Japanese were invincible, and they controlled the peninsula within two months, but the situation soon changed. A guerrilla war sprang up throughout Korea as an estimated 22,000 irregulars began harassing Japanese supply lines.[14] These raids cost the Japanese dearly as men died and smaller fortified positions fell.

More importantly, Admiral Yi Sun-sin, commander of the Korean fleet, engaged Japanese ships along the coast. Although usually outnumbered, he never lost.[15] The Korean ships were strong, reasonably fast, and had excellent armament. The Japanese hoped to close with the enemy and board their ships to defeat the crews in combat. Instead, the Koreans kept their distance and raked the enemy with the superior gunfire of their armored "turtle boats" that wrecked havoc on the Japanese ships. On August 16, 1592, Yi met the Japanese fleet off the island of Hansando and destroyed sixty ships; two days later he sank eighty more. The Japanese fleet was utterly crushed.[16] The samurai commanders realized the significance of the defeat—their sea lines of communication were severed, so reinforcements and supplies from Japan were unlikely to arrive in a timely manner.

Although the war lurched on, the Japanese were unable to regain the initiative. In September 1598, Hideyoshi died. His death gave his successors a pretext to end the war—it was obvious that the conquest of Korea, much less China, would never succeed. The Imjin War was over, and little had been achieved except the destruction of the Korean peninsula. The Japanese lost at least 80,000 men, but the Koreans suffered far more—perhaps 2 million died.

After the war, Japan entered upon a period of peace and isolation. This was Japan's only overseas invasion in a thousand years, and it ended in defeat. For the next 250 years Japan would remain at peace.[17]

Yorktown (1781)

The American colonies began to chafe under British rule after the French and Indian War. The core issue was taxation. The war had been expensive, so London increased taxes to help pay the bill. The colonies resented this, and over the next decade there occurred a series of demonstrations against the new taxes, such as the Boston Tea Party in December 1773.

The British tightened the screws, and in April 1775 a force of redcoats marched out of Boston to confront the rebels at Lexington and to confiscate military stores at Concord. Fighting broke out and blood was spilled: the Revolution had begun.

Over the next three years George Washington, commander of the Continental Army, fought several inconclusive battles against the British, and neither side seemed close to victory. American success at Saratoga in October 1777 was, however, a turning point in the war: it brought in the French, who supplied essential funds, arms, troops, and a fleet.

In 1778 the war shifted to the southern colonies, where the British captured the ports of Savannah and Charleston. A British army under Charles Cornwallis moved into the interior and attempted to destroy colonial resistance. Washington then sent Nathaniel Greene to take command in the south. Cornwallis pushed for a conclusive victory, but Greene cleverly refused to fight anything but delaying actions. Exasperated, in April 1781 Cornwallis abandoned the Carolinas and moved north into Virginia. Arriving at Yorktown in August, he intended to resupply and reinforce his troops by sea, but Yorktown turned into a trap.

In a crucial engagement in Chesapeake Bay, the Royal Navy was driven off by the French fleet, which then blockaded Yorktown. Simultaneously, Washington marched south with a large contingent of American and French troops to bolster Greene's forces, who had invested Cornwallis by land. Washington took command of the combined allied army of 17,000 men and laid siege to Yorktown. After an abortive attempt to break free, Cornwallis realized the hopelessness of his situation. On October 19 he surrendered his 8,000 men.[18]

The loss of another major army in the American colonies after Saratoga, combined with the active involvement of the French fleet, caused consternation in London. The war had become increasingly expensive and unpopular, and in 1783 Britain sued for peace. Yorktown had won independence for the United States of America.

Marne (1914)

Europe had been edging toward conflict for decades. The French sought revenge after their losses in 1870. Factors such as a naval arms race between Germany and Britain, competition over colonies in Asia and Africa, an alliance system that pitted one half of Europe against the other, and inflexible war plans all contributed to trouble. One example of this inflexibility was Germany's Schlieffen Plan.

As chief of the German General Staff, Field Marshal Alfred von Schlieffen assumed that war with France would eventually occur. He devised a plan that envisioned a massive wheeling movement through the Netherlands, Belgium, and northern France. It was expected French armies would be located primarily to the south, and they would be pushing into Germany itself. Schlieffen's intent was for his center troops to give way slowly to the advancing French, while the great wheel on his right would sweep down from the north, encircle Paris, and smash into the French from the rear. On paper it looked elegant—a modern day Cannae—but it was far too reliant on everything working precisely on schedule—a situation that seldom prevails in war.[19]

Although Schlieffen retired in 1906, his ideas survived and a version of his plan was used in August 1914.[20] Unfortunately, Germany was now in a two-front war with France and Russia, and this required an alteration of the original scheme. Even so, initially, all went well for Germany. The right wing, consisting of five armies, swept through Belgium and northern France, pushing back the French and British troops in its path. The commander of the German First Army on the western flank, Alexander von Kluck, then amended the plan, going *east* of Paris so as to destroy the fleeing French and British forces. This was a mistake: not only did he not bag these troops, his maneuver left the Sixth French Army on his western flank. The Sixth attacked, causing von Kluck to turn and meet the threat, thus opening a gap between his army and that of the German Second Army to his east. This gap was discovered by air reconnaissance, and the British Expeditionary Force moved into it. The Germans halted and fell back to restore their front. The French commander, Marshal Joseph Joffre, hurled all his forces at the Germans, now poised at the Marne River, to make the halt permanent. It was a close-run thing. In a legendary story, hastily assembled French troops were hurried to the front by a fleet of Parisian taxicabs. Over 2.5 million troops fought ferociously at the Marne for five days. The result was stalemate, but that was good enough.[21]

Air reconnaissance, combined with fortuitously located French and British forces, and an overly ambitious German war plan, led to the climactic battle at the Marne. France was saved. Although four long years of horrific trench warfare lay ahead, Germany's best chance of knocking out France had passed.

Battle of Britain (1940)

The Treaty of Versailles was merely a truce. When Adolf Hitler was appointed chancellor in 1933, he began rearmament and introduced a more bellicose foreign policy. In 1936 Germany reoccupied the Rhineland; in 1938 it annexed Austria and then moved into the Sudetenland of Czechoslovakia. When Hitler invaded Poland in September 1939, France and Britain declared war—but did little actual fighting. Poland fell, then so did Denmark, Norway, the Netherlands, Belgium, and France in blitzkrieg strikes. Britain was alone.

Hitler intended to invade Britain, and Operation SEA LION was the plan to mount such an amphibious assault. Before he could attempt the effort, however, he needed to ensure control of the English Channel, and for that he needed air superiority *over* the Channel.

In August 1940 the Luftwaffe under *Reichsmarschall* Herman Göring mustered 1,000 aircraft; the Royal Air Force's Fighter Command under Air Chief Marshal Hugh Dowding had about the same number. Fighter Command did, however, have significant advantages: superior leadership, excellent aircraft, fighting in its own airspace, and a radar and communications network that allowed Fighter Command to see and then counter German attacks.

The German onslaught began on August 12 when Göring sent over several hundred bombers escorted by fighters. The intent was to bomb targets so vital to Britain that the RAF would be required to defend them. The German goal was to bring Fighter Command to battle and then destroy it. Initially, Germany targeted the radar sites, whose loss would pose a serious danger to the RAF. After only three days, however, Göring switched targets and began concentrating on airfields. This too was a major concern for Fighter Command, and over the next month "the few" found themselves "gasping on the ropes." They were saved when Hitler, angered over the bombing of Berlin, directed his bombers to concentrate on British cities. On September 15 a force of 200 heavily escorted bombers attacked London but suffered 25 percent casualties; these were unsustainable losses. This raid, which occurred on the date originally set for the invasion, was the Luftwaffe's last major daylight attack: the Blitz moved to the safety of night. This decision spelled the end of German attempts to gain air superiority for an invasion.[22]

By the end of October the Battle of Britain was over. One of history's great negative decisive victories, it saved Britain. When Hitler realized he could not achieve air superiority over the Channel, he knew an invasion was impossible. His attention turned toward Russia.

Hiroshima/Nagasaki (1945)

After Pearl Harbor, the Japanese swept to victory throughout Asia. Much of China and Indochina fell into their hands, as did Korea, the Philippines, Singapore, Malaysia, the Dutch East Indies, and a host of other islands. The Battle of Midway in June 1942 was a turning point, but there was still a long slog ahead. In June through August 1944 the Mariana Islands were recaptured, and airbases were built to house long-range B-29s, which then began hitting the Japanese home islands. Invasions of these islands were planned: the assault on Kyushu was scheduled for November 1, 1945, and an invasion of Honshu was slated for the following March. A new weapon would make them unnecessary.

Since early 1942 scientists had been studying the possibility of splitting the atom to release an astounding amount of energy. A major scientific endeavor, the Manhattan Project, built an atomic weapon, and the Army Air Forces formed a special B-29 unit to deliver the new weapon. The 509th Bomb Group, commanded by Colonel Paul W. Tibbets, moved to Tinian in the Marianas in May 1945 and trained to deliver the top-secret bomb.[23]

On July 26 President Harry Truman sent Japan an ultimatum: surrender or suffer destruction. This "Potsdam Declaration" was rejected, and orders were issued to prepare for a launch. On August 6 the *Enola Gay,* piloted by Tibbets, lifted off from Tinian and at 0815 local time dropped an atomic bomb on the industrial city of Hiroshima. Crewmembers would later refer to the purple cloud building upward for ten miles, and the cauldron below that resembled a "pot of bubbling hot tar."[24] The center of Hiroshima was destroyed, and over 60,000 died.

Japan still resisted, and a second atomic bomb was dropped on Nagasaki on August 9. Emperor Hirohito then made a radio address to his people citing "a new and most cruel bomb" that contained a power to do "incalculable" damage. He was surrendering.

Ever since, debate has raged about the necessity and morality of the atomic strikes, but at the time there was little disagreement. Moreover, the statistics are stark. There were 900,000 Japanese defenders on Kyushu awaiting an attack by 760,000 Allied troops. On the main island of Honshu there were over 2 million Japanese defenders poised to receive an attack by over 1 million Allied troops. Given the experiences of the war until then, the scheduled invasions would have cost millions of Allied and Japanese lives, both military and civilian.[25]

The atomic strikes on Japan ended World War II and proved to be one of the most decisive victories in history. Over seventy years later Japan remains a close ally of the West.

* * *

This is my list of decisive battles—those engagements, both positive and negative, that decided the outcome of major wars. These wars were in turn monumental events in world history. As noted, not all battles or wars that end in victory can be termed decisive—and thus that term is overused. Often, battlefield victories are termed decisive if the casualties are disproportionate.

This is a poor standard. Recall that great battlefield victories such as Cannae, Austerlitz, and Tannenberg were not decisive simply because they did not appreciably alter the war in which they occurred. Time is important: how long did the results of the victory last? If an enemy is able to raise new armies and continue to fight, then the battlefield victory was not decisive at all. Key to all decisive victories in battles or in wars is that they were able to attain conclusive political objectives, and, ultimately, a better peace. That after all is the object of war.

7

Time in War

Go sir, gallop, and don't forget that the world was made in six days. You can ask me for anything you like, except time.

—Napoleon

TIME HAS ALWAYS BEEN considered a key element in war. Speed, by definition, derives from time—"distance traveled divided by the time of travel." Two millennia ago Sun Tzu remarked on its importance, noting that "speed is the essence of war" and "divine swiftness" is to be "esteemed."[1] Carl von Clausewitz believed similarly, commenting that time had a major psychological effect that would help provide secrecy as well as speed.[2] Not just theorists, but practitioners, such as Napoleon in the epigraph above, have recognized the importance of time and timing in war. But what is time?

There are several ways to describe the concept, but most consider time to be a straight line. Things begin, they develop, and they end. One can remember or read about the past, but we cannot go back—time marches inexorably forward, and the future remains unknown. Albert Einstein introduced the notion that time was flexible and relative. Physicists have adapted this bendable concept of time when discussing cosmology. For theologians, God is both timeless and endless; He always was and always will be. Moreover, God's time is not an arrow but a circle: He sees all—past, present, and future whichever way He chooses to look.[3]

Besides its physical and theological aspects, time also has a psychological component that we all experience. Although the clock ticks on rhythmically, we often feel it differently. On some days the clock appears to move very slowly—when we are waiting in anticipation for something to occur. On other occasions, time appears to accelerate—as when we are enjoying ourselves and want to prolong the moment but cannot.

For the military, it is the notion of time as an arrow—the orderly sequencing of events—that matters most. Yet, the psychological aspect of time, especially its apparent suddenness, is also of great importance in military operations. John Boyd, an airman and theorist of war, devised his OODA Loop—Observe, Orient, Decide, Act—to illustrate the cycle through which the human mind makes decisions. Boyd posited that the side in war whose OODA Loop was quicker—who acted most appropriately in the fastest time—would have an advantage.[4] Militaries also use terms like "tempo" and "synchronization" to explain the importance of conquering and best utilizing time in their operations.[5]

An example of time's psychological impact concerns the fates of Carthage and Hiroshima. The Third Punic War ended with the defeat of Carthage at the hands of Rome. When decisively defeating the African power in 146 BC, the Romans razed Carthage, killed its inhabitants or sold them into slavery, and then, as tradition has it, sowed the ground with salt so nothing would grow.[6]

On August 6, 1945, a B-29 aircraft took off from Tinian. At 0815 it arrived over Hiroshima and dropped an atomic bomb. In its final toll on the structures, people, and land of the Japanese city, the bomb's blast and radiation were not all that dissimilar from the effects of the Romans at Carthage two millennia earlier.[7] The difference between the events was that the destruction of Hiroshima was affected virtually instantaneously by one weapon, and not over a period of months by several legions. It was the conquest of time, not of matter, that so stunned the world—both then and since.

Time and Land Warfare

There have been many examples when time played a key role on the battlefield. In September 1812, Napoleon met the Russian army at Borodino. He thought it could be the decisive battle of the war—a victory that would open the door to Moscow and force the czar to surrender. Yet, the emperor was reluctant to use all his troops in the battle, especially his Old Guard. One general on the scene reported that Napoleon said: "I want to see more clearly. . . . My battle hasn't begun yet. . . . The day will be long. You have to know how to wait. Time always has to be considered. . . . Nothing is clear yet." He then asked an aide what time it was, and when told Napoleon remarked: "The time for my battle hasn't come yet. It will begin in two hours."[8] But the emperor had miscalculated: in two hours the battle was already decided; his timing was off, and the Russian army survived to fight again; Napoleon would lose the war.

On the second day at Gettysburg, Lieutenant General James Longstreet was to attack the Union left at Little Round Top to coincide with assaults on the right and center, but his corps took the wrong road and was late getting into position. What if he had attacked in coordination with his comrades? One historian summed the day by stating: "Lee's offensive, based upon attacks in progression until it developed into a giant pincers squeezing both enemy flanks, required careful coordination and expert timing."[9] For the Confederates, the timing was off.

The Schlieffen Plan originated in Germany in the last decade of the nineteenth century by the chief of the General Staff, Field Marshal Alfred von Schlieffen.[10] When adapted for use in 1914, it was part of a two-front war. To be successful, Germany must hold in the east against Russia, and then strike quickly in the west against Belgium and France—knocking them out of the war so as to enable a turn back to the east to meet the lumbering Russian army. It was assumed the Russians would take two months to mobilize and thus not initially be a threat. The war in the west had to be concluded within two months. Schlieffen retired in 1906, and over the next decade his successor, Field Marshal Helmuth von Moltke (the younger), tinkered with the plan. Unfortunately, the need to maintain a rigid time schedule for the huge military turning movement driving through Belgium and northern France remained a dominant feature.[11]

When war broke out in July 1914, von Moltke realized the Russians were mobilizing and advancing more quickly than had been anticipated, so he ordered two army corps detached from the western arm to bolster the east. For this and other reasons, the rigidly timed attack in the west went awry. The German armies fell behind schedule and had to readjust their timing. A French flank attack on the westernmost German army caused gaps to develop between the armies as they maneuvered to readjust; the French and their British allies noticed the faulty German dispositions and hurried to act. Even so, events hung in the balance. As the German armies moved to the Marne River shielding Paris, a hastily cobbled together French army was rushed to the front just in time and managed to deliver a pivotal check to the enemy.[12] The carefully timed Schlieffen Plan had fallen apart, and the Western Front soon devolved into a stagnant trench war of attrition that would last for much of the next four years.

In June 1950, North Korea attacked across the 38th parallel demarcation line into the south. Caught unprepared, Republic of Korea forces precipitously retreated south. General of the Army Douglas MacArthur, the US commander in Japan, was appointed by the United Nations to lead a coalition against the aggression, and he began deploying US troops and air assets based in Japan into South Korea to help stem the tide while reinforcements were hastily ordered from the United States. Initially, this did not work, and UN troops were pushed into a perimeter at Pusan on the southern tip of the peninsula, but MacArthur was planning a counterstroke. Operation CHROMITE was to be an amphibious assault at Inchon, the port city near Seoul, to take place in mid-September. As one historian phrased it: "One of General MacArthur's outstanding attributes, demonstrated quite often in World War II, was a keen sense of timing."[13] His forces would not be ready for the operation until mid-September, but waiting until October would be too late for his forces in Pusan. The window of opportunity was narrow.

The obstacles at Inchon were formidable. Tides there averaged thirty feet, and when the tide was out the mudflats left behind were so soft and deep as to preclude movement. Twice a day the tide came in, but the time available for an assault was only three hours. After that, the retreating waters would leave the attackers and their craft stranded on the mud for the next twelve hours, sitting ducks for the defenders. On September 15, 1950, the UN forces landed at Inchon, totally astonishing North Korean defenders. The assault force landed at high tide, disgorged its troops, and the landing craft backed out before the waters began to recede. It was a brilliant maneuver, perfectly timed against what many thought were hopeless odds.[14] The aggressors fled north to escape the trap even faster than they had moved south.[15]

Timing and Air Warfare

Between the two world wars, airpower thinkers at the Air Corps Tactical School in Alabama devised a doctrine for employing bombers in war. They projected an "industrial web" theory that likened an economy to a spider's web—all was interconnected and damage anywhere in the web would reverberate throughout the entire structure with dramatic effects. This theory also hypothesized that certain resources, facilities, or activities were more important to the successful operation of an economy at war than were others. Typical ideal targets included oil refineries, the electric power grid, steel plants, armament factories, and the transportation network.[16] In addition, it was believed that gaining air superiority was crucial; therefore, destroying aircraft and engine factories was just as important as destroying the aircraft themselves.

Germany had very little internal oil resources, and during peacetime most had to be imported. When Hitler launched the war, one of his first objectives was to secure the oil fields and refineries of Romania through alliance. These resources, centered at Ploesti, subsequently supplied over 60 percent of Germany's crude oil supply.[17] Air planners argued that knocking out this complex would have a disastrous effect on Germany's "web."

From the nearest Army Air Force (AAF) bases in Africa, this would be a deep strike (1,200 miles each way); moreover, the refineries were heavily defended by antiaircraft artillery (AAA) and fighters. Planners therefore suggested a low-level attack at 300 feet using B-24s to strike in a coordinated fashion. Nearly 200 bombers would be used, and given the unusual tactics, as well as the extreme distance, the B-24s were fitted with extra fuel tanks and low-level bombsights. The crews practiced over the Libyan Desert, flying low and dropping practice bombs on a dummy complex built to resemble that at Ploesti. Rehearsals were flown on July 28 and 29, and on both days the mission went flawlessly, "completely destroying" the dummy site.

On August 1, 1943, 177 planes in five groups took off from Libya and headed east. Beforehand, crewmen were told to write letters home and leave them on their cots—if they did not return the letters would be mailed. Not long after takeoff things began to go awry. The weather was far different from the clear skies over Libya, and thunderstorms en route broke up the formation. Radio calls would have assisted a rejoin, but the crews were told to maintain radio silence so as not to tip off the enemy. Things worsened.

As a result of the disruption in timing caused by the formation breakup, two bomber groups arrived over the target well before the rest of the force, thus alerting the defenses for those coming behind. Two other groups misidentified a checkpoint and turned early, flying all the way to Bucharest before realizing their mistake and turning back. This too alerted defenses and scrambled Luftwaffe fighters. Another group encountered heavy AAA approaching Ploesti so it deviated to the east to avoid the threat. The result of these snafus was an uncoordinated attack as bombers flew in piecemeal from different directions and at different times, as opposed to arriving en masse in a single formation. Colonel Leon Johnson—awarded the Medal of Honor for his actions that day—later wrote: "We flew through sheets of flame, and airplanes were everywhere, some of them on fire and others exploding."[18] Upon departing the area, instead of reforming, the groups pressed on home by themselves. Stretched out over a hundred miles, they were easy prey for enemy fighters. By the time it was over and the B-24s straggled back to Africa, fifty-four aircraft were lost as well as 532 airmen. Only three of the 177 bombers that had started the mission were fit to fly the following day. To illustrate the harrowing nature of the mission, five Medals of Honor were awarded—the most ever for a single air operation.

The keys to success at Ploesti were to be "surprise and razor-sharp timing," but both were lost and the result was carnage. It would not be until April 1944 that the AAF again attacked Ploesti—and those attacks were conducted at high altitude in standard air group formation. Besides oil, ball bearings were also a promising target system identified before the war.

Schweinfurt was Germany's major ball bearing production center; this was a "bottleneck" target whose destruction prewar air planners believed would have a disproportionate effect on the German economy. Regensburg, a nearby city, had a large Messerschmidt factory that produced 48 percent of the Luftwaffe's fighter aircraft. In the summer of 1943, planners thought they knew how to neutralize them.[19] Due to the lack of long-range escort fighters to accompany the bombers deep into Germany—a major shortcoming of airpower thinking before the war—it was concluded the bombers would suffer heavy losses at the hands of the Luftwaffe fighter force. It was therefore decided to throw the enemy a curveball. There would be two separate waves of bombers. The first would depart England and head directly for Regensburg. Spitfires and P-47s would accompany them for the first part of their journey, but would be forced to turn back when low on fuel. The bombers would then be hit by interceptors, but after striking the target they would turn south for North Africa rather than reverse course and return to England. It was hoped this would so surprise and confuse the defenders that the second half of the bombers' journey would be fairly easy.

A second wave of bombers would depart England ten minutes after the first and head for Schweinfurt. The close arrival of the second wave was timed to arrive over the target while the Luftwaffe was on the ground refueling and rearming. The German fighters would be airborne again within thirty minutes, but the planners figured this would allow the bombers to get to the target relatively unscathed. However, they would have to fight their way back to England afterward.

In other words, the timing of the assault meant the first wave (Regensburg) would only have to defend itself on the way into the target; whereas, the second wave (Schweinfurt) would only have to fight on the way home. It made sense.

Crews were awakened at 0130 and served *real* eggs and bacon for breakfast —they knew something was up, and many referred to it as "the Last Supper."[20] In the briefing room the map showing their target for the day was covered by a cloth, but they had learned that a string with a bob at the end would trace their route of flight; more string left hanging at the bottom of the chart meant the target would be close to the coast and therefore include fighter escort. Today, there was no string showing. This would be a deep strike, unescorted.

Unfortunately, heavy fog rolled into England the morning of August 16, 1943. The first wave of 146 bombers had to take off in order to land at the unfamiliar North African bases before dark. Fortuitously, Colonel Curtis LeMay, who led the first contingent, had trained his men rigorously on instrument takeoffs and climb outs. The training paid off and not a single bomber was lost during the form up.

The takeoff of the second wave of 230 bombers, led by Brigadier General Robert Williams, was then delayed for over three hours due to the fog. The crewmembers knew what this meant: they would engage a freshly fueled, armed, and rested fighter defense not only into their target, but on the return as well. Their escort fighters would not offer much help and would turn back before reaching the German border. There would be hell to pay.

As expected, LeMay's first wave endured heavy attacks inbound to Regensburg—losing fourteen aircraft while still 100 miles from the target. Ten more went down over the city, but their turn south did catch the defenders by surprise. As a result, the bombers' five-hour journey to North Africa was largely uneventful.

Williams's unescorted Schweinfurt crews were hammered both to and from the target and were pounced on by 300 enemy fighters. Overall, the Eighth would lose sixty bombers that day, with over 550 aircrew dead, missing, or captured. Another 100 bombers were so heavily damaged they would not fly again. This was over 20 percent of the attacking crew force and 60 percent of the airframes—unsustainable losses. It was not difficult for even the most mathematically challenged crewman to figure his odds: such losses meant the entire aircrew force would theoretically be annihilated in five missions; yet they were required to fly twenty-five combat missions to complete their tour.

In short, the air missions to Ploesti and Schweinfurt/Regensburg had relied on superb timing to achieve success, but in both cases that timing broke down and resulted in disaster.

A basic tenant for airmen concerns the importance of air superiority. In order for aircraft to operate effectively, the opposing air force and air defenses must be neutralized—this was a major reason for attacking the manufacturing plants at Regensburg. Other methods of achieving air superiority are defeating enemy interceptors in the air or attacking the aircraft while they are still on the ground and at their most vulnerable.

During ROLLING THUNDER, the air interdiction campaign against North Vietnam between 1965 and 1968, US aircraft were met by extremely heavy enemy air defenses—AAA, surface to air missiles (SAMs), and MiG fighters. These defenses were deadly, yet they could not be systematically attacked. The rules of engagement stated that SAM sites could not be hit while being built and still harmless—the sites had to be operational. Similarly, MiG airbases were off limits—enemy aircraft could only be attacked if actually airborne. Achieving air superiority under these rules appeared impossible.

In 1966, airmen at bases in Thailand devised a plan to destroy MiGs while still adhering to the rules of engagement. Colonel Robin Olds, the commander of the 8th Tactical Fighter Wing at Ubon, took the lead in this effort. Olds was a legend in the Air Force; he had been an All-American football player at West Point, an ace in World War II with thirteen victories, and had married movie actress Ella Raines. Olds devised a plan, Operation BOLO, to sucker the MiGs into air combat.

When bomb-ladened F-105s (nicknamed "Thuds" supposedly because of the sound they made when hitting the ground) were sent north to strike various targets, they were usually escorted by F-4s and "Iron Hand" assets—F-105s equipped with electronic jamming pods and anti-radiation missiles to suppress the SAMs. If MiGs showed up, the bombers would continue to their targets while the Phantoms engaged the MiGs. The North Vietnamese were aware of these tactics, so they avoided the deadly Phantoms whenever possible.[21]

BOLO proposed that F-4s mimic the actions of an F-105 strike package. The Phantoms would be loaded with air-to-air missiles but no bombs; they would use standard Thud routing, altitudes, speeds, tactics, and call signs. It was hoped North Vietnamese radar operators would paint the incoming aircraft and assume they were unescorted F-105s. They would then scramble MiG interceptors from the five airfields ringing Hanoi and direct them against the incoming bombers. Not until sighting the Phantoms would the MiGs realize they had been duped. It was expected they would then peel off and head for home, knowing their landing fields were protected sanctuaries. Olds was prepared for that: F-4s stationed at Da Nang airbase in South Vietnam, also mimicking F-105s, would head toward Hanoi from the east. Enemy radar would assume these aircraft were also bombers intending to strike targets near the capital. Instead, the Da Nang fighters would head for the MiG bases and orbit overhead. Their intention: when the MiGs fled from the Thailand-based F-4s to recover at their airfields, the Da Nang F-4s would be there waiting. The MiGs would be forced to fight.[22]

Timing was crucial for the plan to succeed. Not only did the F-4s need to mimic the airspeed, altitude, and tactics of the F-105s, they had to arrive in separate waves. Studying the actions of the MiGs over the previous months, Olds knew they remained airborne for only fifty minutes, less if using afterburner. The F-4s, even though hitting tankers just prior to entering North Vietnamese airspace, still had only five minutes to engage over the target. Accordingly, the MiGs would encounter several waves of USAF fighters—arriving at five-minute intervals—allowing successive aircraft to continue the fight while others departed for home.[23] In addition, the Da Nang aircraft also had to arrive over the MiG airfields in a series of waves so as to meet enemy aircraft attempting to flee. If those F-4s arrived too soon, they would run low on fuel before the MiGs showed up; if they arrived too late, the MiGs would have already landed.[24]

Other activities had to be precisely timed as well. To ensure secrecy, aircraft in Thailand and South Vietnam had to continue their regular routines—combat missions were flown against normal targets. Some of the F-4s would also have to mount the anti-SAM pods carried by Iron Hand—if their electronic emissions were not detected, enemy radar operators would be suspicious—but the switch could not be made too soon. The pods were removed from the F-105s at Korat and Takhli and flown to Ubon and Da Nang. There, maintenance crews worked all night installing them so they would be ready for BOLO in the morning.

As is often the case, the mission did not go as planned. Bad weather kept the Da Nang aircraft from arriving over the MiG bases. Nonetheless, Olds led his wing as scheduled; the North Vietnamese were tricked; twelve MiG-21s scrambled to intercept what they supposed were unescorted F-105s; and they did run into a buzz saw. At no loss to the Ubon F-4s, seven MiGs were downed, one by Olds. Unfortunately, the lack of the Da Nang force meant the remaining MiGs were able to recover safely.

What It Means

Time has always been a crucial factor in war, and commanders and planners should give it great consideration when developing strategy and tactics.

Inchon was an example of excellent timing carefully planned and artfully executed. In some instances, however, commanders have too quickly discounted or ignored the importance of time, while on other occasions they have given it too much importance. The Schlieffen Plan was built on a foundation of quicksand: it presumed an ability to maintain an impossible time schedule given the nature of man, beast, vehicles, and human nature. Things usually go wrong in war, yet German generals thought they could proceed with rigid precision. The result was calamity. The same belief in timing was seen at Ploesti and Schweinfurt/Regensburg. Timing was crucial to the successful outcome of these plans, but air planners failed to account for a situation in which the timing went awry. Too much weight was placed on this one pillar of timing; it could not support the pressure, and when it buckled, so did the entire edifice.

Certain factors become clear when studying the issue of time in war. The conquest of time can produce other qualities that can turn the tide. The first of these is *speed*. Theorists and commanders have realized since antiquity that moving quickly is crucial both in approaching the battlefield and during the battle itself. Speed often grants *surprise*, which contains both physical and psychological elements, and most would argue the psychological impact is more powerful. The shock of arriving in force when and where an enemy does not expect it can often cause panic, as was the case for the Prussian Army at Leuthen in 1757, the arrival of Admiral Horatio Nelson's fleet at Aboukir Bay in 1798, or the drive through the Ardennes by German forces in 1940. In addition, time is crucial in the collection and dissemination of accurate intelligence. Most commanders would argue the value of intelligence is directly proportional to the speed of its gathering and dissemination.

The conquest of time also grants *flexibility* and *mobility*. It is not surprising the great captains of history—Alexander, Hannibal, Genghis Khan, Frederick, Napoleon, Nelson, Wellington, Lee, Rommel, Patton, etc.—were known for their rapidity of movement and ability to adjust quickly to events. With the arrival of the airplane, the ability to move rapidly and conquer time was multiplied by an order of magnitude. Even in World War I aircraft struck targets hundreds of miles behind enemy lines, with several tons of bombs, while traveling twenty times faster than infantry. It has been a facet of modern air warfare that this ability to quickly strike deep allows parallel warfare—speed and PGMs permit a multitude of enemy targets to be struck throughout a theater in a remarkably short period of time. Thus, airstrikes hit more Iraqi targets in the first twenty-four hours of DESERT STORM in 1991 (152 separate targets, including fifty in the first ninety minutes) than the Eighth Air Force had been able to hit in its first year of operation over Europe in 1942–43.[25] It is not unreasonable to suggest that Iraq was defeated on the first day: Saddam Hussein was cut off from his forces and knocked off balance to such an extent he was never able to recover. The speed of the Coalition air attack conquered time and made it virtually impossible for Iraq to avoid defeat.

Time can in some instances substitute for *mass*. The speed and accuracy of modern air weapons can now ensure density and mass precision, and such attacks in a short period of time allow simultaneity. And those attacks generally neutralize targets due to the accuracy of PGMs. This means lowering risk: less aircraft in a danger zone for less time means fewer casualties. Since DESERT STORM in 1991, the United States has sustained but a handful of casualties in air operations despite hundreds of thousands of combat sorties flown around the world.

As noted, telescoping time can provide great psychological impact. Because of the speed with which airpower can operate, psychological effect has always been touted by airmen. Air Marshal Hugh Trenchard stated that its impact was twenty times greater than the physical effect of bombing.[26] Although an exaggeration, Trenchard was not alone in his belief regarding these psychological repercussions.

It was one of airmen's great irritants of the Vietnam War that civilians in Washington devised a strategy of "gradual escalation" against North Vietnam. This policy was intended to serve as a carrot and a stick: the United States would bomb some valuable targets in the north with the clear implication that if enemy leaders would not modify their behavior and cease fomenting war in the south, the bombing would increase in volume and include higher value targets. If the North did ease off, then carrots—favorable political or economic terms—would be forthcoming. A National Security Council document from December 1964 explained:

> Such a program would consist principally of progressively more serious air strikes, of a weight and tempo adjusted to the situation as it develops (possibly running from two to six months) and of appropri-

> ate US deployments to handle any contingency. Targets in the DRV would start with infiltration targets south of the 19th parallel and work up to targets north of that point. This could eventually lead to such measures as air strikes on all major military-related targets; aerial mining of DRV ports, and a US naval blockade of the DRV. The whole sequence of military actions would be designed to give the impression of a steady, deliberate approach, and to give the US the option at any time (subject to enemy reaction) to proceed or not, to escalate or not, and to quicken the pace or not. Concurrently, the US would be alert to any sign of yielding by Hanoi, and would be prepared to explore negotiated solutions that attain US objectives in an acceptable manner.[27]

This strategy of gradual escalation was deeply resented by the airmen because it robbed airpower of one of its greatest weapons—the psychological impact of dominating time. Worse, the strategy did not work: the stick used in gradually escalating air attacks was never big enough or swift enough to prevent the North Vietnamese from stealing the carrot.

* * *

Time has been a key factor in war since antiquity, and commanders have repeatedly tried to harness it to their advantage. To do so would grant them speed, secrecy, surprise, and shock. Great commanders were those most adept at conquering time. This quest took on new vigor with the invention of the airplane. The conquest of time, as well as the medium in which aircraft operate, was recognized as revolutionary within the first decade of manned flight. A century later, that revolution is even more apparent as speed, accuracy, range, and secrecy continue to increase. Joint commanders must recognize this capability and factor it into their military plans.

8

Jointness and the Norwegian Campaign, 1940

THE NORWEGIAN CAMPAIGN IN the spring of 1940 was the first major joint and combined operation of World War II. Not only did the British and French work together to attack the German occupiers, but the forces of the participants included land, air, and sea elements. Yet this campaign was marked by major errors. Both sides had yet to develop a joint perspective on war—the centuries-old tradition of working alone and only grudgingly succumbing to "cooperation" with each other would be hard to break. Joint training and doctrine had not yet been sufficiently developed to allow diverse elements to work together effectively. Moreover, in Germany the unique power of *Reichsmarschall* Hermann Göering, head of the Luftwaffe, added to the poisonous effects of service parochialism—Göering would not allow his air forces, whatever the necessity, to be subservient to another arm.

The Campaign

Although Britain and France had declared war on Germany in September 1939 after the invasion of Poland, they were loath to strike the enemy along the Western Front. The French had learned from the Great War that defense had become supreme; they intended to sit behind the Maginot Line and allow the Germans to bleed themselves white in fruitless attacks. This passivity while Germany was occupied in the east devouring Poland was scathingly referred to as "sitzkrieg," to distinguish it from the German blitzkrieg. Instead, the Allies looked for a less risky venue to strike Germany, and Norway came to mind.

Germany was heavily dependent on the high-quality iron ore of Sweden that was usually shipped by rail through Norway to the ice-free port of Narvik on the Norwegian Sea. From there it traveled south by freighter to Germany.[1] Although Sweden and Norway were declared neutrals, the Allies nonetheless considered denying this resource to Germany, by force if necessary. Two weeks after the outbreak of war, First Lord of the Admiralty Winston Churchill suggested mining Norwegian territorial waters to force German ore freighters into the open sea, where they could be destroyed by the Royal Navy.[2] As the months passed, this option, and even the thought of occupying Norway, were increasingly considered and then planned because it was feared Germany might act first and invade Sweden and Norway to ensure access to the iron ore and to protect the supply lines for its shipment. On April 8, 1940, the Royal Navy began laying mines in Norwegian territorial waters. This was against international law, as it violated the rights of a neutral country, but Britain deemed it essential for its security.[3]

The Germans *were* concerned about their access to Swedish ore and safe access from Norwegian ports. The Allied starvation blockade of the First World War, coupled with violations of neutral shipping rights during the first year of the current conflict, had taught them that international law provided flimsy protection. German planners also thought Norway could serve as a valuable submarine basing site and provide bomber airbases that would outflank the Allies and allow strikes on Britain's industry and lines of communication.[4] On March 3, 1940, Hitler ordered plans drawn up to occupy Denmark and Norway to protect Nazi access to the Baltic Sea and to ensure that the ore supply lines along the Norwegian coast remained intact. The invasion of Denmark and Norway was set for April 9—coincidentally, the Allies began their mining operations the day before this assault was to take place.[5]

The German plan called for a series of quick, powerful, and wide-ranging attacks. Denmark would be seized and its two airfields at Aalborg would be used by the Luftwaffe to ferry troops and supplies into Norway and to serve as a base for long-range strike aircraft. (Thirty thousand German troops were airlifted into Norway by the Luftwaffe—the first major airlift of the war.) The five major port cities of Norway would be attacked simultaneously: Oslo, Bergen, Trondheim, Kristiansand, and Narvik, as well as the major airfield at Stavanger. These attacks would employ most of the German surface fleet, six army divisions, a paratroop battalion, and approximately 1,000 aircraft.[6]

The plan went off well despite bad weather and determined Norwegian resistance. By the end of the first day the Germans had the situation under control. Denmark surrendered in a nearly bloodless assault, and the five major Norwegian cities fell, as did the airfields near Oslo and Stavanger. (The first combat paratroop drop in history secured the airfield at Stavanger.)[7] The next day Allied help arrived, but it was too little and too late.

Allied plans were deeply flawed. Historian John Terraine later wrote that the joint planning staff "displayed an amateurishness and feebleness which to this day can make the reader alternatively blush and shiver."[8] Like the Germans, the Allies did not institute a joint command for Norway; instead, each service maintained control over its own forces. In the Narvik area, for example, Admiral Lord Cork commanded naval forces and Major General P. J. Mackesy headed the ground troops. Both, however, received orders from London—sometimes contradictory. Cork, for example, thought the army should assault Narvik forthwith, but Mackesy considered that "sheer bloody murder" and refused. Unknown to Cork, Mackesy had been told by his army superiors *not* to land on an opposed shore.[9] Instead, Mackesy landed forty-five miles away on an undefended island and approached Narvik by land. All the while, Cork chaffed at the "delay."[10] Coordination problems were aggravated when Mackesy established his headquarters ashore while Cork remained afloat. Mackesy was eventually relieved in the hope joint cooperation would improve, but by then the campaign was virtually over.

The other Allied task force was directed to liberate Trondheim. This port, however, was well within range of Luftwaffe aircraft, and Allied operations there were a disaster. The Royal Navy cruiser *Suffolk* was so badly mauled by German bombers that it barely limped back to port. This convinced the Admiralty that a direct assault on Trondheim was impossible in the face of enemy air superiority. Instead, landings were made north and south of the city, and it was hoped these two pincers would march on Trondheim and retake it by land assault.[11] This was soon seen as impossible, again due to the Luftwaffe controlling the skies. Major General Carton de Wiart, commander of the northern pincer, signaled London the day following his landing: "I see little chance of carrying out decisive, or indeed, any operations unless enemy air activity is considerably restricted."[12] The following day, April 21, he was even more emphatic: there was "no alternative to evacuation" unless he could gain air superiority.[13] With its nearest airbase 600 miles distant, the Royal Air Force (RAF) could not intervene, and the Fleet Air Arm (FAA) was outmatched—its aircraft, neglected during the interwar years, were obsolescent in comparison to those of the Luftwaffe. On May 1 the Royal Navy moved two aircraft carriers toward the area, the *Ark Royal* and *Glorious,* in an attempt to gain air superiority over the landing areas, but these ships were driven off by the Luftwaffe. Because the Germans controlled the sky over the littoral, the ground forces were soon evacuated.

The situation at Narvik was not quite as dismal for the Allies—despite the disagreements between Cork and Mackesy—simply because it was so far north that the Luftwaffe had difficulty covering the area. The RAF, through Herculean efforts, carved three air strips out of the snow and ice and deployed Gladiators and Hurricanes that had been transported by aircraft carrier. The German garrison had been resupplied by seaplane and flying boat, but these were quickly neutralized by the RAF. As a result, Allied ground forces made some headway.[14]

Unfortunately, on May 11 the Battle of France began and Norway became a sideshow. Before the Allies had even retaken Narvik they were planning its evacuation. The city fell on May 25, but the Allies embarked and departed two weeks later. The Germans quickly moved back in, and the campaign was over. Norway would remain in Nazi hands until the end of the war.

Observations

- Germany's strategic plan was logical and achievable. Swedish iron ore, which comprised 40 percent of the German supply, was an essential war resource that needed to be ensured.[15] This goal justified its campaign to seize Denmark and Norway. Similarly, the plan to use Norway for a submarine base was wise; the U-boat pens at Trondheim became a thorn in the Allied side for the rest of war. On the other hand, the plan for Luftwaffe bases from which to bomb Britain proved to be a chimera—they were too distant from Britain to be useful.[16] The strategic concept of the Allies also made sense. Liberating Norway and avoiding the main enemy deployed opposite France was logical. For the same reasons that Norway was valuable to Germany, so too was its denial to the Nazis of great import to the Allies. Without Swedish iron ore, Germany would have serious difficulties manufacturing the armaments it needed for a total war. The problem for the Allies was in the execution.
- Although the Germans were no more experienced in joint planning than the Allies, they had greater foresight in their net assessment. Airpower was realized as essential, as were the innovative tactics of airlifting troops and supplies, as well as employing paratroops. Both air missions

were pioneered during this campaign. The Allies failed to appreciate the fundamental change that airpower had made to modern war. RAF aircraft did not have the range to operate effectively over Norway from their bases in Britain, and the aircraft of the Royal Navy's FAA were obsolescent and no match for the Luftwaffe fighters they would encounter.[17] This campaign would open British eyes to the need for more air assets more creatively used.

- British planning was poor. One observer noted that "The British had only the vaguest ideas as to those two most important elements in coming up with a workable operational plan: the enemy and the terrain." Troops departing for Norway were told there was little snow in the Narvik area, but upon arrival they found several feet of it piled up all the way to the water's edge! Mackesy's orders from his superiors were not shared with the navy or air force. One observer, General Hastings Ismay, summarized the problem clearly: "The Chief of the Naval Staff and the Chief of the Imperial General Staff acted with sturdy independence. They appointed their respective commanders without consultations with each other; and worse still, they gave directives to those commanders without harmonizing them. Thereafter they continued to issue separate orders to them. Thus was confusion worse confounded."[18]
- Unity of command is a recognized principle of war, and is especially necessary in an amphibious assault against a defended shore. There must be a single commander in charge, and all components must recognize that authority. During the Norwegian campaign both sides were deficient in this area: at times component commanders received conflicting orders from their respective services back home. In addition, there must be no conflict between sea and land commanders during such hazardous joint operations—which again was the case in Norway. Today, US doctrine insists on such unity, embodied in a "joint force commander" for whom all components—air, land, sea, space, and special forces—are explicitly subordinate at all times.[19]
- Although the Germans encountered a hostile Norwegian population, the typically no-nonsense approach that the *Wehrmacht* took to such occupations ensured there were no serious problems. This passivity allowed the Germans to establish a solid base for extended operations within the country. The Allies, on the other hand, were only successful in the far north at Narvik, where they were able to build rudimentary

airfields from which to base aircraft and establish a supply and staging area. The intent was to use Narvik as a stepping-off point to attack German forces to the south. This plan, which would have been difficult to implement in any event, was never attempted due to the invasion of France and subsequent Allied withdrawal.

- It is difficult for an invader to launch an amphibious operation against a defended shore. In the Norwegian campaign, British commanders refused to land at Trondheim or Narvik for this very reason—and they were supported in those decisions by superiors in London. When a vigorous enemy defense is expected, the attacker must soften up enemy positions through a prolonged and heavy artillery bombardment from sea, aerial bombing, or both. The alternative is to achieve near total tactical surprise—a rare occurrence.
- The Allied forces attempting to liberate Norway were inadequate for the task. Not only were the ground troops insufficient to dislodge the Germans from their entrenched positions, but the air forces—both land- and sea-based—were likewise too sparse, and in the case of the FAA were of poor capability. Luftwaffe superiority at the point of attack was a critical factor in Allied failure.
- Joint military leadership underwent a transformation as a result of this campaign. The addition of airpower made joint planning and command essential. Previously, a grudging cooperation between sailors and soldiers might have been sufficient, but the advent of airpower, which was necessary for the successful conduct of both land and sea operations, made coordination essential. Land- and sea-based aircraft operated in the same airspace—a serious danger unless the air arms closely coordinated their efforts. Simple factors of efficiency and effectiveness were also apparent. There was no unity of command in Norway—on either side—and conflicting orders were often sent to the component commanders, who generally maintained separate headquarters. What today is termed "jointness" was barely present in this campaign. As the war progressed, the Allies learned more quickly than did the Germans. The German official history ruefully admits this: "The successful conclusion of Weserübung [the German codeword for the Norwegian/Danish invasion] did not encourage critical analysis; rather, it tended to divert attention from the shortcomings of the German command organization and the weaknesses of the *Wehrmacht*."[20]

- Services doctrines were seldom compatible, and the lack of joint training exercises during peacetime became painfully obvious. This was especially apparent in the poor results gained by naval gunfire in support of troops ashore, and in the inadequacy of close air support by the RAF. Such myopia had to be cured by the harsh teacher of combat.
- This campaign demonstrated that intelligence was vitally important for success. The Allies had superior intelligence-gathering assets and also enjoyed the supreme advantage of having broken the German codes used by the Enigma machine that transmitted Ultra intelligence. Yet, intelligence was poorly shared among the services and even within each service, so numbers, quality, and location of enemy aircraft, vessels, and shore batteries were often unknown to the key parties.[21]
- The notion of sea superiority underwent a fundamental and irreversible change as a result of the Norwegian campaign. It was now realized that command of the air was essential to ensure command of the sea. The Luftwaffe controlled the sky, and the Royal Navy could not maintain a presence in the face of that control. The Royal Navy's official historian concluded: "if effective air cover was lacking, warships could not be maintained overseas."[22] This was a startling admission. General Alan Brooke, later field marshal and chief of the Imperial General Staff, concurred with this assessment, writing that Norway demonstrated "the undermining of sea power by air power."[23] The sole bright spot for the Allies was at Narvik, but only because the Luftwaffe was unable to intervene effectively and the RAF was able to gain localized air superiority.

It had been a major tenet of naval theory that one of sea power's strengths was its ability to prevent an enemy from conducting a major amphibious operation. If such an attack were initiated, a fleet could strangle it by preventing resupply to the troops ashore—a major lesson demonstrated in Bonaparte's Egyptian campaign of 1798 when his entire fleet was destroyed at Aboukir Bay. But this Mahanian concept of neutralizing an enemy fleet in order to gain sea control did not take into account the emerging importance of airpower. The British cabinet initially believed sea power would dispose of German forces in Norway in "a week or two."[24] Instead, the tone of the campaign was set on the first day when the British fleet was intercepted by the Luftwaffe. Without air cover, one destroyer was quickly sunk and the battleship *Rodney* was damaged. In response, the fleet moved north, out of range of German aircraft: the

Royal Navy was thus unable to lend effective support to the troops landing on the coast.[25]

The Major Lesson of the Campaign

World War II demonstrated almost from its outset that control of the sea was difficult if not impossible to maintain if the air above the sea was not controlled as well. This had been the belief of many airmen between the wars, but they had no historical precedents to back it up. Soon after World War II began, however, the truth of this new proposition became apparent. It was certainly the case in Norway. RAF aircraft, based in England and Scotland, had not the range to extend an air control bubble over the landing areas, and the aircraft of the Fleet Air Arm were underpowered and obsolescent. Only in the far north, at Narvik, was the RAF able to scrape out rudimentary airfields and contest command of the air.

The need for air superiority over the littoral was shown repeatedly during the war. At Crete in May 1941 over 23,000 German invaders, transported mostly by air, landed on the island, which was defended by over 42,000 British, Commonwealth, and Greek troops. Despite being heavily outnumbered, the Germans were successful in less than a week, largely because the Luftwaffe had command of the air. The Royal Navy aircraft carrier *Formidable* was driven off with heavy damage, thereby eliminating use of its aircraft. As in Norway, the RAF's aircraft did not have the range to cover the island from their bases in Egypt, and the result for the Royal Navy was catastrophic. The Luftwaffe sank three cruisers and six destroyers, while heavily damaging an aircraft carrier, three battleships, and fifteen other major ships. Counting smaller ships in the harbor at Suda Bay, a total of forty-two vessels were sunk or damaged with a loss of over 2,000 lives due to German air attacks.[26] The words of the British land and sea commanders are compelling. Major General Bernard Freyberg cabled his superior during the battle: "A small ill-equipped and immobile force such as ours cannot stand up against the concentrated bombing that we have been faced with during the last seven days."[27] The Royal Navy commander in the Mediterranean, Admiral Andrew Cunningham, wrote at the time of the debacle: "As I have always feared, enemy command of the air, unchallenged by our own Air Force, and in these restricted waters, with Mediterranean weather, is too great odds for us to take on except by seizing opportunities of surprise and using the utmost circumspection—It is perhaps fortunate that H. M. S. *Formidable* was immobilized, as I doubt if she would now be afloat."[28]

In one of the war's greatest shocks to Winston Churchill, Japanese land-based aircraft sank the battleship *Prince of Wales* and battle cruiser *Repulse* on December 9, 1941, off the coast of Malaya. Those were the Royal Navy's only two capital ships in the Pacific. Admiral Tom Phillips, the task force commander, had not commanded operationally since the Great War, and clearly the air revolution had missed him. Not only did he not wait for air cover when steaming out, but when Japanese aircraft were first sighted he refused to break radio silence to call for help from RAF airfields within range. It was a fatal mistake.[29]

Historian Michael Howard saw this shift in war clearly, writing that the Second World War in Europe involved the transportation and continued supply of massive armies from small and fragile port facilities. As a result, the defender moving up reserves by road and rail enjoyed the customary flexibility of internal lines of supply, but "it was the new weapon of air-power, rather than the traditional one of sea-power, that had to be called upon to counter it."

The specific impact of airpower on amphibious operations was also first revealed in Norway. For the rest of the war commanders realized that amphibious operations could not succeed if the enemy controlled the sky—regardless of the size of the flotilla supporting the landings. American amphibious assaults in the Pacific were dependent on air superiority; indeed, it was not a coincidence that General Douglas MacArthur's "island-hopping" campaign consisted of jumps of around 300 miles—the radius of most US fighter aircraft at the time. In addition, the islands chosen for assault either already had a runway in operation or the terrain allowed one to be rapidly built. In the Central Pacific Area, the invading forces of Admiral Chester Nimitz were always accompanied by multiple aircraft carriers to ensure air control over the beaches. As a consequence, the aircraft carrier replaced the battleship as the center of the US fleet. Air superiority was no less crucial in Europe. It was an integral part of the Allied landings in North Africa, Sicily, and Italy. In June 1944 the Allies landed on the coast of France. General Dwight Eisenhower would later testify before Congress regarding the importance of air superiority for the Normandy invasion:

> The Normandy invasion was based on a deep-seated faith in the power of the air forces, in overwhelming numbers, to intervene in the land battle. That is, a faith that the air forces, by their action, could have the effect on the ground of making it possible for a small force of land troops to invade a continent. . . . Without that air force, without

> the aid of its power, entirely aside from its anticipated ability to sweep the enemy air forces out of the sky, without its power to intervene in the land battle, that invasion would have been fantastic. . . . it would have been more than fantastic, it would have been criminal.[30]

Field Marshal Erwin Rommel, Eisenhower's opponent in Normandy, admitted the accuracy of the above, stating: "Anyone who has to fight, even with the most modern weapons, against an enemy in complete command of the air, fights like a savage against modern European troops, under the same handicaps and with the same chances of success."[31] The noted historian Paul Kennedy summed this new fact of war succinctly: "Airpower in the Second World War created winners and losers; either they had it or they didn't."[32]

Lieutenant General Claude Auchinleck, who succeeded Mackesy in command of the Narvik operation, wrote of airpower's importance in his campaign report: "He [the enemy] used it first, to support his troops by low-flying attacks, by bombing, [in the latter stages by dive-bombing], by surprise landing of combat troops by parachute, and from seaplanes. The enemy advanced detachments were supplied by air. And secondly, [air power was used] to deny us the use of sea communications in the narrow coastal waters in the theatre of operations."[33]

He summed this issue by stating: "to commit troops to a campaign in which they cannot be provided with adequate air support is to court disaster."[34] Air superiority allowed the Luftwaffe to conduct interdiction, close air support, reconnaissance, resupply, and reinforcement with little interference. Also of importance, the psychological impact of having enemy aircraft continually overhead was a severe blow: "in some cases, frustration built up to a sense of hopelessness and a serious lowering of morale."[35]

Germany's campaign in Norway proved to be highly successful at relatively low cost; for the British and French, the opposite was the case.

One other and vitally important result of this failed Allied campaign: the government of Neville Chamberlain fell. The new prime minister was Winston Churchill.

Part III
American Military Experiences

9

American Military Culture and Its Influence on Strategy

CULTURE IS SOCIALLY TRANSMITTED behavior patterns, arts, beliefs, and institutions that shape a community or population. Culture influences the way people fight, effecting not only goals and strategies, but also methods, technologies, weapons, force structures, and even tactics—not always favorably. At the Battle of Agincourt in 1415, French knights treated the English archers with disdain—they were not aristocrats but commoners unworthy of notice. That cultural mind-set proved to be a deadly miscalculation.

US military culture, although partly inherited from its European forebears, has developed in its own distinctive ways over the past two centuries. Events following the end of the Cold War have signaled changes in this culture, fine tuning it to the demands of domestic and international politics. A heightened sensitivity to the use of force has impacted the way Americans fight—emphasizing speed, precision, power projection, discrimination, and information fusion to produce decisive results quickly and with remarkably low casualties. In addition, the tension between a professional military and one composed of citizen-soldiers—a National Guard—remains politically charged, and civilian control of the military engenders continued debate.

* * *

Observers have stressed certain themes in American culture and their impact on military organization and strategy. The nineteenth-century French traveler Alexis de Tocqueville noted that Americans emphasized democracy, individualism, and the rule of law. Americans believed they had a God-given mandate to further those concepts throughout the world, prompting Tocqueville to write in exasperation: "Nothing is more embarrassing in the ordinary intercourse of life than this irritable patriotism of the Americans."[1] This ethnocentrism would become an American trait.

Regarding the military, Tocqueville noted that geography, in the form of a huge land mass bounded by oceans and weak neighbors, meant that a standing army was unnecessary. Consequently, military affairs were little discussed by the average American or politician. This in turn caused naivete and unpreparedness when a crisis did arise: "There are two things that a democratic people will always find very difficult, to begin a war and to end it."[2] These were prescient observations, especially the latter.

Another foreigner who observed America at close hand was Alfred Vagts. He had served in the German Army during World War I and then immigrated to the United States. A historian, he defined two related but fundamentally different terms. The "military way" was marked by the use of men and materiel to achieve specific objectives in war with efficiency and dispatch. It was limited in scope and inherently scientific in its methods. "Militarism," on the other hand, was a combination of "customs, interests, prestige, actions, and thought associated with armies and war and yet transcending true military purposes." Militarism was an evil, focused on "caste and cult" rather than science, and was often antithetical to the military way.[3] The Germany of his youth was militaristic; his adopted country was not: "The American system at the outset was a military system, not a militaristic system. It conceived of the army as an agent of civil power, to be organized and disciplined with that purpose in view, not as an end in itself."[4]

Samuel P. Huntington's *The Soldier and the State* covers a wide range of topics, including the nature of a profession, military professionalism, and civilian control of the military. He too noted the distinction between the military way and militarism, the security of the United States that stunted strategic thought, and the tension between professional soldiers and the National Guard. He viewed the Guard as an inherently political instrument. Commanders were generally appointed by state governors, and such positions were often seen as a form of patronage.[5] Senior officers thus had a dual loyalty—to their state and to the federal government. Because the regular military force was small and the nation had to rely on its Guard and Reserve forces, there arose continual tension regarding the political nature and influence of the US military.

Other factors characterize American military culture.[6] First was the fear of a standing army that might prove dangerous to the liberties of a free people. Related to this fear was an affinity for the citizen-soldier. It was a strongly held belief that most able-bodied men in America were capable of taking up arms to defend their homes. During the colonial era this was not an unreasonable assumption. Colonial America was a dangerous place, and most men, especially those in frontier areas, had to be proficient with firearms to ensure their own safety. The English were aware of this latent military capability, and one magistrate warned London that these were "a people numerous and armed."[7] The United States was born in war, and this had a defining effect on its subsequent military culture.

At the same time, Americans were not militaristic in that the rigid discipline characteristic of European armies was not present in the Colonies. General William von Stueben, who helped train George Washington's Continental Army, noted that Americans wanted to be told *why* they were doing certain things—simple orders were insufficient.[8] This trait meant that American military personnel of all ranks were imbued with an unusual degree of independence and sense of initiative—something seldom encouraged in other armies. This independent streak would also be a lasting trait.

The United States, due largely to English influence, was founded on the rule of law, so the role of the military was carefully circumscribed.[9] The law similarly governed the way the military conducted itself. It is significant that one of the first legal treatises governing the conduct of an army in war was drawn up by Francis Lieber for the US Army in 1861.[10] This mandate to follow the law is even more pronounced today.

Isolationism, to a great extent fostered by geography, has been a characteristic strain in the American spirit. George Washington warned of foreign entanglements in his "farewell speech" of 1796, and it was not until 1948 that the US joined a military alliance in peacetime. Americans viewed war as an aberration not to be taken lightly. This sense of commitment often led to a policy of unconditional surrender—allegedly what the initials of U. S. Grant stood for.[11] If wars were total and the subjugation of the enemy was necessary, then it followed that the aftermath of war—indeed its goal—should be the spread of the American spirit, of democracy and an abhorrence of war. Democracy was therefore the desired end state for Mexico in 1847, Cuba and the Philippines in 1898, for Europe as articulated by Woodrow Wilson in his Fourteen Points of 1918, and after World War II in Germany and Japan. Even in Korea, Vietnam, Iraq, and Afghanistan, free and democratic societies were the ultimate US policy goals. Unfortunately, it was also a characteristic of the "aberration" mentality that when wars ended, things were expected to return to normal. The troops would come home and be demobilized, the defense budget cut, America would return to isolationism, and the budding democracy in the recently defeated/liberated country would be left to fend for itself.[12] Post-conflict pacification and stabilization efforts were often given short shrift, usually with unfortunate results.

* * *

US military strategies over the past two centuries have been shaped by these characteristics and traits. Through the end of World War II at least, American soldiers held a narrow definition of the term "strategy." To them it meant merely "the art of bringing forces to the battlefield in a favorable position," and generals did not consider broader issues, such as the political, economic, or social implications of battle. Using this narrow definition, soldiers tended to see battle as an end in itself.[13] Clausewitz had said much the same thing, so American soldiers could at least claim a dubious pedigree.[14]

American strategy focused on how the battle should be set up, and how it should then be fought. Much time was spent thinking through problems of logistics, command and control, staff work, and battle tactics—although usually at the small unit level. The goal was to get there first, get there fast, and get there heavy. If one did so, then annihilation might result—the enemy army would be defeated, and peace, whatever politicians meant by that term, would then ensue. This meshed with an American military culture that saw war as an aberration to be quickly ended and then forgotten.

A corollary of this emphasis on annihilation was that America would rely on its massive industrial and natural resources to overwhelm an enemy. For America, there would always be an unlimited supply of weapons, ammunition, fuel, steel, etc. In short, technology could substitute for manpower.

American military strategy thus involved massing forces for a climactic battle that would lead to the defeat of the enemy army and victory. Some generals got quite good at this; by the end of the Civil War, Grant was battering Robert E. Lee's army to bits—as well as his own. In the Great War, John Pershing followed the same unimaginative strategy used by the British and French—a series of bloody frontal assaults against German trenches. As for World War II, many believe that Eisenhower's refusal to move beyond the Elbe River toward Berlin was the epitome of myopic strategic thinking. Eisenhower would not listen to the entreaties of Winston Churchill regarding the importance of Berlin as a political prize in the postwar settlement: his job as a soldier was to defeat German military forces, preferably with as low a butcher's bill as possible. Taking the German capital would cost many lives, and they were not worth the seizure of the city for "mere" political ends.[15]

Korea was a turning point, because the world had changed. The American and Soviet colossi faced each other, armed with atomic weapons, across the devastated but invaluable landscape of Europe. When North Korea moved south in June 1950, Western leaders saw the attack as a feint dictated by Moscow to distract America from Europe. Chinese intervention a few months later aggravated these fears. Such concerns were either not shared or not understood by the soldier in Tokyo. Douglas MacArthur believed that his mission was to destroy the enemy's forces. Clausewitz and his experiences in two world wars had taught him there was "no substitute for victory." Harry Truman thought otherwise, and the Old Soldier faded away.

American military leaders learned from MacArthur's experience in Korea, but it would take time. Dwight Eisenhower succeeded Truman as president and declared a new US strategy of massive retaliation, dependent on nuclear weapons delivered from land, sea, and air. The Army's chief of staff, General Matthew Ridgway, disputed such a notion and was increasingly vocal about his objections. In the words of one observer: "Between the autumn of 1953 and the summer of 1955, the United States Army took it upon itself to mount an explicit challenge to civilian control. Through a determined effort aimed at overturning the national security policies promulgated by President Dwight D. Eisenhower, himself a career military officer who had risen to five-star rank, Army leaders sought to restrict the ability of senior civilian leaders to determine basic national strategy. They did so by attempting to undermine the credibility of the Eisenhower administration's declared strategy of massive retaliation."[16]

This is a serious charge, hardly mitigated by the author's argument that Ridgway and his officers engineered such a confrontation for the "right" reasons. Ridgway was pushed into early retirement, but the repercussions of the affair were disturbing: "the ultimate effect of the tugging and hauling between Eisenhower and his generals was not to affirm civilian control but to accelerate the politicization of the senior military leadership."[17] Unfortunately, more vital strategic issues were not grasped, and Vietnam was the result.

Presidents Kennedy, Johnson, and Nixon saw Vietnam as another proxy war pushed by Moscow and Beijing to distract attention from Europe. To avoid falling into this trap, the presidents decided there would be no attempt to annihilate or overthrow the enemy by invading North Vietnam. LBJ confined himself to a land war in the south and bombing North Vietnam, although the bombing was never enough and seldom at the right targets. Indeed, it is a fascinating paradox that Johnson chose airpower to coerce North Vietnamese leaders precisely because of its greatest perceived weakness—its inability to hold ground. Invasion by an American army would send too strong a signal to the world. Airpower, on the other hand, would be seen as less provocative, especially if employed in a measured and circumscribed fashion.[18] In an unusually candid passage, Johnson explained his reasoning for a military strategy that promised something less than victory:

> I saw our bombs as my political resources for negotiating a peace. On the one hand, our planes and our bombs could be used as carrots for the South, strengthening the morale of the South Vietnamese and pushing them to clean up their corrupt house, by demonstrating the depth of our commitment to the war. On the other hand, our bombs could be used as sticks against the North, pressuring North Vietnam to stop its aggression against the South. By keeping a lid on all the designated targets, I knew I could keep the control of the war in my own hands. If China reacted to our slow escalation by threatening to retaliate, we'd have plenty of time to ease off the bombing. But this control—so essential for preventing World War III—would be lost the moment we unleashed a total assault on the North—for that would be rape rather than seduction—and then there would be no turning back. The Chinese reaction would be instant and total.[19]

General William Westmoreland was thus placed within rigid constraints. As the heir to the tradition of decisive battle and annihilation, he struggled to reconcile divergent goals. He had drawn up plans for invasions of Laos, Cambodia, and North Vietnam and suggested this to President Johnson, but was rejected. He was certain the reason for this denial, fear of Chinese intervention, was unfounded: "Surely they would back down in the face of a threat or token commitment of forces by the world's greatest power; had not even the Russians backed down over Berlin and Cuba?"[20] The president chose not to gamble. Unable to widen the war or cut off supplies and reinforcements streaming south (and with no control over the aerial interdiction campaign against North Vietnam that was run from Washington), Westmoreland devised a strategy emphasizing body counts, search and destroy operations, free fire zones, and an astonishing use of firepower. The US Air Force dropped 5 million tons of bombs on South Vietnam, while the Army and Marine Corps fired 8 million more tons of artillery rounds.[21] And South Vietnam was on our side. Had the enemy been the German Army of 1944 this kind of strategy might have made sense; in 1968 against the Viet Cong it most certainly did not. The political and cultural components of military strategy were barely considered, largely because American military leaders had not been educated to worry about such things.

This shortcoming was fatal because much had changed since 1945, but military leaders had not understood. America had become a superpower and was engaged in a Cold War that saw a "balance of terror" enforced by nuclear weapons. The "sneak attack" at Pearl Harbor had left a deep scar on the American psyche. The cultural tendency toward isolationism that permitted military weakness was a luxury no longer tenable. America needed a "force in being" to protect itself, because a nuclear Pearl Harbor could mean the death of the nation. And so, military policy emphasized forward basing, deterrence, and a "cocked" strike force consisting of nuclear-tipped missiles, ballistic missile submarines, and heavy bombers. If American strategy was based on a strategy of annihilation, then "mutual assured destruction" was that cultural predilection writ large.

Fortunately, such apocalyptic visions soon became "unthinkable."[22] Instead, wars took place in far-off lands, and, for the United States at least, for limited ends. These small wars had international political repercussions that had to be understood by military leaders, but it was a lesson slow to take root. America would need to use its mighty military power in a most circumspect fashion. American strategy needed to be reexamined.

* * *

It is an unusual paradox of American military culture that although American military leaders were not sufficiently broad-minded when relating strategy to political factors, they were hardly apolitical. The opposite has tended to be the case.

When General Winfield Scott took Mexico City in 1847, he ran the country for several months and was so adept that Mexican leaders offered him the position of dictator and the sum of $1.25 million—as well as an annual salary![23] During the nineteenth century, Army officers served as military governors in Florida, Louisiana, New Mexico, and California.[24] During the First World War,

General John Pershing insisted, largely for political reasons, on maintaining a separate American army and command structure on the Western Front, rather than allowing his troops to be integrated into French and British units. He also pushed for an invasion of Germany to demonstrate to its people that they had indeed been defeated.[25] And of course, Douglas MacArthur, the "proconsul" of Japan for five years, was nothing if not political. His conduct during World War II and the occupation of Japan, but also his views during the Korean War, demonstrated a deep involvement in domestic and foreign political affairs. MacArthur was fired not because he lacked an appreciation for the political implications of military power, but because his understanding of how they should be implemented differed from those of his president.

Military services are unique entities formed and shaped by diverse traditions, experiences, and beliefs. The Navy, for instance, has a tradition of independence formed by virtual autonomy while at sea and out of direct contact with Washington. This led to a spirit of initiative, but also of disdain for politicians who attempted to "meddle" in their affairs. The Army saw itself as an obedient and willing servant of the people. Although often neglected by its masters, it remained steadfastly loyal and dependable. The Air Force as the youngest service boasted that its only tradition was its refusal to have any traditions. It saw itself as technologically oriented and therefore progressive.[26]

Granted, these characterizations are too facile, but the services *are* different. Their histories and traditions have induced mind-sets that shape their views on strategy and war. The Army follows a Clausewitzian bent, and its basic doctrine manual announces: "The ability to close with and destroy enemy forces, occupy territory, and control populations achieves moral dominance over enemy will and destroys means to resist."[27] Clausewitz would have found little to disagree with in that statement.

The Navy looks at war differently. It seldom refers to armies or territory as centers of gravity in its doctrine but defines such centers as sources of strength, "but not necessarily strong or a strength in itself." It posits that "a lengthy resupply line supporting forces engaged at a distant front could be an enemy's center of gravity." In consequence, the Navy's first job is to control the sea lanes.[28]

Airmen believed similarly. Billy Mitchell wrote: "The advent of air power, which can go straight to the vital centers and either neutralize or destroy them, has put a completely new complexion on the old system of making war. It is now realized that the hostile main army in the field is a false objective, and the real objectives are the vital centers."[29] A century later, an Air Force chief of staff expressed it as follows: "There is an aerial view. By instinct and training, even the most junior pilot sees it. The battlefield looks different from 40,000 feet, and it is a difference of kind, not simply degree."[30]

In essence, sailors and airmen argue there are centers of gravity other than the enemy army. Moreover, such key targets are often beyond the range or influence of ground forces. Naval blockade was a form of economic warfare, as was the Allied strategic bombing campaign in World War II; both were designed to sap German and Japanese strength and will to fight.

Airmen also tend to be technological determinists and believe in the power of the machine. This reliance on technology to solve problems is an American trait, and air and space power is the epitome of advanced technology. Meanwhile, soldiers advocate "boots on the ground" and occupation of territory as the solution to military problems.

Differing service cultures shape the way soldiers, sailors, and airmen view war—its purpose, its strategies, and its tactics. For decades these diverse views generated confusion. After Vietnam and missteps in the Iran hostage rescue attempt of 1980 and the invasion of Grenada in 1983, the services made concerted efforts to adopt a more joint approach to warfighting. This move toward "jointness" accelerated with the end of the Cold War. The reduced threat resulting from this event thrust the United States into the role of the world's sole superpower. Such a position in the global spotlight subjected US military actions to intense scrutiny. Image became crucial. To minimize mistakes, military operations became more centralized and more joint. At the same time, a technological breakthrough in the area of precision-guided munitions was taking place.

Munitions that routinely land within feet of their aimpoint has been a revolution. The emergence of these new weapons resulted in an increasing demand for the discrete application of force. "Annihilation"—the US goal in the past—became inappropriate. Instead, operations were planned to minimize casualties to enemy forces: the objective became to dissuade them from fighting at all, or to paralyze them so they were unable to fight effectively and would quickly surrender. More importantly, eliminating collateral damage to civilians became a prime mandate. Any bomb that went astray or any civilian killed by accident could be reported on the nightly news, worldwide, thereby harming US foreign policy. Significantly, the US and its allies are held to higher standards than the adversaries they face. It is now expected that enemies will use terrorism, human shields, and other illegal practices; such actions are not options for the United States and its allies.

Other technological advances continued the transformation of military culture. In addition to precision weapons, stealth, networked operations, and near-instantaneous global communications and intelligence have revolutionized the way the United States fights, beginning with DESERT STORM in 1991. Besides suffering remarkably few casualties, the US military achieved its objectives with unusual speed: DESERT STORM lasted six weeks, and the air-war over Kosovo less than three months.

America's overwhelming military might generated a predictable response: enemies did not disappear; they morphed into a new form. Taking on the United States in a conventional fight was seen as out of the question, so adversaries began to use asymmetrical strategies and weapons. This meant the US military began to worry seriously about weapons of mass destruction, cruise and ballistic missiles, information warfare, and terrorism. The catastrophe of 9/11, like the Pearl Harbor attack six decades earlier, forced changes in American military culture by accelerating the move toward greater technological development and more joint command and control.

Saddam Hussein's Iraq offered unique problems. In 2003, the US-led Coalition hoped for a quick military campaign to stun, paralyze, and overwhelm the Iraqi leadership, both civilian and military. In a rapid campaign relying on less than one-fourth of the ground troops used in 1991, the Coalition struck with a combined force of land, sea, air, and special operations units. Iraqi leaders were unable to mount a serious defense or even coordinate their forces. The Coalition encountered only sporadic resistance, and within two weeks Baghdad had begun to totter. A week later it was over—at least the United States thought it was. And that echoes the concern advanced by Tocqueville nearly two centuries ago: Americans have difficulty getting out of wars.

It is useful to ask to what extent did the way in which the Coalition fought in Iraq contribute to the problems that occurred afterward? Did the Coalition win too easily and bloodlessly, thereby leaving the Iraqi populace with the impression they had not been defeated? In this argument, a slower, more deliberate and more brutal campaign to destroy the Iraqi Army and occupy the major population centers would have been more desirable—even though requiring significantly more ground troops.

The counterargument maintains that it is not that serendipitous things had gone better in Bosnia and Kosovo after major hostilities ended, but rather it was precisely because the American ground presence was so slight. From this perspective, the wisest strategy is to place as few of our troops—infidels to the Muslims—in harm's way as possible.

Military service culture will probably determine where one falls on the complex (and over simplified) issue outlined above. Clearly, the clash of service cultures is apparent and has potentially serious implications on how America fights.

* * *

In sum, it appears the peculiarities of American culture have indeed helped shape a distinctive American way of fighting. But culture changes as a result of new directions in society's circumstances, attitudes, beliefs, and behaviors. The American military culture has thus changed as well, especially in the years following World War II and then again following the Cold War. The days of US isolationism are gone—one cultural paradigm that has been irrevocably shattered.

Other cultural artifacts have not disappeared. The long-standing belief in the efficacy of the citizen-soldier is deeply ingrained. American youngsters know of the "Minutemen," those rugged colonials who grabbed the long rifle hanging over the fireplace and went off to fight when necessary. Although professional soldiers since George Washington have decried the reliance on the militia/National Guard and termed its utility a myth, the concept endures. And it endures for good reason. The armies that fought US wars over the past two centuries were populated largely by draftees, short-term volunteers, and the reserve forces, stiffened by a small cadre of professionals.[31]

That has now changed. The demise of the draft after the Vietnam War means that for the first time in US history much of the fighting is done by long-term professionals.[32] Even so, this issue is not clear-cut. The Guard and Reserves now play a greater role because of increased military commitments overseas. For example, over 50 percent of airlift and air refueling missions in Afghanistan and Iraq up through 2003 were flown by Air National Guard and Air Force Reserve crews. During the Iraqi campaign the US Army mobilized 150,000 Reservists and Guardsmen; the Marine Corps activated 20,000 Reservists, and the Navy 10,000.[33] Even so, there endures a tension between a professional military and one made up of citizen-soldiers, airmen, and sailors. In a democracy, both types are necessary. The dilemma of ensuring a highly capable military force that can react to crises quickly, but that also remains above political influence, is an enduring one.

The change in American military culture since the end of the Cold War in 1989 has affected the way Americans fight. Still, questions remain regarding the role of the military in US society. What is the appropriate role of senior military leaders in political decision-making? The combatant commanders, those four-star officers assigned regional commands around the world, have enormous political influence. They deal routinely with foreign leaders, as well as their military counterparts, regarding issues as diverse as status of forces agreements, force structure, contingency plans, and local terrorist threats.[34] Counteracting terrorism, with its emphasis on all aspects of this problem—political, economic, religious, ethnic, cultural, and military—means these officers are destined to play a greater role in future crises. Are they trained for such roles? Are they given sufficient guidance from Washington to help them navigate the shoals?

This leads to the broad yet critical issue of civil-military relations—more specifically, civilian control of the military. This is a huge topic, but its essence was perhaps best expressed by Peter Feaver: "The civil-military challenge is to reconcile a military strong enough to do anything the civilians ask them to with a military subordinate enough to do only what civilians authorize them to do."[35]

This is an emotional subject that has generated much ink. Some have written passionately about a crisis in American civil-military affairs.[36] The Clinton and Obama years were seen as troubling because it appeared the military did not like their commander in chief.[37] Studies indicated the American military was increasingly conservative and identifying itself with the Republican Party. President Donald Trump, for example, has been viewed favorably by the military, raising many eyebrows.[38] Of greater concern to some, two-thirds of military personnel surveyed thought the military had higher moral standards than did society at large.[39] It was feared an ideological gulf was developing between society and the military chartered to protect it, and this spelled danger. Others have argued just as strenuously that there is no crisis at all.[40] This is a vitally important subject that strikes at the very core of American military culture. Civilian control of the military is fundamental to our political and cultural system.

And yet, the issue of the political education, abilities, and sensitivities of senior military commanders is brought into sharp relief by policies that emphasize an active democratization process around the world. This desire to spread the "good news of freedom" was an American trait noted by Tocqueville and implemented after most of the nation's wars, but the goal of bringing democracy to Afghanistan and Iraq, and seeing them as harbingers of a wider democratic sweep throughout the Middle East, gave this traditional inclination an increased vigor. Paradoxically, the instrument of this democratization process was the US military. To some, this tendency smacks of a yen to be "the world policeman." And yet, as a previous chapter argued, military force has been effective in *imposing* peace on troubled areas. How to achieve a correct balance?

Fewer US politicians have military experience now than previously. In 2016, only 19 percent of senators and congressmen had served in uniform—compared to 77 percent and 71 percent respectively in 1977.[41] Three of the last four presidents have had no military experience. This is not to say such individuals are uninformed or incapable of making wise decisions regarding military issues, but it does mean that such knowledge must be gained in other ways than personal experience in uniform.[42] How do we ensure this education occurs? If politicians do not understand the military, will a vacuum be created in the decision-making process that will be filled by military leaders?

Other distinctive traits remain. The military continues to conduct itself in a rigidly legal fashion. If anything, the growth of a global news media has made this requirement even more compelling. Americans also continue to view war as an aberration that should be undertaken only with reluctance and that should be ended quickly. Regrettably, as Iraq and Afghanistan demonstrate, war's aftermath is still often given scant consideration until it is too late.[43]

* * *

A society's culture has an important impact on its military—the way it views war, its goals, and its strategy and tactics. This is certainly true in the United States. In addition, the individual services have their own unique notions and traditions, and these differences can bring confusion and disagreements. Many changes in this military culture have occurred over the past few decades. The tendencies to regard battle as an end in itself, to see annihilation of the enemy as a desirable goal, and for military commanders to be blind, or at least naive, to anything on a plane higher than the tactical level of war are no longer valid. The US military today is far more attuned to the political, social, and cultural implications of its activities than ever before. It also relies more heavily on technology as a way to achieve objectives quickly and efficiently, with the least possible loss of life. The campaigns in the Balkans, Afghanistan, Iraq, Libya, and Syria show this trend. Most important of all, the American military has embraced the concept of jointness. This is a seemingly obvious lesson that took a depressingly long time to learn. As for the future, although specific weapons and tactics will most certainly change in the decades ahead, the basic cultural trends noted above probably will not.

10

Soldiers and Politics

Exposing a Myth

AMERICANS TODAY COULD NOT imagine the country's senior military officer running for political office while on active duty. They would think it absurd for a serving general to run for the presidency, lose, and then quietly resume his position in the Pentagon while continuing in uniform for another decade, receiving not only promotion but wide respect and acclaim from Congress, the people, and the news media. Yet that is what occurred in the mid-nineteenth century. Major General Winfield Scott, the commanding general of the US Army and hero of the Mexican War, contested with President Millard Fillmore to win the Whig Party's presidential nomination. Upon receiving that nomination, Scott then ran against his erstwhile subordinate, former Brigadier General Franklin Pierce. Scott did not resign his commission to run for president, and indeed made several trips around the country to visit his troops and give speeches, preceded by a Whig advance party to ensure suitable crowds were on hand.[1] He lost the election of 1852 but continued as the Army's top general for another decade. In 1856 Congress promoted him to lieutenant general—the first officer to hold that rank since George Washington.

This was not Scott's first foray into politics. In 1840 he coveted the presidency, but William Henry Harrison was the candidate that year.[2] In 1848 he lobbied for the Whig presidential nomination, but the party chose another general, Zachary Taylor, a Mexican War hero and commander of the Army's Western Division. Taylor remained in uniform throughout the campaign. The election was held on November 7, but General Taylor did not submit his resignation from the Army until December 21—to take effect four days before his inauguration.[3]

These were not isolated incidents. Throughout most of our history this type of conduct *was* the American military tradition. It is a myth to argue that the military has been divorced from political affairs. On the contrary, military leaders have been deeply involved in politics throughout much of the past two centuries. Yet, one of the foremost observers of civil-military relations in US History, Richard H. Kohn, argues in his seminal essay on the subject that a crisis is unfolding because the military is becoming politicized. It was not always so, says Kohn: "Historically, one of the chief bulwarks of civilian control has been the American military establishment itself. Its small size in peacetime, the professionalism of the officers, their political neutrality, their willing subordination, and their acceptance of a set of unwritten but largely understood rules of behavior in the civil-military relationship—all had made civilian control succeed, messy as it sometimes was and situational as it must always be."[4]

The US military was anything but politically neutral during much of its history; its leaders were not always willingly subordinate to civilian authority; and they did not often agree to an unwritten standard of behavior. Rather, there was a "permeable membrane" between the military and political spheres that allowed men to pass back and forth between the two as it suited their purpose—and the purpose of the political parties and even the nation.

* * *

America's founding fathers were fearful of a standing army. The Declaration of Independence railed against King George III because he "kept among us, in times of peace, standing armies without the consent of our legislature" and he imposed an occupying force that "affected to render the military independent of and superior to the civil power." It was therefore no surprise that the issue of an army was highly contentious in the newly independent United States. Debates at the Constitutional Convention in 1787 were heated. When the Constitution was agreed upon, it included several provisions designed to regulate the powers and limitations of an army. The president was to be the commander in chief and appoint officers, but Congress would approve these appointments, control the purse strings, and declare war. The Second Amendment ensured the right of the people to keep and bear arms, while the Third Amendment put restrictions on quartering troops among the populace—a grievance mentioned in the Declaration of Independence. The American people were averse to a standing army, which was viewed as a threat to liberty.[5] On the other hand, the founding fathers feared the possibility of internal problems—like those which they themselves had fomented against England—and so they included in the Constitution that federal troops could be used to suppress insurrection and domestic violence.[6] Indeed, federal troops would be called out dozens of times over the next two centuries to suppress rebellion, implement federal laws, break strikes, quell draft, railroad, and mining riots, and enforce civil rights.[7]

Paradoxically, the distaste of a professional army did not extend to its leaders. The officer corps was viewed with respect, and a military career was seen as a stepping stone to political office. That trend began with George Washington. After the war he was universally referred to as General Washington—even while serving as president of the Constitutional Convention in 1787. In fact, his official portrait by Charles Wilson Peale while serving as president shows him in the uniform of a lieutenant general.[8] Upon being elected, Washington chose cabinet officers who had served with him during the war—John Knox, Edmund Randolph, Timothy Pickering, and Alexander Hamilton.[9] After leaving the presidency, *General* Washington was recalled to active duty in 1798 by President John Adams to command the army during the "Quasi War" with France. In the years ahead a number of soldiers, and a few sailors, would attempt to parlay success in uniform into a political career. Of the first twenty-five men to hold the presidency, twenty-one had military experience.[10]

Politicians understood this connection, so it was no surprise when presidents selected military officers based on their political leanings. President John Adams, for example, wanted Federalists in the officer corps, and shortly before leaving office in February 1801 he nominated eighty-seven men to fill Army vacancies. Virtually all were known Federalists.[11] The new president, Thomas Jefferson, would have none of it. He had Captain Meriwether Lewis do a survey of all officers on active duty, ranking not only their professional ability but also their political affiliation. The Federalists were purged and Republicans were advanced.[12]

While serving as commander of the Southern District, Major General Andrew Jackson was determined to incorporate West Florida into the United States. Although receiving clear orders from the secretaries of war and state in 1818 *not* to move against the Spanish forces in the area, he attacked two Spanish forts, killed most of the inhabitants, and even executed two British citizens he came across. London and Madrid were outraged, and so were Jackson's civilian superiors for his presumption at taking American diplomacy into his own hands. Yet, the majority of Americans supported him: "In the end, Jackson's popularity made him invulnerable."[13] Jackson suffered no repercussions for his insubordination; in fact, he was appointed Florida's military governor after it was annexed by the United States. In 1828 he was elected president.

Major General Jacob J. Brown, the Army's commanding general from 1821–1828, fancied himself a kingmaker. In the presidential election of 1824 he vocally promoted John C. Calhoun for president. When the results were in, no one had a majority in the Electoral College, and Calhoun came in third behind Andrew Jackson and John Quincy Adams. Brown then threw his support to Adams. When Adams won and announced that Henry Clay would be his secretary of state, Brown remonstrated with him that Clay was a poor choice; he pushed instead for DeWitt Clinton, an old friend and governor of New York. Adams kept Clay.[14]

In 1845 President James K. Polk was in a quandary over who to appoint as commander in the war against Mexico: whoever landed this assignment would have the inside track for the presidency. His two top generals, Winfield Scott and Zachary Taylor, were Whigs and therefore politically unacceptable. In an attempt to stack the deck, Polk appointed thirteen new generals—all democrats and nine of them politicians. One of those was Gideon J. Pillow. It was a reward for his services in helping Polk get elected.[15] The president also nominated Democratic senator Thomas Hart Benton, a career politician, to the rank of lieutenant general. If approved, Benton would outrank Scott and Taylor and, presumably, be in line for the presidency after the war. The Senate understood the game Polk was playing with these political appointments but balked at Benton's proposed rank, which until then only George Washington had earned. Senator Benton had to be satisfied with the rank of major general. The entire point of the commission now rendered meaningless, General Benton played no role in the war, and as Polk feared, the two Whigs vied for the White House in 1848.[16] Taylor won.

Others taking the path from high command to political office included Jackson, the hero of New Orleans and the Seminole Wars, previously mentioned. He aroused strong feelings in opponents, who considered him autocratic. The Whig Party, successor to the Federalists, wanted someone more conservative, but they liked the idea of a military hero. Their first candidate would be former general, congressman, and senator William Henry Harrison. In addition to being a veteran of the War of 1812, General Harrison was also the victor over the Prophet at the Battle of Tippecanoe. He won the presidency in 1840.

Jefferson Davis went back and forth between the military and politics.

After graduating from West Point in 1828 he served five years in the Army. After resigning he later ran for Congress, taking office in 1845. He soon quit the House to serve as a colonel during the Mexican War, where he won acclaim for his bravery under fire. Afterward he was elected to the Senate in 1848 and was named secretary of war in 1852; after four years he returned to the Senate. In January 1861 he left office again to become a major general in the Mississippi militia when his state seceded from the Union; one month later he was appointed president of the Confederate States of America. He later won election to a full six-year term.[17]

Colonel John C. Frémont was a noted explorer while in the Army during the 1840s. The son-in-law of Senator Benton, Frémont used this family relationship to further his political career. In 1846 he was appointed military governor of California. In fact, California was ruled by the military for over three years between 1846 and 1850. One historian notes this was not a period of martial law, but of military law—the Army did not support the civilian government in place; it supplanted it.[18] In 1850 Frémont was elected to the Senate by California, and in 1856 he was the first Republican candidate for president, losing to James Buchanan. When the Civil War broke out, he returned to uniform and was promoted to major general. He continued to dabble in politics while in uniform, and when appointed commander in Missouri he freed all slaves within the state—a policy well in advance of President Abraham Lincoln's thoughts on the subject. Frémont was relieved of duty.[19] In 1864 he ran for president as the candidate of the Radical Democracy Party, but he withdrew a few months later when his campaign gained no traction. In 1878 he was appointed governor of the Arizona Territory by President Rutherford Hayes.

In 1858, Major P.G.T. Beauregard was posted to New Orleans and became disgusted with the corrupt leadership of the Know Nothings political party in charge. He decided to run for mayor of New Orleans that year on a reform platform "out of a sense of duty to his city." He lost the election but remained in New Orleans for another three years.[20]

The Constitution permits such political activities. Article I, Section 6, prohibits members of Congress from simultaneously holding another federal office, but it does not bar anyone already holding federal office—such as a military officer—from *running* for Congress or the presidency, as long as they resign one commission before taking up another.[21] (The courts have ruled that this "ineligibility clause" does not apply to officers of the National Guard or the Reserves, who may serve simultaneously as members of Congress.)

The relationship between the military and politics underwent a transformation during the Civil War. Such intrastate conflicts are inherently political, and politicians became heavily involved in military affairs while military officers meddled in politics. It was part of the genius of Abraham Lincoln that he intuitively realized this political nature. A huge army needed to be built, and this was initially accomplished through the raising of volunteer regiments in each state. The officers of such units were generally elected by the men, and the commanders (colonels) appointed by the governors. As the regiments were combined into brigades and divisions, however, Lincoln appointed the generals himself. His choices were an attempt to balance the necessity of combining military proficiency with political expediency. Significantly, of the 110 Union generals in 1861, eighty were known Democrats. In the words of one historian: "Most Union generals, through whatever mixture of conviction and self-interest, displayed rather than disguised their political leanings."[22] Lincoln was well aware of this.

During the war, Lincoln nominated 583 generals: of these, 217 were West Point graduates and another 178 had some military background; but 188 (32 percent) had no military experience.[23] Lincoln realized it was essential to maintain a united front in the North, keep a strong war coalition in Congress, and ensure that the border states—Missouri, Maryland, Kentucky, western Virginia, and even southern Illinois—remained in the Union. To achieve these varied aims, Lincoln chose politicians to be generals so they could inspire patriotism, raise troops, and hold Congress together. Thus, Benjamin Butler of Massachusetts was selected for general rank specifically because he was a prominent Democrat who supported the war. He raised thousands of troops and was soon made a major general. He was not successful as a field commander, but his organizational and administrative abilities were formidable, especially in New Orleans, where he took command in 1862.[24] Other political generals included Nathaniel Banks, John Dix, John Logan, Jacob Cox, Andrew Hamilton, John McClernand, Francis Blair, and dozens of others. The "professional soldiers" who had graduated from West Point were opposed to these "amateurs" and complained to friends, Congress, the president, and each other that the political generals were useless and would get men killed. In truth, the political generals often did do poorly in battle, but the fact that the major battles lost by the Union were all commanded by West Pointers tended to undermine their argument. Despite complaints, Lincoln backed his appointees through most of the war: he needed the legitimacy with the electorate they provided him. It was not until after his reelection in 1864 that Lincoln gave General U. S. Grant great powers and the West Point clique was able to remove the political generals from command.

After Fort Sumter, scores of politicians at the federal and local level left office to don the uniform. In the 36th Congress of 1859–61, 9.8 percent of the members had military experience, but seventy-three then resigned to join the army—both armies.[25] Numerous veterans ran for office in the war's aftermath. Of the 516 Union generals surviving the war, 134 (26 percent) eventually held public office, and nearly 200 more wartime brevet brigadier generals entered public service as well.[26] In the South, this propensity was even greater: of the 412 surviving Confederate generals, 150 (36 percent) entered politics after the war.[27] Some of the more notable men who moved from political office to soldiering and back to politics included the following men.

- Carl Schurz was a German immigrant who campaigned for Lincoln in 1860 and was rewarded with an ambassadorship to Spain. During the Civil War he joined the Army and was made a major general. After the war he was elected senator from Missouri and in 1877 was named secretary of the interior.[28]
- Nathaniel P. Banks was a congressman elected speaker of the house and was governor of Massachusetts. During the conflict he was a major general, and at war's end he returned to politics to serve six more terms in Congress.
- John B. Logan was an Illinois Democratic congressman who joined the Union Army as a private at the outbreak of war. He rose to major general and was the only non-West Point graduate to command a corps. After the war he served in the House and Senate and was the Republican candidate for vice president in 1884.
- John McClernand was an Illinoisan and close friend of President Lincoln who served in the House of Representatives as a Democrat before the war. He was appointed a major general and fought at Fort Donelson, Shiloh, and Vicksburg. Always a political intriguer who played shamelessly on his relationship with the president, he was eventually removed from command by Grant. After the war he reentered politics.
- John McCauley Palmer was a state senator from Illinois prior to the war.

During the conflict he was appointed a major general; afterward he was elected governor and then to the US Senate. In 1896 he ran for president on the National Democratic ticket.

- Daniel E. Sickles served in the New York state senate for two terms before being elected to the US House. During the war he was a major general and fought at Gettysburg, earning the Medal of Honor.[29] After the war he was appointed minister to Spain, elected sheriff of New York City, and eventually returned to the House.
- Lew Wallace was an Indiana politician who served in uniform during the Mexican War. He was elected as a Democrat to the Indiana Senate and at the outbreak of the Civil War was appointed a brigadier general and soon after a major general. His performance was credible, especially at the Battle of Monocacy. After the war he served on the committee to investigate the Lincoln assassination, was governor of the New Mexico Territory, and consul to the Ottoman Empire. He also found time to write *Ben-Hur*.
- Rutherford B. Hayes was elected solicitor in Cincinnati in 1859, then joined the Union Army and rose to brevet major general. He was wounded in battle seven times. While still on active duty he was elected to Congress in 1864. After two terms he was elected governor of Ohio, and in 1876 he won the presidency.
- James A. Garfield was elected to the Ohio state senate in 1859. At the outbreak of the war he joined the Union Army and rose to major general. While on campaign he was elected to Congress; in December 1863 he arrived at the Capitol in uniform to take his oath of office. He was later elected to the US Senate and in 1880 to the presidency.
- Benjamin Harrison, grandson of President William Henry Harrison, was elected city attorney of Indianapolis, was secretary of the Indiana Republican Party, and was elected reporter of the Indiana Supreme Court. In July 1862 he resigned his offices to join the Union Army, and by war's end he was a brevet brigadier general. He then returned to Indiana to be governor, senator, and in 1888 was elected president.

Of note, forty-five Union generals were foreign-born, and although some had prior military experience, usually in Prussia or France, others did not and became generals largely because of their ability to raise troops among immigrant groups. These generals included Carl Schurz, Franz Sigel, Gustave Koerner, Henry Bohlen, Friedrich Salomon, Michael Corcoran, Thomas Meagher, Wladimir Krzyzanowski, and Albin Schoepf.[30]

There were other military officers who rose to high rank during the Civil War and then used the fame gained to run for office afterward. Examples include:

- George B. McClellan, West Point class of 1846, served in the Mexican War and was twice commander of the Army of the Potomac during the Civil War as well as commanding general of the Army. In 1864 he was the Democratic Party's nominee for president and ran against Lincoln. He submitted his resignation from the Army on Election Day. In 1878 he was elected governor of New Jersey.
- U. S. Grant, West Point class of 1843, ended the war as a lieutenant general and commanding general of the Army. He retired from the Army, effective March 4, 1869, the day of his inauguration as president.
- Winfield Scott Hancock, West Point class of 1844, was a hero at Gettysburg. In 1880 the major general was the Democratic Party's nominee for president, while still commanding the Army's Atlantic Division. He lost the election to former Major General James Garfield, but was graciously invited to the inauguration, which he attended. Hancock remained in uniform and died at his desk on Governors Island in 1886.
- Simon Bolivar Buckner, West Point class of 1844, fought in the Mexican War and upon secession joined the Confederate Army, rising to become a lieutenant general. In 1887 he was elected governor of Kentucky, and in 1896 he was former Major General John McCauley Palmer's vice presidential running mate, losing to William McKinley.
- Joshua Lawrence Chamberlain was a professor of rhetoric at Bowdoin College before the war. He joined the Army and was made a lieutenant colonel. At Little Round Top he won the Medal of Honor. He was wounded six times during the war, finishing as a major general; he returned to Maine to serve four terms as governor.
- John B. Gordon had no military experience before the war but was steadily promoted up to major general and became an outstanding corps commander for the Confederacy. Following the war he was elected to the US Senate and as governor of Georgia.[31]

- Wade Hampton, not a Military Academy product, became a lieutenant general in the Confederate Army and a corps commander. After the war he was elected governor of South Carolina and then to the US Senate.

Aside from these examples, other events during the war demonstrated that the American tradition *was not* one of separation between the military and politics. In March 1861, before the war began, Lieutenant General Winfield Scott wrote Lincoln regarding the situation at Fort Sumter in Charleston harbor. The garrison there was in dire straits and under the guns of the newly secessionist South Carolinian military forces. Scott suggested that Sumter be evacuated, which would "instantly soothe and give confidence to the eight remaining slave-holding States, and render their cordial adherence to this Union perpetual." Clearly, Scott was giving his president political not military advice.[32] Lincoln rejected it.

In May 1862, Major General David Hunter, commander of the Southern Department, apparently having not learned from Frémont's mistake the previous November, issued a similar edict freeing the slaves in South Carolina, Georgia, and Florida. Lincoln read of the order in the newspaper and immediately voided it, stating he had no foreknowledge of the general's action; moreover, neither Hunter nor anyone else had the authority to free slaves. In addition, Hunter had begun enlisting "freed" blacks into the army—also contrary to presidential policy.[33]

After the disaster of Chickamauga in September 1863, the incompetence of Major General William S. Rosecrans was obvious, and Grant wanted to cashier him. Lincoln asked him to delay such an action: "the popular Rosecrans hailed from Ohio, and Lincoln preferred to temporize until after the Ohio gubernatorial election on October 13, which Republicans won."[34]

In January 1863 President Lincoln relieved Major General Ambrose E. Burnside as commander of the Army of the Potomac following the disaster at Fredericksburg. In his letter appointing Major General Joseph Hooker, the president wrote: "I have heard, in such a way as to believe it, of your recently saying that both the army and the government needed a dictator. Of course, it was not for this, but in spite of it, that I have given you the command. Only those generals who gain successes can set up dictators. What I now ask of you is military success, and I will risk the dictatorship."[35]

This stunning letter shows the president was well aware of political maneuverings among his generals. Similarly, Major General John A. Pope, the loser at Second Manassas, often wrote his fellow Illinoisan President Lincoln for favors. He was never hesitant in advancing his own political views, writing to Lincoln of what he "*had* to do, in both military and civil matters."[36] Such intrigues and meddling were no doubt unsavory to Lincoln but were expected. Indeed, his appointment of political generals ensured that he would receive a steady barrage of unsolicited advice from the field. An even clearer example showing Lincoln's understanding of the close relationship between the military and politics is seen in his reelection campaign of 1864.

Lincoln's opponent that year was Major General George B. McClellan, formerly the commanding general of the Union Army, but who had not been reassigned since the Battle of Antietam. He remained on active duty while residing in New Jersey. McClellan's political beliefs had been known since July 1862 when he wrote the president that he did not think the war should be about slavery, but about saving the Union. He argued that "neither confiscation of property, political executions of persons, territorial organization of states or forcible abolition of slavery should be contemplated for a moment." He concluded that "A declaration of radical views, especially upon slavery, will rapidly disintegrate our present Armies."[37] McClellan, like Hooker, Pope, and many other professional soldiers, had strong feelings regarding domestic politics and was not shy about expressing them. It should be noted that Lincoln did not feel secure in his position. Not only did he worry about reelection, but he could not assume he would even receive his party's nomination. Republican Party leaders wanted a successful military officer to run, and they raised the prospect of nominating Generals U. S. Grant, William T. Sherman, Benjamin Butler, Joseph Hooker, or Admiral David Farragut. Although Lincoln deflected these moves, he remained worried about the election versus General McClellan.[38]

Five Northern states did not have absentee ballots in 1864; if a man wanted to vote he had to do so in person in his home district. Soldiers were encouraged to exercise the franchise, but their ability to do so seemed impossible while away at war. Lincoln made it easier. In August 1864 he had his secretary of war wire Sherman in Georgia, asking him to furlough his soldiers—while in the middle of a campaign—so they could return home to vote. Free railway passes were issued to get soldiers to and from their home states. The president also ensured the soldiers "were assessed a fraction of their pay for the support of the [Republican] party."[39] Similarly, Grant, who was then besieging Richmond, was prevailed upon to furlough his soldiers so they could go home to vote.[40] In some cases, prominent officers were sent home to campaign for Lincoln: Major General Logan to Illinois, Colonel Harrison to Indiana, Major General Banks to Massachusetts, and Major General Schurz to several states due to his popularity among immigrant groups. McClellan similarly used his uniform to solicit votes. He had friends in the Army distribute his campaign literature to their troops and encouraged the formation of military clubs to support his election. The fall of Atlanta to Sherman's troops in September sealed the election for Lincoln: he won handily and was especially popular among the soldiers, 78 percent of whom voted for his reelection.[41]

There were other examples of political intrigue: in 1862 Major General John Dix, the commander at Fort Monroe in Virginia, banned from voting all but whites who supported the Union.[42] In Kentucky, Major General Jeremiah Boyle "ruthlessly" punished anyone suspected of being disloyal and used his troops to control elections.[43] In 1863 Major General Burnside announced that anyone who committed an act benefitting the Confederacy would be arrested and charged with treason. He also ordered the suppression of the *Chicago Times* because of its antiwar stance.[44] In 1864 Major General Stephen Burbridge, the military governor of Kentucky, began arresting "persons suspected of opposing the reelection of Lincoln."[45]

The Army's involvement in politics did not end with the war. A difficult example of the Army's role in civil affairs occurred during Reconstruction. In the war's aftermath the Army occupied the defeated Southern states, and military commanders governed there until 1877. Their task was daunting: all wanted to restore civilian control and bring the rebellious states back into the Union fold, but it was just as important that the hard-won gains of the war not be jettisoned. The bloodiest war in American history had been fought over slavery, and the North was loath to see blacks returned to a position of subservience. These conflicting aims had Army commanders torn between political factions in Washington. On one side were "conservatives" following President Andrew Johnson, a former slave owner from Tennessee who wished a speedy return to normalcy, which to him meant white supremacy. He was opposed by the "radicals," who insisted that de facto slavery not be reinstituted. The White House and the Capitol were at constant odds, and it became a pattern for Congress to pass laws imposing stringent rules on an unrepentant South, for Johnson to then veto them, and for Congress to then override the vetoes.

When the war ended, General Grant was the most popular man in America. In the North he was a hero, and in the South his dignified and lenient treatment of the surrendering rebels eased a difficult passage. Congress promoted him to full general—the first in American history—and he continued as the commanding general. He was in a hard spot: his personal tendencies were on the side of the radicals—he abhorred the vicious and widespread violence being wrecked on freed blacks, while local white leaders did nothing and allowed the Ku Klux Klan to proliferate. He was subordinate to President Johnson but also answerable to Congress. Which of these two Constitutional obligations took precedence? Grant opted for Congress. His military secretary wrote that he "was as anxious to frustrate Johnson's maneuvers as he had ever been to thwart those of Lee."[46] Congress passed four Reconstruction Acts dividing the South into military districts, each under the martial law of a general officer. Grant and his subordinates increasingly took their cue from Congress, to the chagrin of the president. Johnson had his attorney general prepare an opinion severely limiting the powers of the military governors, despite the new laws. Grant instructed his generals to instead interpret their congressional mandate freely. As one biographer explained the commanding general's response: "Although Grant was usually dutiful in following civilian policy, he believed Johnson had subverted the will of Congress in a way that bordered on treason."[47] Grant had thrown in his lot with Congress.

This was a melancholy period for the Army that saw it assuming a role for which it was not prepared. Problems had begun in March 1865 when Congress created the Bureau of Refugees, Freedmen, and Abandoned Lands. The Freedmen's Bureau was placed under the secretary of war, and its director was Major General Oliver O. Howard. A West Pointer known as "the Christian General" because of his piety and humaneness, Howard's mandate was to provide food, clothing, and medical supplies to destitute Southerners as well as to settle freed people—former slaves—on abandoned estates.[48] Unfortunately, when the war ended, angry whites returned from the war expecting to reoccupy their former plantations and farms and reclaim their slave laborers. Instead, they often found that the Freedmen's Bureau had confiscated their homes and lands, designated them "abandoned," and then given them to their former slaves, who were in no mind to give them back. Violence often ensued.

During Reconstruction, military commanders were empowered by Congress "to supervise the enrollment, determine the qualifications of voters, monitor elections, and convene constitutional conventions." They were authorized to replace inept or disloyal public officials, to act as policemen in protecting the persons and property of citizens against violence, and to transfer cases from civil courts to military tribunals at their discretion. In short, the military commanders became the supervisors of both the political process and the administration of justice in the South.[49]

Examples of commanders exercising these considerable powers over civilians are legion. In July 1865 a white man in Mississippi was arrested for killing a black man. The accused appealed to a local judge, who ordered the man released. The military commander, Major General Henry W. Slocum, not only refused to release the man, he then arrested the judge. That same month the Army set aside the results of an election in Richmond, Virginia, because "too many unpardoned rebels had been elected." In September 1865 Major General Alfred H. Terry closed down a Virginia newspaper and had its editor arrested for publishing what Terry believed was "an indecent insult" to the memory of President Lincoln. Major General George H. Thomas was offended by an Alabama bishop who advised that a prayer in support of "all in civil authority" not be said, because the civil authority was composed of Yankees who did not deserve prayers. Thomas ordered the bishop suspended. On July 3, 1866, General Grant directed military commanders to arrest anyone in the South for crimes in situations where "civil authorities either could not or would not do so."[50] In April 1867 Major General John Pope annulled elections in Tuscumbia, Alabama, and appointed a new mayor himself. In July, Major General Philip Sheridan ousted Texas governor James Throckmorton for being "an impediment" to Reconstruction. Sheridan then installed the loser in the recent gubernatorial election. Between July and December 1867 Major General John M. Schofield intervened twenty-one times in civil court cases. In some instances he simply halted proceedings, while in others he ordered the cases turned over to military commissions for trial. As the history of the Army's role in Reconstruction states, the "viceroy generals" garnered "a fearsome amount of political power."[51]

The Civil War and Reconstruction were periods of civil-military intermingling greater than any in American history, and its effects were felt for decades.[52] Six presidents following the war had been Union Army generals, including Andrew Johnson, who was a brigadier general in Tennessee before being tapped as Lincoln's running mate. A seventh, Chester Arthur, had been a brigadier general in the New York militia but saw no action, and William McKinley had also fought in the Civil War, finishing as a brevet major.

It is true that the period between the end of the Civil War and the beginning of World War I was a golden age for the US Army. While commanding general, Sherman pushed for more professionalism and increased education in the officer corps. Branch schools were opened for infantry, cavalry, and artillery. Around the turn of the century Secretary of War Elihu Root established the General Staff as a deliberate move to break the hold of the bureau chiefs and give more skill to planning and administration.[53] These moves were not without their own issues. One historian argues that increased professionalism in the Army and Navy (the Naval War College was opened in 1884) made officers more inclined to resent the "interference" of politicians who did not understand military affairs: "The more that officers viewed themselves as members of a distinct vocational group with special training and a common set of values, the more likely they were to question military decisions made by those outside the profession."[54] Commander Bradley Fiske (later an admiral) published an article stressing these sentiments, comparing military officers to the clergy and the law for their unique professionalism. He complained of "the refusal of the civil authorities to give the navy the responsibility and authority which it needs."[55] He added that this failure was the result of "the non-acquaintance of civilians with naval conditions." More to the point, despite such moves toward professionalization, many officers continued to involve themselves in politics.

Nelson A. Miles had been a competent officer during the Civil War, but his overweening ambition was legendary. He peppered various senators and General Sherman incessantly for promotion or better assignments, even proposing that he should be named secretary of war.[56] As a lieutenant general in the 1890s, Miles suggested to New York governor Theodore Roosevelt that they run for the White House on the same ticket—Miles as the presidential nominee. Roosevelt rejected the idea as "fatuous," but when William McKinley won the Republican nomination in 1896 Miles approached him and offered to be his running mate.[57]

One of the few sailors to actively aspire for the White House was Admiral George Dewey, the hero of Manila Bay during the Spanish-American War. He made it known he would entertain a nomination, but a number of ill-advised comments to the press, such as the presidency "was not such a difficult office to fulfill," quickly diminished his chances. He withdrew his name from consideration and remained a full admiral, serving as president of the General Board of the Navy until his death in 1917.[58]

Major General Leonard Wood's well-known political ambitions and vocal calls for preparedness ensured that President Woodrow Wilson would not give him a high command during World War I. Instead, the former chief of staff was exiled to Kansas for most of the war. Wood had met with Republican leaders to explore the presidency in 1916, and did so again in 1920—while still on active duty. (He did not resign from the Army until 1921.)[59] During World War II, General Douglas MacArthur sent Lieutenant General George Kenney and other senior aides to Washington, D.C., in April 1943 to secretly discuss nomination possibilities with Republican Party leaders.[60] In 1951 General of the Army Dwight Eisenhower planned and organized his presidential campaign from his office outside Paris while serving as Supreme Allied Commander Europe.[61] The editor of his multi-volume *Papers* states that although Eisenhower avoided saying anything in public about presidential aspirations, he visited Washington in October 1951 to meet secretly with Republican Party leaders and "Privately . . . Eisenhower was nurturing the informal political staff that would carry him to the nomination as the Republican candidate for the presidency." This staff included senators, generals, and old friends.[62] In the decades following, retired senior officers running for the White House or the vice presidency included Curtis LeMay, James Stockdale, Alexander Haig, and Wesley Clark. John McCain had been a more junior naval officer, although both his father and grandfather had been full admirals.[63]

* * *

The belief that the American military has been uninvolved in politics is traditional and long-held. In his work on the subject of civil-military affairs, Samuel P. Huntington stated flatly that "after the Civil War officers unanimously believed that politics and officer-ship did not mix."[64] Such an assessment is simply not true. Rather, senior military officers were continually and deeply involved in political affairs before, during, and after the Civil War. More importantly, such a relationship was not seen as either un-American or unconstitutional. On the contrary, for most of our nation's history the close relations between soldiers and politics has been encouraged and accepted.

To be clear, the issue here is *not* civilian control of the military. That is a separate matter and one not at play in most of the cases cited above.[65] Soldiers understood they were subject to civilian control; what they wanted was to win public office so they would themselves *be* the civilians in control. Few times in our history have military commanders confronted their civilian superiors: Winfield Scott and his squabbles with Secretary of War Jefferson Davis; generals following the Civil War in their confrontation with President Johnson over

Reconstruction; and Douglas MacArthur's challenge to President Truman during the Korean War are the most notable.

The issue is not even whether active-duty military officers *should* be involved in political affairs. The consensus today is that such involvement is inappropriate. Rather, this essay shows that the military, for much of our nation's history, has been deeply involved in politics. Partly this had been a result of the enormous power given to our military commanders, especially those designated as combatant commanders in geographic areas.

Dana Priest of the *Washington Post* commented on the power these officers hold: "[They are] the modern-day equivalent of the Roman Empire's proconsuls: well-funded, semi-autonomous, unconventional centers of US foreign policy." William Pfaff argues they "have become more important agents of US foreign policy than the embassies in their regions because of their wealth and their lack of congressional scrutiny."[66] When the commander in Iraq was raised to four-star level in 2004, the rationale given was "making sure the civilian-military effort is consistent and well-integrated" and that the "military and civilian pieces fit together."[67] It was not explained why a civilian diplomat could not ensure cooperation. The commanders in Iraq and Afghanistan became well-known public figures, and this is partly why such commanders were feared by some who saw a crisis unfolding in American civil-military affairs. Moreover, the past two decades have seen an increase in retired military officers expressing their opinions in public. Numerous retired officers campaigned for presidential candidates in the last several elections, and in April 2006 six retired generals publicly called for the firing of their former boss, Defense Secretary Donald Rumsfeld.[68]

Military forces have been used in domestic disturbances throughout the nation's history. After the terrorist attacks of 9/11, the Defense Department began planning responses to major terrorist incidents and catastrophes on American soil. A recent study posits several such response scenarios: tactical combat against terrorists, protection of critical infrastructure facilities, logistical support in disaster response, enforcing quarantines and providing triage care, and quelling civil disturbance or enforcing laws when civilian institutions are unable to do so.[69] On November 13, 2001, President George W. Bush used his commander in chief powers to order the military to arrest and detain suspects without charges, access to counsel, or other Constitutional protections—a deliberate attempt "to prevent imprisoned suspects from seeking relief in U.S. courts." He also directed the National Security Agency to intercept email traffic and private phone calls without judicial warrants.[70] As during Reconstruction, the military was given an enormous amount of power due to unprecedented events.

These types of activities are not new in our nation's history. Theater commanders today have no more power than did General Winfield Scott in Mexico City in 1847, military governors in Florida, Louisiana, New Mexico, and California, and in the South during Reconstruction, Lucius D. Clay in Germany from 1947 to 1949, or Douglas MacArthur in Japan from 1945 to 1950.[71] Our collective memory has simply forgotten these events. As the facts show, the US military has always been deeply involved in political affairs. For most of our past such involvement has been condoned and even encouraged.[72] It may be true that such involvement is no longer desirable. Theater commanders today have a great deal of power at their disposal, and ensuring that such power is kept on a short leash is an understandable response. But if that is our policy, then we should rely on reasoned arguments regarding changes in the nature of the world, the country, and our political environment. Policy should not be based on a flawed and mythological version of American history.

11

Unity of Command in the Pacific during World War II

A myth of World War II is that, unlike in Europe, unity of command was lacking in the Pacific. The argument goes that the Southwest Pacific Area had one commander, General Douglas MacArthur, and the Pacific Ocean Areas had another, Admiral Chester Nimitz. MacArthur complained that the Pacific Ocean Areas drained resources for little gain that he could have put to better use. In his memoirs, he railed against the command structure: "Of all the faulty decisions of war perhaps the most unexplainable one was the failure to unify the command in the Pacific . . . [it] cannot be defended in logic, in theory, or in common sense. . . . It resulted in divided effort, the waste, diffusion, and duplication of force, and the consequent extension of the war, with added casualties and cost."[1]

For its part, the Navy believed that the Pacific war was "a naval problem." Admiral Ernest King, commander of the fleet and chief of naval operations, insisted that "the entire Pacific Ocean should constitute a single theater with a unified Naval command headed by Nimitz."[2] Because MacArthur and Nimitz were so powerful, unity could not be achieved. As a result, a fundamental principle of war was ignored and the result was inefficiency, confusion, waste, and an "ad hoc" and "piecemeal strategy."[3] Another historian is even more critical, arguing that the US effort in the Pacific was "hamstrung" because of its inability to appoint a single theater commander. The result was "a wasteful allocation of resources, a dispersion of effort, and a consistent failure to pursue the most effective and economical strategy against the Japanese." The compromise of appointing two commanders for what should have been a single theater was "grotesque."[4] In truth, a basic assumption of the above argument is false. There was no unified command in Europe, and so the ideal to which the critics of the Pacific war allude never existed.

Regarding the term "unity of command": principles of war, in one form or another, have been claimed since Sun Tzu wrote over 2,000 years ago. As noted in an earlier chapter, the first twentieth-century effort to enumerate such principles was by a British Army officer, then-Captain J.F.C. Fuller, who published his list in 1916. These principles were soon enshrined in British Field Service Regulations, and in 1921 they were adopted with minor revision by the US Army. These early doctrinal writings referred to a principle of "cooperation" allowing diverse fighting forces to work efficiently and effectively toward success.[5] By 1931 the US Army had substituted the term "unity of command" for this idea, stating authoritatively: "It is a well-established principle that there shall be only one commander for each unit, and one commander in each zone of action, who shall be responsible for everything within his unit or within his zone of action."[6] This principle was not, however, established in a joint environment. Theater commanders were not yet common in American military operations; rather, Army and Navy commanders were expected to "cooperate" when circumstances dictated. This would lead to problems as late as 1941, when the services disputed who should be the commander for the Caribbean Theater.

This was a crucial region for the United States because it guarded the Panama Canal, vital to hemisphere defense as well as providing the necessary route to reinforce the Atlantic and Pacific fleets (sailing around the tip of South America would have added weeks to the deployment schedule). Yet, when Lieutenant General Daniel Van Voorhis was appointed commander of the Caribbean Defense Command in February 1940, he quickly discovered the Navy had other ideas. Whenever Van Voorhis attempted to exert the authority given him by President Franklin Roosevelt over the naval forces in the theater, local admirals replied tartly that "he was not in their chain of command."[7]

Pearl Harbor changed things. Global war against powerful enemies necessitated dramatic improvements. In October 1942, US planners preparing for the Casablanca Conference issued a definition to guide Allied leaders regarding future joint and combined commands: "Unified command is the control, exercised by a designated commander, over a force integrated from combined and joint forces allocated to him for the accomplishment of a mission or task. This force will include all the means necessary for the mission's successful execution. Unified command vests in the designated commander, the respon-

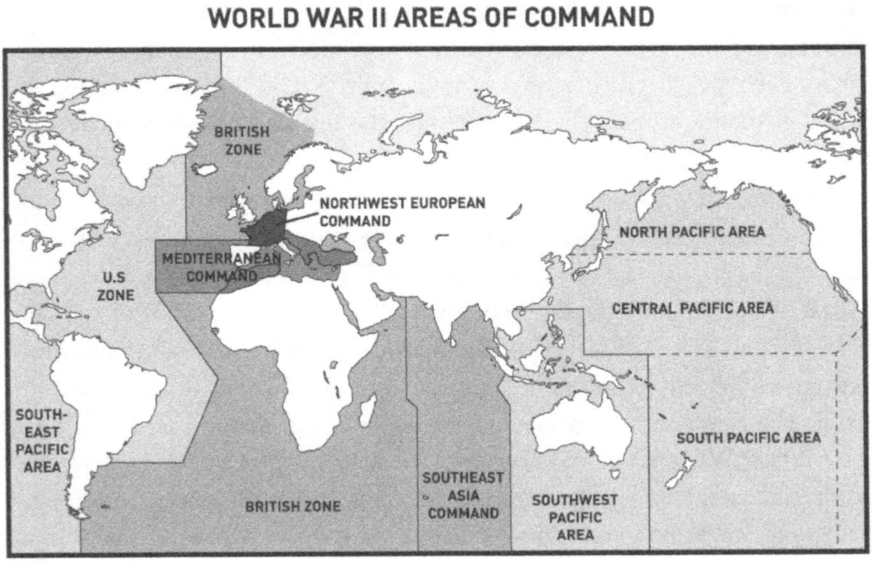

World War II Allied Theater/Area Command Boundaries.

sibility and authority to control the organizations of all arms and services composing his force, by the organization of task forces, assignment of missions, designation of objectives, and the exercise of such control as he deems necessary to insure the success of his mission."[8]

It was such unity of command that existed in Europe. Or did it?

Italy is part of Europe, as are the Balkans and Poland. Other nations included in the European family are Iceland and Greenland, key island outposts serving as stepping stones between America and the Continent. Yet, the Supreme Allied Commander of Europe, General Dwight D. Eisenhower, had no authority over the Mediterranean Theater of Operations, which included Italy and the Balkans; it was led by British Field Marshal Harold Alexander, a theater commander in his own right who was coequal to Eisenhower, not subordinate. Nor did Eisenhower control the Atlantic sea lanes or the vital bases in Iceland and Greenland, which fell under the authority of Admiral Max Horton at Allied Naval Forces in the Atlantic. Finally, Eisenhower had no say over (indeed, was barely informed about) Soviet operations in Central and Eastern Europe. A look at the map illustrates this issue.

As is apparent, the European and Mediterranean theaters combined were much smaller than the Central Pacific or Southwest Pacific Areas. If, therefore, one argues that the theaters of Eisenhower and Alexander were too large to be commanded effectively by one man, then how much more impossible would it have been for any one person to run the entire Pacific?! Moreover, also note that the Atlantic Ocean—far smaller than the Pacific—was divided into US and British zones with no overall commander.

Similarly, it is specious to contend that effective coordination between the Pacific Ocean and Southwest Pacific Areas was unattainable. Successful coordination certainly existed in Europe and was exercised by the Combined Chiefs of Staff (CCS)—the union of the British chiefs and the US Joint Chiefs of Staff (JCS). The CCS met regularly throughout the war to draft grand strategy and to allocate resources between the theaters. Debates were often vociferous. The chiefs would then recommend a course of action to their political superiors in Washington and London, who would approve or disapprove and order implementation.[9] Although the CCS system was not perfect, and many would argue that national and service politics too often shaped its decisions, the system worked in Europe. If landing craft or forces had to be moved from the Mediterranean Theater to reinforce the European, or if air assets from Europe were needed to bolster the Middle East (as was the case for Operation TORCH in North Africa), the CCS directed such changes—often overruling the wishes of the theater commanders involved.[10]

In the Pacific, command relationships were less cumbersome. Both the Pacific Ocean and Southwest Pacific Areas were largely American affairs. The British played almost no role for most of the war, and when they attempted to interject themselves into operations near the end of hostilities, US military leaders rejected their offer.[11] At the Potsdam Conference in May 1945, the British announced they could deploy more of the Royal Navy to the Pacific so as to take part in the planned invasions of the Japanese home islands scheduled for November 1945 and March 1946. Admiral King objected, arguing that he could neither use nor support additional British vessels.[12] It was apparent that the Americans wanted to control all operations relative to the invasions. If Britain wanted to play a role in the Pacific, they could confine themselves to operations in the south—perhaps liberating Borneo for example.[13]

In addition, the Australians were steadfast allies throughout World War II, but US leaders denied them much of a voice in Allied planning or command—despite the fact that in 1942 and 1943 Australians comprised fifteen of MacArthur's eighteen divisions.[14] In short, Pacific military operations were controlled almost totally by the JCS, so it was not necessary to go through the time-consuming and politically charged process of securing the approval of allies like in Europe. The JCS—with presidential approval—would adjudicate any disagreements between the theater/area commanders and issue orders to those involved.

Another anomaly that existed throughout the war regarded the status of the British and American strategic air forces. In Europe, the Royal Air Force's Bomber Command, led by Air Chief Marshal Arthur Harris after February 1942, enjoyed a special status. Harris was a favorite of Prime Minister Winston Churchill, who ensured that Bomber Command existed as a separate force, answerable directly to the CCS, and thus was treated as an equal of the various theater commands.[15] On January 1, 1944, the United States established a similar system. General Carl Spaatz became commander of the US Strategic Air Forces (USSTAF), consisting of the Eighth Air Force, based in England (European Theater), and the Fifteenth Air Force, based in Italy (Mediterranean Theater). Cutting across theater boundaries, USSTAF ensured unity of command of the American strategic air forces, but focused that unity on the target—Germany—rather than in the different theaters where the bombers were based. This system was modified prior to Operation OVERLORD, when the CCS gave General Eisenhower temporary targeting authority over both USSTAF and Bomber Command to support the Normandy invasion. After the invasion was launched and successful, Eisenhower relinquished control of the heavy bombers in September 1944, and they returned to the overall direction of the CCS for the remainder of the war.[16]

The situation was similar in the Pacific, although only American air units were involved. In April 1944, B-29s began deploying to India and staging bases were established in China. B-29s of XX Bomber Command would depart from their Indian bases, land in China to refuel, continue on to bomb targets in Japan, and then return to India via China. In mid-1944 the Mariana Islands were liberated by Allied forces and airfields were immediately built on Guam, Saipan, and Tinian to accommodate the B-29s of the newly formed XXI Bomber Command. This meant that B-29 bases were established in two different theaters—in the Southeast Asia Theater commanded by Admiral Louis Mountbatten (Royal Navy) and in the Central Pacific Area under Nimitz (US Navy)—while transiting the theater of General Joseph Stilwell (US Army) in China.[17] Who was in overall command of the B-29s?

In an unusual move, General "Hap" Arnold, the commanding general of the Army Air Forces in Washington, formed the Twentieth Air Force, composed of the XX and XXI Bomber Commands, and then elected to command the Twentieth himself; he then dual-hatted his Washington staff to serve as the staff of the Twentieth. Arnold argued that, as in Europe, unity of command over the *target area*—Japan—was far more important than unity of command in the *basing areas*. He maintained it would be impossible to delegate authority to three different theater commanders and have any hope that an effective, coordinated strategic air campaign could be conducted against Japan. And one should note, had control of the heavy bombers been parceled out to those three theaters, that would have meant MacArthur in the Southwest Pacific would have been shut out—an unacceptable situation.[18] When selling his command idea to his fellow chiefs, Arnold noted that much the same system in the US Navy allowed Admiral King to command the US Antisubmarine Command, redesignated the Tenth Fleet—which spanned different theaters and had a global mission—while remaining in Washington as chief of naval operations. King concurred with Arnold's plan.[19]

As in Europe, it was formally stipulated that if the combat situation was such that the heavy bombers were needed for ground support, Arnold would place them at the disposal of the theater commander involved. This happened in March and April 1945 when the Twentieth Air Force was diverted from its strategic bombing campaign against the Home Islands to support the invasion of Okinawa; targeting authority then passed temporarily to Admiral Nimitz.[20] By the end of the war, AAF air assets were consolidated even further. Upon arrival of the Eighth Air Force in the Pacific—newly outfitted with B-29s and based on Okinawa—a new command was formed combining the Eighth and Twentieth Air Forces. This new echelon, the United States Army Strategic Air Forces, was placed under the command of General Carl Spaatz, who moved from Europe to Guam after the Nazi surrender.[21] Of note, this new command had no authority over the tactical air forces under General George C. Kenney in the Southwest Pacific Area.

In sum, in both Europe and the Pacific, strategic air forces operated side by side with the theater commanders, all of whom took their guidance from the CCS or, in the case of the Pacific, from the JCS. If the situation required, forces or resources (such as the crucial landing craft or air assets needed for TORCH) were shifted from one theater to another, or air assets were temporarily placed at the disposal of a theater commander if the tactical situation made it necessary. The system worked.

The combination of Nimitz, MacArthur, and Arnold working under the guidance of the JCS operated effectively. Indeed, there is no evidence that not settling on either a central Pacific thrust or one coming up through New Guinea and the Philippines delayed Allied victory. On the contrary, simultaneous attacks on the central and southern fronts—as well as the strategic bombing offensive, the US Navy's unrestricted submarine warfare campaign, and military operations in China and Burma—stretched the Japanese defenders to the breaking point. Had the Allies focused on a single thrust, the Japanese would have been able to use their interior lines to concentrate their forces to meet that threat. Instead, they were forced to disperse and defend against continual attacks from several different directions. The Allies had the forces to conduct such a multiprong strategy; the Japanese did not.

In such a view, redundancy is the true American way of war. The United States had the personnel, materiel resources, and logistics capability to follow several different strategies simultaneously. To put it more cynically, indecision became the key to flexibility. Because US political and military leaders refused to decide on a supreme commander in the vast Pacific region, they unwittingly introduced enormous flexibility into Allied planning—and consternation into Japanese defensive problems. The Joint Chiefs seemed to understand this notion intuitively. When debating whether sound strategy demanded favoring a Central Pacific thrust or one coming up through New Guinea, discussions became heated, but then an inevitability seemed to take hold. In truth, issues of tempo, pace, the stated priority of operations in Europe, public opinion, command personalities, and resource allocation pushed the chiefs into compromise. It was not clear in 1943 which strategic offensive—that of MacArthur or Nimitz—would prove the most effective. As a consequence, "the JCS determined to maintain the momentum of both until the strategic picture was clearer."[22] As events played out, the JCS made a conscious decision to retain this broad front strategy for the remainder of the war.

In truth, the competition between Nimitz, MacArthur, and even Arnold spurred them and their staffs to heightened efforts. All wanted to claim it was *their* command that had been the decisive instrument in bringing Japan to its knees.[23] Indeed, this has been a central issue in postwar historical debates ever since.

One should also note that the entire grand strategy of attacking the enemy simultaneously on several different fronts was a deliberate and essential aspect of the war against Nazi Germany. The one time this notion was violated was during the "rapier thrust" to Berlin by Field Marshal Bernard Montgomery in

Operation MARKET GARDEN—a bridge too far. When it failed, Eisenhower reverted to a "broad front strategy" to stretch German defenses. And of course the Allies were also battling in Italy, as were the Soviets on the Eastern Front.[24] Why should such a multipronged offensive be considered inspired in Europe but a "grotesque compromise" in the Pacific?

In reality, the entire "unity of command in the Pacific" argument is nothing more than an interservice turf battle. Because it would look unseemly for one service to admit that it wanted command priority simply to enhance its prestige, however, the debate has acquired the fig leaf of centering on a hallowed principle of war—unity of command. As the facts show, there was actually far greater unity of command in the Pacific than there was in Europe during World War II, and operations against the Japanese undoubtedly benefitted as a result of the flexibility inherent in the Pacific command situation.

12

Analysis, Intelligence, and Targeting in Strategic Air Operations

AMERICAN AND BRITISH PRE–WORLD War II air doctrine posited strategic bombing against an enemy's industrial centers that would prove "decisive." It was a faith-based theory, unsupported by evidence.[1] Because strategic bombing had barely been conducted before 1939, it was inevitable that things would not work out as planned. How did air commanders cope?

First, they realized that basic questions regarding tactics, procedures, and cause and effect begged answers. How did you, for example, disrupt a rail system, or what size or type of bombs would best disable a factory? What was the ideal bomber formation to maximize accuracy while minimizing risk? To address these types of questions a discipline was founded called Operations Research (OR), the use of scientific and mathematical methods to study military operations with the intention of making them more efficient and effective.

* * *

OR was first employed in World War I when the British Admiralty asked scientists to study how to combat German submarines. After the war the scientists returned to academia and the military turned to other matters, but World War II identified the need for such methods once again. The Royal Air Force (RAF) began attaching scientists to operational commands, and by autumn 1941 they had been organized into sections responsible to the unit commander. Section leaders were scientists, while their staffs contained personnel trained to "think numerically."[2]

The problems studied were tactical or technical—the most effective use of aerial photography, camouflage, aerial mines, searchlights, radio, radar, etc.

They also began studying strategic bombing. Specifically, OR sought to improve accuracy and effectiveness while also lowering aircrew risk.

Prewar doctrine was quickly disproved in combat. Bomber Command's history was blunt in summing the problem: "More was learnt about the potentialities and limitations of the day bomber formation in a few months of war experience than had been gained from the previous twenty years of theorizing on the basis of fragmentary and often obsolete evidence derived from the First World War, the Sino-Japanese War and the Spanish Civil War."[3] Bomber Command could not fly in daylight without sustaining heavy losses; yet, it had difficulty locating cities at night—much less specific factories—so accuracy was poor. The Butt Report of August 1941 noted these shortcomings: only one in three aircraft dropped bombs within five miles of the target, and on moonless nights accuracy dropped to one in fifteen.[4] This led to navigation aids such as *Gee, Oboe,* and radar that became increasingly effective: by the end of the war 95 percent of bombs fell within three miles of the target, and 50 percent hit within a mile of the aim point.[5]

OR determined that the concentration of the bomber stream over the target should be increased. British night bombers did not fly in a large formation to the target as US bombers did. Rather, they proceeded individually in a trail stretching over a hundred miles. Analysts calculated that the odds of a midair collision were barely one per hour and that the chances of being struck by the bombs of an aircraft above were negligible.[6] Concentration of aircraft in the bomber stream then increased from ten aircraft per minute to thirty over the target area, thus decreasing the bomber stream's exposure to enemy fire.

Similarly, OR determined that evasive action over the target was "meaningless." Although heading and altitude changes made aircrews feel better, it did nothing to lower their vulnerability. Worse, it increased the odds of a collision while also decreasing accuracy. If the resultant accuracy was so poor as to require a repeat strike, then aircrew risk actually *increased* as a result of evasive action.[7] In short, crews were told that flying straight and level and putting bombs on target were the best ways to ensure their survival.

The Americans borrowed heavily from the British. In September 1942 Major General Ira Eaker, commander of the Eighth Air Force, set up an OR section for studying bombing accuracy and loss rates. At the same time, General "Hap" Arnold established the Committee of Operations Analysts (COA) in Washington, composed of lawyers, mathematicians, and engineers. The types of problems examined were similar to those studied at Bomber Command. The first task was to determine accuracy and suggest ways to improve it. Results showed that the better the weather, the better the accuracy: electronic bombing aids were therefore essential because of the chronically poor weather over Germany. Nonetheless, bombing through weather never equaled visual bombing in accuracy, regardless of the electronic aids employed. By October 1944, 41.5 percent of the Eighth Air Force's bombs were falling within 1,000 feet of the aim point when bombing visually. Using only radio or radar aids, accuracy plummeted to 5 percent falling within 1,000 feet.[8]

As in Bomber Command, the COA tackled specific problems dealing with range extension, tactical formations, bomb weights and fuses, the utility of incendiary bombs, the optimal strike mission size, and so forth.[9]

One problem involved determining the relative danger of enemy interceptors versus antiaircraft artillery (AAA) fire. The worst situation existed for stragglers; when a bomber fell out of formation, it was quickly pounced on by fighters.[10] The bombers usually fell out of formation, however, because their engines had been hit by AAA, resulting in aircraft power loss. The solution: put armor around the engines to reduce AAA damage, which would then reduce the number of stragglers. In another study, post-strike photographs revealed that bombing accuracy would be enhanced if an entire group dropped when its leader did, rather than if each bombardier chose his own drop point.[11]

Such technical problems had not been ignored before the war. A review of the curriculum at the Air Corps Tactical School (ACTS) reveals the concern over issues such as accuracy and bomb types. Unfortunately, very little practical work was done, and this led to assertions that were later proven absurd, such as one bombardment text stating that 100-pound demolition bombs were "particularly efficacious against the average factory or warehouse."[12] Such small bombs proved useless in combat.

It was because of such muddled thinking before the war that OR proved essential. Commanders like Air Marshal Arthur Harris, General Carl Spaatz, and Eaker recognized this and gave the scientists their full support. The commanders also faced a more difficult problem. Doctrine *assumed* that bombing enemy industry would have decisive results. OR provided guidance on how to destroy specific parts of that infrastructure effectively and efficiently. The broader question remained: what effect did destroying an oil refinery or rail yard have on the enemy's ability to fight? Because you know *how* to destroy a factory does not necessarily mean you *should* destroy it. OR told air commanders how to hit the target right; they now needed to know how to hit the right target.

Airmen tried to focus on results, but they did not have the tools necessary to determine them in strategic air operations. As a result, they began solving tactical and technical problems, hoping that by doing things efficiently they would also be doing them effectively. Airmen were not intellectually lazy in thinking through these challenges; rather, they lacked the requisite experience and methodologies.

* * *

In 1917 Lieutenant Colonel Edgar S. Gorrell of the US Army Air Service in France wrote the first American concept paper regarding strategic bombing. He noted that German artillery mercilessly pounded Allied positions, but these millions of shells were produced in only a few factories. If these factories were destroyed, shell production would cease. In other words, if one wanted to halt artillery attacks, maybe it was not necessary to destroy German artillery pieces on the Western Front. Rather, destroying the factory that made the guns and shells would have the same result but could be achieved more quickly and with less loss of life. The same was true of any number of critical war industries. Regrettably, Gorrell was vague on specifics.

In 1925 Brigadier General Billy Mitchell wrote that air forces should strike the enemy's "manufacturing and food centers, railways, bridges, canals, and harbors."[13] Clearly, he had made little improvement on Gorrell's thinking of eight years previous.

Giulio Douhet was similarly vague, identifying "peacetime industrial and commercial establishments; important buildings, private and public; and certain designated areas of civilian population as well."[14] He admitted that the selection of objectives was "the most difficult and delicate task in aerial warfare, constituting what may be defined as aerial strategy."[15] Indeed, this was where an air commander must prove his genius. Frustrating about these theorists was their assurance that decisive effects would result from bombing, without discussing the key targets or how their destruction would lead to victory.

As a result, the doctrine the AAF and RAF took into World War II offered little more than laundry lists of broad categories. US Army Field Manual 1-5, "Employment of Aviation of the Army," stated that "important objectives may be found in the vital centers in the enemy's line of communication and important establishments in the economic system of the hostile country." Besides concentrating on enemy forces, the manual suggested rail communications, bridges, tunnels, rail yards, power plants, oil refineries, and "other similar objectives."[16]

The RAF's 1940 "War Manual" stated that a nation was defeated when its people or government no longer retained the will to continue. This could be achieved partly by strategic bombing, which would concentrate on what had by then become the usual suspects: the enemy's industrial and economic infrastructure, which included such things as public utilities, food, fuel supplies, transportation networks, and communications.[17]

Such bromides were insufficient: at some point airmen needed to devise actual plans. In truth, throughout the interwar period airmen grappled with the problem of how they would actually go about conducting a strategic air campaign.

It is an oft-told anecdote that one day ACTS instructors were unable to fly because their planes were grounded. There had been a failure of a certain spring in the propeller assembly, but replacement parts were on back order. The springs were manufactured in Pittsburgh, but due to recent floods that factory was temporarily closed. No factory; no springs; no flying.[18] This seemed important. If an enemy wished to gain air control over the United States, it wasn't necessary to attack every airfield or shoot down every plane. Perhaps it was only necessary to destroy one factory in Pittsburgh.

This was insufficient for a theory of war, but there was more to it. During the Great Depression businesses and banks were closing on a daily basis; the nation was nearly brought to its knees, but not a shot had been fired. It seemed that economies were fragile instruments, so perhaps it was not unreasonable to expect airpower to destroy an economy. But one couldn't destroy *every* factory, power station, rail line, etc. in an enemy country. What targets were more important than others? The propeller spring incident implied there were key nodes within a system that were more important than others. All targets were not created equal. The propeller spring became a metaphor for a way of looking at air warfare—the search for the strategic bottleneck.

Before the war, it was difficult for American airmen to obtain information on the economies of potential enemies. There was no funding for such an intelligence organization, and US isolation policy made it inappropriate. ACTS instructors therefore looked at the industrial northeast. Via letters, phone calls, and visits, they gathered information on how American power grids, steel mills, oil refineries, and transportation systems worked.[19] More importantly, they tried to ascertain how they *did not* work. Airmen would take this knowledge with them into the war.

To summarize, air leaders entering World War II believed in the importance of achieving results through bombing, but they did not have the analytical tools at hand to determine the results of such attacks.

* * *

Once at war, the AAF focused on combat air operations. Businessmen, engineers, and bankers were contacted for information regarding factories in Europe that American banks had financed or that American construction companies had built. In other cases, experts instructed planners on how US systems and networks operated, assuming those in Germany would be similar. There was a danger here: the types of intelligence available and examined will shape one's view on how a system operates. If planners had copious information on the German ball bearing industry, for example, then they might place too much emphasis on its role in the war economy while overlooking other target systems. But it was a beginning.

Three organizations were established to study vulnerabilities within the German economy. The first was formed prior to the war, the British Ministry of Economic Warfare (MEW). The second group was the COA noted earlier. A third organization, created in the American embassy in London, was the Enemy Objectives Unit (EOU). These three groups would serve as advisers to Allied air leaders throughout the war.

All three of these organizations suffered from similar problems. They did not have access to the types of information necessary to make reasoned judgments on the German economy. As the AAF official historians eloquently phrased it: "But there existed in almost every instance a serious shortage of reliable information, and the resulting lacunae had to be bridged by intelligent guesswork and the clever use of analogies. In dealing with this mass of inexactitudes and approximations the social scientist finds himself in a position of no special advantage over the military strategist or any intelligent layman; and an elaborate methodology may even, by virtue of a considerable but unavoidably misdirected momentum, lead the investigator far afield."[20]

To overcome these impediments, analysts initially looked for information in German magazines and newspapers as well as industrial and financial contacts located in the United States or Britain.[21] Such sources led to a misconception: the German economy was drawn taut and therefore susceptible to air attack with devastating results. Actually, early in the war the German economy was poorly organized and run. Once the economy and industry were effectively rationalized, production increased dramatically despite Allied bombing.[22] On the other hand, some air planners believed oil offered a special case.

Germany had limited oil resources—only about 7 percent of peacetime needs were met by domestic sources. She therefore had to gain access to it through conquest, alliance, or devising a substitute. In 1940, Germany allied with Romania, which then supplied 60 percent of her crude supplies.[23] In addition, German scientists produced oil from coal in a process called Bergius hydrogenation.[24] Allied air planners therefore saw Germany as oil vulnerable. It was not known how much oil Germany had in reserve or how much it was consuming. Based on little more than guesswork, the COA estimated that Germany had somewhere between 2.4 and 6.0 million tons of oil in reserve. That's quite a range. The MEW put the figure at 3 million tons.[25] The compromise solution: Germany had 4 million tons of oil reserves. As a result, when air planners met at Casablanca in January 1943 to determine targets for the bomber offensive, oil was placed fourth on the list because Germany had so much oil in reserve that it made little sense to make it a high priority. The Americans would later question that decision.

Over time methods for determining the effects of air attacks improved. Analysts looked at such issues as indispensability of the product, total production of a given commodity, operational requirements, surplus capacity, ability to substitute other materials, time needed to repair damaged facilities, and the ratio between pool and production.[26] This last noted the distinction between commodities that could be stored, stockpiled, or used for an appreciable length of time versus a commodity quickly expended. Thus, oil was initially seen as a large "pool" and destroying production would have little immediate effect; hence, the initial decision to give it a low priority. Similarly, U-boat production was slow and most submarines were in service, so hitting the factories would have little immediate effect. On the other hand, German aircraft were used up quickly; there was no pool to draw from, so destroying aircraft factories would have an immediate effect on the Luftwaffe's combat status.[27]

Eventually, the EOU became adept at examining industries in detail and preparing "aiming-point reports" that gave instructions on how best to destroy those industries.[28] For example, regarding oil refineries, the gas plant was critical, followed by the distillation units, power houses, and boiler plants. The least effective targets were the tanks and pipes. They were the most visual elements of a refinery complex, but also the most easily repaired.[29] Once planners determined which industries or commodities were more important than others, and OR provided guidance on how to attack them, they then had to determine if the bombing was actually working. There were two questions to be answered: were air strikes neutralizing their intended targets; and if so, was that destruction having the effect throughout the German economy that had been predicted?

The first question did not have an obvious answer. As noted, the accuracy of early bombing efforts was poor.[30] In addition, the related question of how much damage was achieved when the bombs did hit the target was also problematic. Post-strike photographs showed, for example, that the strikes against Schweinfurt's ball bearing factories in 1943 caused extensive damage. After the war it was discovered, however, that most bombs detonated upon hitting factory roofs. This collapsed the roofs, making post-strike photos look impressive, but the machines on the floors below were largely untouched. Less than 5 percent were damaged, and most of those were quickly repaired.[31]

Planners also had to confront indirect effects. To do that it was necessary to specify measures of effectiveness linking objectives to targets.[32] What type of evidence should be examined to determine if goals were being achieved? There were several instances during the war when answering this question caused disagreements, such as during the oil plan versus rail plan controversy of 1944.

The argument over targets began at the Casablanca Conference of January 1943. There, President Roosevelt and Prime Minister Churchill agreed to a charter guiding the heavy bombers. The Casablanca Directive stated the objective of the Combined Bomber Offensive was "the progressive destruction and dislocation of the German military, industrial and economic system, and the undermining of the morale of the German people to a point where their capacity for armed resistance is fatally weakened."[33]

This was deliberately ambiguous and allowed the reader to take from it whatever he wished. Harris saw the order to "undermine the morale of the German people" as a vindication of his night area-bombing strategy. Spaatz saw "the progressive destruction and dislocation of the German military, industrial and economic system" as the goal of his daylight bombing campaign. But General Dwight Eisenhower, commander for OVERLORD, focused on the invasion, so in his view the bombers' main function was to support that assault—to ensure that "armed resistance was fatally weakened."

By early 1944 planning for the Normandy invasion was in full swing, and the question of how best the bombers could support the landings was discussed. By this point American analysts had revised their estimates of the German oil situation and decided it should become a top priority. If the oil refineries and hydrogenation plants were knocked out, the enemy war machine would be halted. Other air planners focused on the German rail network. Troops, supplies, equipment, and raw materials all moved primarily by train. If the rail lines were cut and trains stopped, especially in France, it would be difficult for the Germans to resupply the coast.

This debate broke along national lines, with the Americans pushing for oil and the British advocating rail. The question was resolved on March 25, 1944, when Eisenhower opted for the rail plan.[34] The key factor to him was time: he wanted the beachhead isolated from German reinforcements *before* the invasion, not sometime in the months that followed. Although Eisenhower agreed that a lack of oil would be catastrophic to the German war machine, such a collapse could not occur until late 1944—too late for his troops in Normandy. The rail plan won the day for the logical reason that it promised a solution to an immediate problem.

A difficulty concerned mirror imaging. Allied air planners and analysts, in the absence of hard data or credible intelligence, made decisions based on their own experience. Sometimes this worked, but on other occasions it induced errors. For example, it was assumed German hydrogenation plants operated like Allied oil refineries. They did not. To improve efficiency, the Germans folded rubber and chemical production into their plants. Thus, a strike on one of these plants affected not only gasoline production but that of rubber and chemicals as well. In turn, these chemicals were used in other applications, so there was a cascading effect in the explosives industry. Allied planners were not aware of this symbiotic relationship until after the war.[35] This is precisely the type of effect prewar planners had hoped to achieve. Had this been known, it would no doubt have moved oil targets higher up the priority list.

Even among rail plan advocates there was a spirited debate. If it was desired to halt rail traffic, then what specific parts of the rail system should be targeted? There were numerous possibilities: rail cars, locomotives, repair facilities, switching mechanisms, marshalling yards, and rail bridges.

Solly Zuckerman, a British scientist on Air Chief Marshal Arthur Tedder's staff in the Mediterranean, examined results of bombing rail bridges versus marshalling yards in Sicily and Italy during 1943 and concluded that rail yards were better targets because they were larger. Given bomber accuracy, bridges would take a disproportionate tonnage to knock out. Because marshalling yards were so large, however, bombers were likely to hit *something* of value when the yards were targeted. Zuckerman concluded that bombing marshalling yards was more *efficient* than bombing bridges.[36] Tedder agreed and directed planners to concentrate on marshalling yards.

When Tedder and Zuckerman left the theater, the new air commander, Lieutenant General Eaker, reviewed that decision. His analysts concluded Zuckerman had been mistaken. Using data from more operations than Zuckerman had sampled, they discovered that bridges were not as difficult to hit as thought, especially when using medium bombers. In addition, the results of bridge bombings were more lasting than those of marshalling yards. In the latter case, repairs were often affected within days, but when a rail bridge was dropped, it generally took several weeks to repair.[37]

This discovery became important as planners grappled with the same issue in preparing for the Normandy invasion. If it was desired to isolate the beachhead by preventing German reinforcements from reaching the area, then how best could airpower do so? Tedder and Zuckerman, now in London, dusted off their earlier analysis and pushed for marshalling yards. Other analysts, led by Charles Kindleberger and Walt Rostow in the EOU, differed.[38] Using the more recent analysis from the Mediterranean, they argued for a bridge campaign.

As with the broader question of oil versus rail, the specific question of "what rail" broke down by nationality and generated bitter debate.[39] In the event, air leaders resolved the issue in their usual manner—they bombed *both* marshalling yards and bridges. There was enough Allied airpower by mid-1944 to follow a number of targeting strategies: rail bridges *and* marshalling yards, as well as oil refineries, submarine pens, rocket-launcher sites, airplane and engine factories, and the enemy front lines.

But the story is not over. In January 1945 the German railroad system, which had been employing its own teletype network for transmitting status reports, began using the top secret Enigma machine because their teletype system had been knocked out by bombing. Intelligence personnel had ignored rail messages, believing them of little import, but when it began using Enigma—not by design but necessity—analysts started paying attention.[40] Enigma revealed the crucial role played by coal in the German economy, powering 90 percent of industrial production. More to the point, coal was moved largely by train after Bomber Command had mined German rivers and canals, eliminating barge traffic.[41] Since the rail plan had been in effect, coal shipments had slowed, causing a serious decline in German production. The implication was clear. To deliver a death blow to German industry and military capability, the Allies had to stop the flow of coal. The best way to do so was by stopping the trains.[42]

Tedder may have been right, although for the wrong reasons. He had not identified coal as the key commodity that made the Reich function. His plea for a rail campaign stressed disrupting the flow of supplies and reinforcements, to "rapidly produce a state of chaos which would vitally affect not only the immediate battle on the West Wall, but also the whole German war effort."[43] Coal was never mentioned. Tedder was not interested in studying intelligence related to its shipment until his staff did so serendipitously. But the evidence had been there all along. It merely required someone to establish coal as the crucial link, and then to realize the necessity of halting its movement by rail. Once this relationship was articulated, the bombing campaign could focus on its achievement.

Another example of using appropriate measures of effectiveness concerned the issue of air superiority. Control of the air was an "intermediate objective of overriding priority" as determined at Casablanca, but how does one measure its attainment? There are several possibilities: the number of enemy aircraft destroyed or Allied bombers shot down; the ability of bombers to hit their targets; the number of aircraft produced versus how many are operational; or the number of sorties flown versus tonnage dropped. All of these are important data points, but what determined air superiority?

One criticism of the bomber offensive was that production of German fighters rose throughout 1944 despite the growing intensity of Allied bombing. If one were to use German fighter production figures as the key for measuring air superiority, one could conclude the air offensive was a failure. But was that the appropriate metric?

First, analysts discovered large discrepancies between the number of aircraft allegedly produced and those delivered.[44] In addition, Luftwaffe combat losses were so enormous that even increased production could not keep pace. By D-Day there were only 300 German fighters in France to oppose the 12,000 Allied aircraft. The German official history paints an even bleaker picture. At the time of D-Day there were 30,000 enemy aircraft ringing Germany, and as Luftwaffe Fighter Command's General Adolf Galland put it eloquently: "Germany was a house without a roof."[45] During the first twenty-four hours of OVERLORD the

Allies flew 12,015 sorties, versus 319 for the Luftwaffe.[46] Despite statistics purportedly showing increasing fighter production, it was obvious by D-Day that the Allies controlled the skies. Aircraft production was an inadequate metric for determining the effectiveness of the air superiority campaign.

Was there a key node the heavy bombers missed? At various times there were several contenders for a magic bullet: oil, coal, rail, electricity, and ball bearings. Were these truly key, or were they mere "panacea targets" as Harris suggested?

It is useful to ask what the Germans thought. Albert Speer, the German minister of armaments and war production, later wrote: "I shall never forget the date May 12, [1944] . . . On that day the technological war was decided. Until then we had managed to produce approximately as many weapons as the armed forces needed in spite of their considerable losses. But with the attack of nine hundred and thirty-five daylight bombers of the American Eighth Air Force upon several fuel plants in central and eastern Germany a new era in air war began. It meant the end of German armaments production."[47] On the other hand, that same November he wrote Hitler regarding the bombing attacks on the Ruhr that focused on rail lines: "We are on the verge of the most serious coal production crisis since the beginning of the war. . . . For more than six weeks now, in the matter of transport the Ruhr has become more and more cut off from the areas it supplies. . . . It is clear from Germany's overall economic structure that in the long run the loss of the industrial area of Rhineland-Westphalia would be a mortal blow to the German economy and to the conduct of the war."[48] It appears that Speer, like the Allies, was ambivalent about targeting.

To summarize the World War II experience: Operations Research was instrumental in studying the *tactics* of air warfare, but for matters of air *strategy* a higher level of analysis was necessary. Going into the war, air planners had no precedents for determining appropriate objectives, targets, and measures of effectiveness for strategic bombing. At the same time, they had almost no experience with gathering the types of intelligence necessary to conduct such a campaign. These processes, which required massive resources and conceptual skill, had to be created from scratch.

* * *

It is important to look closer at the role of intelligence in all of this—specifically, the high-grade ciphers used by the Germans.

The British had broken the Enigma codes early in World War II and established a center at Bletchley Park near London to decode and analyze this Ultra intelligence and pass it on to Whitehall and the military. When the United States joined the war they shared this intelligence. However, the British jealously guarded their control of the Enigma machines and their decoding apparatus, a fact that irritated their allies. Meetings were held, veiled threats were made, and in May 1943 an agreement was reached giving the United States equal access, even allowing Americans to work at Bletchley Park.[49]

The story of Ultra has been told elsewhere, but its role in the air campaign has received less coverage.[50] As with surface operations, it proved invaluable to the air war, but gave little information directly associated with targeting issues: this was economic and industrial data seldom transmitted by the Enigma machines. (The exceptions were German rail traffic and coal shipments discussed earlier.) Ultra did provide the Luftwaffe's order of battle and the movement of air units around the Reich.[51] This noted the increasing number of fighter units detached from the Eastern and Mediterranean Fronts and sent west for use against Allied bombers.[52] This emphasis on favoring air defense was seen in other Ultra traffic: in August 1942 Luftwaffe bomber pilots were being transferred to fighter units to replace heavy losses, thus lowering the capability of their offensive arm.[53]

One of the trends picked up by Ultra in the spring of 1944 was the increasing concern shown by German leaders regarding attacks on oil.[54] Flight training and flights supporting headquarters were cut, and even dispersal efforts were reduced due to the lack of fuel. In June 1944, the British official intelligence history states, "for the first time in the war a vital target system had been chosen [at a time] when the force and skill necessary to destroy it were available. The system was German oil."[55] As the oil situation worsened, the ability of the Luftwaffe to defend German airspace vanished.

The situation regarding Bomber Command and Ultra is interesting. Initially, decrypts were forwarded to the war ministries, but not to operational commands. After complaints, distribution was widened to include "overseas commands." This decision made sense: a theater commander had an immediate need for accurate, high-grade intelligence. Routing it through the War Office was time consuming. However, because Bomber Command was not "overseas" but based in the British Isles, it was not given Ultra. (But, of course, its *targets* were overseas!) Instead, the Air Ministry received decrypts from Bletchley and forwarded what it thought relevant. The absurdity of this decision was revealed in 1943 when the Americans arrived in England. The Eighth Air Force was provided Ultra because it was, by definition, an overseas command. Bomber Command and the Eighth Air Force were thus headquartered a few miles apart but did not receive the same intelligence even though both worked for the Combined Chiefs and had similar directives for conducting their bombing campaigns! By the end of the war there were twenty-five to thirty analysts at Eighth Air Force headquarters working with Ultra intelligence—and none at Bomber Command.[56]

* * *

Following World War II, the US Air Force's Strategic Air Command (SAC) formed the Joint Strategic Target Planning Staff to study Warsaw Pact economic and military structures. This secretive body, based on wartime organizations like the EOU, had access to the intelligence sources and analysts to conduct an in-depth study of the Soviet economy and infrastructure. At the end of the war, for example, intelligence personnel had discovered the Germans had penetrated Soviet signals operations. A group of agents therefore rushed into Germany to snatch these hundreds of German agents—and their tons of equipment—before they could fall to the Russians. This intelligence windfall was shipped to the United States and became one of the core aspects of what would soon become the National Security Agency.[57]

Even so, the mechanics of translating raw intelligence into a coherent targeting plan was a major undertaking. SAC decided that the Soviet oil industry should be the main target to be struck if war broke out, but the Joint Staff disagreed, pushing instead for the electrical system. A decade earlier similar arguments had been made regarding the vulnerability and importance of the German oil and electrical networks.[58]

A member of the Air Staff's intelligence division spoke to the Air War College in 1948 on how planners went about the targeting issue. Lieutenant Colonel W. J. Smith began by recalling the tale of King Richard III, who was killed at the Battle of Bosworth when his horse was hobbled after losing a shoe—"for want of a nail" a kingdom was lost. The goal of air planners was to discover the appropriate "nails" in an enemy nation that would have similarly major effects.[59] Recall that a similar analogy was behind the Tactical School's theories of the 1930s. Smith's office gathered and cataloged data to form a coherent picture. The result was a "bombing encyclopedia," a multivolume work that contained, for example, an entire book on the Russian aircraft industry divided into both airframe and engine plants. Each installation was entered with location coordinates, floor space, capacity, number of workers employed, products produced, date information was gained, and other available facts.[60] According to Smith, a modern nation had at least 70,000 targets. The task of the air planner was to find the 700 that were most vulnerable to attack while also providing the greatest payoff.[61]

The process used to develop a target plan was much like that employed at the Eighth Air Force. The enemy economy was viewed as a system, and the goal was to find its critical nodes. In some cases, as with petroleum, it would be necessary to hit refineries and oil pumping stations.[62] The recuperation capability and excess capacity potential of each industry had to be factored in as well. Here the briefer admitted the limits of his branch's knowledge. They had useful information on European Russia gained from German sources, reconnaissance flights, and Russian newspapers, but activities taking place in "never-never land" (Siberia) were almost completely unknown. It was feared that construction was going on there to relocate Soviet industry and make it impervious to anything less than a massive atomic attack.[63]

Two years later another lecturer at the Air War College stated the purpose of any strategic bombing mission was to achieve the greatest effect at the least cost—the minimum number of bombs. Using the example of a steel plant, it was necessary to know not just its size and location, but also its internal makeup—the location of blast furnaces, open-hearth buildings, where ingots were produced, etc. Obtaining such information was difficult but not impossible. "In many cases we have complete drawings of all the buildings within the plant, complete schedules of the materials used in the construction and as much detail as we would have on any industrial plant in the US." This knowledge was often gained from engineering firms in the United States that had helped build the plants prior to World War II.[64] This was the same process used before and during the late war to gain a picture of German industry.

For SAC, this process tasked hundreds of individuals. Unfortunately, the emphasis on the Soviet Union and reliance on nuclear weapons made the Target Planning Staff of limited utility when conventional wars broke out in Korea and Vietnam.

* * *

In Korea, air planners hoped to repeat their success of World War II. Although strategic targets in China and the Soviet Union were off limits, airmen believed they could isolate enemy forces. The Air Force therefore launched a series of interdiction campaigns with impressive code names like STRANGLE and SATURATE. Around 50 percent of all Air Force combat sorties were interdiction. Including the Navy and Marine Corps, the United States flew over 320,000 sorties in Korea—nearly 9,000 per month.[65] What were the results of this massive effort? If destruction of enemy equipment was desired, then the results were impressive. Airmen claimed they destroyed or damaged 5,087 bridges, 2,345 locomotives, 41,882 rail cars, and 111,623 vehicles.[66] Even assuming exaggeration, one could expect the enemy would have been virtually immobilized by such destruction. Yet, in July 1951 the enemy fired 8,000 artillery rounds at United Nations forces, and less than a year later (after ten months of air interdiction) they were able to fire over 100,000 rounds.[67]

Clearly, something was wrong. The bugbear of the previous war—determining a useful measure of effectiveness—had returned. If the metric used was destruction of equipment, the number of sorties flown, or the tonnage of bombs dropped, then air interdiction was a success, but if the criterion was the ability of the enemy to fight, the conclusion was different. This problem continued during the next "minor war" in Asia.

During the Vietnam War it was common to criticize the US Army for its "body count" mentality. This was the epitome of a measure of effectiveness gone wrong. But airmen were just as guilty. Vietnam became an exercise in counting—sorties, bomb tonnage, jungle trails cut, trucks/water buffalos destroyed, and bridge spans dropped. The drive to gather data became an end in itself.[68]

Virtually all pre-planned targets struck by air in South Vietnam were selected by Military Assistance Command Vietnam, located in Saigon. This was largely a US Army organization—80 percent of its personnel—and because it selected targets based on a ground situation it alone saw, the effects desired were unclear.[69] So airmen invented their own metrics: aircraft readiness rates, tons of ordnance dropped, rapidity of response, and sortie rates. The Air Force serviced a list of targets for the Army, and the criteria for success became a determination of how quickly and efficiently they could service that list. The divided responsibility for selecting, planning, conducting, and evaluating air strikes meant that targets were divorced from the military objectives sought.

The problem of counting things and mistaking that for effectiveness was true regarding the air war over North Vietnam as well. After the LINEBACKER II strikes of December 1972, the Air Force stated that North Vietnamese rail yards had suffered greatly: "a damage level of 60 percent or better was achieved against two-thirds of the railroad yard targets representing damage to the most important rail facilities, other than bridges, in North Vietnam." But the study also noted that due to earlier air strikes most traffic had already been moved from rail to roads.[70] In short, was the aim to limit movement of supplies, or to destroy marshalling yards and rolling stock?

The core issue, as it had been in World War II, revolved around effectiveness. The US goal was to stop the communist insurgency in the South, so the Viet Cong had to be eradicated and the supply of troops, ammunition, and equipment from the North eliminated. If those were the military goals to fulfill the political mandate, then the data points noted above had relevance, but which metrics indicated whether the American strategy was succeeding or failing?

Following Vietnam the USAF underwent a fundamental reorientation. The doctrine of nuclear strike receded to the background, as did the bomber pilots who had held most of the key leadership positions within the service. Fighter pilots, who had borne the brunt of the war in Vietnam, took over the top slots in the Air Force.[71]

One result of this organizational and doctrinal shift was a renewed emphasis on strategic conventional air operations. Two Air Force colonels—both fighter pilots—led the intellectual journey back to serious thinking about air strategy—John Boyd and John Warden. Both men moved away from an air strategy focusing on an enemy's economy, and instead centered on an enemy's leadership. What made them capable of coercion? In some cases attacking an industry might impact a leader's mind. In other cases an attack on the leaders themselves, even if unsuccessful, might prompt a desirable change in behavior.

This targeting shift introduced new problems. A coercive strategy is dependent on cultural, psychological, and political factors that are difficult to measure.[72] The problem with such operations lies in the realm of predicting human behavior in a crisis. It is difficult to model uncertainty, randomness, chance, and the nonlinear and often seemingly irrational thinking of human organisms, because different people respond differently to the same stimuli, and some people respond differently to the same stimuli at different times.

Nonetheless, by the Persian Gulf War in 1991 operations that focused on effects had become ingrained in key airmen. One participant tells of initial plans calling for each Iraqi air defense control center to be targeted by eight F-117s. This would have required a great many sorties for the high-demand stealth bombers. He then postulated that a single bomb would no doubt shut down operations physically, while also causing any technicians still alive inside to flee. The number was then reduced from eight sorties per facility to two.[73] The desired effect was to shut down the air defense system, not necessarily destroy it. Not everyone was on board, however.

Colonel John Warden, a key Pentagon air planner during the war, tells of talking to a bomb damage assessment officer regarding strikes against electricity. The analyst gave a damage assessment of only 10 percent effectiveness. When Warden asked why he had given such a low estimate, the analyst replied that there were a specified number of electrical power plants in Iraq, and Coalition bombs had destroyed 10 percent of them. The arithmetic was pretty simple. Warden remonstrated that the lights were out in Baghdad, and indeed throughout most of Iraq. Wasn't that the result desired? What did it matter how many smoking holes there were across Iraq? Clearly, the bombing of electricity had been virtually 100 percent effective! The analyst hung up.[74]

* * *

Air strategy remains an argument over targeting. Early air thinking had focused on an economic theory of war. Airpower was seen as a more direct and more rapid form of traditional sea power—although few airmen or sailors would ever admit that.

There have been variations. Arthur Tedder focused on the transportation system to produce paralysis. John Boyd and John Warden looked at leadership. Political scientist Robert Pape and US Army generals Wesley Clark and Gordon Sullivan have argued that wars are won the old fashioned way, by killing armies, but that airpower can kill armies faster and with less risk than armies can kill armies.[75]

The tendency to count things, although sometimes necessary, can distort the analytical process. There must be a method of translating "statistical destruction" into a broader strategic context or else it will be easy to fall into the trap of being efficiently ineffective—of destroying targets that don't matter.

Combatant commanders must think through these issues and recognize it is an iterative process—desired effects and metrics selected one day may be wrong or change later as conditions or appraisals change. Unfortunately, there is a tendency to select criteria based on traditional methods that may no longer apply. The ability to measure results, especially for military operations above the tactical level, has always been a challenge. It has taken high-speed computers, systems analysis methodology, and the revolution in precision weapons to finally make strides in this area.

Air planners in World War II needed to know the structure of an enemy's society and economy. Today, globalization has made this information more transparent than in the past. In addition, there has been an explosion in the growth, pervasiveness, and complexity of intelligence-gathering sensors and methods. These new capabilities have provided an enormous amount of information for military planners to absorb.

The development of precision-guided munitions has been one of the revolutionary breakthroughs in warfare during the past few decades. The accuracy problem in World War II bombing operations is now solved. Precision weapons now consistently achieve accuracies of less than ten feet. The next question, did hitting the target have the desired effect, is also being worked.

Challenges remain: the need for adequate intelligence and cultural sensitivity regarding adversaries and the need for simulations that adequately account for cognitive, cultural, political, and social factors. For much of the first century of air warfare, adequate fidelity, effectiveness, and efficiency were beyond reach, due to the technological limitations of aircraft and weapons, but also because of inadequate analytical tools. The tools and technology have caught up.

13

Determining the Effects of the Allied Air Offensive

THE UNITED STATES SPENT $183 billion on armaments during World War II, and the Army Air Forces (AAF) share was $45 billion (24.6 percent). With that money it bought 230,175 aircraft, of which 34,625 were heavy bombers—15 percent of the aircraft purchased. These bombers cost $9.2 billion—20.4 percent of AAF expenditures and 5 percent of the US total.[1] Did the taxpayers get their money's worth? That question has been debated for decades, but those arguments shed more heat than light. There was, however, a massive effort conducted at the end of the war to answer the question of strategic airpower's effectiveness. That effort was the US Strategic Bombing Survey (USSBS). Its findings are difficult to dispute because of the massive amount of facts and details that were uncovered and recorded.

* * *

When war broke out in Europe in September 1939, Britain was not well prepared. As in the Great War, its small army was sent to France, but this time that strategy failed. France fell in six weeks and Britain was alone against Germany. It fought on doggedly, but there was little it could do to hurt its enemy. The British Army had been expelled from France at Dunkirk—leaving behind most of its heavy equipment—and the Royal Navy was battling German submarines in the Atlantic. Bomber Command was too small and ill-equipped to do much damage, despite its prewar doctrine calling for an air offensive. Losses were heavy due to enemy fighters and antiaircraft artillery (AAA), so Bomber Command retreated to the relative safety of night operations, for which it had been neither trained nor equipped. The result was predictable: area bombing became the new doctrine because of navigation and instrument limitations.[2]

When the United States entered the war in December 1941, the AAF also had a doctrine emphasizing precision daylight strategic bombing of industrial targets. But the AAF was small—nearly half of its aircraft production had been given to the British during the previous two years—so the buildup in England was slow.[3] Moreover, the Eighth Air Force in England was denuded to supply aircraft and crews to the newly formed Twelfth Air Force for Operation TORCH. Its P-38 escort fighters were transferred as well, leaving the bombers largely alone against the Luftwaffe, except for short-range Spitfires that could barely reach into France.

The Eighth carried on, but it was costly; the bombers found the Luftwaffe daunting, and prewar doctrine was wrong—the heavy formations were *not* self-defending. Rather than switch to night operations, the Eighth instead pushed for long-range escort fighters. Eventually, the P-47 and P-51 equipped with drop tanks would solve the problem. Before then, bomber losses mounted. In August 1943 a mission to Schweinfurt to hit ball bearing factories was a disaster—sixty bombers were lost. In October the Eighth went back to Schweinfurt, again with horrible results. At that point the Eighth took a pause, bombed targets in France that could be covered by fighter escort, and waited for the planes noted above. From the spring of 1944 on, things changed dramatically. The around-the-clock bombing of Germany with the RAF operating at night and the AAF during the day was devastating, and, according to the German history, "the superiority of the Allies became oppressive."[4] The Nazi economy fell hard over the next six months.[5]

* * *

In early 1944 airmen pushed for a major study to ascertain the effects of strategic bombing on Germany and Japan. This study became the US Strategic Bombing Survey. It was the brainchild of Major General Muir Fairchild, who had been an instructor at the Air Corps Tactical School in the late 1930s and who served in Washington during the war on the Air Staff and Joint Staff. He remained keenly interested in the bombing offensive and the effect it was having on the German war effort. He had been instrumental in forming the Committee of Operations Analysts and in early 1944 believed a bombing survey was essential to answer questions regarding effectiveness. At the same time, General Carl Spaatz in England was having similar thoughts. He sent a letter to General "Hap" Arnold suggesting a study, emphasizing it must be done by impartial civilians. Spaatz wanted the survey to be an American effort, arguing that the differences between RAF and AAF efforts were so distinct as to demand separate studies.[6] Arnold approached Robert Lovett, the assistant secretary of war for air, who in turn approached the president. On September 9, President Roosevelt gave his approval to form a bombing survey team. As Spaatz suggested, the RAF would conduct its own survey.

The following month Arnold offered the job as survey chief to Franklin D'Olier, president of Prudential Insurance Company. D'Olier expressed his unsuitability for the job—he was not an aviator. Arnold countered that was precisely why he was ideal; he wanted "a nationally prominent man of affairs, with no axes to grind, pro or con." Arnold argued that the AAF needed an impartial report to be used "as a basis for planning the postwar composition and strategical principles of the Army Air Forces." The survey would also guide the bomber offensive against Japan. The general concluded by stressing, "This is your job, and when you're finished, you report not to me, but directly to Secretary Stimson and the President."[7]

D'Olier accepted and organized his team—which would eventually number 1,600 officers, enlisteds, and civilian personnel—into three broad groups dealing with military, economic, and civilian studies, with those divided into thirteen smaller divisions for categories such as physical damage, oil, munitions, transportation, morale, and so forth. All of the groups and divisions were headed by civilian businessmen, lawyers, bankers, or engineers. The quality of the men chosen was exceptional and included Paul Nitze, John Kenneth Galbraith, Henry Alexander, George Ball, and Edward Meade Earle. Most were chosen for their specific expertise; for example, Robert Russell of the Standard Oil Company was to be director of the oil division, Theodore Wright, the director of US Civil Aeronautics, was appointed head of the aircraft division, and Frank McNamee, deputy of US Civil Defense, was to head the civil defense division. The military advisers to the survey were also first-rate and included Generals Omar Bradley and Lucius Clay and Admirals Richard Byrd and Robert Ghormley.

Over the next year, USSBS teams visited hundreds of bombed sites, measuring, photographing, and collecting data while also interviewing hundreds of individuals, from top generals and diplomats to civilian workers. In June 1945, D'Olier met with Spaatz—who was moving to Guam to take command of AAF strategic air forces in the Pacific—and advised him on targeting priorities for the bombing of Japan. D'Olier said that based on their findings in Germany, the target that should be given the highest priority was the Japanese transportation system. He also listed oil and chemical plants and the electrical power system.[8] For reasons discussed below, the targeting priorities set forth by the USSBS were scarcely used.

D'Olier and his staff deployed to Japan upon enemy surrender and conducted a similar survey of the Japanese economy and its destruction by the bombing campaign. Overall, they published 324 reports—216 for the European theater and 108 for the Pacific—between May 1945 and June 1947. These reports were often controversial, especially in the Pacific theater. The US Navy had played a supporting role in the defeat of Germany but felt it had exercised a dominant role against Japan. It therefore insisted on writing a lengthy report detailing naval and amphibious operations in the South Pacific and Central Pacific Areas. In the Navy view, these operations were essential preludes to the bomber offensive that began in November 1944 from bases in the Mariana Islands.[9] Clearly, both services were looking ahead to peacetime, when the major issue of a separate air force would be decided.

* * *

Regarding the war in Europe, the survey concluded that "Allied air power was decisive in the war in Western Europe."[10] But airpower was not the only decisive factor: Soviet armies on the Eastern Front chewed up German divisions at an astonishing rate. The American and British forces in the west faced fewer German troops, but the Normandy invasion caught Germany in a vise it could not escape. Bombing had a catastrophic effect on the German economy and transportation system, which in turn fatally impacted the German armed forces.

USSBS presented scores of charts, graphs, and tables illustrating the impact of bombing. At its peak, the Allied air campaign employed 1.34 million personnel and over 27,000 aircraft. Bombers flew 1.44 million sorties and dropped 2.7 million tons of bombs—54.2 percent by the AAF and the remainder by the RAF. The bombing campaign was costly—nearly 160,000 airmen were lost by the British and the Americans (almost exactly the same number by each), and 40,000 aircraft were destroyed (22,000 RAF and 18,000 AAF). Losses for the Eighth Air Force alone were a staggering 44,472 men.[11] Indeed, the Eighth suffered greater losses than did the entire US Marine Corps or Navy during the war.[12] Significantly, 85 percent of all bombs dropped by the AAF on Germany fell *after* D-Day.[13] In truth, the Combined Bomber Offensive did not really begin until the summer of 1944—the third year of war for the Americans and the fifth for the British.

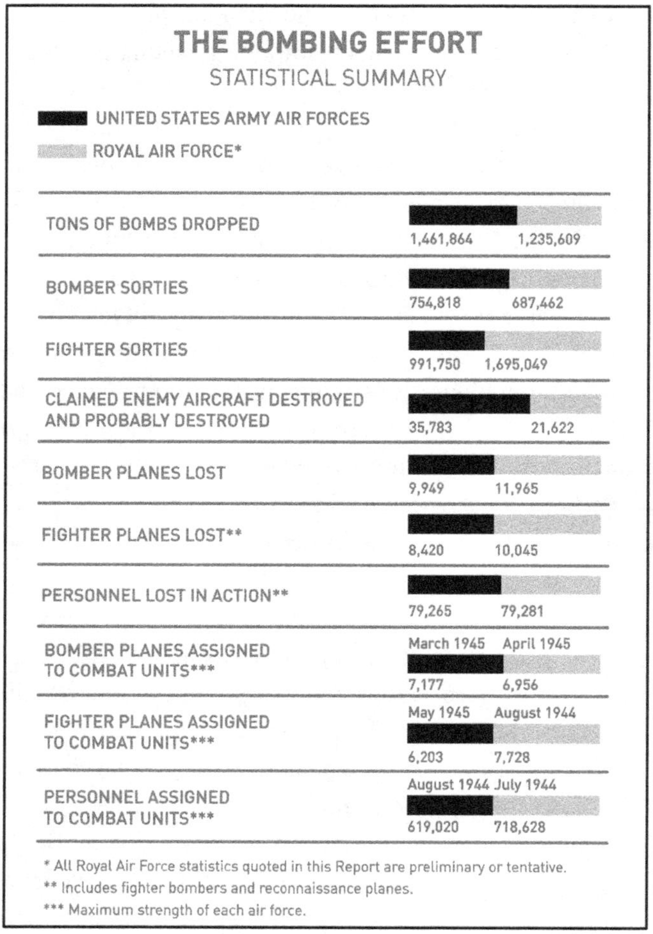

The Allied Bombing Effort. USSBS, "European Over-All Report."

Graphs regarding production in key industries are dramatic—virtually every major commodity necessary to the German war effort began a severe decline in the summer of 1944. Production of aviation fuel, for example, plummeted from 316,000 tons/month to 107,000 tons in June and 17,000 tons by September. Synthetic fuel dropped from a high of 175,000 tons in April 1944 to 30,000 tons by July and just 5,000 tons in September—a 90 percent drop in four months. The largest oil refinery, Leuna, was bombed twenty-two times, ultimately reducing its output to 10 percent of its previous capacity. The effects

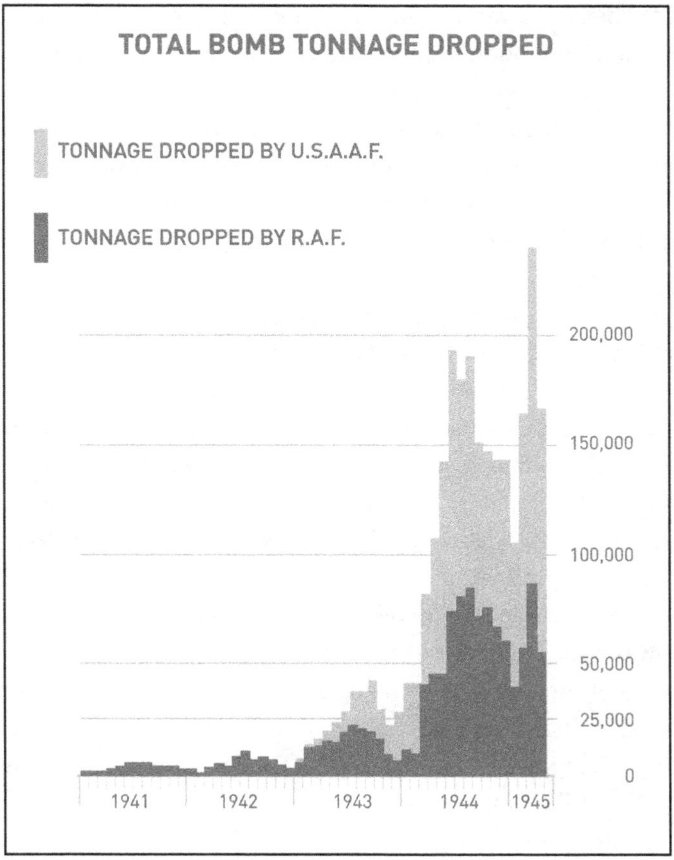

Allied Bomb Tonnage. USSBS, "European Over-All Report."

of this fuel drought were felt throughout the *Wehrmacht*—aircraft stopped flying and tanks stopped driving. In March 1945 the Soviets overran 1,200 German tanks that had run out of gas. Because of the aviation fuel shortage, new Luftwaffe pilots entered combat with perhaps 145 flying hours compared to 525 for the AAF.[14]

Given the critical nature of the Battle of the Atlantic, German U-boats were a key target for the bombers throughout the war. This had been an oversight for Allied planners. Although submarines had come close to bringing Britain to its knees in the Great War, surprisingly little was done to prepare for their threat two decades later. It would be a combination of convoy tactics, sonar and weaponry, long-range patrol aircraft, and frequent bombing of U-boat ports and facilities that would win this battle. There were 138 strikes on these ports and factories, amounting to over 100,000 tons of bombs—4 percent of all tonnage dropped. By the end of 1944 submarine construction plummeted by 57 percent.[15] Of the 1,110 U-boats commissioned during the war, 757 were lost to Allied action. Of these, 204 were sunk by land-based aircraft and another thirty by a combination of ships and land-based aircraft—82 percent of all submarines sunk by airpower. In addition, forty-three boats were destroyed by air attack while in port.[16]

Bombing attacks on the German transportation industry were profound: "The attack on transportation was the decisive blow that completely disorganized the German economy." The survey noted that 40 percent of all rail traffic was coal—21,400 train carloads per day at the beginning of 1944, but by the end of the year that number had fallen to 9,000 cars daily. Rail traffic in general had fallen by 50 percent by mid-1944.[17] Steel production was related to this collapse, suffering an 80-percent drop in three months. Similar declines were experienced in the production of explosives, synthetic rubber, chemicals (nitrogen, chlorine, methane), gunpowder, and combat munitions.[18] Production graphs show output dropping sharply by the end of 1944.[19]

The effect of the bombing campaign on the German labor force was also significant: 2.5 million workers were engaged in "debris clearance, reconstruction and dispersal projects and other types of repair activity necessitated by the bombing." One million more workers were assigned to produce civilian goods that had been destroyed in the bombing attacks, and another million were devoted to the production of antiaircraft guns. Germany had over 55,000 AAA batteries in 1943, and they consumed 20 percent of all ammunition produced. Indeed, that much aluminum could have produced an additional 40,000 fighter planes.[20]

Did bombing weaken morale? The survey said yes: "bombing appreciably affected the German will to resist. Its main psychological effects were defeatism, fear, hopelessness, fatalism, and apathy. It did little to stiffen resistance through the arousing of aggressive emotions of hate and anger." The report continued that "War weariness, willingness to surrender, loss of hope in German victory, distrust of leaders, feelings of disunity, were all more common among bombed than among un-bombed people."[21] In addition, bombing affected German troops, becoming "a chronic cause of fear, discouragement and confusion, and potentially disrupter of discipline . . . Air power when employed against lines of communication and transportation plays a vital role not

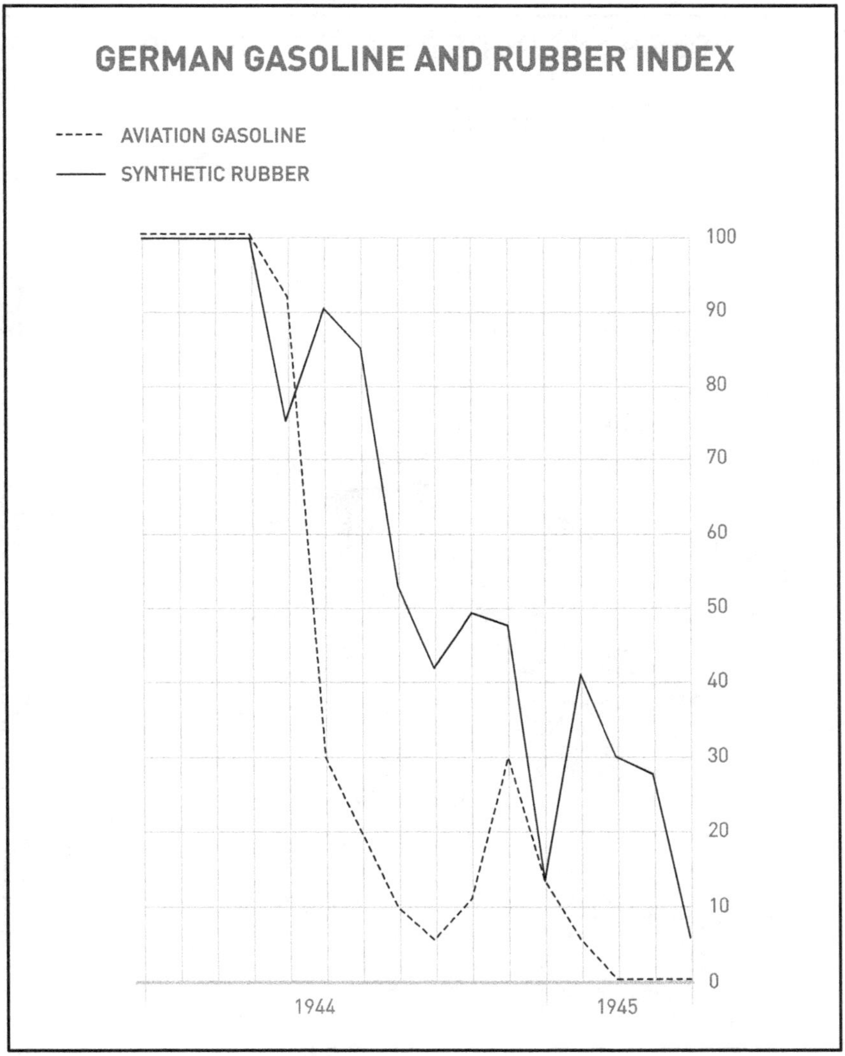

German Gasoline and Rubber Index. "European Over-All Report."

only in producing the more obvious military isolation of the battlefield, but intensifying feelings of anxiety and frustration."[22] Nearly 5 million German civilians became refugees, and this had a cascading effect that put heavy burdens on the transportation system, food distribution efforts, medical and community services, etc.[23]

Yet, a valid question remains: was low morale a meaningful measure of merit? Absenteeism would seem to be more appropriate. Regardless of wheth-

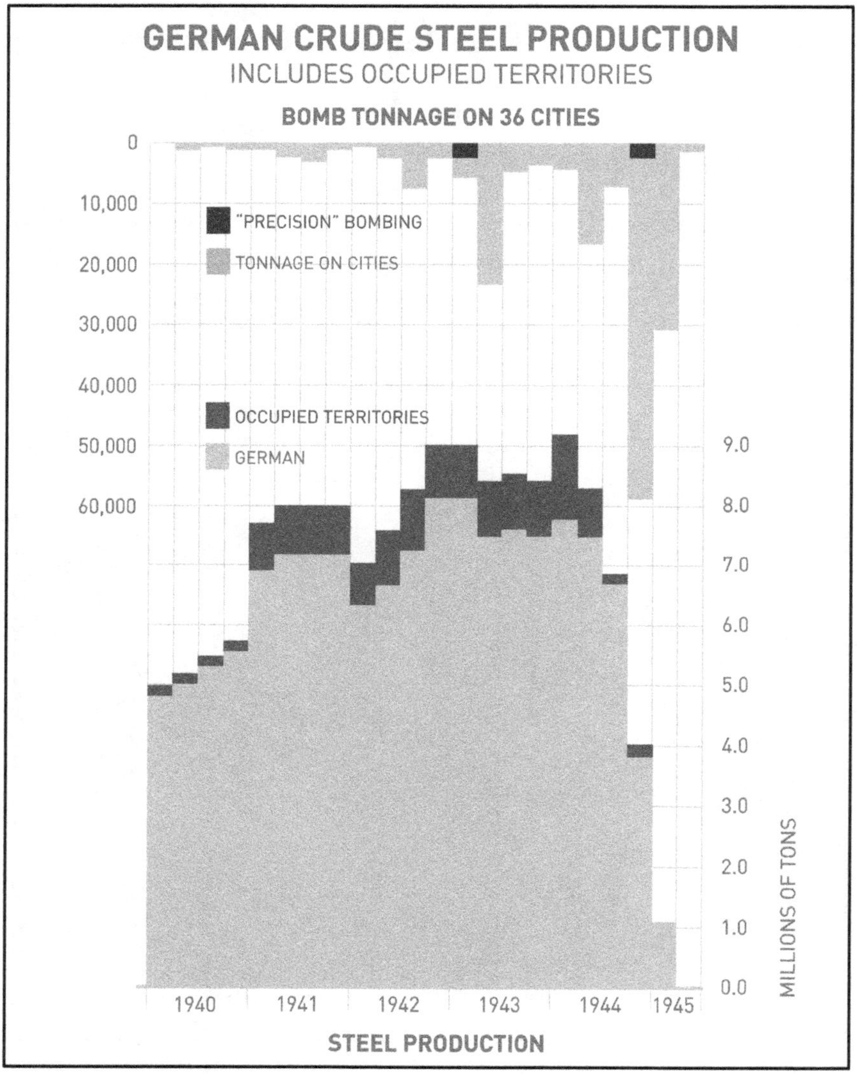

German Steel Production and City Tonnage. USSBS, "European Over-All Report."

er a worker admits to having low morale, does he or she report for work? In Germany, absenteeism approached 25 percent in key factories, causing a corresponding loss in productivity.[24] Not only did production decrease, it also shifted in focus. German assets were increasingly devoted to air defense. By D-Day, defense against Allied air attack—which ultimately proved futile—absorbed one-third of the German war economy.

The survey argued that air superiority was essential to the bombing campaign's success. This air dominance was achieved in early 1944 (the "Big Week" air campaign in February that broke the back of the Luftwaffe), allowing the bombing campaign to achieve its dramatic results. The German official history echoes this conclusion: "As a deterrent factor during the days of the invasion, the Luftwaffe's fighter force in the west had practically ceased to exist." It added "there was no Luftwaffe combat presence worth the mention in Normandy."[25] Indeed, it is important to remember that the planned invasion of France was pushed back from 1942 to 1943 and finally occurred in June 1944. One reason for this delay was that air superiority over the beachhead was deemed essential for success, and that was not gained until the spring of 1944. At that point the Luftwaffe was scrambling to produce more fighters in an effort to halt the bomber offensive. Bombers, which had consumed over half of all German aircraft production in 1942, declined to only 18 percent by mid-1944.[26]

USSBS analysts also concluded it was better to focus on one target system and destroy it rather than hit numerous systems with a small amount of tonnage on each. Every industry had built-in slack, so light bombing was simply absorbed, resulting in little decline in production.[27] The transportation network, the recipient of greater tonnage than any other target system, 32.1 percent, was key to the enemy economy because it moved resources to the factories and then finished goods to the front. Disruption of railroads brought everything to a crawl. Especially important was the movement of coal that powered the German economy.[28] Close behind the destruction of transportation was the ruination of oil refineries, which was especially fatal to the *Wehrmacht*'s mobility on land and in the air (9.3 percent of the total tonnage).

Area attacks were deemed less effective in reducing industrial production than were "precision" attacks.[29] Bombing accuracy of the Eighth Air Force was initially not impressive and was the subject of a separate study by USSBS. Some findings appeared obvious: an increase in altitude or in bomber formation size decreased accuracy. Cloud cover decreased precision—the more cloud cover, the poorer the results. Navigation aids, such as *Gee, Oboe*, and H2X radar, significantly increased accuracy in bad weather, but visual bombing was still more precise. Medium bombers, because they flew lower and in smaller formations, generally had better accuracy than did the heavy bombers.[30] The Eighth and Fifteenth Air Forces were approximately equal in precision, and improved dramatically throughout the war: in late 1942 the circular error probable was close to 3,400 feet, but by 1945 it was down to 900 feet.[31]

Another survey of bombing accuracy completed at the Eighth Air Force headquarters found that by October 1944, 41.5 percent of its bombs were falling within 1,000 feet of the aimpoint when bombing visually. Using radio or radar aids, the accuracy diminished to only 5 percent falling within 1,000 feet.[32]

Although German morale plummeted and absenteeism was endemic, USSBS argued that the "terroristic" practices of the Nazi regime—relying on slave labor and a 72-hour work week—kept factories operating, albeit at a greatly reduced rate.[33] The survey also confirmed the notion of an industrial web (a prewar targeting concept) focusing on key targets within the overall system that had a disproportionate importance to the whole. In the USSBS phrasing, "The most serious attacks were those which destroyed the industry or service which most indispensably served other industries."[34] There was a synergism between target sets; bombers destroyed the steel mills as well as rail lines leading to and from those factories, along with marshaling yards serving the railroads. Taking down oil refineries meant there was little fuel to power the airplanes and tanks that were produced, and Allied aircraft destroying military equipment in combat also contributed to the German military collapse. In other words, although specific bottleneck targets existed, repeated heavy attacks against several components of the industrial system collapsed the enemy infrastructure.

The German economy was akin to a living organism that adapted to attacks against it. The Germans changed behaviors and produced work-arounds. German resiliency was a disturbing surprise. Even so, when the bombing campaign launched powerful attacks beginning in mid-1944, the result was dramatic: the USSBS reports depict a cascading, cataclysmic failure throughout the German economy, a failure that spelled doom for the enemy war effort.

USSBS analysts wrote that some targets should have been struck more heavily—specifically, the German electrical system. It had been considered early on as a bottleneck target (it had topped the initial air war plan list), but its dispersed nature and the small size of individual power plants made it a low-priority target. This system, with minor exceptions, was never made a primary target for strategic bombing, but analysts argued it should have been—a relatively small amount of tonnage would have had "catastrophic" effects on the economy.[35] Similarly, USSBS argued that the ball bearing industry, hit hard in 1943 but at grievous cost to the AAF (the Schweinfurt/Regensburg strikes), was indeed a choke-point target system that should have been revisited.[36] Other key nodes susceptible to cascading effects were aircraft engine factories, fuselage assembly plants, propeller facilities, and tetraethyl lead plants.[37] The survey also determined that attacks on engine factories paid higher dividends than strikes on aircraft manufacturing plants. Moreover, it noted a key node in the aircraft industry entailed "certain highly complicated specialized castings for jet engines" that were the "Achilles heel of jet fighter production."[38] Nonetheless, the overall effect of strategic bombing on Germany, concentrated in the last nine months of a six-year war, was devastating.[39]

Significantly, the United States entered the war with a small number of heavy bombers—which could have been built six years earlier. The B-17 first flew in July 1935, but when war broke out in Europe in September 1939, the Air Corps had only twenty-seven heavy bombers. Over the next two years the air arm enjoyed a huge buildup—21,000 aircraft were built—but only 300 were big bombers (1.8 percent.)[40] The Army hierarchy refused to buy the heavy bombers that airmen proposed. The result: in mid-1943 the Allies together could muster barely 1,000 heavy bombers on a given day. One year later that number had tripled. By the fall of 1944, the combined bomber forces numbered 5,250 aircraft.[41] That is why the "Crescendo of Bombing" that began in mid-1944 was so utterly devastating. Airmen wondered if those astounding results could have been achieved earlier and with significantly less loss of life.

The bottom line: the strategic bombing offensive against Germany was worth the cost: it measurably shortened the war and saved tens of thousands of American and Allied lives.

The British Bombing Survey Unit

In May 1944, about the same time as the Americans considered establishing a bombing survey, the British were having similar thoughts. Prime Minister Winston Churchill was against the notion, however, believing it a waste of time and money. The RAF pressed on, using its own funds to establish a survey team. Given the lack of support, the RAF's effort was smaller than its American counterpart—consisting of only a few dozen people. In addition, given the lack of resources, the RAF relied heavily on the data already accumulated by USSBS. The one-volume report, replete with charts, graphs, and 173 pages of text, was titled "The Strategic Air War against Germany, 1939–1945." Completed in 1947, the report was classified and not released until 1956. In 1998, the RAF's Historical Branch published the *Report of the British Bombing Survey Unit,* with Sebastian Cox writing an excellent introduction.[42]

Cox pointed out a major concern with the report: it was written by Solly

Zuckerman, an advisor to Air Chief Marshal Arthur Tedder during the war. At the time the report was written, Tedder was a marshal of the Royal Air Force and chief of the Air Staff. Zuckerman, while working for Tedder both in the Mediterranean and northwestern Europe, was the main architect of the Rail Plan. Cox argues this background had a significant effect, as the bias of the two is clearly reflected in the report.[43]

There were other problems. The RAF relied too heavily on USSBS data, which thus skewed the report, as the Americans were focused on "precision" bombing and were not receptive to studying the efforts of Bomber Command's area campaign. As a result, Cox argues, the report followed USSBS tendencies and denigrated the effectiveness of area bombing on both German production and morale.[44] Cox believes this was erroneous.

There were, of course, many positive aspects to the report. It compared the various British bombers and determined, not surprisingly, that the Lancaster was the premier weapon of Bomber Command. Accuracy, which was dismal when night operations began, improved throughout the war due to electronic aids, and by the end of the war night bombing with instruments was equal to that of AAF daylight visual bombing. The report argued that from spring 1944 onward, Bomber Command's accuracy was "unequalled by any other Air Force operating in Europe."[45] Bomber Command, although absorbing a mere 5 percent of the total British war effort (coincidentally, the same as the US percentage), achieved enormous and disproportionate results—especially after D-Day, when the vast majority of bombs actually fell on Germany.[46] The report gives detailed numbers on the tonnage dropped by Bomber Command on specific target systems: the main target was towns (45.7 percent), and second was the enemy transportation system (13.9 percent).[47] The conclusion of the British Bombing Survey Unit was that the air war "was the over-riding cause of the collapse of the German industrial machine."[48]

* * *

Allied war plans anticipated a Europe-first strategy. After Pearl Harbor, however, the public demanded action against Japan, and the AAF examined ways to hit Nippon. B-17s and B-24s did not have the range to reach the Japanese Home Islands from then existing US bases: the AAF needed a bomber with a range of 3,000 miles. This was to be the B-29. Even so, due to the extreme distances extant in the Pacific theater, bases in China and the Mariana Islands would be necessary for B-29 operations.

The first B-29s of the US XX Bomber Command deployed to India in April 1944. The bombers based in India, staged through airfields in China, bombed Japan, and then returned to India via China. Immediately, however, logistical problems arose as supplies had to come over the Himalayas. Flying the massive amounts of supplies necessary over the Hump was a terrific aerial feat, and this requirement added to the difficulties of the XX. The B-29s hauled fuel, and 85 percent of the bombers' flying was on logistics missions. Although this helped solve one problem, it put a heavy strain on the over-stretched maintenance system.[49] At the same time, base construction was slow due to the low priority of the theater. Finally, the B-29s, which had been rushed into production, suffered severe teething problems with their engines.[50]

As a consequence, XX Bomber Command combat operations proceeded slowly. Arnold sent a new commander to India, Major General Curtis LeMay, but the problem was the concept itself. Attempting to operate a strategic bombing campaign over such vast distances in a remote theater was simply unrealistic. The tale is told in the tally: in the forty-nine combat missions flown by the XX over five months, only 800 tons of bombs were dropped on Japan. Operations from India were halted in January 1945.[51] On the positive side: some bugs were worked out of the new aircraft; the campaign bolstered Chinese morale; and LeMay gained valuable Pacific and B-29 experience. Clearly, however, Mariana bases were essential for the strategic air campaign against Japan, and it was from the islands of Guam, Saipan, and Tinian that the B-29s of the XXI Bomber Command would strike major blows against the enemy.

Building on the lessons and experiences of the European theater, air planners identified several key systems in Japan to be targeted. Coke ovens, essential for the production of steel, were singled out for attack. Other targets included merchant shipping, oil refineries, the transportation network, munitions factories, and aircraft and engine complexes. USSBS analysts reinforced these targeting priorities after studying the effects of Allied bombing on Germany, as well as suggesting ideas of their own.

The first three months of XXI Bomber Command operations based out of the Marianas were not impressive: by January 1945 it had dropped only 1,500 tons of bombs on Japan, and only one out of fifty hit within 1,000 feet of the aimpoint. Tonnage continued to lag, and only 7,180 tons had been delivered prior to March 9, 1945. Once again, Arnold ran out of patience.[52]

LeMay was brought from India to take over. In a stunning reversal of two decades of theory and practice, LeMay jettisoned prewar doctrine and most of what he and others had learned over Germany. He stripped his B-29s of guns, ammunition, and armor plating and launched them at night and at low altitude in area bombing attacks, using incendiaries against Japanese cities. The Japanese were unprepared for fire bombing, and the results were devastating.[53] Intelligence determined the Japanese economy was organized into "cottage industries," unlike the large factory complexes prevalent in Europe; indeed, half of all Japanese workers were employed in factories of less than 100 people.[54] LeMay's area bombing was suited to destroying these small factories scattered throughout the major urban areas.

* * *

USSBS revealed that the AAF entered the war deficient in strategic intelligence, worldwide, but the problem was greater in Japan because of the closed nature of its society. In many cases, air planners had to rely on old maps, an occasional tourist report, or prewar insurance data.[55] There were also mechanical troubles with the B-29s required to span the great distances inherent in Pacific theater of operations, and meteorological phenomena like the 200-miles-per-hour high-altitude jet stream that played havoc with navigation and bombing accuracy.

Yet, the size of the attacks continued to rise, and in July 1945 the Eighth Air Force, newly outfitted with B-29s, arrived in theater under the command of Lieutenant General Jimmy Doolittle. The Eighth was just gearing up when the war ended, but as a portent, the two air forces carried out a 1,000 plane strike on August 14. To illustrate the crescendo of bombing, the B-29s had dropped 14,000 tons in March (with 385 aircraft available), and 43,000 tons in July (with nearly 900 aircraft on hand). This figure would rise to an astonishing 115,000 tons in September with the combination of the Eighth and Twentieth Air Forces in full operation.[56]

On August 6, 1945, a B-29 dropped an atomic bomb on Hiroshima. Three days later a second atom bomb hit Nagasaki. In an unprecedented move, the Japanese emperor went on radio and announced surrender on August 15, citing the new bomb as his reason for capitulating.[57]

The dropping of the atomic bombs caused controversy, and USSBS added to this debate by noting in an oft-quoted statement that Japan would have surrendered by November 1, 1945, without the use of atomic bombs, without an invasion, and without Russia entering the war—thus implying the bombs were unnecessary and that there was an effective and seemingly more humane alternative.[58] But the survey's prediction of a Japanese surrender by November was based on the assumption that the crescendo of bombing just noted would soon begin: the tonnage dropped on Japan was scheduled to nearly triple beginning in September. As it was, sixty-six of Japan's urban centers had already been burned out; the increase of tonnage would have dramatically increased that figure. This hardly seems a preferred strategy.

What if there had been no bombing and no invasion? Would the US Navy's starvation blockade have been more humane? The survey revealed that food rationing had started in 1941 and by 1945 the situation was "critical."[59] How long would a blockade have lasted and how many civilians would have starved before military leaders gave in? Indeed, B-29 mine-laying operations in Japanese coastal waters had had devastating results. A Japanese officer in charge of countermine operations later testified, "The result of B-29 mining was so effective against the shipping that it eventually starved the country. I think you probably could have shortened the war by beginning earlier."[60] What of the millions of Chinese, Koreans, Indonesians, and other Asians who would have suffered under continued Japanese occupation? (It is estimated that 6 million died under oppressive Japanese rule throughout Asia.[61]) It is likely such a delaying strategy would have been seen as a deliberately racist strategy of American leaders unconcerned for Asian life. Finally, what of the 145,000 Allied prisoners of war held in Japanese prison camps? The mortality rate in these camps was 40 percent—ten times that of German camps.[62] Delay would have been a disaster for them. It should also be noted that several high-ranking Japanese officers were actually hoping the Allies would invade, envisioning a bloodbath on the beaches. The Japanese deputy army chief of staff, Lieutenant General Masakuzu Kawabe, later stated: "I desired a landing operation . . . we would have inflicted heavy casualties. . . . It was my desire that that would result not in an unconditional surrender but probably a compromise. . . . I would say it [this belief] was pretty well general throughout the Army."[63]

As in Europe, interviews, site visits, photographs, and data accumulation went into USSBS analysis. Statistically, the numbers were illuminating. B-29s dropped 91 percent of all bombs on Japan, and 96 percent of all tonnage fell in the last five months of the war.[64] The attacks destroyed 600 factories and thousands of "feeder shops." The Japanese attempted to disperse into underground factories and caves to avoid air attacks, but this further dissipated scarce resources. Overall, production dropped by 53 percent between November 1944 and July 1945. In cities that had *not* been bombed, production in July 1945 was at 94 percent of its wartime peak, but in cities that *had* been bombed, production had fallen to 27 percent of its acme. By July 1945 aluminum production was at 9 percent, while oil refining and ingot steel production were at 15 percent of their high points.[65] Production at aircraft engine plants was down 75 percent, army ordnance plants by 30 percent, and naval ordnance by 28 percent.[66] The USSBS concluded: "By July 1945 Japan's economic system had been shattered. Production of civilian goods was below the level of subsistence. Munitions output had been curtailed to less than half the wartime peak, a level that could not support sustained military operations against our opposing forces. The economic basis of Japanese resistance had been destroyed."[67]

An estimated 8.5 million people evacuated Japanese cities. This was one-quarter of the entire urban population, although in big cities like Osaka and Kobe over half fled. One-third of the 8.5 million evacuees were factory workers, so the absentee rate in factories was at 49 percent by the end of the war.[68] This trend toward flight was spurred by LeMay, who in July began dropping leaflets on Japanese cities stating they would be bombed in the next few days. One Japanese official said these leaflet drops caused panic and contributed to the evacuation of the cities. Of those remaining, hundreds of thousands were pressed into service to fight fires, restore utilities, and clear rubble, which further hindered production and attempts to disperse the armaments industry. Morale and hope plummeted. Survey polls indicated that in June 1944, 2 percent of the Japanese population thought they would lose the war; by December it was 10 percent; in June 1945 it was 46 percent; and by August it had climbed to 68 percent. As for the reasons for surrender: 50 percent said it was due to air strikes; 25 percent said food shortages; and 20 percent blamed it on other military losses.[69]

As in Europe, there were synergies in this industrial collapse, and the US Navy's unrestricted submarine warfare campaign was critical in reducing the supply of raw materials to the Home Islands. Japan was extremely resource poor and relied on raw materials from China, Korea, Indochina, and the East Indies. The air-sea blockade strangled the flow of these resources to the Home Islands.[70] Victory was a joint effort. For example, B-29 airbases were won by the combined efforts of the Army, Navy, and AAF. The bombers then struck Japanese aircraft factories, but these factories were already low on aluminum supplies due to the blockade. Even if aircraft were built, there were few engines to power them because bombing had destroyed the power plant factories. If

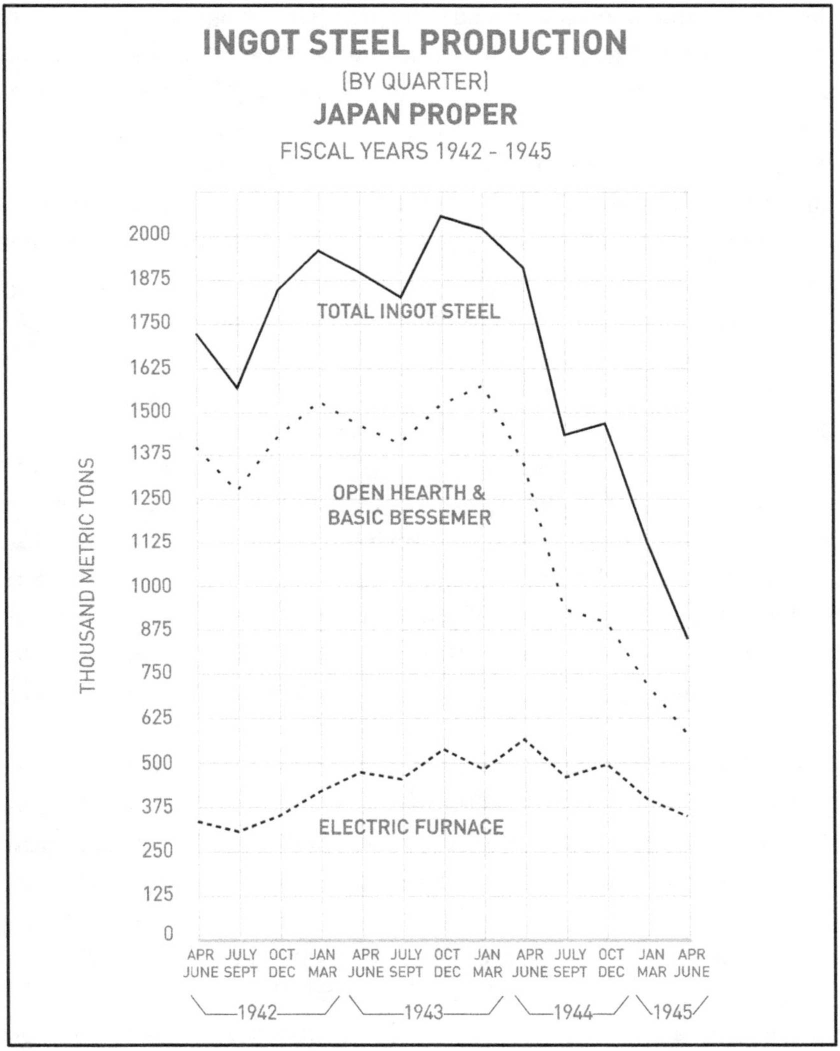

Japanese Ingot Steel Production. USSBS, "Effects of Bombing on Japan's War Economy."

engines had been available, there was little petroleum to fuel them because of the blockade; if there had been petroleum, there would have been no gasoline, because the oil refineries had been destroyed from the air.[71] The Navy's strangulation blockade was assisted by the B-29 campaign that mined inland waterways. And so on.

Similarly, the Japanese food situation was precarious. As the war progressed, more and more farmers had to leave the land to fight or to work in the factories, thus causing food shortages. The cutting of sea lines by submarines and aerial mines lowered imports, and the bombing cut fertilizer production by two-thirds; this in turn cut the yield per acre. The need to rebuild bombed factories pulled more farmers off the land, and by the end of the war over 1 million acres of arable land had been abandoned. Due to a consequent lack of food, worker productivity was lowered as the amount of calories available in their diet plummeted.[72]

There were many such examples demonstrating a vicious and ever tightening downward spiral from which Japan could not recover. Japanese leaders were presented with multiple catastrophic failures they could not handle; one or two of the above might have been worked around, but not all of them.

As in Europe, air superiority was essential. Japan had excellent aircraft that were further improved as the war progressed, but they did not have enough of them, the fuel to operate them, or the pilots to fly them. USSBS recognized this: "Japan understood the importance of air power and especially air superiority, but failed to appreciate the full scope and complexity of the requirements for continuing control of the air."[73] Significantly, there were 9,000 aircraft in the Home Islands that could have been used as Kamikazes had the war not ended in mid-August.[74]

About 2.5 million Japanese homes were destroyed, and 600,000 more were pulled down to create firebreaks.[75] The masses forced to relocate placed impossible burdens on transportation, food distribution systems, and medical facilities. USSBS estimated that at least 330,000 Japanese civilians were killed in air attacks—more than in Germany, although the losses occurred in less time and with only one-tenth the tonnage. Of these deaths, the survey estimated that 45 percent were in the labor force. One source totals the civilian deaths worldwide due to air attack during World War II and arrives at a number of under 2 million. Since 40 million civilians died during the war, this means that less than 5 percent of the total was the result of air attack. In other words, the more traditional forms of land and sea warfare, as well as genocide and starvation, accounted for more than 95 percent of all civilian deaths.[76]

USSBS noted errors: the B-29s should have struck railroads and inland waterways (via mining) sooner.[77] These attacks would have thoroughly disrupted internal transportation and curtailed the influx of reinforcements to Kyushu—the site of the proposed invasion in November 1945 that so concerned ground planners. As in Europe, such a transportation plan would have

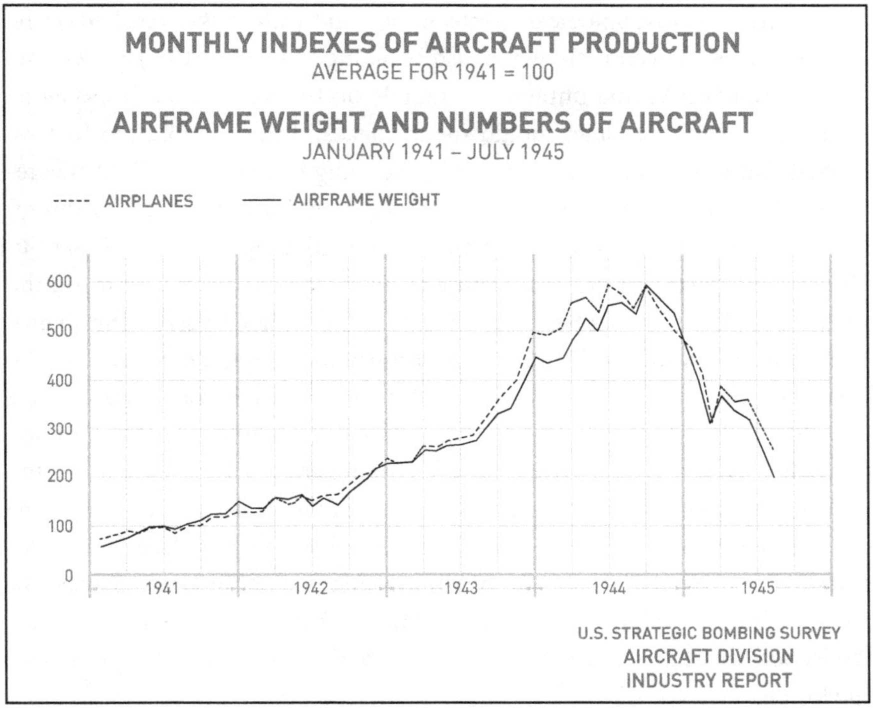

Japanese Aircraft Production. USSBS, "Aircraft Division Industry Report."

made beachhead defense much more difficult. The amount of Japanese merchant shipping was never enough to sustain the flow of materials from China and the southern islands, and that situation worsened as the war progressed and the air-sea blockade took its toll on the fleet.[78] An earlier focus on this target by the B-29 mining effort would have provided an earlier collapse. Even so, results of the bombing campaign, especially the atomic strikes, were disastrous for Japan. Surrender occurred without a bloody invasion being necessary.[79]

* * *

The B-29s played a decisive role in the defeat of Japan. This was partly because they reinforced the blockade that so disrupted the economy of the country as a whole, but also because they made ultimate victory seem hopeless to the Japanese people and their leaders.[80] No doubt Japan could have gone on for months and perhaps years if the only threats had been the blockade and the slow but inexorable march of Allied armies toward the Home Islands, but the physical and psychological effects of the nightly air strikes resulted in the destruction of the economy while also breaking the will of the Japanese. As Premier Kantarō Suzuki phrased it, "merely on the basis of the B-29s alone I was convinced that Japan should sue for peace." Prince Fumimaro Konoye echoed that statement: "Fundamentally, the thing that brought about the determination to make peace was the prolonged bombing of the B-29s." Admiral Osami Nagano, supreme naval advisor to the emperor, stated, "If I were to give you one factor as the one leading to your victory, I would give you the Air Force." Chief Cabinet Secretary Hisatsune Sakomizu argued: "The chance had come to end the war. It was not necessary to blame the military side, the manufacturing people, or anyone else—just the atomic bomb. It was a good excuse."[81] Admiral Soemu Toyoda, chief of the naval combined forces, echoed this belief, stating, "I do not think it would be accurate to look upon use of the Atomic Bomb and the entry and participation of Soviet Russia into the war as direct cause of termination of the war, but I think that those two factors did enable us to bring the war to a termination without creating too great chaos in Japan."[82] The psychological effect of the atomic bombs created a climate within the leadership that allowed the emperor to overrule his military advisers and sue for peace.

* * *

Although USSBS was supposed to be apolitical, this hope was naive. Strategic bombing was freighted with politics: inter-allied (United States vs. United Kingdom), inter-service (AAF vs. the Navy and Army), and intra-service (bombers vs. fighters). No matter what the survey teams wrote, they would offend someone. Moreover, the Survey did have problems: its focus on strategic bombing slighted tactical airpower—although a strategic focus was after all its specific charter. The civilian specialists chosen were mostly from management rather than labor, and this might have skewed results regarding worker productivity and morale. One author scored the survey team for being biased and a tool of the AAF to secure a separate air force following the war.[83] Regarding Germany, USSBS researchers were too easily swayed by prewar Nazi data regarding the mobilization of the economy. Germany entered the war in a semi-mobilized state, and it was only after two years that Hitler realized he was in for a long war and put the economy on a total war footing. Because of this, the Survey passed off the ineffectiveness of early bombing efforts by arguing there was so much slack in the German economy that although the bombing was having results, they were mitigated by the swelling production due to Hitler's mobilization directive. In truth, early bombing efforts appeared ineffective largely because they were.[84]

And yet, the overwhelming authority of the US Strategic Bombing Survey is unassailable. Nothing like it has ever been attempted after a war. The mountain of evidence obtained, the thousands of interviews conducted, the painstaking measurements taken—it is simply too massive and detailed to refute. The statistics do not lie. Seldom does a victor have the opportunity to range across a defeated country, examine its archives and records, tour its cities and factories, and interview its people. As the Navy feared, USSBS provided the unimpeachable evidence needed to carry on the fight for the Air Force's institutional independence after the war. The Survey's reports, especially the easy-to-read, concise, and readily obtainable summary volumes, were oft cited in the years ahead. The most repeated quotation regards the war in Europe: "Allied airpower was decisive in the war in Western Europe." But there is so much more to be gained from these documents. The hundreds of detailed surveys provide a rich and deeply authoritative mother lode of information regarding the effectiveness of the bombing effort in both theaters—for those willing to actually read the reports.

14

Summation

The Emergence of a Paradigm

THE STUDY OF MILITARY history has largely been a study of land warfare. This was logical in the past because generals leading great armies in violent battle were the stuff of legends. Emphasis was given to such events by Carl von Clausewitz. He had participated in the Napoleonic wars and sought to make sense of them. To his mind, the wars were political acts, whole nations at war, but they were defined by bloodshed and violence. His seminal work, *On War*, stressed these factors and did not even mention sea power, a fundamentally different form of war than that on land, and this distortion took root.[1] For the past two centuries his view of war has prevailed among too many military leaders.

Clausewitz wrote of many things that were insightful and even profound. But his main theme, stressed repeatedly, was the necessity of fighting major battles involving large forces. He argued that war was slaughter and there was no easy way around that fact. As a way of softening this sanguinary message, he also wrote of war's inherently political nature—an idea he intended to expand on in later renditions of *On War*. He died before doing so; thus, we are left with a draft that perhaps unduly emphasized certain aspects of war while downplaying others. We should not try to imagine what he *might* have written.

Europeans shared a common culture, and the notion that policy defined war was understood by them. Regrettably, the guerrilla warfare practiced by the Spanish and Russians that had such a deadly impact on Napoleon's armies was largely ignored by Clausewitz. This type of war was far different than that he had witnessed, and it was to take on increased significance in the decades ahead.

A century after Clausewitz wrote, the generals of the Great War found themselves immersed in a conflict for which they had not planned. There were harbingers, notably the Russo-Japanese War of 1904–5. One observer of that war wrote with insight: "Battles are no longer the spectacular heroics of the past. The army of to-day and to-morrow is a sombre [*sic*], gigantic machine devoid of all melodramatic heroics, but in itself all-heroic, silent and terrible: a machine that requires years to form its separate parts, years to assemble them together, and other years to make them work smoothly and irresistibly. Then, when it is set in motion, naught shall stop it but a similar machine stronger and better."[2]

Military leaders in 1914 expected fast-moving operations of maneuver and firepower—classic Napoleonic warfare. Instead, they quickly mired in stagnation, and the "machines" of war took over. In retrospect over a century later, one can sympathize with the generals. They attempted to break out of the trench deathtraps employing various tactical and strategic ploys, but none worked or were pursued vigorously enough: it was simply too comfortable to fall back on the Clausewitzian dictum of hitting the enemy's main force and destroying it—so 8 million in uniform died in the Great War.[3]

In the aftermath, intelligent, experienced, and sober officers studied the war in depth, trying to make sense of what had happened and seeking to ensure such horror would not recur. Ironically, the answers reached by the Germans and French were diametrically opposed—despite the fact they had shared the same war and the same experiences over the same ground. The Germans decided that mobility could be restored to the battlefield by the use of new weapons, the tank and the aircraft working in concert. Their notion would later be dubbed blitzkrieg, lightning war.[4] The French envisioned another war of attrition, and because their population and resources were less than those of their likely enemy, the sane response was a concrete trench, the Maginot Line. If the Germans wished to attack again, they would have to bleed themselves white against massive fortifications at the border.[5]

There were other solutions proposed during the interwar years. Some in Britain and the United States took to the air for a solution to trench stalemate. They theorized that air bombardment would be the antidote to the Western Front. Aircraft could fly over fortifications and trenches and strike directly at the heart of an enemy at the outset of war. It too would be deadly, but the theory assumed a war's quick end, and this would mean far fewer casualties in the long run. Serious thinkers and military men like Hugh Trenchard, J.F.C. Fuller, and Basil H. Liddell Hart in Britain, and Billy Mitchell, Henry "Hap" Arnold, and Alexander de Seversky in America, were advocates of this new form of war. Fuller and Liddell Hart, after flirting with strategic airpower, settled back into their infantry culture—they envisioned future war as focusing on the ground, aided by new technologies. Fuller even devised a list of Principles of War to help guide future commanders, and these would become ingrained in military doctrine.

These men were products of their service and national cultures. As soldiers, they assumed war would be decided through major land operations. Yet, both also realized that for centuries Britannia had ruled the waves, and this gave it a unique flexibility in war. In the words of Francis Bacon: "he that commands the sea is at great liberty, and may take as much and as little of the war as he will."[6] Major battles were often still required, but it was not the main object to be sought. Taking the war elsewhere—to a different theater—often made more sense, especially because that enemy was usually France. This was a time-honored policy for sea powers that stretched back to antiquity. Although it did not always work, many believed it was still preferable to a Clausewitzian bloodbath. The Iberian campaign during the Napoleonic wars was a successful example of this strategy, and Liddell Hart argued that a similar move should have been used in the Great War. In truth of course it was employed—at Gallipoli and Salonika, with little effect, but were those operations pushed forcefully? To Liddell Hart, the answer was no. Decisive war using an indirect approach was still possible—if by decisive it was meant that a nation was able to achieve its political goals.[7] This notion is important: simply killing large numbers of enemy troops and controlling the battlefield afterward was not good enough: long-term policy objectives had to be secured.

World War II taught other important lessons. Campaigns in Crete and Norway demonstrated that the services needed to work together to secure common objectives, especially because war had moved into the third dimension. What today is termed jointness became a necessity in a global war versus powerful opponents. In addition, commanders realized that the air weapon was crucial to success. Old lessons regarding the need for control of the sea were modified to reflect the need for control of the air over the sea.

In the United States, the cultural aspects of war were ambiguous. Military traditions were to a great extent inherited from the British and emphasized a fear of standing armies and militarism—even if the officer corps was held in high esteem. It is a myth that American tradition called for the strict separation of the military and politics: for much of the nation's history that was not the case. Successful generals were routinely pursued by political parties and many—Washington, Jackson, Taylor, Scott, McClellan, Grant, Hayes, Garfield, Hancock, Eisenhower, Haig, Clark, and others—were attracted to politics, and that attraction often occurred while they were still in uniform. At the same time, the service cultures of the Army, Navy, and Air Force were deeply ingrained and impacted how officers thought about war—its goals, strategy, tactics, and technology. These cultures clashed in the Second World War.

Military commanders envisioned different ways and means of defeating Germany, Italy, and Japan. Great armies, invasions, amphibious assaults, unrestricted submarine warfare, and aircraft were eventually employed worldwide. Strategic airpower was used extensively for the first time and showed powerful results. It was a hard path to success. Such a form of war had not been seriously attempted before, thus making it susceptible to theoretical flights of fancy and technological determinism. And yet, once organizations were put in place to study enemy economies, and an intelligence apparatus was formed to analyze the tactics and techniques of air attack, the results were impressive. The US Strategic Bombing Survey compiled unassailable data to prove strategic bombing's effectiveness.

The Pacific campaigns were remarkable in that the huge distances involved—many times greater than those in Europe—were spanned by airpower, and the radius of tactical aircraft determined strategy to a great extent, in both the Central Pacific and Southwest Pacific Areas. Air superiority over a beachhead, provided by carrier-based or land-based air, was vital.

Time, a critical factor in war and often the difference between victory and defeat, was conquered by the atomic bomb, and this shaped the future.

* * *

The atomic bombs' ending the war against Japan had a profound psychological effect on the world. Although the US monopoly in atomic weapons lasted barely four years, the ensuing "balance of terror" has ensured that nuclear weapons have not been employed since. War has been deterred down to the conventional level. War itself has not been eradicated; rather, major belligerents have used limited means to achieve limited goals. Conflict dropped back two centuries, to when limited war was the norm. The Thirty Years War in the seventeenth century moved the great powers to lower the scale of violence.

Wars were to be fought for colonies, provinces, or trade rights. This would last until the Napoleonic era. Afterward, limited wars once again became the norm. The cataclysms of the world wars changed things, but the aftermath repeated the cyclical nature of war. Nations were loath to wage war against peers. Indirect means or asymmetrical strategies were sought that held hope of success but with lowered risk.

* * *

The Korean War was the first test for the United States and its allies in the post–World War II era. It did not go well. The South Korean armed forces were initially ineffectual in comparison to their northern neighbors. Although the United States had forces in nearby Japan, it was similarly unready. The mission of those forces was occupation duty: the Army and Air Force elements were not prepared to conduct major combat operations or to work together effectively.[8] Air units, for example, were structured and trained for air defense against a possible Soviet attack.[9] The results of this myopia were immediately apparent on the Korean peninsula when US forces were sent to South Korea to repel the invaders but were instead pushed steadily back.

Eventually the United Nations forces held. General of the Army Douglas MacArthur then launched his brilliant flank attack at Inchon. While the North Korean forces were battering Pusan, UN forces landed near Seoul, cut enemy supply lines, and then turned south to hit the North Koreans in the rear. Caught by surprise, the North Koreans broke. Fleeing north, they crossed back into their own country, and the war should then have been won and over. But President Harry Truman convinced the UN to continue into North Korea, destroy the remaining enemy forces, and then unite the peninsula under one government—the political aim ostensibly sought by all sides since the end of World War II. It was a fundamental change of strategy and a classic example of "mission creep."[10]

The Peoples Republic of China warned the United States that it would not stand by idly while foreign troops approached its borders, but Truman and the UN paid no mind.[11] The Chinese intervened in force in November 1950, smashed UN forces, and drove them back across the 38th parallel. America was presented with a new war.

Korea cost well over a million civilian and military casualties and hundreds of billions of dollars, while achieving little more than the status quo ante bellum.[12] Airpower was used extensively but with mixed results. Initial air operations defeated the small North Korean Air Force, established air superiority over the battlefield, conducted close air support operations, and then launched massive air interdiction operations. Close air support probably saved the UN forces from initial disaster and allowed the beleaguered ground forces to hang on at Pusan, but air interdiction was of limited utility. Chinese and North Korean lines of supply were never totally cut, and there was always enough material getting through to allow enemy operations.

Strategic bombing was largely a non sequitur. North Korea had few strategic targets, and most of those were off limits for much of the war. Instead, the war became one of prolonged attrition, reminiscent of World War I. A static front was established that was characterized by massed artillery, frontal infantry assaults, and ground attack by UN airpower.

* * *

Vietnam was a completely different war, although American military leaders attempted to force it into a conventional model with which they were familiar. US ground forces had fought insurgencies for well over a century—the Army during the endemic Indian Wars and the Marine Corps in Central America between the world wars. These were not experiences that earned much glory or required extensive force structure. One authority notes that between the Civil War and 1900, "neither in the schools nor in instructional manuals was the unconventional warfare practiced by Indians addressed. West Point had no courses addressing the subject. The emphasis was on the next conventional war, to be fought by orthodox strategy and tactics."[13] The decades-long Indian wars should have been fruitful areas for study, but they were ignored and their lessons forgotten.

Some observers have argued that the United States should have fought the North Vietnamese as a conventional foe. They criticized the administration of President Lyndon Johnson for worrying too much about guerrillas; he should have invaded North Vietnam, Laos, and Cambodia to isolate the battlefield and prevent movement of men and supplies into South Vietnam.[14] Others argued the opposite—that the American response should have focused on counterinsurgency and not conventional operations.[15]

Airpower was misused. The president and his civilian advisors concocted a strategy employing airpower in a carefully constrained ratcheting of force to "signal" North Vietnamese leaders to modify their behavior. If the enemy did so, the airstrikes would relent; if they did not, the strikes would increase.[16] The air campaign against North Vietnam between 1965 and 1968 was an unsuccessful attempt to coerce the North Vietnamese into acquiescence.

Of importance, President Johnson chose airpower for coercion precisely because of its alleged greatest weakness. Airpower cannot occupy ground, but in Vietnam that was the last thing he desired. Proposals were made for an invasion of the North, but he rejected those suggestions, believing such an action would draw in China—as had happened in Korea.[17] Instead, he chose airpower against North Vietnam because it could not occupy ground and was therefore less provocative. It was a poor strategy, but it nonetheless suggested an original strategic thought: armies of occupation had become less useful simply because they were so visible, physically present, and obtrusive. An army's greatest strength was becoming a liability because of the cost and risk it entailed.

* * *

The American way of war began to change in the aftermath of the Vietnam debacle, and that change was evidenced in the Gulf War of 1991. When Saddam Hussein sent his forces into Kuwait in June 1990, he believed there would be no serious response from the West. Instead, virtually the entire world was outraged, and in greater or lesser degrees dozens of nations coalesced to expel the Iraqis from Kuwait.

Hussein was not concerned. His large army had been battle-hardened in an eight-year war against Iran. He was dug in along the Kuwaiti border adjoining Saudi Arabia, and had large stocks of aircraft, tanks, missiles, and weapons of mass destruction—which he had already used against Iran and his own Kurdish population. Hussein assumed that only a bloody ground assault would be used in an attempt to dislodge him; and he doubted the West would have the stomach for such a fight. Many in the United States agreed, and some opined that Coalition casualties would total as many as 30,000 if such a strategy were employed.[18] Hussein believed just the thought of "a mother of all battles" would cause the West to lose enthusiasm.[19]

General Norman Schwarzkopf asked his Central Command staff for options to liberate Kuwait but was disappointed. His planners produced a scheme to fulfill the worst fears of those predicting a bloodbath—a massive ground assault into the center of the Iraqi defenses. Schwarzkopf was irritated, so he turned instead to an unlikely source—the Air Force. He wanted an air plan that would dislodge the dug-in Iraqi Army without a huge butcher's bill.[20]

The result was an air plan dubbed "Instant Thunder." The choice of name was deliberate. Most high-ranking airmen had fought in Vietnam as junior officers and witnessed the debilitating strategy of "gradual escalation" devised by the White House. They loathed the idea and its air campaign code named ROLLING THUNDER, but nonetheless attempted to carry it out. The results were unsuccessful, and two decades later airmen were against trying it again. Instead, "Instant Thunder" was to be a furious and rapid application of airpower against the center of Iraq.[21]

Schwarzkopf liked the idea, but modified it by making the Iraqi Army a key target. The vast majority of air sorties and ordnance expended would be against fielded forces. In this sense, airpower was used in a somewhat traditional fashion: to destroy the enemy army. Only, modern airpower was able to destroy that army more quickly and cheaply than could another army.

The result was an astounding success. After six weeks of continuous pounding from the air, the Iraqi Army was devastated. When the ground offensive finally began at the end of February 1991, Schwarzkopf's intelligence directorate estimated that all of Iraq's forty-eight frontline divisions had been reduced by airpower to below 50 percent strength. That assessment was confirmed by the CIA.[22] In essence, the Iraqi Army was "combat ineffective"—defeated—before major ground operations even began. Iraq's air force was similarly devastated, and hundreds of aircraft were destroyed in the air or on the ground, while over 130 others fled to Iran to escape a similar fate.

Coalition ground forces found a defeated enemy at their front: over 80,000 troops had deserted and another 86,000 were quickly taken prisoner virtually without a fight.[23] Then-Secretary of Defense Richard Cheney, when asked why Iraq was defeated so quickly and thoroughly, replied: "It was crushed, I think, by the air campaign, and the way in which we went about the [air] campaign meant that when we finally did have to move our ground forces in, and we sort of kicked in the door, they collapsed fairly rapidly."[24]

Following surrender, Coalition air units remained in Turkey, Kuwait, and Saudi Arabia to impose an air blockade on Iraq. Fixed-wing flight by Iraqi military aircraft was severely circumscribed, and even the movement of ground units was limited. These air operations, termed NORTHERN and SOUTHERN WATCH, were successful. They kept Hussein in a box and prevented him from threatening his neighbors. Moreover, as we now know, they and UN inspectors kept Iraq from building weapons of mass destruction or harboring al Qaeda terrorists. The cost for this decade-long air blockade was negligible: no lives were lost despite nearly 200,000 combat sorties flown, and operations cost slightly over $1 billion per year—a pittance compared to the trillions spent in the ground operations that followed.[25]

Unfortunately, we learned little from those experiences. In Somalia the nation was imploding and warlords were in charge. People were dying, so the United States sent in troops to restore order and permit the distribution of food and medicine. Mission creep then occurred, and we attempted to depose warlord Mohamed Farrah Aideed. In a show of force in October 1993, US troops drove into Mogadishu but were immediately ambushed and trapped. Two Army helicopters flying in to rescue the soldiers were shot down and three others damaged. In the ambush and subsequent firefight, eighteen Americans were killed and their bodies mutilated while another eighty-two were wounded; between 500 and 1,000 Somalis were also gunned down.[26] America pulled out and left Somalia to its fate.

In 1995 Yugoslavia began to disintegrate, and thousands of civilians were caught in the middle of the vicious ethnic violence that followed. NATO, with the Balkans on their doorstep and recalling that this area had served as the tinderbox for the Great War, acted decisively. Rather than send in ground troops, however, the alliance relied on airpower. In a three-week campaign over Bosnia, ethnic Serbians backed by Belgrade were stopped and peace was restored. Croatian ground forces had also moved against the Serbs, and this combination of airpower and indigenous ground forces ended the conflict on NATO's terms.[27] Serbian leader Slobodan Milosovic attested to the surgical precision of the air strikes, commenting that perhaps twenty-five civilians were killed.[28] NATO's political goals were achieved at low cost or risk.

Three years later ethnic violence erupted again. The Serbs drove 800,000 Muslims out of Kosovo so as to repopulate it with their own people. Once again NATO relied on airpower. During the ensuing seventy-eight-day air campaign, Serbian forces in Kosovo were pummeled and driven back. Air strikes on infrastructure targets in Serbia, including Belgrade, brought the war home to the aggressors. Milosevic surrendered and eventually died in a prison cell awaiting trial for war crimes. The Kosovars returned to their homes.[29]

This series of wars, beginning with DESERT STORM in 1991 and ending with Serbia in 1999 (with the exception of the disaster in Mogadishu), seemed to usher in a new form of war, one dominated by airpower employing precision strikes, supported by the use—or the threat of use—of conventional ground forces. Air operations were timed to coincide with those of indigenous ground forces, such as the Kosovar Liberation Army. Although this emerging model was used initially in Afghanistan in 2001 and Iraq in 2003, military leaders then reverted to the past.

* * *

The terrorist attacks of September 11, 2001, signaled a major change in US foreign policy. Afghanistan was attacked and invaded; the objective was to kill or capture al Qaeda operatives, while also toppling the Taliban regime that had supported and protected them. Afghanistan, a huge, land-locked country with little in the way of paved roads, rail lines, or industry, offered significant challenges for the United States and its allies. Once again, reason combined with austere conditions to produce remarkable results.

On October 7, less than a month after 9/11, US aircraft hit thirty-one separate targets in Afghanistan, including early warning radars, ground forces, command and control facilities, terrorist barracks and training camps, and Taliban airfields.[30] Air strikes continued for the next ten days against such fixed targets. On the fifth day objectives began to include caves in which the Taliban and al Qaeda were hiding. On October 19 the first special operations forces (SOF) team was air-dropped into Afghanistan.

The arrival of SOF was crucial. The teams established contact with the anti-Taliban Northern Alliance and began spotting targets for Coalition aircraft.[31] Over the next few weeks, seventy-eight SOF troops were air-dropped into Afghanistan. The Northern Alliance found new strength as Coalition aircraft bombed the Taliban, who then began to melt away: on November 9 the Alliance captured the northern stronghold of Mazar-e-Sharif. Three days later the capital of Kabul fell. One high-ranking Taliban official who defected during the assault on the capital stated that "Kabul has seen many rockets, but this was a different thing. The American bombing of the Taliban trenches, cars, and troops caused us to be defeated."[32]

It was a stunning victory. Moreover, the Northern Alliance, even with the smattering of SOF troops present, were always outnumbered by the Taliban—at Mazar-e-Sharif, for example, 5,000 Taliban in defensive positions confronted 2,000 Northern Alliance troops.[33] But the Northern Alliance had airpower behind it, and that proved the decisive factor.

In March 2003, Coalition forces attacked Iraq to destroy weapons of mass destruction it believed Saddam Hussein was building, and to root out al Qaeda fighters thought to be training there. All started well and air-delivered precision weapons and sensors were used with great effect, as during the sandstorm that halted Coalition forces en route to Baghdad. These conditions in times past would have kept airpower grounded and ineffective. This time, radar penetrated the sand and pinpointed Iraqi targets, which were then struck from the air by GPS-guided weapons.[34] To the stunned Iraqis below, the delivery of these weapons with such accuracy in near-zero visibility was a major psychological blow.

One Iraqi general attested to the importance of airpower: "This [the bombing campaign] affected the morale of the troops. . . . The Iraqi will to fight was broken outside Baghdad."[35] The Al Nida Republican Guard Division, for example, originally consisted of 13,000 men and 500 vehicles; it was reduced by airpower to 2,000 troops and 50 vehicles by the time the marines engaged it. Similarly, the Hammurabi Division was reduced to 44 percent effectiveness, and the Medina Division to 18 percent.[36] One US Army brigade commander later said simply: "We never really found any cohesive unit of any brigade, of any Republican Guard division."[37] As in the previous decade, the bulk of the Iraqi Army was rendered "combat ineffective" by airpower before it was ever engaged by Coalition ground forces. Overall, one report states that up to 90 percent of the Iraqi Army in some units deserted in 2003 because of the devastating air strikes.[38]

As in the first Gulf War, the Iraqi Air Force was a non-player: none of its 400 aircraft even took off to challenge the Coalition; indeed, the Iraqis attempted to save their best aircraft by burying them in the desert.[39] Baghdad fell in three weeks, with only 139 Coalition deaths and just one fixed-wing aircraft lost to enemy fire.[40]

Things then went awry. The head of the Coalition Provisional Authority, Paul Bremer, issued edicts prohibiting Baath Party members from holding administrative offices, while also disarming and disbanding the Iraqi military forces and police.[41] These decisions exacerbated the long-simmering enmity between the majority Shias and the minority Sunnis. Saddam Hussein and his chief advisers, administrators, and military officers were Sunnis and Baath Party members. They had kept an iron hand and boot on the Shias. When the regime fell, the Shias expected that balance would be restored, but American leaders feared that a Shiite state would come under the influence of Iran. Once again, we had not thought through what our goals were and how we could achieve them, given the deep-seated divisions in Iraq. Chaos ensued.

The US military compounded this shortsightedness by inserting large numbers of conventionally trained and equipped ground troops into an explosive situation that demanded instead the expertise of those schooled in counterinsurgency.

Journalist Tom Ricks criticized some units for taking an overly aggressive stance when dealing with the Iraqi populace. When troops went into an area, they often did so in mass, heavily armed, and usually at night. In contrast, Ricks lauded the activities of SOF, contending that success occurred when small numbers of highly trained troops acted with restraint. Unfortunately, big battalions fighting aggressively dominated Army doctrine, and this was on display in Iraq. One study traces the experience of the US Army in low-intensity conflict since Vietnam and concludes: "Defeat in Vietnam led the Army to consciously turn away from its experience there and discard what it had learned about counterinsurgency."[42]

Following DESERT STORM, the United States experimented with a new paradigm: the use of airpower, SOF, indigenous ground troops, and robust intelligence assets. The employment of conventional US ground troops was avoided due to their cost and risk. This emerging paradigm proved successful in Bosnia, Kosovo, Afghanistan, and northern Iraq.[43] Given the political and military risk of putting ground troops in harm's way, it should be the aim of all joint planners to devise ways of achieving national objectives with the least cost in blood and treasure. This means that using large numbers of conventional ground troops should be the last resort rather than the first.

The successful paradigm of relying on airpower and SOF was ignored in Iraq following the collapse of the Saddam Hussein regime. The result should have been expected. In a poll taken in October 2003, two-thirds of Iraqis saw the Coalition as "occupying powers," while only 15 percent saw them as "liberators."[44] Four years later, polls had 69 percent of Iraqis saying the US presence was making things worse; only 21 percent thought the Americans were making things better.[45] Hearts and minds were not being won.

And then the Islamic State of Iraq and Syria (ISIS) raised its ugly head in 2014. Composed largely of Sunni Arabs who had been disenfranchised by the Shias in Iraq after the fall of Saddam Hussein, ISIS launched devastating attacks across Iraq and Syria. At its peak, ISIS had 7.5 million people under its control, and its forces numbered 30,000.[46] At first, Iraqi forces were unsuccessful in stopping these assaults, and major cities like Mosul fell and ISIS established a Caliphate in Raqqa, Syria. Fortunately, indigenous forces in Iraq, Kurdistan, and Syria were turned around. They teamed with small numbers of SOF, were provided real-time intelligence from myriad sensors, and US airpower was employed with devastating effect. ISIS began to retreat. Mosul was liberated and Raqqa was recaptured in October 2017.[47] Air strikes against ISIS peaked during this period as the terrorist organization crumbled. In addition, local forces recaptured Syrian oil fields that had been held by ISIS and which helped finance its operations.[48] By February 2018, ISIS was largely destroyed, and this was accomplished without the use of large numbers of US conventional ground forces.[49] Instead, the winning combination was airpower, SOF, robust intelligence, and indigenous ground forces.[50] Political objectives were achieved with almost no loss of American lives. Our SOF have now proven useful not only in counterinsurgency operations, but in restoring functioning governance, reducing corruption, negotiating with tribal leaders, working with local forces, and keeping the peace.

Yet, the tale is not over. The continued division and animosity among Iraqi factions leaves fertile ground for rebellion. After the Iraqi government declared victory over ISIS, the terrorists fled to isolated regions of the country, where they continue the fight. It appears they are also moving into Afghanistan with the support of Iran. As in Iraq, serious ethnic divisions make it seemingly impossible to reach a solution to the endless violence.[51] How can we solve this difficult and complex problem and bring peace to a chronically troubled region?

* * *

Political scientists say that democracies seldom fight other democracies. Although that statement often hinges on definitions—was 1914 Germany an autocracy because of the Kaiser or a democracy because of an elected *Reichstag*—it is still largely valid.[52] It has thus been a tenet of US diplomacy to urge the spread of democracy worldwide to foster peace. Former Deputy Secretary of State Richard L. Armitage noted: "every President except John Quincy Adams has been involved in the belief that the world is made better by a U.S. that is involved in the protection of human freedoms and human rights across the board." He added: "every postwar President has believed we have a duty to spread democracy."[53] At times that "duty" has been a major factor in foreign policy. After President George W. Bush invaded Iraq, he stated that "freedom and democracy will always and everywhere have greater appeal than the slogans of hatred."[54] That is an unquestioned assumption in the United States, and many presidents have believed that force was often necessary to produce freedom and democracy.

In the turmoil following World War II, President Harry Truman saw the emerging Cold War as a Manichean struggle. He stated in 1947 that the American way of life was based on the will of the majority, "and is distinguished by free institutions, representative government, free elections, guarantees of individual liberty, freedom of speech and religion and freedom from political oppression." He argued that people looked to the United States for support: "If we falter in our leadership, we may endanger the peace of the world."[55] This had been classical liberal ideology for the previous two centuries or more. Freedom equaled democracy and vice versa, and often it would take active intervention by outside powers to achieve those goals.

Six decades later, President Barack Obama accepted the Nobel Peace Prize in 2009 and gave a surprising speech. Like Truman and others before him, he extolled democracy, but argued that talking would not force terrorists to lay down their arms; rather, "force is sometimes necessary [and that] is not a call to cynicism—it is a recognition of history." He argued that "the instruments of war do have a role to play in preserving the peace" and that "force can be justified on humanitarian grounds, as it was in the Balkans, or in other places that have been scarred by war. . . . That is why all responsible nations must embrace the role that militaries with a clear mandate can play to keep the peace."[56] The key phrase was the requirement that militaries have "a clear mandate"—force can no longer be used without international approval, even if the motive for intervention is a humanitarian concern for human life.

There are lessons for the West in the still troubled regions of Africa, Asia, and the Middle East. Peace can be imposed on peoples with a history of endemic strife. Warlike tendencies can be curbed, and populations can be coerced into living in harmony with neighbors. Obviously, the excessive policies used in the past by colonial powers are unacceptable, but the end result of peace is so important that perhaps it might be acceptable to *impose* such a modern-day Pax Romana. In a remarkable report, Refugees International argues that the military capability of the West allows it to intervene in civil wars or to counter aggression with low risk to all involved. In fact, the authors argued that the West now has a "responsibility" to intervene in internal conflicts in order to save lives: "Our hypothesis is that new military technology and tactics can be used to increase the effectiveness and reduce the costs and risks of forcible humanitarian interventions. If such operations can be made more effective and less costly, the political barriers to undertaking them should be lower, making it easier for individual countries and the UN to fulfill their responsibility to protect."[57]

In March 2011 the Libyan situation had deteriorated to the point that the United Nations decided to take action. In approving a no-fly zone over Libya to be enforced by NATO airpower, Secretary-General Ban Ki-moon said the international community must "act with speed and decision" to save civilian lives: "The international community has acted together to avert a potential large-scale crisis. . . . In all my meetings, public and private, I took special care to stress that action under resolution 1973 is governed by an overriding objective—to save the lives of innocent civilians."[58]

One observer argues that the UN Security Council reinterpreted the law regarding the use of force. Muammar Gaddafi was abusing the rights of his people, and that brutality had reached an unacceptable level. The League of Arab States, however, rejected an invasion of Libya as a violation of the country's territorial integrity and therefore against the UN charter. Significantly, however, it went along with the idea of *air* invention. Angeline Lewis argues: "the initiating argument of the League of Arab States was that an air-only operation in the form of an enforceable no-fly zone would be lawful (and thus legitimate) because it preserved Libyan territorial integrity." Lewis notes that an air intervention was no different legally than a land invasion, but it was *perceived differently* by virtually the entire world. The UN Security Council implicitly agreed with this view, and when the air invention escalated from enforcing a no-fly zone to air strikes designed to help topple the regime, it continued to grant the operation legitimacy.[59] Another observer states that "never before was aerial intervention pursued so intentionally as a strategy—introducing ground forces into the Libyan civil war was proscribed not only by the desire to avoid another quagmire in the region, but explicitly by the very U. N. resolution that the operations were conducted to enforce."[60] This was an important precedent for the legitimization and legalization of force, specifically airpower, to achieve humane objectives in ways that traditional surface forces could not.

Four years later, the United Nations unanimously adopted resolution 2170 condemning the ISIS terrorist organization and calling on all UN members to "join the fight against the Islamic State in Syria and Iraq and redouble efforts to prevent further attacks by the militant group." The Security Council specifically authorized nations to combat ISIS in *whatever territory they were located.*[61] In December 2018 the UN announced an investigation into the "heinous" war crimes committed by ISIS in Iraq and elsewhere and asked for all member states to assist in bringing the culprits to justice.[62]

As noted, it was President George W. Bush's goal to establish democratic governments in Afghanistan and Iraq to encourage the spread of democracy throughout the region. This "inverse domino theory" imagined that nascent democracies would bring peace to a troubled area of the world, because the theory goes that democracies seldom fight each other. That was a useful vision, even if so badly implemented. Is there another way to achieve peace without the excesses incurred in the past? Richard Armitage, quoted earlier, notes the necessary preconditions for allowing democracy to grow: the rule of law, transparency, party-building, and a free press.[63] Also needed is security. This last is the greatest problem facing the peoples and governments of the Middle East today. Tens of thousands of people, mostly fellow Muslims, died at the hands of ISIS. This terrorist group and its vicious treatment of all dissenters had to be eradicated.

Given President Donald Trump's proactive strategy against ISIS, it appears he too believes that peace and democracy should sometimes be imposed on lawless areas. Yet, we need to think through such a strategy and its implementation. Is democracy a realistic goal in Iraq, Afghanistan, or Syria, and if so, how can it be achieved—bearing in mind that "freedom and democracy" have different meanings to Muslims than they do to those in the West. Indeed, such notions are antithetical to Muslims who believe in Sharia law. Are the Libyan and ISIS interventions, including United Nations mandates that *did not* include the country's occupation by foreigners, a model for the future?

There is a danger to such humanitarian interventions. Historian Michael Howard traced the history of Western liberal ideology over the past several centuries and argued this ideology took as a postulate that freedom led to democracy, and this in turn led to world prosperity.[64] Peace was a necessary prerequisite in this formula. Yet, there were numerous factors that led to war, and over time various culprits were named as impediments to peace: the aristocracy, militaries, balance of power strategists, imperialists, capitalists, fascists, communists, etc. There seemed an endless supply of such wreckers, but one by one they were forcibly confronted and pushed aside. Yet, global peace and its incumbent prosperity seemed always just out of reach. There was a dangerous paradox here: though peace was the desired end-state, enemies of peace were ever-present, and to overcome them force had to be employed. In short, those who were viscerally inclined to hate the use of force nonetheless found themselves tending to employ that force—if only to achieve peace. It was a dilemma President Obama noted in his Nobel Peace Prize speech quoted earlier; two months later he deployed 34,000 combat troops into Afghanistan to enforce peace there. For much of the world, Western intervention is viewed as a pretext for exploitation cloaked in hypocrisy. At best, Western liberal ideology has often been seen as simple naivete.

Also inherent in these ideals is the assumption that people everywhere and in every culture thirst for freedom, and that democracy is intrinsically viewed as a good. We now know, or at least we should, that this is not always the case. If jihadists today want a return to a caliphate and Sharia law, how are we to proceed? The pitfalls Howard mentions have an underlying theme—a cultural insensitivity to those we seek to help. As was discussed in an earlier chapter, the world does not always accept the goals, desires, and aspirations of the West.

* * *

In sum, our world at the end of the second decade of the twenty-first century involves peer competitors that must remain deterred. A major conventional war—or worse, one using nuclear weapons—must always remain a concern. It is probable that a major reason why nuclear weapons have not been employed since 1945 is that so many nations have them and state their intention of using them if attacked. Maintaining the nation's nuclear deterrent is essential.

Conventional strength is also necessary. Although the Cold War is over, the competition, to use a benign word, between the West and Russia and China is not. The past several years have seen those traditional adversaries increase their military budgets and assume a bellicose foreign policy. Conventional deterrence requires conventional strength.

Nonetheless, it is also true that the majority of conflicts that will see US involvement are punitive or UN-sanctioned protection missions. We should not rush into such missions that so often contain the danger of mission creep. One RAND study noted that a decade ago there were eighty-two insurgencies taking place around the world and thirty-five of those involved militant Islamists.[65] The majority of those eighty-two insurgencies did not involve the United States. Our interests, and especially our vital interests, were not at stake. In such conflicts we must not squander our political, economic, or moral capital; we must walk away and refuse to engage.

If, however, political leaders determine that US involvement is necessary, the conflicts in the Balkans, Middle East, and Libya are relevant because they reveal effective and efficient methods of achieving political goals at low risk. At such times, *United Nations approval and legitimacy should be a primary goal of*

Western leaders. That is what occurred in Libya in 2011 and against ISIS beginning in 2014. At the same time, modern technology and the constraints of law, culture, the media, geography, and economics necessitate that we adapt new methods, strategies, and doctrine. We cannot expect wars to be bloodless or without risk, but we can make them *less* bloody and *less* risky. It should always be the goal of a military planner—from any service—to devise strategies and tactics that achieve political goals with the least cost.[66] It should not be a planner's aim to deliberately deploy large numbers of America's sons and daughters to within range of enemy guns if an alternative is available. Airpower plus SOF plus indigenous ground forces plus robust intelligence, surveillance, and reconnaissance will not guarantee victory, but as the events since World War II have repeatedly demonstrated, neither will hundreds of thousands of boots on the ground.[67]

We must constantly search for new ways of fighting, and not merely using new weapons to fight in the old ways. We must use our great asymmetrical advantages to achieve our political goals at low cost and low risk.

Notes

1. Busting the Icon

1. The majority of his writings dealt with military history. For a discussion, see Peter Paret, "The Function of History in Clausewitz's Understanding of War," *Journal of Military History* 82 (October 2018): 1049–66.

2. Besides the fact that governments are not always reasonable, the trinity concept is difficult to understand, leading some to treat it as profound. For example: "But the continual twisting about that fills *On War* is not just a case of Clausewitz's being ponderous and wordy. Instead, the apparently irresolute to and fro of his prose conforms fully to his metaphor of theory floating among competing points of attraction." Alan Beyerchen, "Clausewitz, Nonlinearity, and the Unpredictability of War," *International Security* 17 (winter 1992/93): 85. Another observer sees it in theological terms, and, like the mystical "Holy Trinity" of Christian doctrine, it is not intended to be understood. Bruce Fleming, "Can Reading Clausewitz Save Us from Future Mistakes?" *Parameters* 32 (spring 2004): 67.

3. Carl von Clausewitz, *On War,* trans. and ed. Michael Howard and Peter Paret (Princeton, N.J.: Princeton Univ. Press, 1976), 580. Discussions of "total" or "absolute" war are relative. Although the Napoleonic wars were more total than those preceding them, they were less total than either world war of the twentieth century.

4. Although there are scattered references to Charles XII, Hannibal, Turenne, and others in *On War,* the majority of historical examples refer to Frederick the Great or Napoleon.

5. Clausewitz wrote in 1827 that Books I through VI were "a rather formless mass that must be thoroughly reworked once more"; Book VII was a "rough draft"; and Book VIII was a "rough working over of the raw material." Clausewitz, *On War,* 68–69.

6. One analyst refers to an Old and New Testament for the "old" ideas of Clausewitz and the new ones to be introduced in revisions. Antulio J. Echevarria II, *Clausewitz and Contemporary War* (New York: Oxford Univ. Press, 2007), 4–5. The use of a biblical reference is telling.

7. Clausewitz, *On War,* 313. He hints at the topic by referring to the "elemental fire of war" so fierce that "all forces press unremittingly toward the great decision."

8. Vanya Eftimova Bellinger, *Marie von Clausewitz: The Woman behind the Making of* On War (New York: Oxford Univ. Press, 2016), 232–33.

9. Azar Gat argues that *On War* may actually be more finished than supposed. He wants to date the damning 1830 note by Clausewitz regarding the unfinished nature of his work to 1810. See his *The Origins of Military Thought: From the Enlightenment to Clausewitz* (Oxford, UK: Clarendon Press, 1989), appendix.

10. Echevarria, *Clausewitz,* 191.

11. Clausewitz, *On War,* 608fn. Bernard Brodie stated in his introductory essay that the term "absolute war" is used far less "than others have in their translations" (47). Does this mean that Howard and Paret deliberately toned down Clausewitz's prose to make it more palatable to our sensitive ears? Or is Brodie claiming that earlier translators accentuated brutality? In either case, Brodie is telling us *On War* is as much an *interpretation* as it is a translation. Bellinger also argues that after Marie von Clausewitz's death, her brother undertook a new publication of *On War* that made significant changes regarding the primacy of politics in conflict, presumably because he thought that's what his brother-in-law actually believed. Bellinger, *Marie von Clausewitz,* 225–26.

12. Clausewitz, *On War,* xi. The editors do not address why Hahlweg's version should be considered accurate, since we do not have the manuscript upon which it was supposedly based.

13. One analyst uses his own translation throughout his book, hoping to eliminate some of these problems. But does that introduce others? Echevarria, *Clausewitz,* 8, fn1.

14. Some might argue that Napoleon benefited from advances in mobile artillery.

15. Julian S. Corbett, *Some Principles of Maritime Strategy* (Annapolis, Md.: Naval Institute Press, 1988), 94. Clausewitz makes a reference to naval tactics in Book III.

16. US Navy submarines sank 1,314 Japanese ships, 1,113 of which (85 percent) were merchantmen. Joel Ira Holwitt, *"Execute against Japan": The U.S. Decision to Conduct Unrestricted Submarine Warfare* (College Station: Texas A&M Univ. Press, 2009), 166. For the U-boat, an excellent website listing all Allied ships attacked, damaged, and sunk is https://uboat.net/allies/merchants/warships.html. (The number of Allied ships sunk was 3,137, of which 93 percent were merchants.)

17. Clausewitz, *On War,* 102.

18. Basil H. Liddell Hart, *The Ghost of Napoleon* (London: Faber and Faber, 1933), 120.

19. See for example, Hoffman Nickerson, *The Armed Horde, 1793–1939* (New York: Putnam's, 1942); Lynn Montross, *War Through the Ages* (New York: Harper, 1944); John U. Nef, *War and Human Progress* (Cambridge, Mass.: Harvard Univ. Press, 1952); Gordon Craig, *The Politics of the Prussian Army* (Oxford, UK: Oxford Univ. Press, 1956); R. Ernest and Trevor N. Dupuy, *The Military Heritage of America* (New York: McGraw-Hill, 1956); Walter Goerlitz, *The German General Staff, 1657–1945* (New York: Praeger, 1966); Russell F. Weigley, *The American Way of War: A History*

of United States Military Strategy and Policy (New York: Macmillan, 1973); Larry H. Addington, *The Patterns of War since the Eighteenth Century* (Bloomington: Indiana Univ. Press, 1984); and Brian Bond, *Pursuit of Victory: From Napoleon to Saddam Hussein* (New York: Oxford Univ. Press, 1996). In a typical assessment, Nickerson wrote that Clausewitz advocated a form of war that entailed "the utmost violence and the most fearful sacrifices" (52).

20. Clausewitz, *On War,* 258.

21. Ibid., 259–60, 262, 75.

22. Echevarria, *Clausewitz,* 6.

23. Clausewitz, *On War,* 92.

24. Ibid., 94–97, 529. This was classic Napoleonic strategy against the various coalitions arrayed against him.

25. Carl von Clausewitz, *Principles of War,* trans. Hans W. Gatzke (Harrisburg, Pa.: Military Service Publishing, 1942), 15.

26. Ibid., 45.

27. Ibid., 69.

28. Ibid., 99, 254. Emphasis in original. Paret states in his introductory essay to *On War* that "Clausewitz denied that limited aims justified a limitation of effort" (21). Howard echoes this conclusion in his own essay, stating: "there is no reason to suppose that Clausewitz would in his revision have abandoned any of the beliefs expressed in Book Four" (29). Azar Gat, who does not always agree with Howard and Paret, does so in this instance. See his *The Development of Military Thought in the Nineteenth Century* (Oxford, UK: Clarendon Press, 1992), 107.

29. Clausewitz, *On War,* Howard introduction, 36. See the essay on Foch by Etienne Mantoux in Edward Mead Earle's *Makers of Modern Strategy* (Princeton, N.J.: Princeton Univ. Press, 1944). When testifying before the commission on responsibility for the war, Ludendorff stated flatly: "The German General Staff is based upon the teachings of the great war philosopher Clausewitz." Major General Sir Frederic Maurice, *British Strategy: A Study of the Application of the Principles of War* (London: Constable, 1929), 45.

30. Christopher Bassford, "John Keegan and the Grand Tradition of Trashing Clausewitz: A Polemic," *War in History* 1 (November 1994): 319–36.

31. Arden Bucholz, *Hans Delbrück and the German Military Establishment: War Images in Conflict* (Iowa City: Univ. of Iowa Press, 1985), passim. On the other hand, Raymond Aron in *Clausewitz, Philosopher of War* (Englewood Cliffs, N.J.: Prentice-Hall, 1985), chapter 10, argues that Delbrück was the one mistaken. Michael Howard in his introductory essay also condemns von Moltke (the elder), von der Goltz, and Foch for misunderstanding Clausewitz (30–32).

32. See, for example, Michael I. Handel, ed., *Clausewitz and Modern Strategy* (London: Frank Cass, 1986), passim. For MacArthur, see John W. Spanier, *The Truman-MacArthur Controversy and the Korean War* (Cambridge, Mass.: Belknap, 1959). The last five names were listed by Echevarria as having "misunderstood" Clausewitz. Echevarria, *Clausewitz,* 58, fn6.

33. Ralph Peters, in review of Bassford's *Clausewitz in English, Parameters* 24 (winter 1994/95): 148.

34. Jon Tetsuro Sumida, *Decoding Clausewitz: A New Approach to* On War (Lawrence: Univ. Press of Kansas, 2008), xvii, 181.

35. Colonel Harry G. Summers Jr., *On Strategy: A Critical Analysis of the Vietnam War* (Novato, Calif.: Presidio, 1982), 25, 59, 77, 88, 104, 119, 123–24. Ironically, one critique of Summers accused *him* of misreading Clausewitz. Fleming, "Can Reading Clausewitz Save Us from Future Mistakes?," 65.

36. Summers, *On Strategy,* 12, 19, 22, 25, 28.

37. Faculty instructor notes handed out for teaching the lessons on Clausewitz at the US National War College assert that if instructors could get students to understand the points made in these notes, "maybe they could be the first generation of leaders not to misinterpret the master." Teaching notes provided by a NWC faculty member in 2006.

38. Michael Howard, *Clausewitz* (Oxford, UK: Oxford Univ. Press, 1983), 46.

39. Echevarria, *Clausewitz,* 143.

40. General Wesley K. Clark, *Waging Modern War: Bosnia, Kosovo, and the Future of Combat* (New York: PublicAffairs, 2001), 183.

41. To track this, see the Gallup Poll website: http://poll.gallup.com/.

42. Martin Blumenson, "A Deaf Ear to Clausewitz: Allied Operational Objectives in World War II," *Parameters* 23 (summer 1993): 16–27.

43. General Gordon R. Sullivan and Colonel James M. Dubik, "War in the Information Age," pamphlet (Carlisle Barracks, Pa.: US Army War College, Strategic Studies Institute, 1994), 12.

44. General Gordon R. Sullivan and Colonel James M. Dubik, "Envisioning Future War," pamphlet (Fort Leavenworth, Kans.: US Army Command and General Staff College, 1995), 23.

45. Thomas Bruscino, "Naturally Clausewitzian: U.S. Army Theory and Education from Reconstruction to the Interwar Years," *Journal of Military History* 77 (October 2013): 1274–75.

46. For a discussion of centers of gravity, see Echevarria, *Clausewitz,* chapter 8.

47. US Army, Field Manual 1, "The Army," June 2005, paragraph 3-27.

48. US Army, Field Manual 3-0, "Operations," June 2001, paragraph 1-36.

49. US Marine Corps, Fleet Marine Field Manual 1, "Warfighting," March 1989, 11.

50. Ralph Peters, "In Praise of Attrition," *Parameters* 32 (summer 2004): 24–32.

51. Christopher Bassford traces the influence of Clausewitz in the US Army's school system in *Clausewitz in English: The Reception of Clausewitz in Britain and America, 1875–1945* (Oxford, UK: Oxford Univ. Press, 1994).

52. Lieutenant Colonel Andrew F. Krepinevich Jr., *The Army and Vietnam* (Baltimore, Md.: Johns Hopkins Univ. Press, 1986), passim.

53. Gregory A. Daddis, *Westmoreland's War: Reassessing American Strategy in Vietnam* (New York: Oxford Univ. Press, 2014), 171–72, 183.

54. For an excellent discussion of how this paradigm succeeded in Afghanistan, see Richard B. Andres, Craig Wills, and Thomas E. Griffith Jr., "Winning with Allies: The Strategic Value of the Afghan Model," *International Security* 30 (winter 2005/2006): 124–60.

55. See updated statistics at https://www.statista.com/statistics/262894/western-coalition-soldiers-killed-in-afghanistan/.

56. General Wesley Clark was reportedly pushed into early retirement after Kosovo because of his mistaken belief that a massive ground invasion of Serbia was necessary to achieve victory. See Peter J. Boyer, "General Clark's Battles," *New Yorker*, November 17, 2003, 70–88.

57. Niccolò Machiavelli, *The Ruler* (London: The Bodley Head, 1954), 34.

58. See the interview with *Atlantic Monthly* defense correspondent James Fallows at http://www.pbs.org/wgbh/pages/frontline/shows/invasion/interviews/fallows.html.

59. Evan Thomas and John Barry, "Anatomy of a Revolt," *Newsweek*, April 24, 2006, 28–32; and Michael Duffy, "The Revolt of the Generals," *Time*, April 24, 2006, 41–42.

60. See, for example, Thomas E. Ricks, "Officers Question Visibility of Army in Iraq," *Washington Post*, July 26, 2004, 1; and Greg Jaffe, "As Chaos Mounts in Iraq, U.S. Army Rethinks Its Future," *Wall Street Journal*, December 8, 2004, 1.

61. For an excellent discussion of how airpower plus SOF plus indigenous Kurdish forces overcame twelve Iraqi divisions in northern Iraq, see Richard Andres, "The Afghan Model in Northern Iraq," *Journal of Strategic Studies* 29 (June 2006): 395–422.

62. In testimony before the Senate, then-CENTCOM commander General John P. Abizaid stated: "Our long-term strategy in the region will not likely be furthered by the continuing presence of a large U.S. military footprint in the Middle East." See his testimony from March 2006 at https://www.cbsnews.com/news/general-grilled-by-congress/.

63. Clausewitz refers to Spain and the insurgency briefly, but there is no discussion or insight. Clausewitz, *On War*, 220, 350, 592, 615.

64. Ibid., 487. Emphasis in original.

65. It is surprising that Clausewitz never mentions in his lengthy Book VI ("Defense") the serious impact that guerrillas can have on an occupying army's supply lines, especially given that such effects were demonstrated so dramatically in Spain and Russia.

66. Michael Howard makes a cute comment regarding the common assertion that Clausewitz would have said this or that had he lived to revise his book: "an argument frequently used by admirers of Clausewitz—the present writer not excepted—who find aspects of his work not wholly to their liking." Clausewitz, *On War*, 33.

67. John Keegan, *A History of Warfare* (New York: Knopf, 1993), chapter 1, passim.

68. A similar thesis is advanced by Martin Van Creveld. In his *The Transformation of War* (New York: Free Press, 1991), ix, he writes: "contemporary 'strategic' thought . . . is fundamentally flawed; and, in addition, is rooted in a 'Clausewitzian' world-picture that is either obsolete or wrong." Clausewitz backers were offended. In reviewing

Van Creveld's book, Harry Summers confronted Van Creveld's ideas by attacking him as being "known for his ill-manners and overweening arrogance" and someone who "never heard a shot fired in anger." *Strategic Review* 19 (spring 1991): 58–60.

69. Clausewitz, *On War,* 86.

70. Michael Howard opined: "Fascists regarded war not just as an instrument of policy but as a thoroughly desirable activity in itself." Michael Howard, *The Invention of Peace: Reflections on War and International Order* (London: Profile, 2001), 68.

71. Eric Carlton, *War and Ideology* (Savage, Md.: Barnes and Noble, 1990), 17. Emphasis in original.

72. Elizabeth Rosenthal and David Sanger, "US Plane in China after It Collides with Chinese Jet," *New York Times,* April 2, 2001, 1. See also http://www.cnn.com/2001/US/04/01/us.china.plane.02/index.html.

73. The charge that a slow and cumbersome four-engine cargo plane could ram a small and nimble jet fighter is risible.

74. Michael R. Gordon, "Collision with China: 'A Dangerous Game,'" *New York Times,* April 3, 2001, 1. For a provocative discussion of how the unique Chinese culture impacts their military strategy, see William H. Mott and Jae Chang Kim, *The Philosophy of Chinese Military Culture: Shih vs. Li* (New York: Macmillan, 2006).

75. Of course, because a decision is rational does not mean it is correct. We should not assume rationality in our adversaries that may not exist.

2. Is War an Instrument of Policy?

1. "Rage over Cartoons Perplexes Denmark," *Los Angeles Times,* February 9, 2006, 1.

2. Although the Vatican called for a boycott of the film, it had little effect.

3. In February 1989, Iran's Ayatollah Khomeini issued a death sentence on novelist Salman Rushdie, a British citizen, for the alleged crime of blasphemy against Islam for his book *The Satanic Verses.* Although Rushdie remains alive, several others associated with the publication of his novel were murdered. For the tale of his thirteen years spent in hiding, see Salman Rushdie, *Joseph Anton: A Memoir* (New York: Random House, 2012).

4. It is small consolation that adversaries are similarly obtuse regarding how we think.

5. For these various translations, see Colonel J. J. Graham, *On War* (London: Cassell, 1918); Anatol Rapoport, *On War* (New York: Penguin, 1982); Otto J. Jolles, *On War* (New York: Modern Library, 1943); Michael Howard and Peter Paret, trans. and ed., *On War* (Princeton: Princeton Univ. Press, 1976); Major General T. D. Pilcher, *War According to Clausewitz* (London: Cassell, 1918); A.M.E. Maguire, *General von Clausewitz on War* (London: William Clowes and Sons, 1909); and Gordon Craig, *The Politics of the Prussian Army* (New York: Oxford Univ. Press, 1956).

6. See, for example, Ralph Peters, "In Praise of Attrition," *Parameters* 32 (summer 2004): 24–32; and Colonel Bruce J. Reider, "Strategic Realignment: Ends, Ways, and Means in Iraq," *Parameters* 35 (winter 2007/2008): 46–57.

7. Christopher Bassford, "John Keegan and the Grand Tradition of Trashing Clausewitz: A Polemic," *War in History* 1 (November 1994): 326.

8. Clausewitz spent little time discussing what he termed "partisan warfare," and his comments were derogatory. He does not mention at all such operations by the Russian guerrillas attacking French supply lines and only barely refers to Spain.

9. Richard Wrangham and Dale Peterson, *Demonic Males: Apes and the Origins of Human Violence* (Boston: Houghton Mifflin, 1996), chapter 1. Research reveals that most mammals practice this system of "propagating their genes" by murdering the offspring of male competitors. Carl Zimmer, "Unraveling Why Some Mammals Kill off Infants," *New York Times,* November 13, 2014, http://www.nytimes.com/2014/11/13/science/unraveling-why-some-mammals-kill-off-infants.html?_r=0.

10. Wrangham and Peterson, *Demonic Males,* chapter 1.

11. Stephen Peter Rosen, *War and Human Nature* (Princeton, N.J.: Princeton Univ. Press, 2005), 74.

12. Ibid., 135–36.

13. Thomas E. Ricks, *Fiasco: The American Military Adventure in Iraq* (New York: Penguin, 2006), 238.

14. Amy Chua, *Political Tribes: Group Instinct and the Fate of Nations* (New York: Penguin, 2018).

15. Ibid., 2.

16. Ibid., 54–55.

17. Ibid., 60.

18. For discussions, see Lawrence H. Keeley, *War before Civilization: The Myth of the Peaceful Savage* (New York: Oxford Univ. Press, 1996); Steven A. Le Blanc, *Constant Battles: The Myth of the Peaceful, Noble Savage* (New York: St. Martin's, 2003); John Keegan, *A History of Warfare* (New York: Knopf, 1993); Keith F. Otterbein, *How Wars Began* (College Station: Texas A&M Univ. Press, 2004); and Azar Gat, *War in Human Civilization* (New York: Oxford Univ. Press, 2006).

19. Wrangham and Peterson, *Demonic Males,* chapter 4, "Raiding."

20. Keegan, *History of Warfare,* and Gat, *War and Civilization,* argue this position particularly well.

21. It is interesting that a near-contemporary of Clausewitz, philosopher Immanuel Kant, wrote: "Often war is waged only in order to show valor; thus an inner dignity is ascribed to war itself, and even some philosophers have praised it as an ennoblement of humanity." Quoted in Sainab Bahrani, *Rituals of War: The Body and Violence in Mesopotamia* (New York: Zone Books, 2008), 131.

3. The Mutable Nature of War

1. Carl von Clausewitz, *On War,* trans. and ed. by Michael Howard and Peter Paret (Princeton, N.J.: Princeton Univ. Press, 1976), 77, 87, 95, 101, 122, 231, 259. Emphasis in original.

2. John A. Lynn, *Battle: A History of Combat and Culture* (Boulder, Colo.: Westview, 2003), xv.

3. Victor Davis Hanson, *Carnage and Culture: Landmark Battles in the Rise of Western Power* (New York: Doubleday, 2001), 7.

4. Martin Van Creveld, *The Culture of War* (New York: Ballantine, 2008), xv and chapter 6.

5. Basil H. Liddell Hart, *Thoughts on War* (London: Faber and Faber, 1944), 158.

6. Adrian R. Lewis, *The American Culture of War* (New York: Routledge, 2007), 40.

7. US Army, Field Manual 100-5, "Operations," June 1993, 1–3.

8. US Army and Marine Corps, Field Manual 3-24/MCWP 3-33.5, "Counterinsurgency," December 2006, 1.

9. US Marine Corps, Fleet Marine Field Manual 1, "Warfighting," March 1989, chapter 1, "The Nature of War."

10. "Battle Plan under Fire," an interview with Lieutenant General Paul Van Riper, NOVA, August 2002, http://www.pbs.org/wgbh/nova/wartech/nature.html.

11. "Panel Touts Robots' Future Combat Role," *Virginian-Pilot,* January 28, 2009, 13. The speaker was General James Mattis, a secretary of defense under President Donald Trump.

12. For an excellent overview, see Lance E. Davis and Stanley L. Engerman, *Naval Blockades in Peace and War: An Economic History since 1750* (New York: Cambridge Univ. Press, 2006).

13. A. C. Bell, *A History of the Blockade of Germany, 1914–1918* (London: HMSO, 1937), 672. See also Louis Guichard, *The Naval Blockade, 1914–1918* (New York: Appleton, 1930), 294, who notes the blockade remained in place for two years after the Armistice and continued to starve Germans to pressure them into signing a peace treaty and making required reparations payments.

14. UNICEF, "Child and Maternal Mortality Survey, 1999, Preliminary Report" (New York: UNICEF, July 1999), 10; Fourth Freedom, "Morbidity and Mortality among Iraqi Children" (Washington, D.C.: Fourth Freedom, March 1999), 1.

15. David E. Weekman, "Sanctions: The Invisible Hand of Statecraft," *Strategic Review* 26 (winter 1998): 40.

16. John Mueller and Karl Mueller, "Sanctions of Mass Destruction," *Foreign Affairs* 78 (May/June 1999): 43–53.

17. Daniel T. Kuehl and Robert A. Miller, "Cyberspace and the 'First Battle' in 21st-Century War," *Defense Horizons* (September 2009): 3.

18. Rebecca Grant, "The Cyber Menace," *Air Force Magazine,* March 2009, 24–28.

19. "Taiwanese under Siege from Blitz of Chinese Cyberattacks," *Asia Times,* April 6, 2018, 6.

20. Martin C. Libicki, *Cyberspace in Peace and War* (Annapolis, Md.: Naval Institute Press, 2016), 14–18.

21. John Rollins and Clay Wilson, "Terrorist Capabilities for Cyberattack: Overview and Policy Issues," Congressional Research Service report (Washington, D.C.: Congressional Research Service, January 22, 2007), 1–4, 10–11; and "Homeland Security:

DHS's Progress and Challenges in Key Areas of Maritime, Aviation, and Cybersecurity," Government Accountability Office report GAO-10-106 (Washington, D.C.: GPO, December 2, 2009), 8, 18. Note these warnings were before the Stuxnet attack.

22. "Electric Grid Cybersecurity," Congressional Research Service report (Washington, D.C.: Congressional Research Service, September 4, 2018), passim.

23. Bryan Krekel, "Capability of the People's Republic of China to Conduct Cyber Warfare and Computer Network Exploitation," US-China Economic and Security Review Commission report (Washington, D.C.: US-China Economic and Security Review Commission, October 9, 2009), 6; Libicki, *Cyberspace in Peace and War,* chapter 8.

24. Richard B. Andres, "Air Power and Cyber," in *Routledge Handbook of Air Power,* ed. John Andreas Olsen (London: Routledge, 2018), 207.

25. Deb Riechman, "Intel Official: Cyber Threat Warnings 'Blinking Red,'" Associated Press, July 16, 2018, https://www.militarytimes.com/flashpoints/2018/07/15/intel-official-cyber-threat-warnings-blinking-red/?utm_source=Sailthru&utm_medium=email&utm_campaign=ebb%2016.07.18&utm_term=Editorial%20-%20Early%20Bird%20Brief.

26. Data derived from Gulf War Air Power Survey and various USAFE, AFCENT, and USAF fact sheets. For example, the USAF flew 37,567 combat sorties in DESERT STORM, 1,066 in DELIBERATE FORCE, over 189,000 in NORTHERN and SOUTHERN WATCH, 24,345 in OEF/OIF during 2005, 38,026 in OEF/OIF during 2008, etc.

27. The program for arming Predator UAVs was begun by the USAF in 2000, and the CIA joined the effort soon afterward. For the background, see Thomas H. Kean (chairman), "The 9/11 Commission Report" (Washington, D.C.: GPO, July 22, 2004), 210–13. For the Predator's effectiveness against terrorists, see Michael Evans, "Death from Above: How Predator Is Taking Its Toll on al Qaeda," *London Times,* January 3, 2009, http://www.timesonline.co.uk/tol/news/world/middle_east/article5435471.ece. For updated statistics on drone missions and results, see the website of the Bureau of Investigative Journalism at http://www.thebureauinvestigates.com/category/projects/drones/. The MQ-1 Predator was retired in July 2018 after having flown for seventeen years in constant combat—over 135,000 sorties. Brian W. Everstine, "Elegy for the Predator," *Air Force Magazine,* July 2018, 18–22.

28. Four different agencies, worldwide, have compiled statistics on drone strikes, but all are fairly consistent. Avery Plaw, Matthew S. Fricker, and Carlos R. Colon, *The Drone Debate* (New York: Rowman and Littlefield, 2016), 30, 38.

29. Predator/Reaper operations have dual control: they are launched, recovered, and maintained by teams in theater, but during the flight itself they usually are controlled from bases in the United States.

30. Major General Charles J. Dunlap Jr., "Lawfare: A Decisive Element of 21st-Century Conflicts?" *Joint Force Quarterly* 54 (3rd quarter 2009): 36.

31. Human Rights Watch, "Off Target: The Conduct of the War and Civilian Casualties in Iraq" (New York: Human Rights Watch, 2003), 13.

32. Sarah B. Sewall, *Chasing Success: Air Force Efforts to Reduce Civilian Harm* (Maxwell AFB, Ala.: Air Univ. Press, 2016), vii. Sewall notes, however, that not all nations have followed the USAF lead. Russian air operations in Chechnya have been utterly devastating, and the capital city of Grozny has been labeled "the most destroyed city on earth" (ibid., 15).

33. The Iraq Body Count website updates its figures at www.iraqbodycount.org. The overall numbers could be considered high because IBC does not always differentiate between civilians killed by war or by other violence. For example, a businessman killed and robbed in a drive-by shooting in Baghdad on February 27, 2018, is considered war-related, but is it instead merely a homicide?

34. "Afghanistan: Protection of Civilians in Armed Conflict," United Nations Assistance Mission in Afghanistan report (New York: United Nations Assistance Mission in Afghanistan, February 15, 2018), https://unama.unmissions.org/afghanistan-10000-civilian-casualties-2017-un-report-suicide-attacks-and-ieds-caused-high-number.

35. Eric V. Larson and Bogdan Savych, *Misfortunes of War: Press and Public Reactions to Civilian Deaths in Wartime* (Santa Monica, Calif.: RAND Corp., 2007), 2–3.

4. Starting with a Blank Sheet

1. For a good account, see Pierre Razoux, *The Iran-Iraq War* (Cambridge, Mass.: Belknap, 2015).

2. Diane T. Putney, *Airpower Advantage: Planning the Gulf War Air Campaign, 1989–1991* (Washington, D.C.: Air Force History and Museums Program, 2004), 332; Thomas A. Keaney and Eliot A. Cohen, *Revolution in Warfare? Air Power in the Persian Gulf* (Annapolis, Md.: Naval Institute Press, 1993), 92–93.

3. Michael R. Gordon and Lieutenant General Bernard E. Trainor, *The Generals' War: The Inside Story of the Conflict in the Gulf* (Boston: Little, Brown, 1995), 283–88.

4. General Merrill A. McPeak made this claim in his DoD news briefing of March 15, 1991. A copy of that briefing can be found in his, *Selected Works 1990–1994* (Maxwell AFB, Ala.: Air Univ. Press, 1995), 15–50.

5. The Thanh Hoa Bridge near Hanoi was a distressingly difficult target to hit. Over a period of three years the US Air Force flew 873 sorties against the bridge, losing eleven aircraft, and never dropped a span. In April 1972, laser-guided bombs were used for the first time: five aircraft dropped the bridge with no losses. Wayne Thompson, *To Hanoi and Back: The USAF and North Vietnam, 1966–1973* (Washington, D.C.: Air Force History and Museums Program, 2000), 234–35.

6. JDAM and the Small Diameter Bomb—a glide bomb with a 250-pound warhead—are GPS guided and individually targeted from the cockpit; the latter is reported to have better than three-meter accuracy.

7. Thomas R. Phillips, ed., *The Roots of Strategy* (Harrisburg, Pa.: Military Service Publishing, 1940), 22.

8. The definitive work on the history of principles of war, and on which this sec-

tion draws heavily, is John I. Alger, *The Quest for Victory: The History of the Principles of War* (Westport, Conn.: Greenwood, 1982).

9. Adapted from Alger, *Quest for Victory,* 22–23.

10. J. L. Harsh, "Battlesword and Rapier: Clausewitz, Jomini, and the American Civil War," *Military Affairs* 38 (October 1974): 133–38. The best treatment of Jomini is by John Shy in Peter Paret, ed., *Makers of Modern Strategy: From Machiavelli to the Nuclear Age* (Princeton, N.J.: Princeton Univ. Press, 1986). For an update on Jomini's influence, see Carol Reardon, *With a Sword in One Hand and Jomini in the Other: The Problem of Military Thought in the Civil War North* (Chapel Hill: Univ. of North Carolina Press, 2012).

11. For an overview of staff development, see J. D. Hittle, *The Military Staff* (Harrisburg, Pa.: Military Service Publishing, 1961); for the managerial and administrative revolutions, see Walter Millis, *Arms and Men: A Study of American Military History* (New York: Putnam, 1956).

12. Alan Clark, *The Donkeys* (New York: William Morrow, 1962).

13. J.F.C. Fuller, *The Army in My Time* (London: Rich and Cowan, 1935), 53.

14. Alger, *Quest for Victory,* 232–33.

15. Ibid., 241.

16. Ibid., 253.

17. Ibid., 255–56.

18. Robert Frank Futrell, *Ideas, Concepts, Doctrine: Basic Thinking in the United States Air Force, 1907–1960,* 2 vols. (Maxwell AFB, Ala.: Air Univ. Press, 1989), 1, 369. The references are to Brigadier General "Billy" Mitchell, General of the Air Force "Hap" Arnold, and Major General Hugh J. Knerr.

19. US Air Force, Air Force Doctrine Document 1, "Air Force Basic Doctrine," February 27, 2015, 45–75.

20. The problem of IEDs (improvised explosive devices) in Iraq led to an increased use of airlift to avoid the truck columns that were favorite targets of jihadists.

21. For a definitive examination, see Martin C. Libicki, *Cyberspace in Peace and War* (Annapolis, Md.: Naval Institute Press, 2016).

22. Rachel Martin, "Sounding the Alarm about a New Russian Cyber Threat," National Public Radio, *Morning Edition,* April 24, 2018.

23. For an important discussion of this emerging condition, see William C. Banks and Stephen Dycus, *Soldiers on the Home Front: The Domestic Role of the American Military* (Cambridge, Mass.: Harvard Univ. Press, 2016).

24. Steven T. Ross, *European Diplomatic History, 1789–1815: France against Europe* (Malabar, Fla.: Krieger, 1981), chapter 11; Christopher D. Hall, *British Strategy in the Napoleonic War, 1803–15* (Manchester, UK: Manchester Univ. Press, 1992), passim.

25. L. Paul Bremer, head of the Coalition Provisional Authority, was a career diplomat in command of all diplomatic and military forces in Iraq, but his tenure was a disaster.

26. See the 2006 Quadrennial Defense Review report, http://www.defenselink.mil/qdr/report/Report20060203.pdf.

27. Norman H. Schwarzkopf with Peter Petre, *It Doesn't Take a Hero* (New York: Bantam, 1992), 479. Horner told this anecdote when visiting the School of Advanced Airpower Studies in 1993.

28. This is articulated in Basil H. Liddell Hart, *The Way to Win Wars: The Strategy of Indirect Approach* (London: Faber and Faber, 1929).

29. Robert D. Heinl Jr., *Dictionary of Military and Naval Quotations* (Annapolis, Md.: Naval Institute Press, 1966), 17.

30. For the definitive account of this legislation's history, see James R. Locher III, *Victory on the Potomac: The Goldwater-Nichols Act Unifies the Pentagon* (College Station: Texas A&M Univ. Press, 2004).

31. "'Nuke Sniffer' Fleet's Availability Too Low," *Air Force Magazine*, July 2018, 16.

32. For a discussion, see Robert P. Haffa Jr. and Jasper Welch, "Command and Control Arrangements for the Attack of Time-Sensitive Targets," Northrop Grumman Analysis Center paper (Roslyn, Va.: Northrop Grumman, November 2005).

33. Vice Admiral Arthur K. Cebrowski and John J. Garstka, "Network-Centric Warfare: Its Origins and Future," *US Naval Institute Proceedings* 124 (January 1998): 28–35.

34. There are a number of websites listing such data; for example, http://globalfirepower.com.

35. The Civil Reserve Air Fleet was also activated—civilian airliners under the control of the USAF—to assist with this massive airlift.

36. Eliot A. Cohen, ed., *Gulf War Air Power Survey*, 5 vols. (Washington, D.C.: GPO, 1993), 3:177–86.

37. The Focused Lethality Munition's goal is to not cause "any significant damage" outside 100 feet of detonation. It relies almost entirely on blast effect rather than fragmentation to neutralize its target. Amy Butler, "Sharpening Focus," *Aviation Week and Space Technology*, February 26, 2007, 28. See also the Global Security website at https://www.globalsecurity.org/military/systems/munitions/sdb-flm.htm.

38. Moreover, it is the nature of PGMs that they are more accurate when dropped from medium to high altitude, above enemy ground fire.

5. Second Fronts

1. Other second front operations include British operations against the French in North America in the eighteenth century, Bonaparte's invasion of Egypt in 1798, Allenby and Lawrence in the Middle East during World War I, the Salonika front in World War I, and the Allied landings in Sicily and Italy in 1943.

2. One of Alcibiades's biographers describes him as "Vicious, insolent, adorable, detestable, brilliant and fickle, with the face and body of a god and the wit of Aristophanes, he was the very incarnation of the spirit of Athens." E. F. Benson, *The Life of Alcibiades: The Idol of Athens* (New York: D. Appleton, 1929), 47.

3. Thucydides, *The Landmark Thucydides: A Comprehensive Guide to the Peloponnesian War*, ed. Robert B. Strassler (New York: Free Press, 1996), 367–68.

Thucydides admits he was not present for most such speeches, "so my habit has been to make the speakers say what was in my opinion demanded of them by the various occasions" (15). In other words, Thucydides invented the speeches. It is wise to take the words of Nicias and others throughout this account with some reserve, although their general tenor may be accurate.

4. Benson, *The Life of Alcibiades,* 141.

5. Thucydides, *The Landmark Thucydides,* 375.

6. P. J. Rhodes, *Alcibiades* (London: Pen and Sword, 2011), 46.

7. It has never been determined whether the charges had validity—Alcibiades was infamous for his lavish and decadent lifestyle—but he was not a fool, and the crimes he was charged with were punishable by death.

8. John R. Hale, *Lords of the Sea: The Epic Story of the Athenian Navy and the Birth of Democracy* (New York: Viking, 2009), 194.

9. Victor Davis Hanson, *Warfare and Agriculture in Classical Greece* (Berkeley: Univ. of California Press, 1998), concluding chapter.

10. John Aberth, *Plague in World History* (Lanham, Md.: Rowman and Littlefield, 2011), 6–9, 76.

11. Donald Kagan, *The Fall of the Athenian Empire* (Ithaca, N.Y.: Cornell Univ. Press, 1987), 2–3.

12. Hans Delbrück, *History of the Art of War: Within the Framework of Political History,* 4 vols. (Westport, Conn.: Greenwood, 1975–85), 1:143.

13. Thucydides, *The Landmark Thucydides,* 387.

14. Nic Fields, *Syracuse 415–413 BC: Destruction of the Athenian Imperial Fleet* (Oxford, UK: Osprey, 2008), 34.

15. Hale, *Lords of the Sea,* 189.

16. Thucydides, *The Landmark Thucydides,* 434.

17. Richard Mansfield Haywood, *The Ancient World* (New York: David McKay, 1971), 240.

18. Benson, *The Life of Alcibiades,* 307–11.

19. For the background, see David Gates, *The Spanish Ulcer: A History of the Peninsular War* (New York: Norton, 1986), chapter 1.

20. David Chandler, *The Campaigns of Napoleon: The Mind and Method of History's Greatest Soldier* (New York: Macmillan, 1966), 620.

21. At the same time, Britain launched the largest amphibious assault in history to that point at Walcheren in Holland. Over 40,000 troops landed in the Scheldt estuary to capture Napoleon's major port at Antwerp. The operation was a disaster. Although only 106 men were killed in fighting, the British lost nearly 8,000 dead to disease before the force was ignominiously withdrawn. Martin R. Howard, *Walcheren 1809: The Scandalous Destruction of a British Army* (London: Pen and Sword, 2012), 201.

22. Moore was killed during the evacuation, but most of his army—26,000 men—escaped. See Richard Humble, *Napoleon's Peninsular Marshals* (New York: Taplinger, 1973), 87–96; and Joshua Moon, *Wellington's Two-Front War: The Peninsular Campaigns, at Home and Abroad, 1808–1814* (Norman: Univ. of Oklahoma Press, 2011), 26–28.

23. Christopher D. Hall, *Wellington's Navy: Sea Power and the Peninsular War, 1807–1814* (London: Chatham, 2004), 70–74.

24. Saragossa fell after a two-month siege marked by house-to-house fighting and a casualty toll of over 50,000 Spanish dead.

25. Moon, *Wellington's Two-Front War,* 54–55, 221.

26. Of the thirty-three ships of the line destroyed or captured by Nelson at Trafalgar, fifteen were Spanish. Hall, *Wellington's Navy,* 38.

27. Gates, *The Spanish Ulcer,* 9–10.

28. Ibid., 33.

29. Ronald Fraser, *Napoleon's Cursed War: Popular Resistance in the Spanish Peninsular War* (London: Verso, 2008), xi–xiii.

30. For a good evaluation of the various French commanders, see Humble, *Napoleon's Peninsular Marshals.*

31. Moon describes the labyrinthine tangle of the British military system. To give two examples: "A single request for reinforcements required the correspondence and approval of no fewer than six cabinet ministers and the commander in chief" (Moon, *Wellington's Two-Front War,* 9). Of Wellington's eight primary staff officers, seven answered directly to London and not to him (ibid., 10).

32. Napoleon chose his marshals and generals based largely on merit; Wellington had no input into which commanders he was sent—all such personnel decisions were made in London.

33. Moon, *Wellington's Two-Front War,* 95.

34. Gates, *The Spanish Ulcer,* 220. Another source termed the French command system "military anarchy." Humble, *Napoleon's Peninsular Marshals,* 7.

35. Gates, *The Spanish Ulcer,* 35.

36. Huw J. Davies, "Diplomats as Spymasters: A Case Study of the Peninsular War, 1809–1813," *Journal of Military History* 76 (January 2012): 37–68.

37. Hall, *Wellington's Navy,* 137.

38. Ibid., 1–2.

39. Stalemate was caused by increased firepower from rapid-fire artillery and machine guns. The standard method of achieving mobility, cavalry, had no chance in the face of such firepower. In addition, the introduction of the airplane for reconnaissance meant that tactical surprise became increasingly difficult to achieve. Finally, the growth of huge armies ensured an endless supply of troops to feed the meat grinder. The result was trench warfare and stalemate.

40. In current US parlance, the First Lord was the secretary of the navy, and the First Sea Lord was the chief of naval operations.

41. Robin Prior, *Gallipoli: The End of the Myth* (New Haven, Conn.: Yale Univ. Press, 2009), 10.

42. Basil H. Liddell Hart, *A History of the World War* (Boston: Little, Brown, 1935), 185.

43. Admiral Fisher had directed a study a decade prior that argued a navy-only operation to open the strait was impossible: troops were essential. Obviously, Fisher

changed his mind due to Churchill's arguments. Dan van der Vat, *The Dardanelles Disaster: Winston Churchill's Greatest Failure* (London: Duckworth Overlook, 2009), 20.

44. Bulgaria had attempted to capture the Dardanelles in 1913. This experience caused the Turks to beef up their defenses in the area, much to the Allies' detriment in 1915. Edward J. Erickson, *Gallipoli: The Ottoman Campaign* (Barnsley, UK: Pen and Sword, 2010), 5–9.

45. Van der Vat, *The Dardanelles Disaster,* 99.

46. Prior, *Gallipoli,* 45.

47. The trawlers were fishing boats, crewed by civilians, commandeered by the Admiralty; regular minesweepers were thought better used in the North Sea and English Channel.

48. Van der Vat, *The Dardanelles Disaster,* 85.

49. The troops sent to Gallipoli included French, British, and British Commonwealth forces, notably the ANZAC Corps, which was comprised of Australian and New Zealand divisions. For a breakdown, see Prior, *Gallipoli,* 93.

50. Liddell Hart, *A History of the World War,* 187.

51. Van der Vat, *The Dardanelles Disaster,* 136. Erickson argues that Allied victory would also have meant there would have been no Russian Revolution and no Versailles Treaty to help prompt World War II. Erickson, *Gallipoli,* xiv.

52. Major General Donald M. Weller, "The Development of Naval Gunfire Support in World War Two," in *Assault from the Sea: Essays on the History of Amphibious Warfare,* ed. Lieutenant Colonel Merrill L. Bartlett (Annapolis, Md.: Naval Institute Press, 1983), 267.

53. Van der Vat, *The Dardanelles Disaster,* ix.

54. Liddell Hart, *A History of the World War,* 187.

55. Ibid., 183.

56. Prior, *Gallipoli,* 38.

57. Van der Vat, *The Dardanelles Disaster,* 122.

58. Basil H. Liddell Hart, *The War in Outline* (London: Faber and Faber, 1936), 87.

59. US State Department, *The Conferences at Washington, 1941–1942, and Casablanca, 1943,* Foreign Relations of the United States (Washington, D.C.: GPO, 1968), 214.

60. Maurice Matloff and Edwin Snell, *Strategic Planning for Coalition Warfare, 1941–1942,* United States Army in World War II (Washington, D.C.: Office of the Chief of Military History, 1956), 185. Another historian argues more colorfully that Marshall sought a *mano a mano* fight with the *Wehrmacht* on the beaches of northern France. Douglas Porch, *The Path to Victory: The Mediterranean Theater in World War II* (New York: Farrar, Straus, and Giroux, 2004), 334.

61. Matloff and Snell, *Strategic Planning,* 233. The British and Americans also argued they were already fighting on multiple fronts: in the Pacific, Burma, North Africa, and of course in naval wars in the Atlantic and Pacific, as well as the strategic bombing campaign of the Royal Air Force and the US Army Air Forces.

62. Securing the Mediterranean meant Allied shipping would not have to sail

around the Cape of Good Hope, thus drastically improving efficiency. Keith Sainsbury, *The North African Landings, 1942: A Strategic Decision* (Newark: Univ. of Delaware Press, 1976), 21.

63. Michael Howard, *Grand Strategy,* vol. 4, *August 1942–September 1943,* History of the Second World War (London: HMSO, 1970), xxi–xxii; Matloff and Snell, *Strategic Planning,* 221, 283.

64. Howard, *Grand Strategy,* 4:119; Matloff and Snell, *Strategic Planning,* 287–93.

65. Howard, *Grand Strategy,* 4:118. After conquering France, Hitler permitted the southern part of the country to maintain a degree of autonomy. This government was located at Vichy and led by Marshal Henri Petain.

66. George F. Howe, *Northwest Africa: Seizing the Initiative in the West,* United States Army in World War II (Washington, D.C.: Center of Military History, 1957), 54–58.

67. Howard, *Grand Strategy,* 4:118; Porch, *The Path to Victory,* 353.

68. Ralph Bennett, *Ultra and Mediterranean Strategy* (New York: William Morrow, 1989), 188.

69. Howe, *Northwest Africa,* 666, 676. For the Tunisia campaign, see David Rolf, *The Bloody Road to Tunis* (Harrisburg, Pa.: Stackpole, 2001).

70. F. H. Hinsley, et al., *British Intelligence in the Second World War: Its Influence on Strategy and Operations,* 5 vols. (London: HMSO, 1979–1990), vol. 2, chapter 24.

71. Porch, *The Path to Victory,* 352.

72. Ibid., 341–43; Rolf, *Bloody Road,* 44–45.

73. Carlo D'Este, *World War II in the Mediterranean, 1942–1945* (Chapel Hill, N.C.: Algonquin, 1990), 9–10.

74. Porch, *The Path to Victory,* 327.

75. Hinsley, *British Intelligence,* 2:469–70.

76. Ibid., 2:479–81; Howard, *Grand Strategy,* 4:138.

77. Wesley Frank Craven and James Lea Cate, eds., *The Army Air Forces in World War II.* 7 vols. (Chicago: Univ. of Chicago Press, 1948–58), 2:55–58.

78. Ibid., 2:33.

79. The Ottoman Empire was neutral at the start of the war, but one event had major consequences and drove it closer to Germany. Constantinople had ordered two battleships to be built by Britain. In August 1914, however, Churchill reneged on the contract, arguing the ships were needed for the Royal Navy. The Turks were outraged. Peter Hart, *Gallipoli* (New York: Oxford Univ. Press, 2011), 8.

80. Hinsley, *British Intelligence,* vol. 2, chapter 24.

81. Gates, *The Spanish Ulcer,* 35.

82. Hinsley, *British Intelligence,* 2:425–35.

6. Decisive Victories and What They Mean

1. A belligerent's goals can change during a war based on a variety of factors. That does not necessarily mean the original goals were ill-advised or unattainable; circumstances change.

2. The finest account of Napoleon's military career remains David Chandler, *The Campaigns of Napoleon: The Mind and Method of History's Greatest Soldier* (New York: Macmillan, 1966).

3. Russell F. Weigley, *The Age of Battles: The Quest for Decisive Warfare from Breitenfeld to Waterloo* (Bloomington: Indiana Univ. Press, 1991), xi–xiii, 536–40.

4. Barry Strauss, *The Battle of Salamis* (New York: Simon and Schuster, 2004), chapters 8–11.

5. Hans Delbrück, *History of the Art of War: Within the Framework of Political History,* 4 vols. (Westport, Conn.: Greenwood, 1975–85), vol. 1, book 1, chapters 8 and 9.

6. Delbrück, *Art of War,* vol. 1, book 3, chapter 4; J.F.C. Fuller, *The Generalship of Alexander the Great* (London: Eyre and Spottiswoode, 1958), 163–80.

7. H. H. Scullard, *Scipio Africanus: Soldier and Politician* (Ithaca, N.Y.: Cornell Univ. Press, 1970), chapters 6 and 7; J. F. Lazenby, *Hannibal's War* (Norman: Univ. of Oklahoma Press, 1978), 215–27.

8. Little is known about the Battle of Tours, but for useful accounts see J.F.C. Fuller, *A Military History of the Western World,* 3 vols. (New York: Minerva, 1954), 1:340–49; and Charles Oman, *A History of the Art of War in the Middle Ages,* 3 vols. (London: Methuen, 1924), 1:57–59.

9. Jonathan Phillips, *The Fourth Crusade and the Sack of Constantinople* (New York: Viking, 2004); Matthew Bennett et al., *Fighting Techniques of the Medieval World, AD 500–AD 1500* (New York: Thomas Dunne, 2005), 226–32.

10. Prince Philip and Queen Mary were wed in July 1554; Philip succeeded his father as king of Spain in 1556. Thus, Philip was both king of England and of Spain, although Parliament insisted that if Mary were to die before him—which is what occurred—he would *not* continue to serve as king of England.

11. David Wason, *Battlefield Detectives: Unearthing New Evidence on the World's Most Famous Battlefields* (London: Carlton, 2014), 97–100.

12. David Howarth, *The Voyage of the Armada: The Spanish Story* (New York: Viking, 1981); Winston Graham, *The Spanish Armadas* (New York: Doubleday, 1972).

13. Kitajima Manji, "The Imjin Waeran: Contrasting the First and the Second Invasions of Korea," in *The East Asian War, 1592–1598: International Relations, Violence, and Memory,* ed. James B. Lewis (New York: Routledge, 2015), 73.

14. Stephen Turnbull, *Samurai Invasion: Japan's Korean War, 1592–1598* (London: Cassell, 2002), 51.

15. Admiral Yi Sun-sin, *Nanjung Ilgi: War Diary of Admiral Yi Sun-sin,* translated by Ha Tae-hung (Seoul: Yonsei Univ. Press, 1977), viii.

16. Yi Min'ung, "The Role of the Chosŏn Navy and Major Naval Battles during the Imjin Waeran," in *The East Asian War, 1592–1598: International Relations, Violence, and Memory,* ed. James B. Lewis (New York: Routledge, 2015), 125–26.

17. Etsuko Hae-Jin Kang, *Diplomacy and Ideology in Japanese-Korean Relations* (New York: Macmillan, 1997), 138–42.

18. Don Higginbotham, *The War of American Independence* (New York: Macmillan, 1971), 352–88.

19. For a discussion of the plan and its limitations, see Gerhard Ritter, *The Schlieffen Plan* (New York: Praeger, 1958).

20. Another account argues that Schlieffen had not actually written a detailed plan, but rather a "concept" to be used to coerce the War Ministry and the Reichstag into raising more troops. In this account the operation that unfolded in 1914 was the design of Helmuth von Moltke. See Terence Zuber, *Inventing the Schlieffen Plan: German War Planning, 1871–1914* (New York: Oxford Univ. Press, 2002).

21. Martin Gilbert, *The First World War: A Complete History* (New York: Henry Holt, 1994), 55–77; Holger H. Herwig, "1914: The Marne in the Balance," *MHQ* 22 (spring 2010): 26–33.

22. John Terraine, *A Time for Courage: The Royal Air Force in the European War, 1939–1945* (New York: Macmillan, 1985), 169–213; Richard Overy, *The Battle* (London: Penguin, 2000).

23. For the development of the atomic bomb, see Vincent C. Jones, *Manhattan: The Army and the Atomic Bomb* (Washington, D.C.: Center of Military History, 1985).

24. For his personal account, see Paul W. Tibbets, *Return of the Enola Gay* (Columbus, Ohio: Mid Coast Marketing, 1998).

25. For an excellent discussion regarding casualty figures, see D. M. Giangreco, "Casualty Projections for the U.S. Invasion of Japan, 1945–1946," *Journal of Military History* 61 (July 1997): 521–82.

7. Time in War

Epigraph note: Robert D. Heinl Jr., *Dictionary of Military and Naval Quotations* (Annapolis, Md.: Naval Institute Press, 1966), 325.

1. Sun Tzu, *The Art of War,* trans. Samuel B. Griffith (London: Oxford Univ. Press, 1963), 134, 106.

2. Carl von Clausewitz, *On War,* trans. and ed. Michael Howard and Peter Paret (Princeton, N.J.: Princeton Univ. Press, 1976), 198.

3. For excellent discussions of the physical, religious, and psychological dimensions of time, see Paul Davis, *About Time: Einstein's Unfinished Revolution* (New York: Simon and Schuster, 1995); and Colin Wilson, ed., *The Book of Time* (North Pomfret, Vt.: Westbridge, 1980).

4. For the best examination of Boyd's theories, see Frans P. B. Osinga, "The Enemy as a Complex Adaptive System: John Boyd and Airpower in the Postmodern Era," in *Airpower Reborn: The Strategic Concepts of John Warden and John Boyd,* ed. John A. Olsen (Annapolis, Md.: Naval Institute Press, 2015), 48–92.

5. One infantryman also uses terms like frequency and amplitude to describe the effects of time on the battlefield. Robert R. Leonhard, *Fighting by Minutes: Time and the Art of War* (Westport, Conn.: Praeger, 1994), chapter 5.

6. Brian Caven, *The Punic Wars* (London: Weidenfeld and Nicolson, 1980), 273–91.

7. Vincent C. Jones, *Manhattan: The Army and the Atomic Bomb,* United States Army in World War II (Washington, D.C.: Center of Military History, 1985), 534–50.

8. Count Philippe-Paul de Ségur, *Napoleon's Russian Campaign* (Boston: Houghton Mifflin, 1958), 70. For the battle itself, see David Chandler, *The Campaigns of Napoleon: The Mind and Method of History's Greatest Soldier* (New York: Macmillan, 1966), 790–810.

9. Edwin B. Coddington, *The Gettysburg Campaign: A Study in Command* (New York: Simon and Schuster, 1997), 384. Debates over who was at fault for the delays and lack of coordination have raged ever since. Longstreet usually gets the blame, but some argue Lee gave confusing orders and failed to exercise the requisite control over his subordinates. Others blame the guides who failed to scout an appropriate route that would allow Longstreet's corps to move into place without being seen by the Union spotters on the Round Tops. See Noah Andre Trudeau, *Gettysburg: A Testing of Courage* (New York: HarperCollins, 2002), 282–371.

10. Historians have debated the Schlieffen Plan since 1914. In a recent broadside, one author claims that Schlieffen did not really write a war plan, but merely a concept; moreover, the concept was actually an attempt to pry more soldiers out of the War Ministry and Reichstag. In the aftermath of the disaster of 1914, a scapegoat was needed, so senior officers and generals "invented" the "brilliant" Schlieffen Plan that was bungled by the inept von Moltke. For this argument, see Terence Zuber, *Inventing the Schlieffen Plan: German War Planning, 1871–1914* (New York: Oxford Univ. Press, 2002).

11. Gerhard Ritter, *The Schlieffen Plan* (New York: Praeger, 1958). When the plan was studied after the war, most historians decided there were not enough German troops, it was politically foolish, and the plan was so dependent on precise timing of a complex and difficult maneuver as to be impossible.

12. For an overview, see Martin Gilbert, *The First World War: A Complete History* (New York: Henry Holt, 1994), 29–30, 72.

13. James F. Schnabel, *Policy and Direction: The First Year,* United States Army in the Korean War (Washington, D.C.: Office of the Chief of Military History, 1972), 144.

14. Ibid., chapters 8 and 9. For an account of MacArthur and his role in CHROMITE, see D. Clayton James, *The Years of MacArthur,* vol. 3, *Triumph and Disaster, 1945–1964* (Boston: Houghton Mifflin, 1985), 464–85.

15. Schnabel, *Policy and Direction,* 173–77.

16. For an excellent discussion, see Stephen L. McFarland, *America's Pursuit of Precision Bombing, 1918–1945* (Washington, D.C.: Smithsonian, 1995), chapter 5.

17. For the strategic context of this mission, see Wesley Frank Craven and James Lea Cate, eds., *The Army Air Forces in World War II,* 7 vols. (Chicago: Univ. of Chicago Press, 1948–58), 2:477–83. For a more detailed account, see Donald L. Miller, *Masters of the Air: America's Bomber Boys Who Fought the Air War against Nazi Germany* (New York: Simon and Schuster, 2006), 187–92.

18. Miller, *Masters of the Air,* 191.

19. For the strategic context, see Craven and Cate, eds., *Army Air Forces,* 2:681–87, and for more details, see Miller, *Masters of the Air,* 192–205.

20. Miller, *Masters of the Air,* 193.

21. For the beginning of ROLLING THUNDER, see Jacob Van Staaveren, *Gradual Failure: The Air War over North Vietnam, 1965–1966* (Washington, D.C.: Air Force History and Museums Program, 2002).

22. For an overview of BOLO, see Wayne Thompson, *To Hanoi and Back: The USAF and North Vietnam, 1966–1973* (Washington, D.C.: Air Force History and Museums Program, 2000), 52–55. Incidentally, the official name of the F-105 was Thunderchief, but no one called it that.

23. Olds had eight flights of four aircraft each at Ubon. There would be three waves: the flights would arrive on-scene in five-minute intervals with ten minutes between waves. This would ensure there were US fighters on scene for the entire fuel duration of any MiGs that came up.

24. For a detailed account, see Robin Olds, with Christina Olds and Ed Rasimus, *Fighter Pilot* (New York: St. Martin's, 2010), 271–82.

25. Brigadier General David A. Deptula, "Effects-Based Operations: Change in the Nature of Warfare," Aerospace Education Foundation report (Arlington, Va.: Aerospace Education Foundation, 2001), 2; General Merrill A. McPeak, *Roles and Missions* (Lake Oswego, Oreg.: Lost Wingman Press, 2017), 18.

26. "Bombing Germany: General Trenchard's Report of Operations of British Airmen against German Cities," *The New York Times Current History,* April 1919, 152.

27. US Department of State, *1964–1968,* vol. 1, *Vietnam, 1964,* Foreign Relations of the United States (Washington, D.C.: GPO, 1992), 970.

8. Jointness and the Norwegian Campaign, 1940

1. J.R.M. Butler, *Grand Strategy,* vol. 2, *September 1939–June 1941,* History of the Second World War (London: HMSO, 1957), 119–23. Iron ore was also shipped from Swedish ports through the Baltic Sea to Germany.

2. Klaus A. Maier et al., eds., *Germany and the Second World War,* vol. 2, *Germany's Initial Conquests in Europe* (Oxford: Clarendon, 1991), 184–85.

3. Adam A. Claasen, *Hitler's Northern War: The Luftwaffe's Ill-Fated Campaign, 1940–1945* (Lawrence: Univ. Press of Kansas, 2001), 58.

4. Ibid., 3, 5, 11.

5. Maier, *Germany and the Second World War,* 2:192.

6. Claasen, *Hitler's Northern War,* 41, 44.

7. Ibid., 49, 62, 69.

8. John Terraine, *A Time for Courage: The Royal Air Force in the European War, 1939–1945* (New York: Macmillan, 1985), 115.

9. Jack Adams, *The Doomed Expedition: The Norwegian Campaign of 1940* (London: Leo Cooper, 1989), 93.

10. Butler, *Grand Strategy,* 2:132–34, 141. Of note, Cork received orders direct from the Admiralty, bypassing his superior, the Commander-in-Chief Home Fleet.

11. Claasen, *Hitler's Northern War,* 103–5.

12. Denis Richards, *The Fight at Odds: The Royal Air Force, 1939–1945,* 3 vols. (London: HMSO, 1974), 1:86.

13. Ibid.

14. Claasen, *Hitler's Northern War,* 111–15.

15. Ibid., 9.

16. Ibid., 90. Germany never fielded a long-range bomber in quantity during the war, and its medium bombers did not have the range to span the distance from Norway to targets in Britain.

17. The Fleet Air Arm was part of the RAF until 1937, when it was turned over to the Royal Navy. It was not given a high priority by either service, so on entering World War II its aircraft were substandard. See Phillip S. Meilinger, "Between the Devil and the Deep Blue Sea: The Fleet Air Arm before World War II," *Royal United Services Institute Journal* 144 (October 1999): 73–78.

18. Henrik O. Lunde, *Hitler's Pre-Emptive War: The Battle for Norway, 1940* (Philadelphia, Pa.: Casemate, 2009), 245.

19. US Joint Staff, Joint Doctrine Publication 3-02, "Amphibious Operations," August 10, 2009, chapter 2.

20. Maier, *Germany and the Second World War,* 2:219.

21. F. H. Hinsley et al., *British Intelligence in the Second World War: Its Influence on Strategy and Operations,* 5 vols. (London: HMSO, 1979–1990), 1:136–43.

22. Claasen, *Hitler's Northern War,* 118.

23. Ibid.

24. Butler, *Grand Strategy,* 2:128.

25. Geoffrey Till, *Air Power and the Royal Navy, 1914–1945* (London: Jane's, 1979), 15.

26. Gerhard L. Weinberg, *A World at Arms: A Global History of World War II* (Cambridge, Mass.: Cambridge Univ. Press, 1994), 229; George Forty, *Battle of Crete* (Surrey, UK: Ian Allen, 2001), 162–71. Forty notes that 23,464 German troops were moved into Crete by air (162).

27. Alan Clark, *The Fall of Crete* (New York: William Morrow, 1962), 162.

28. Ibid., 120.

29. John Prados, *Combined Fleet Decoded: The Secret History of American Intelligence and the Japanese Navy in World War II* (New York: Random House, 1995), 215–22; David Hein, "Vulnerable: HMS *Prince of Wales* in 1941," *Journal of Military History* 77 (July 2013): 955–989.

30. Testimony of General of the Army Dwight D. Eisenhower to Senate, *Department of Armed Forces, Department of Military Security: Hearings before the Committee on Military Affairs on S. 84 and S. 1482.* 79th Cong., 1st sess., 1945, 360.

31. Basil H. Liddell Hart, ed., *The Rommel Papers* (London: Collins, 1953), 285.

32. Paul Kennedy, *Engineers of Victory: The Problem Solvers Who Turned the Tide in the Second World War* (New York: Random House, 2013), 226.

33. Adams, *Doomed Expedition,* 172.

34. Lunde, *Pre-Emptive War,* 547.

35. Adams, *Doomed Expedition,* 173.

9. American Military Culture and Its Influence on Strategy

1. Alexis de Tocqueville, *Democracy in America,* 2 vols., Everyman's Library ed. (New York: Knopf, 1994), 1:244.

2. Ibid., 2:268.

3. Alfred Vagts, *A History of Militarism, Civilian and Military,* rev. ed. (London: Hollis and Carter, 1959), 13.

4. Ibid., 103.

5. Samuel P. Huntington, *The Soldier and the State: The Theory and Politics of Civil-Military Relations* (Cambridge, Mass.: Harvard Univ. Press, 1957), 169–79.

6. See for example, Walter Millis, *Arms and Men: A Study of American Military History* (New York: Putnam, 1956); Graham A. Cosmas, *An Army for Empire: The United States Army in the Spanish-American War* (Columbia: Univ. of Missouri Press, 1971); Jerry M. Cooper, *The Army and Civil Disorder: Federal Military Intervention in Labor Disputes, 1877–1950* (Westport, Conn.: Greenwood, 1980); Stephen E. Ambrose, *Upton and the Army* (Baton Rouge: Louisiana State Univ. Press, 1964); William B. Skelton, *An American Profession of Arms: The Army Officer Corps, 1784–1861* (Lawrence: Univ. Press of Kansas, 1992); and Edward Coffman, *The Old Army: A Portrait of the American Army in Peacetime, 1784–1898* (New York: Oxford Univ. Press, 1986.

7. John Shy's *A People Numerous and Armed* (New York: Oxford Univ. Press, 1976) is an excellent book on the subject of colonial military affairs.

8. Russell F. Weigley, *History of the United States Army* (New York: Macmillan, 1967), 64.

9. For a concise background to this English tradition in America, see William C. Banks and Stephen Dycus, *Soldiers on the Home Front: The Domestic Role of the American Military* (Cambridge, Mass.: Harvard Univ. Press, 2016), chapter 2.

10. Richard S. Hartigan, *Lieber's Code and the Law of War* (Chicago: Precedent, 1983).

11. Actually, Grant's given names were Hiram Ulysses; he later changed to Ulysses S, but the middle initial did not stand for anything. Most folks called him Sam.

12. World War II was a sea change in this regard: in both Germany and Japan the United States left behind occupation troops, for years, to ensure that democracy took root.

13. Russell F. Weigley, *The American Way of War: A History of United States Military Strategy and Policy* (New York: Macmillan, 1973), xviii.

14. See the first chapter in this book.

15. For critiques of Eisenhower's decision, see John Toland, *The Last 100 Days* (New York: Random House, 1966); and Cornelius Ryan, *The Last Battle* (New York: Simon and Schuster, 1966). For more balanced treatments, see Stephen Ambrose, *Eisenhower and Berlin, 1945* (New York: Norton, 1967); and Forrest C. Pogue, "The Decision to Halt at the Elbe," in *Command Decisions,* ed. Kent R. Greenfield (Washington, D.C.: Office of the Chief of Military History, 1960), 479–92.

16. A. J. Bacevich, "The Paradox of Professionalism: Eisenhower, Ridgway, and the Challenge to Civilian Control, 1953–1955," *Journal of Military History* 61 (April 1997): 307. Bacevich, a West Point graduate, is a retired US Army colonel.

17. Ibid., 333.

18. According to some, US Army leaders continued to press LBJ for an invasion option throughout the war, but the president would have none of it. Lieutenant Colonel Andrew J. Krepinevitch Jr., *The Army and Vietnam* (Baltimore, Md.: Johns Hopkins Univ. Press, 1986), 60, 164–65, 179, 261–62. For the argument that a move with conventional US forces into Laos and Cambodia was a war-winning option, see Colonel Harry G. Summers Jr., *On Strategy: A Critical Analysis of the Vietnam War* (Novato, Calif.: Presidio, 1982), 104, 119, 123–24.

19. Quoted in Dennis M. Drew, "Rolling Thunder, 1965: Anatomy of a Failure," CADRE paper (Maxwell AFB, Ala., 1986), 31.

20. General William C. Westmoreland, *A Soldier Reports* (Garden City, N.Y.: Doubleday, 1976), 410–11. See also Gregory A. Daddis, *Westmoreland's War: Reassessing American Strategy in Vietnam* (New York: Oxford Univ. Press, 2014), for a more nuanced approach to Westmoreland's strategy.

21. Wayne Thompson, *To Hanoi and Back: The USAF and North Vietnam, 1966–1973* (Washington, D.C.: Air Force History and Museums Program, 2000), 5–6.

22. This is a reference to the seminal work by Herman Kahn in 1960, *On Thermonuclear War,* where he advised readers to think the unthinkable.

23. John S. D. Eisenhower, *Agent of Destiny: The Life and Times of General Winfield Scott* (Lawrence: Univ. Press of Kansas, 1997), chapter 28. Scott had some training for political activities: in 1838 he was sent by President Martin Van Buren to negotiate with Canada regarding a border dispute with New York.

24. Theodore Grivas, *Military Governments in California, 1846–1850* (Glendale, Calif.: Arthur H. Clark, 1963).

25. David R. Woodward, *Trial by Friendship: Anglo-American Relations, 1917–1918* (Lexington: Univ. Press of Kentucky, 1993), 181, 200–201, 213.

26. These distinct service cultures have been detailed by Carl H. Builder, *The Masks of War: American Military Styles in Strategy and Analysis* (Baltimore, Md.: Johns Hopkins Univ. Press, 1989).

27. US Army, Field Manual 1, "The Army," June 14, 2001, 4.

28. US Navy, Naval Doctrine Publication 1, "Naval Warfare," March 1994, 35.

29. Brigadier General William L. Mitchell, *Skyways* (Philadelphia, Pa.: J. B. Lippincott, 1930), 155.

30. General Merrill A. McPeak, *Roles and Missions* (Lake Oswego, Oreg.: Lost Wingman Press, 2017), 45.

31. For spirited accounts from the late nineteenth century, see Emory Upton, *The Military Policy of the United States* (Washington, D.C.: GPO, 1912), which argues the need for a professional military, and John A. Logan, *The Volunteer Soldier of America* (Chicago: R. S. Peale, 1887), which extols the virtues of the citizen-soldier. Upton and Logan had been Union generals during the Civil War. Upton was a West Point gradu-

ate and career soldier. Logan had been an Illinois congressman before the war who resigned from office and took up arms, rising to the rank of major general and temporary command of a corps. After the war he returned to politics.

32. Paradoxically, an all-volunteer force is viewed by some as undemocratic because it removes an important check on government power. In this view it is a good thing for political leaders to have to worry about disgruntled draftees—and their families. Thus, it would be a step for democracy if men and women were *forced* into the armed services. See, for example, Diane H. Mazur, "Draft May Be Needed to Rein in All-Powerful Military," *Chicago Tribune*, December 28, 2003.

33. Department of Defense News Release, March 26, 2003, http://www.defenselink.mil/releases/2003/b03262003_bt156-03.html; Air Force Office of Public Affairs, "U.S. Air Force Snapshot," April–June 2004. The US Army and US Air Force have both National Guard and Reserve components; the US Navy and Marine Corps only have Reserve forces.

34. On the *Larry King Live* television program of January 19, 2004, presidential candidate General Wesley Clark boasted: "I'm the only person in this race who has ever done foreign policy, and I know all the domestic issues too. . . . I've negotiated peace agreements. I've won a war." www.CNN.com/TRANSCRIPTS/0401/19/lk1.00.html.

35. Peter D. Feaver, "The Civil-Military Problematique: Huntington, Janowitz, and the Question of Civilian Control," *Armed Forces and Society* 23 (winter 1996): 149.

36. Richard H. Kohn, "Out of Control: The Crisis in Civil-Military Relations," *National Interest* 35 (spring 1994): 3–17.

37. For an alarmist comment, see Edward N. Luttwak, "Washington's Biggest Scandal," *Commentary,* May 1994, 29–33. He refers to the alleged dominance of the Joint Chiefs of Staff in American foreign policy.

38. Paul Sonne and Philip Rucker, "Trump's Visit to Iraq Prompts Concerns about Politicization of the Military," *Washington Post,* December 27, 2018, 4.

39. Gordon Trowbridge, "Today's Military: Right, Republican and Principled," *Army Times,* January 5, 2004, 15.

40. For a response to Kohn, see "An Exchange on Civil-Military Relations," *National Interest* 36 (summer 1994): 23–31. The four respondents were Colin Powell, John Lehman, William Odom, and Samuel Huntington.

41. https://fas.org/sgp/crs/misc/R43869.pdf.

42. Some politicians are very aware of the effects military operations have on their political fortunes. General Wesley Clark stated that he was under pressure to end the war in Kosovo before July, because Vice President Al Gore wanted it over before he began his presidential campaign that month. R. Jeffrey Smith, "Clark Papers Talk Politics and War," *Washington Post,* February 7, 2004, A1, A5. In December 1972 Richard Nixon was anxious to end the war before the new Democratic Congress took office in January. He therefore gave his military commanders great latitude in prosecuting the LINEBACKER II air campaign. Henry Kissinger, *White House Years* (Boston: Little, Brown, 1979), 1458.

43. A US Army study argues that little planning was done for stabilizing Iraq.

Donald P. Wright and Colonel Timothy R. Reese, *On Point II: Transition to the New Campaign: The United States Army in Operation IRAQI FREEDOM, May 2003–January 2005* (Fort Leavenworth, Kans.: Combat Studies Institute, 2008), 76–80.

10. Soldiers and Politics

1. Scott visited New York, Pennsylvania, Ohio, Kentucky, and Indiana, ostensibly to view sites for a potential veterans' hospital. Michael F. Holt, *The Rise and Fall of the American Whig Party* (New York: Oxford Univ. Press, 1999), 739–45; John S. D. Eisenhower, *Agent of Destiny: The Life and Times of General Winfield Scott* (Lawrence: Univ. Press of Kansas, 1997), chapter 30.

2. Timothy D. Johnson, *Winfield Scott* (Lawrence: Univ. Press of Kansas, 1998), 136.

3. K. Jack Bauer, *Zachary Taylor: Soldier, Planter, Statesman of the Old Southwest* (Baton Rouge: Louisiana State Univ. Press, 1988), 219–40. Taylor defeated Lewis Cass, who had been a brigadier general during the War of 1812.

4. Richard H. Kohn, "The Erosion of Civilian Control of the Military in the United States Today," *Naval War College Review* 40 (spring 2002): 26.

5. For the aversion early Americans had for the military, see Richard H. Kohn, *Eagle and Sword: The Beginnings of the Military Establishment in America* (New York: Free Press, 1975).

6. Articles I and IV state these authorities. See also Robert W. Coakley, *The Role of Federal Military Forces in Domestic Disorders, 1789–1878* (Washington, D.C.: Center of Military History, 1988), 3.

7. Ibid., as well as the companion volume: Clayton D. Laurie and Ronald H. Cole, *The Role of Federal Military Forces in Domestic Disorders, 1877–1945* (Washington, D.C.: Center of Military History, 1997).

8. Edward J. Larson, *The Return of George Washington, 1783–1789* (New York: William Morrow, 2014), 106–7, 134, 180, 192, 195–96, 206, 260, 269, 272, 278, 288.

9. Secretary of State Thomas Jefferson had been a colonel in the Virginia militia but saw no action during the war.

10. The exceptions were John and John Quincy Adams, Martin Van Buren, and Grover Cleveland.

11. William B. Skelton, *An American Profession of Arms: The Army Officer Corps, 1784–1861* (Lawrence: Univ. Press of Kansas, 1992), 24.

12. Andro Linklater, *An Artist in Treason: The Extraordinary Double Life of General James Wilkinson* (New York: Walker, 2009), 191–92.

13. John and Mary Lou Missall, *The Seminole Wars: America's Longest Indian Conflict* (Gainesville: Univ. Press of Florida, 2004), 38–51; Samuel J. Watson, *Jackson's Sword: The Army Officer Corps on the American Frontier, 1810–1821* (Lawrence: Univ. Press of Kansas, 2012), 147–51.

14. John D. Morris, *Sword of the Border: Major General Jacob Jennings Brown* (Kent, Ohio: Kent State Univ. Press, 2000), 251–55.

15. Nathaniel Cheairs Hughes Jr. and Roy P. Stonesifer Jr., *The Life and Wars of Gideon J. Pillow* (Chapel Hill: Univ. of North Carolina Press, 1993), chapters 3 and 4.

16. Marcus Cunliffe, *Soldiers and Civilians: The Martial Spirit in America, 1775–1865* (Boston: Little, Brown, 1968), 309; Thomas J. Goss, *The War within the Union: Politics and Generalship during the Civil War* (Lawrence: Univ. Press of Kansas, 2003). 5.

17. William J. Cooper Jr., *Jefferson Davis, American* (New York: Knopf, 2000), passim.

18. Theodore Grivas, *Military Governments in California, 1846–1850* (Glendale, Calif.: Arthur H. Clark, 1963), 16–21.

19. David Roberts, *A Newer World: Kit Carson, John C. Frémont, and the Claiming of the American West* (New York: Simon and Schuster, 2000), chapter 7; Goss, *The War within the Union,* 71.

20. T. Harry Williams, *P.G.T. Beauregard: Napoleon in Gray* (Baton Rouge: Louisiana State Univ. Press, 1954), 43.

21. Leonard W. Levy, ed., *Encyclopedia of the American Constitution* (New York: Macmillan, 1986), 271–73.

22. Charles A. Stevenson, *Warriors and Politicians: US Civil-Military Relations under Stress* (London: Routledge, 2017), 38.

23. Goss, *The War within the Union,* 18. The president nominated, but the Senate confirmed.

24. Dick Nolan, *Benjamin F. Butler: The Damndest Yankee* (San Rafael, Calif.: Presidio, 1991).

25. Data derived from *Biographical Directory of the United States Congress, 1774–1989,* bicentennial ed. (Washington, D.C.: GPO, 1989). Of the seventy-three men who went off to war, six were killed in action and eighteen returned to political office. Of the 583 Union generals of "full" rank (as opposed to brevet rank) during the war, forty-seven (8 percent) were full-time politicians before the war. Ezra J. Warner, *Generals in Blue* (Baton Rouge: Louisiana State Univ. Press, 1964), xix.

26. Roger D. Hunt and Jack R. Brown, *Brevet Brigadier Generals in Blue* (Gaithersburg, Md.: Old Soldier Press, 1990), passim. Brevet rank, no longer used in the US military, was an honorary rank given for merit. It entitled the bearer to prestige, but neither seniority nor extra pay.

27. Ibid.; Warner, *Generals in Blue,* and Ezra J. Warner, *Generals in Gray* (Baton Rouge: Louisiana State Univ. Press, 1959), passim; Bruce S. Allardice, *More Generals in Gray* (Baton Rouge: Louisiana State Univ. Press, 1995), passim. See also James M. Perry, *Touched with Fire: Five Presidents and the Civil War Battles that Made Them* (New York: PublicAffairs, 2003).

28. Details of these generals come from the Warner volumes and the *Biographical Directory of the United States Congress, 1774–1989.*

29. It was Sickles's decision to take his division down from Little Round Top and into the Peach Orchard that nearly lost the battle for the North. He did lose a leg in the battle.

30. Warner, *Generals in Blue,* passim.

31. Gordon is usually listed as a lieutenant general, but Ezra Warner in his authoritative *Generals in Gray* (xvii) states that although Gordon was nominated for a third star, he was never confirmed by the Confederate Senate.

32. James M. McPherson, *Tried by War: Abraham Lincoln as Commander in Chief* (New York: Penguin, 2008), 17.

33. Edward A. Miller Jr., *Lincoln's Abolitionist General: The Biography of David Hunter* (Columbia: Univ. of South Carolina Press, 1997), 99–106. Hunter was a West Point graduate.

34. Ron Chernow, *Grant* (New York: Penguin, 2017), 306. Rosecrans was a West Point graduate.

35. Henry Steele Commager, ed., *Documents of American History,* 7th ed. (New York: Appleton-Century-Crofts, 1963), 422. Both Burnside and Hooker were West Point graduates.

36. Pope also publicly maligned then-President James Buchanan. Robert M. Utley, *The Commanders: Civil War Generals Who Shaped the American West* (Norman: Univ. of Oklahoma Press, 2018), 152. Emphasis in original. Pope was also a West Point graduate.

37. Stephen W. Sears, ed., *The Civil War Papers of George B. McClellan* (New York: Ticknor and Fields, 1989), 344–45. Two months later, Lincoln issued the Emancipation Proclamation. McClellan was incensed, but to his credit he confined his anger to letters to his wife and ordered his Army of the Potomac to faithfully follow the laws of the nation and the orders of the president. Ibid., 481–82, 493. On the other hand, McClellan's low opinion of the president was well known, and in one private letter he referred to Lincoln as "nothing more than a well meaning baboon." Stevenson, *Warriors and Politicians,* 35.

38. John C. Waugh, *Reelecting Lincoln: The Battle for the 1864 Presidency* (New York: Crown, 1997), 124–26.

39. Ibid., 16, 341. The five Northern states without an absentee ballot were Illinois, Indiana, Delaware, New Jersey, and Oregon.

40. Chernow, *Grant,* 452.

41. Sears, *The Civil War Papers of George B. McClellan,* 589.

42. Goss, *The War within the Union,* 124.

43. Warner, *Generals in Blue,* 40.

44. Ibid., 150.

45. Ibid., 54; Goss, *The War within the Union,* 47.

46. Chernow, *Grant,* 583.

47. Ibid., 589.

48. Douglas R. Egerton, *The Wars of Reconstruction: The Brief, Violent History of America's Most Progressive Era* (New York: Bloomsbury, 2014), 101–2.

49. Coakley, *The Role of Federal Military Forces in Domestic Disorders, 1789–1878,* 287. As a direct response to the power of the army during Reconstruction, Congress passed the *posse comitatus* act in 1878 that forbade the use of federal troops in a policing role unless specifically authorized by Congress or the Constitution.

50. Grant, the commanding general, was simultaneously named secretary of war in 1867. The following year, Major General John M. Schofield was also named secretary of war. Of the fifty-seven men who served as secretary of war up to 1947, thirty-three had seen military service (58 percent) and thirteen (23 percent) had been general officers.

51. All examples are taken from James E. Sefton, *The United States Army and Reconstruction, 1865–1877* (Baton Rouge: Louisiana State Univ. Press, 1967), 30, 37, 56, 57, 73, 124, 144, 145, 165. Because most of the political generals had been driven out of the army by the end of the war, most of those running the states during Reconstruction were West Pointers. (Terry was an exception: he was a volunteer who rose to high rank and remained in the army after the war.) Thus, those who had political experience in actually running cities and states were denied the opportunity to do so.

52. Not surprisingly, the military veteran presence in Congress more than tripled after the war. The 42nd Congress of 1871–73 consisted of 329 members, 104 of whom (31.6 percent) had served in uniform during the Civil War. Data from *Biographical Directory of the United States Congress, 1774–1989.*

53. For discussions, see Robert M. Utley, *Frontier Regulars: The United States Army and the Indian, 1866–1890* (New York: Macmillan, 1973), chapters 3 and 4; Russell Weigley, *History of the United States Army* (New York: Macmillan, 1967), chapters 11–14; and Mark R. Grandstaff, "Preserving the 'Habits and Usages of War': William Tecumseh Sherman, Professional Reform, and the U.S. Army Officer Corps, 1865–1881, Revisited," *Journal of Military History* 62 (July 1998), 521–46.

54. Charles A. Byler, *Civil-Military Relations on the Frontier and Beyond, 1865–1917* (Westport, Conn.: Praeger, 2006), 109.

55. Ibid., 158–59. The complete text of Fiske's article is in Byler's appendix.

56. Utley, *The Commanders,* 104, 111, 123.

57. Philip C. Jessup, *Elihu Root,* 2 vols. (New York: Dodd, Mead, 1938), 1:245. McKinley chose Garret A. Hobart as his running mate. After rejection by Roosevelt, Miles petulantly gave a speech announcing that the Rough Rider had *not* led the charge up San Juan Hill during the Spanish-American War. Utley, *The Commanders,* 125.

58. Robert McHenry, ed., *Webster's American Military Biographies* (Springfield, Mass.: Merriam, 1978), 100–101.

59. Jack C. Lane, *Armed Progressive: General Leonard Wood* (San Rafael, Calif.: Presidio, 1978), chapter 16.

60. Thomas E. Griffith Jr., *MacArthur's Airman: General George C. Kenney and the War in the Southwest Pacific* (Lawrence: Univ. Press of Kansas, 1998), 113–14; Thomas Fleming, "The Man Who Would Be President," *MHQ* 31 (winter 2019), https://www.historynet.com/the-man-who-would-be-president.htm.

61. William B. Pickett, *Eisenhower Decides to Run* (Chicago: Ivan R. Dee, 2000), passim.

62. Louis Galambos et al., eds., *The Papers of Dwight David Eisenhower: NATO and the Campaign of 1952,* vol. 12 (Baltimore, Md.: Johns Hopkins, 1989), xviii, 719, 729, 732.

63. Jimmy Carter, the only Naval Academy graduate to be president, was a junior officer before resigning, as was H. Ross Perot (Annapolis, class of 1953), who twice ran for the presidency.

64. Samuel P. Huntington, *The Soldier and the State: The Theory and Politics of Civil-Military Relations* (Cambridge, Mass.: Harvard Univ. Press, 1957), 258.

65. There is a rich literature on this question. For some of the most important, see T. Harry Williams, "The MACS and the IKES," *American Mercury,* October 1952, 32–39; Edward M. Coffman, "The Long Shadow of *The Soldier and the State,*" *Journal of Military History* 55 (January 1991): 69–82; Edward N. Luttwak, "Washington's Biggest Scandal," *Commentary,* May 1994, 29–33; William B. Skelton, "Samuel P. Huntington and the Roots of the American Military Tradition," *Journal of Military History* 60 (April 1996): 325–38; Peter D. Feaver, "The Civil-Military Problematique: Huntington, Janowitz, and the Question of Civilian Control," *Armed Forces and Society* 23 (winter 1996): 149–78; Russell F. Weigley, "The Soldier, the Statesman, and the Military Historian," *Journal of Military History* 63 (October 1999): 807–22; Kohn, "The Erosion of Civilian Control," 10–59; 130–43; Joseph J. Collins, "What Civil-Military Crisis?" *Armed Forces Journal,* February 2010, 18–21; and an anthology, Suzanne C. Nielsen and Don M. Snider, eds., *American Civil-Military Relations: The Soldier and the State in a New Era* (Baltimore, Md.: Johns Hopkins Univ. Press, 2009).

66. William Pfaff, "The Praetorian Guard," *National Interest* 62 (winter 2000/2001): 62. The quote from Dana Priest is in the same article.

67. Rowan Scarborough, "Four-Star Officer Mulled for Iraq," *Washington Times,* January 6, 2004, 1.

68. Perry Bacon Jr., "The Revolt of the Generals," *Time,* April 16, 2006, www.time.com/time/magazine/article/0,9171,1184048-3,00.html; Richard Whalen, "The Revolt of the Generals," *The Nation,* September 28, 2006, available at https://jjwvanwaning.wordpress.com/2006/10/01/revolt-of-the-generals-tegen-bushrumsfeld-cs-the-nation/.

69. William C. Banks and Stephen Dycus, *Soldiers on the Home Front: The Domestic Role of the American Military* (Cambridge, Mass.: Harvard Univ. Press, 2016), 270.

70. Ibid., 274.

71. In 1805, President Thomas Jefferson appointed Brigadier General James Wilkinson, then commanding general of the US Army, to serve also as both the governor of the Louisiana Territory and the commissioner of Indian affairs—combining an enormous amount of military and civil power in one man. Linklater, *An Artist in Treason,* 235.

72. It was the constant pestering of General William T. Sherman to run for president that prompted his famous telegram to the Republican National Convention in 1884: "I will not accept if nominated and will not serve if elected." Lloyd Lewis, *Sherman: Fighting Prophet* (New York: Harcourt, Brace, 1932), 631. On the other hand, Sherman's foster father/father-in-law was a US senator and cabinet secretary, and his younger brother John was also a US senator. He relied on both for support and advice during his military career.

11. Unity of Command in the Pacific during World War II

1. General of the Army Douglas MacArthur, *Reminiscences* (New York: McGraw-Hill, 1964), 172–73. This argument is echoed in the army's official history: Louis Morton, *The War in the Pacific: Strategy and Command, the First Two Years* (Washington, D.C.: Office of the Chief of Military History, 1962), chapter 11.

2. D. Clayton James, *The Years of MacArthur,* vol. 2, *1941–1945* (Boston: Houghton, Mifflin, 1975), 309. Nimitz commanded the Pacific Ocean Areas, which included the Central Pacific, North Pacific, and South Pacific Areas.

3. Stephen T. Ross, *American War Plans, 1941–1945* (London: Frank Cass, 1997), 50.

4. John Ellis, *Brute Force: Allied Strategy and Tactics in the Second World War* (New York: Viking, 1990), 505, 510–11.

5. John I. Alger, *The Quest for Victory: The History of the Principles of War* (Westport, Conn.: Greenwood, 1982), 240.

6. Ibid., 246.

7. Larry I. Bland, Sharon Ritenour, and Clarence E. Wunderlin Jr., eds., *The Papers of George Catlett Marshal,* vol. 2, *"We Cannot Delay," July 1, 1939–December 6, 1941* (Baltimore, Md.: Johns Hopkins Univ. Press, 1986), 257.

8. US State Department, *The Conferences at Washington, 1941–1942, and Casablanca, 1943,* Foreign Relations of the United States (Washington, D.C.: GPO, 1968), 733–34.

9. Vernon E. Davis, "The History of the Joint Chiefs of Staff in World War II, Vol. I: Origins of the Joint and Combined Chiefs of Staff," JCS History Office study (Washington, D.C.: JCS History Office, 1972.

10. Regarding the allocation of landing craft, see US State Department, *The Conferences at Washington and Quebec, 1943,* Foreign Relations of the United States (Washington, D.C.: GPO, 1970), 1146–48. As for air assets, the Eighth Air Force in England was denuded of aircraft and trained crews throughout 1942 in order to stand up the Twelfth Air Force in preparation for the invasion of North Africa. See Wesley Frank Craven and James Lea Cate, eds., *The Army Air Forces in World II,* 7 vols. (Chicago: Univ. of Chicago Press, 1948–58), vol. 2, chapter 2.

11. Charles F. Brower, *Defeating Japan: The Joint Chiefs of Staff and Strategy in the Pacific War, 1943–1945* (New York: Palgrave, 2012), 5.

12. US State Department, *The Conference at Quebec, 1944,* Foreign Relations of the United States (Washington, D.C.: GPO, 1972), 333. It is likely that British involvement in the invasions would have led to their participation in Japanese occupation, as was the case in Europe.

13. John Ehrman, *Grand Strategy,* vol. 6, *October 1944–August 1945,* History of the Second World War (London: HMSO, 1956), 225–29.

14. James, *The Years of MacArthur,* 2:311–14.

15. Max Hastings, *Bomber Command* (New York: Dial, 1979), 136–37.

16. Craven and Cate, eds., *The Army Air Forces in World War II,* 3:79–83.

17. China was technically part of Mountbatten's theater, but Generalissimo Chiang Kai-shek ran things within his country with little interference. To help smooth things out, Stilwell was dual-hatted as the deputy to Mountbatten and the chief of staff to Chiang.

18. In addition, MacArthur's air commander, General George C. Kenney, would have taken such a snub as a deliberate and personal insult. He was the senior air officer in the AAF behind Arnold, outranking Spaatz and the other four-star airman, Joseph McNarney.

19. George W. Baer, *One Hundred Years of Sea Power: The U.S. Navy, 1890–1990* (Stanford, Calif.: Stanford Univ. Press, 1994), 203; Major General Haywood S. Hansell Jr., *Strategic Air War against Japan* (Maxwell AFB, Ala.: Air Univ. Press, 1980), 26–27. Hansell was on the Air Staff at the time the Twentieth Air Force was formed and then took over XXI Bomber Command in the Marianas.

20. Craven and Cate, eds., *The Army Air Forces in World War II,* 5:630–31.

21. Ibid., 5:683–85.

22. Brower, *Defeating Japan,* 46.

23. This was purportedly the deliberate intent of Stalin when he played his two great marshals, Georgy Zhukov and Ivan Konev, against each other to see who would take Berlin first. Max Hastings, *Armageddon: The Battle for Germany, 1944–1945* (New York: Knopf, 2004), 461–476.

24. For a discussion, see Kent Roberts Greenfield, ed., *Command Decisions* (Washington, D.C.: Office of the Chief of Military History, 1960), chapters 18 and 19.

12. Analysis, Intelligence, and Targeting in Strategic Air Operations

1. For the best accounts see Stephen L. McFarland, *America's Pursuit of Precision Bombing, 1910–1945* (Washington, D.C.: Smithsonian, 1995); Robert T. Finney, "History of the Air Corps Tactical School, 1920–1940," USAF Historical Study No. 100, Maxwell AFB, Ala.: Air Univ. Press, 1955; and Thomas H. Greer, "The Development of Air Doctrine in the Army Air Arm, 1917–1941," USAF Historical Study No. 89, Maxwell AFB, Ala.: Air Univ. Press, 1955.

2. Air Ministry, *The Origins and Development of Operational Research in the Royal Air Force* (London: HMSO, 1963), xvii–xx.

3. Charles Webster and Noble Frankland, *The Strategic Air Offensive against Germany, 1939–1945,* 4 vols. (London: HMSO, 1961), 1:190.

4. Ibid., 4:205–13.

5. Air Ministry, *The Origins and Development of Operational Research,* 56–57.

6. Ibid., 63.

7. Ibid., 65.

8. Charles W. McArthur, *Operations Analysis in the U.S. Army Eighth Air Force in World War II* (Providence, R.I.: American Mathematical Society, 1990), 214, 235.

9. There was tension between the COA in Washington and the COA at Eighth Air Force. For simplicity, I refer to both as "the COA," but they were not always in agree-

ment. For insights, see Guido Perera, *Leaves from My Book of Life*, vol. 2, *Washington and War Years* (Boston: Privately printed, 1975), passim. Perera was head of the COA in London.

10. McArthur, *Operations Analysis*, 77–80.

11. Ibid.

12. "Bombardment Aviation," ACTS text, January 4, 1938, File 248.101-9, Air Force Historical Research Agency archives (AFHRA), Maxwell AFB, Ala., 14.

13. Brigadier General William L. Mitchell, *Winged Defense: The Development and Possibilities of Modern Air Power, Economic and Military* (New York: Putnam's, 1925), 126–27.

14. Giulio Douhet, *The Command of the Air*, trans. Dino Ferrari (New York: Coward-McCann, 1942), 20.

15. Ibid., 50.

16. US Army, Field Manual 1-5, "Employment of Aviation of the Army," April 15, 1940, 11, 36.

17. Royal Air Force Manual AP 1300, "War Manual," February 1940, chapter 6, page 12.

18. Greer, "Development of Air Doctrine," 81.

19. McFarland, *America's Pursuit of Precision Bombing*, 93–98.

20. Wesley Frank Craven and James Lea Cate, eds., *The Army Air Forces in World War II*, 7 vols. (Chicago: Univ. of Chicago Press, 1948–58), 2:369.

21. F. H. Hinsley et al., *British Intelligence in the Second World War: Its Influence on Strategy and Operations*, 5 vols. (London: HMSO, 1970–1990), 3:1, 54; "History of the Committee of Operations Analysts (COA)," 1945, AFHRA file 118.01, 28, 52.

22. Alan S. Milward, *War, Economy and Society, 1939–1945* (Berkeley: Univ. of California Press, 1977), 298; Richard J. Overy, *Why the Allies Won* (London: Jonathan Cape, 1995), 203.

23. Craven and Cate, eds., *The Army Air Forces in World War II*, 2:358; Ronald C. Cooke and Roy Conyers Nesbit, *Target: Hitler's Oil* (London: William Kimber, 1985), 15–17.

24. US Strategic Bombing Survey (USSBS), "Over-All Report (European War)," Report 1, February 1947, 39–40. Another process, Fischer-Tropsch, was also used, but hydrogenation was more important while also providing all of the Reich's synthetic aviation gasoline.

25. Stephen Peter Rosen, *Winning the Next War: Innovation and the Modern Military* (Ithaca, N.Y.: Cornell Univ. Press, 1991), 161–63.

26. "War Diary," Research and Analysis Branch, OSS London [Enemy Objectives Unit], 1945, AFHRA file 520.056-167, 36–37; "History of the Committee of Operations Analysts (COA)," 43. See also Walt W. Rostow, *Pre-Invasion Bombing Strategy* (Austin: Univ. of Texas Press, 1981), 99–104; and Mancur Olson Jr., "The Economics of Target Selection for the Combined Bomber Offensive," *Royal United Services Institute Journal* 107 (November 1962): 308–14.

27. "War Diary," Research and Analysis Branch, OSS London [Enemy Objectives Unit], 1945, AFHRA file 520.056-167, 43–46.

28. Ibid., 22–33.

29. Cooke and Nesbit, *Target,* 119.

30. COA History, 20. For the accuracy of the Eighth Air Force, see USSBS, "Bombing Accuracy, USAAF Heavy and Medium Bombers in the ETO," Report 63, January 1947.

31. Perera, *Leaves from My Book of Life,* 2:139; USSBS, "The German Anti-Friction Bearings Industry," Report 53, January 1947, 1, 31, 38.

32. For an excellent discussion of how measures of merit can affect strategy, see Scott S. Gartner, *Strategic Assessment in War* (New Haven, Conn.: Yale Univ. Press, 1997).

33. Craven and Cate, eds., *The Army Air Forces in World War II,* 2:305.

34. Much has been written on the oil/rail plan controversy. For the official histories see Craven and Cate, eds., *The Army Air Forces in World War II,* 3:42–64; Webster and Frankland, *Strategic Air Offensive,* 3:42–64; Lord [Arthur] Tedder, *With Prejudice* (Boston: Houghton Mifflin, 1966), 513–24; Solly Zuckerman, *From Apes to Warlords* (New York: Harper and Row, 1978), chapter 12; and, Rostow, *Pre-Invasion Bombing Strategy,* 88–98, which includes the minutes of the March 25 meeting. For the best overall treatment, see Robert S. Ehlers Jr., *Targeting the Third Reich: Air Intelligence and the Allied Bombing Campaigns* (Lawrence: Univ. Press of Kansas, 2009).

35. USSBS, "Oil Division Final Report," Report 109, January 1947, 1, 3; Burton H. Klein, *Germany's Economic Preparations for War* (Cambridge, Mass.: Harvard Univ. Press, 1959), 226; Rosen, *Winning the Next War,* 165.

36. Zuckerman, *From Apes to Warlords,* 209–10, 220–23.

37. Craven and Cate, eds., *The Army Air Forces in World War II,* 3:371–73; James Parton, *"Air Force Spoken Here": General Ira Eaker and the Command of the Air* (Bethesda, Md.: Adler and Adler, 1986), 380–83; ACM John Slessor, *The Central Blue: Recollections and Reflections* (London: Cassell, 1956), 567–77.

38. "War Diary," Research and Analysis Branch, OSS London [Enemy Objectives Unit], 1945, AFHRA file 520.056-167, 101.

39. For a thorough discussion see Zuckerman, *From Apes to Warlords,* chapter 12; Rostow, *Pre-Invasion Bombing Strategy,* chapter 8; and Richard G. Davis, *Carl A. Spaatz and the Air War in Europe* (Washington, D.C.: Smithsonian, 1992), 403–8. For the caustic response of Harris to Zuckerman's plan see Henry Probert, *Bomber Harris: His Life and Times* (London: Greenhill, 2001), 291–92.

40. Alfred C. Mierzejewski, *The Collapse of the German War Economy, 1944–1945: Allied Air Power and the German National Railway* (Chapel Hill: Univ. of North Carolina Press, 1988), 167–69.

41. Around 60 percent of Romanian oil from was transported to Germany via barge. When the RAF mined the Danube River, it brought this traffic to a halt. One barge of oil was equivalent to a 100-car train, so these mining operations were crucial

in throttling Germany's oil supply. Robert Goralski and Russell W. Freeburg, *Oil and War: How the Deadly Struggle for Fuel in World War II Meant Victory or Defeat* (New York: Morrow, 1987), 271; Cooke and Nesbitt, *Target,* 70.

42. This argument is detailed in Mierzejewski, *The Collapse of the German War Economy.*

43. Webster and Frankland, *Strategic Air Offensive,* 4:290–92, contains the text of Tedder's "Note on Air Policy to be Adapted with a View to Rapid Defeat of Germany," dated October 25, 1944. It is also interesting that in neither the COA nor EOU histories is coal ever mentioned as a target.

44. USSBS, "Over-All Report," 18–22; Richard Overy, *Interrogations: The Nazi Elite in Allied Hands, 1945* (New York: Penguin, 2001), 298, quotes Hermann Göering that the production figures were padded to make the deputy armaments minister, Karl-Otto Saur, look good.

45. Horst Boog, Gerhard Krebs and Detlef Vogel, *Germany and the Second World War,* vol. 7, *The Strategic Air War in Europe and the War in the West and East Asia, 1943–1944/5* (Oxford, UK: Clarendon, 2006), 163, 267.

46. Overy, *Why Allies Won,* 124; John Keegan, *Six Armies in Normandy* (New York: Viking, 1982), 143.

47. Albert Speer, *Inside the Third Reich* (New York: Macmillan, 1970), 346.

48. Webster and Frankland, *Strategic Air Offensive,* 4:349–56, has Speer's November 11, 1944, letter to Hitler.

49. Robert Benson, *A History of U.S. Communications Intelligence during World War II: Policy and Administration* (Fort Meade, Md.: National Security Agency, 1997), chapter 4; Hinsley, *British Intelligence in the Second World War,* 2:55–58.

50. See, for example, Ralph Bennett, *Ultra in the West: The Normandy Campaign, 1944–45* (New York: Charles Scribner, 1980); Ronald Lewin, *Ultra Goes to War* (New York: McGraw-Hill, 1978); and Stephen Budiansky, *Battle of Wits: The Complete Story of Codebreaking in World War II* (New York: Free Press, 2000).

51. US Army Strategic Air Forces, "ULTRA: History of US Strategic Air Force Europe vs. German Air Force," Washington, D.C., Report SRH-013, June 1945, 5–6. This special history series was prepared under the guidance of the National Security Agency. See also Diane T. Putney, *ULTRA and the Army Air Forces in World War II* (Washington, D.C.: Office of Air Force History, 1987); and John F. Kreis, ed., *Piercing the Fog: Intelligence and Army Air Forces Operations in World War II* (Washington, D.C.: Air Force History and Museums Program, 1996).

52. The first such transfer occurred in November 1943 and continued for the rest of the war. US Army Strategic Air Forces, "Ultra," SRH-013, 36. Hinsley, *British Intelligence in the Second World War,* volumes 2 and 3, also documents aircraft transfers away from the Russian and Mediterranean fronts and to the west for use against the American bombers.

53. US Army Strategic Air Forces, "Ultra," SRH-013, 88, 210. Beginning in late 1943, reconnaissance units were also losing their planes and pilots to be converted into defensive interceptors for use against the bombers. Ibid., 105.

54. Ibid., 174, 179, 216, 233, 248, 286, 301.

55. Hinsley, *British Intelligence in the Second World War,* 3:2, 497.

56. Wing Commander John Stubbington, *Kept in the Dark: The Denial to Bomber Command of Vital ULTRA and Other Intelligence Information during World War II* (Barnsley, UK: Pen and Sword, 2010), 273, 350. In truth, Harris knew of Ultra and was passed its secrets, even if most of his staff was not given access. The British official intelligence history states that the Air Ministry "frowned on direct contacts between the Air Section and the commands." Yet, it implies that someone at Bomber Command received this intelligence, even if a major analysis unit was never established there. Hinsley, *British Intelligence in the Second World War,* 1:273 and 3:2, 782.

57. James Bamford, *Body of Secrets: Anatomy of the Ultra-Secret National Security Agency* (New York: Doubleday, 2001), 15–21.

58. Walton S. Moody, *Building a Strategic Air Force* (Washington, D.C.: Air Force History and Museums Program, 1996), 360–64; Walter S. Poole, *The Joint Chiefs of Staff and National Policy,* vol. 4, *1950–1952* (Washington, D.C.: Office of Joint History, 1979), 163–67.

59. Lieutenant Colonel W. J. Smith, "The Strategic Vulnerability of Russia," lecture to Air War College, March 18, 1948, AFHRA file K239.716248-48, 3.

60. For an example of an encyclopedia from April 1952, see AFHRA file K142.6-1.

61. Smith, "Strategic Vulnerability," 4–5.

62. Ibid., 8–9.

63. Ibid., 17–19. Over-flights by high-altitude aircraft like the U-2 and satellites eventually alleviated this lack of information.

64. Richard G. Grassy, "Principles of Weapons Selection and Estimate of Force Requirements," lecture to Air War College, April 11, 1950, AFHRA file K239.716248, 4.

65. Edmund Dews and Felix Kozaczka, "Air Interdiction: Lessons from Past Campaigns," RAND Note N-1743-PA&E, September 1981, 49–51.

66. Ibid., 55. One reason for the disconnect between destruction and the enemy's actual capability was mirror imaging. A US Army division required 500 tons of supplies daily: a Chinese or North Korean division required only forty-eight tons. Even if interdiction was stopping 90 percent of the supplies flowing south, the 10 percent that got through was enough to keep the enemy going. Gregory A. Carter, "Some Historical Notes on Air Interdiction in Korea," RAND Note P-3452, September 1966, 4.

67. Dews and Kozaczka, "Air Interdiction," 57.

68. John Schlight, *The War in South Vietnam: The Years of the Offensive, 1965–1968,* The United States Air Force in Southeast Asia (Washington, D.C.: Office of Air Force History, 1988), 69, 78, 154, 190.

69. Graham A. Cosmas, *MACV: The Joint Command in the Years of Escalation, 1962–1967* (Washington, D.C.: Center of Military History, 2006), 131–32.

70. Pacific Air Forces, "Linebacker II USAF Bombing Survey," April 1973, 5–6.

71. Colonel Mike Worden, *Rise of the Fighter Generals: The Problem of Air Force Leadership, 1945–1982* (Maxwell AFB, Ala.: Air Univ. Press, 1998).

72. For an excellent discussion, see Robert A. Pape, *Bombing to Win: Air Power and Coercion in War* (Ithaca, N.Y.: Cornell Univ. Press, 1996).

73. Brigadier General David A. Deptula, "Effects-Based Operations: Change in the Nature of Warfare," Aerospace Education Foundation paper (Washington, D.C.: Aerospace Education Foundation, 2001), 12.

74. John Warden, "The Enemy as a System of Systems," presentation to the Swedish National Defence College, Stockholm, January 27, 2003.

75. Pape, *Bombing to Win*; General Gordon R. Sullivan, "Lessons That Still Apply," *Washington Times,* March 3, 2001, A31; General Wesley K. Clark, *Waging Modern War: Bosnia, Kosovo, and the Future of Combat* (New York: PublicAffairs, 2001), 221, 241–42, 425.

13. Determining the Effects of the Allied Air Offensive

1. Wesley Frank Craven and James Lea Cate, eds., *The Army Air Forces in World War II,* 7 vols. (Chicago: Univ. of Chicago Press, 1948–58), 6:360; I. B. Holley, *Buying Aircraft: Materiel Procurement for the Army Air Forces* (Washington, D.C.: Office of the Chief of Military History, 1964), 550.

2. For the best account, see Charles Webster and Noble Frankland, *The Strategic Air Offensive against Germany, 1939–1945,* 4 vols. (London: HMSO, 1961); and, MRAF Sir Arthur T. Harris, *Dispatch on War Operations, 23rd February, 1942–8th May, 1945* (London: Frank Cass, 1995).

3. Craven and Cate, eds., *The Army Air Forces in World War II,* 1:134.

4. Horst Boog et al., *Germany and the Second World War,* vol. 6, *The Global War* (Oxford, UK: Clarendon, 2001), 597.

5. For the best account of AAF bombing operations over Europe, see Craven and Cate, eds., *The Army Air Forces in World War II,* vols. 1 and 2. For the Eighth Air Force, see Donald L. Miller, *Masters of the Air: America's Bomber Boys Who Fought the Air War against Nazi Germany* (New York: Simon and Schuster, 2006).

6. David MacIsaac, *Strategic Bombing in World War Two: The Story of the United States Strategic Bombing Survey* (New York: Garland, 1976), 32–36.

7. Ibid., 52. Henry L. Stimson was the secretary of war.

8. Gordon Daniels, ed., *A Guide to the Reports of the United States Strategic Bombing Survey* (London: Office of the Royal Historical Society, 1981). 101.

9. This report, Pacific (P), no. 73, "The Campaigns of the Pacific War," was published over the objections of Paul Nitze, the deputy head of USSBS for the Pacific. MacIsaac, *Strategic Bombing,* 128–30.

10. USSBS, European Theater, "Summary Report (European War)," Report 1, September 1945, 15.

11. USSBS, European Theater, "Over-All Report," Report no. 2, September 1945, 1; USSBS, European Theater, "Statistical Appendix to Over-All Report," Report 2A, February 1947, 1–9.

12. The US Marine Corps lost 24,511 men during World War II; the US Navy lost 36,950.

13. USSBS, "Statistical Appendix," 13.

14. USSBS, "Summary Report (European War)," 8–9.

15. USSBS, "Statistical Appendix," 69–70.

16. Axel Niestlé, *German U-Boat Losses during World War II* (Annapolis, Md.: Naval Institute Press, 1998), 4, 202.

17. Ibid., 12.

18. See the charts depicting this collapse in USSBS, "Over-All Report," passim.

19. RAF's Coastal Command was also sinking a great deal of German shipping bringing raw materials from the Baltic region, and this too affected industrial production. See Christina J. M. Goulter, *A Forgotten Offensive: Royal Air Force Coastal Command's Anti-Shipping Campaign, 1940–1945* (London: Frank Cass, 1995).

20. Horst Boog, Gerhard Krebs, and Detlef Vogel, *Germany and the Second World War,* vol. 7, *The Strategic Air War in Europe and the War in the West and East Asia, 1943–1944/5* (Oxford, UK: Clarendon, 2006), 225–26.

21. USSBS, European Theater, "The Effects of Strategic Bombing on German Morale," 2 vols., Report 64B, May 1947, 1:1.

22. Ibid., 2:41–42.

23. Ibid., 1:7–10.

24. Ibid., 1:59; Richard Overy, *Why the Allies Won* (London: Jonathan Cape, 1995), 133.

25. Overy, *Why the Allies Won,* 301, 325.

26. USSBS, "Over-All Report," 18; Overy, *Why the Allies Won,* 219.

27. USSBS, "Summary Report (European War)," 16–17.

28. For the definitive story on the importance of rail-delivered coal to the German war effort, see Alfred C. Mierzejewski, *The Collapse of the German War Economy, 1944–1945: Allied Air Power and the German National Railway* (Chapel Hill: Univ. of North Carolina Press, 1988).

29. USSBS, "Summary Report (European War)," 16–17.

30. USSBS, European Theater, "Bombing Accuracy, USAAF Heavy and Medium Bombers in the ETO," Report 63, January 1947, 1–7, 10.

31. Ibid., chart labeled "Exhibit I." Circular error probable is defined as the radius of a circle, centered on the mean, whose boundary is expected to include the landing points of 50 percent of the bombs dropped.

32. Charles W. McArthur, *Operations Analysis in the U.S. Army Eighth Air Force in World War II* (Providence, R.I.: American Mathematical Society, 1990), 214, 235.

33. USSBS, "The Effects of Strategic Bombing on German Morale," 1:7; Adam Tooze, *The Wages of Destruction: The Making and Breaking of the Nazi Economy* (New York: Viking, 2007), 632.

34. USSBS, "Summary Report (European War)," 16.

35. USSBS, European Theater, "German Electric Utilities Industry Report," Report 205, January 1947, 4–7.

36. Webster and Frankland, *Strategic Air Offensive,* 4:384.

37. USSBS, European Theater, "Aircraft Division Industry Report," Report 4, January 1947, 7; USSBS, European Theater, "Oil Division Final Report," Report 109,

January 1947, 43–46. Tetraethyl lead was a chemical that raised gasoline's octane rating, making it essential for high-performance aircraft engines.

38. USSBS, "Aircraft Division Industry Report," 7–8.

39. German production did not fall as a result of Allied occupation of German territory; the Allies did not cross the Rhine River until March 7, 1945—long after catastrophic production drops had already occurred.

40. Holley, *Buying Aircraft,* 550.

41. USSBS, "Statistical Appendix," 7.

42. Sebastian Cox, ed., *The Strategic Air War against Germany, 1939–1945* (London: Frank Cass, 1998). This section is derived from Cox's account and the report itself.

43. Ibid., chapter 16, concludes on page 95: "Beginning in the last quarter of 1944, further selective air attacks against the railway system in western Germany led to a precipitous fall in the volume of rail movement, with the result that by the beginning of 1945 almost the whole of industry in western Germany had either ceased to function, or threatened to do so."

44. Ibid., 69. The report states that area attacks decreased production by only 10 percent.

45. Ibid., 7. See also the dramatic chart regarding accuracy on page 49 of the report. The wording of that statement is clever: the AAF was the only other bomber force in Europe!

46. Ibid., 39.

47. Ibid., 56.

48. Ibid., 163.

49. For the best account of this remarkable airlift, see the memoirs of its commander, Lieutenant General William H. Tunner, *Over the Hump* (New York: Duell, Sloan, 1964).

50. For a good discussion of the B-29's mechanical and logistical problems, see Kenneth Werrell, *Blankets of Fire: U.S. Bombers over Japan during World War II* (Washington, D.C.: Smithsonian, 1996), chapter 3.

51. USSBS, Pacific Theater, "Summary Report (Pacific War)," Report 1, July 1946, 16.

52. Ibid., 8–9, 16.

53. The exception was Nagoya. Although hit by nearly the same amount of bomb tonnage as Tokyo throughout the war, it suffered only one-tenth the casualties due to a more effective and efficient fire department and civil defense system. USSBS, Pacific Theater, "Effects of Incendiary Bomb Attacks on Japan," Report 90, April 1947, chapter 8. For an informative discussion of the development of incendiary bombs and their use, see Horatio Bond, ed., *Fire and the Air War* (Philadelphia, Pa.: National Fire Protection Association, 1946).

54. USSBS, "Summary Report (Pacific War)," 18.

55. For more on the problems with air intelligence before and during the war, see John F. Kreis, ed., *Piercing the Fog: Intelligence and Army Air Force Operations in World*

War II (Washington, D.C.: Air Force History and Museums Program, 1996), chapters 1, 2, 6, and 7.

56. USSBS, "Summary Report (Pacific War)," 17.

57. "Emperor's Rescript," *Current History*, September 1945, 191–92. For one of the better discussions of the Japanese surrender, see Sadao Asada, "The Shock of the Atomic Bomb and Japan's Decision to Surrender—A Reconsideration," *Pacific Historical Review* 67 (November 1998): 477–512. USSBS also considered the matter in Pacific Theater, "Japan's Struggle to End the War," Report 2, July 1946. The USSBS claimed that one atom bomb was equal to 229 B-29s carrying 1,200 tons of incendiaries, 400 tons of high-explosive bombs, and 500 tons of anti-personnel fragmentation bombs. USSBS, "Summary Report (Pacific War)," 24.

58. USSBS, "Summary Report (Pacific War)," 26. For specifics re. the atomic bombs, see USSBS, Pacific Theater, "The Effects of Atomic Bombs on Hiroshima and Nagasaki," Report 3, June 1946.

59. USSBS, Pacific Theater, "The Japanese Wartime Standard of Living and Utilization of Manpower," Report 42, January 1947, 1–3.

60. USSBS, Pacific Theater, "Interrogations of Japanese Officials," 2 vols., Report no. 72, July 1946, 1:117.

61. R. J. Rummel, *Death by Government: Genocide and Mass Murder in the Twentieth Century* (New Brunswick, N.J.: Transaction, 1994), table 8.1, page 148.

62. Van Waterford, *Prisoners of the Japanese in World War II* (Jefferson, N.C.: McFarland, 1994), 146; Gavan Daws, *Prisoners of the Japanese: POWs of World War II in the Pacific* (New York: William Morrow, 1994), 360.

63. USSBS, "Interrogations of Japanese Officials," 2:427.

64. USSBS, "Summary Report (Pacific War)," 16.

65. USSBS, Pacific Theater, "The Effects of Strategic Bombing on Japan's War Economy," Report 53, December 1946, 43; USSBS, "Summary Report (Pacific War)," 88. Tokyo lost 58 percent of its population, Osaka 61 percent, Nagoya 56 percent, and Kobe 59 percent. USSBS, "The Japanese Wartime Standard of Living and Utilization of Manpower," 84.

66. USSBS, Pacific Theater, "Effects of Air Attack on Japanese Urban Economy: Summary Report," Report 55, March 1947, 11; USSBS, "Summary Report (Pacific War)," 18.

67. USSBS, "The Effects of Strategic Bombing on Japan's War Economy," 2.

68. USSBS, Pacific Theater, "The Effects of Strategic Bombing on Japanese Morale," Report 14, June 1947, 13; USSBS, "Effects of Air Attack on Japanese Urban Economy: Summary Report," 25.

69. Overy, *Interrogations*, 301.

70. USSBS, Pacific Theater, "Coals and Metals in Japan's War Economy," Report 36, April 1947, 1, 68, 70, 128.

71. Numerous Japanese officials after the war attested to the severe shortage of aviation fuel that impacted air operations. USSBS, "Interrogations of Japanese Officials," 1:120,135; 2:324.

72. USSBS, "The Effects of Strategic Bombing on Japan's War Economy," 53–54; USSBS, "The Japanese Wartime Standard of Living and Utilization of Manpower," 9–11, 24–25; USSBS, Pacific Theater, "The Effects of Bombing on Health and Medical Services in Japan," Report 12, June 1947, 30–32.

73. USSBS, "Summary Report (Pacific War)," 1.

74. Ibid., 10.

75. Ibid., 20; USSBS, "The Japanese Wartime Standard of Living and Utilization of Manpower," 83.

76. Gil Elliot, *The Twentieth Century Book of the Dead* (New York: Scribner's, 1977), 154, 161; Hans Rumpf, *The Bombing of Germany* (New York: Holt, Rinehart and Winston, 1963), 164–65, gives a high estimate of 600,000 German civilian deaths due to air attack.

77. USSBS, "The Effects of Strategic Bombing on Japan's War Economy," 61–65.

78. USSBS, Pacific Theater, "Japanese Merchant Shipping," Report 48, January 1947, 1–4.

79. China, Korea, Indochina, Indonesia, etc. would also need to be invaded and liberated at some point if the Japanese refused to surrender. The death toll would have been enormous.

80. For a good discussion of the abortive contacts in Switzerland, see Gerhard Krebs, "Operation Super Sunrise? Japanese-United States Peace Feelers in Switzerland, 1945," *Journal of Military History* 69 (October 2005): 1081–1120.

81. US Army Air Forces, *Mission Accomplished: Interrogations of Japanese Industrial, Military, and Civil Leaders of World War II* (Washington, D.C.: GPO, 1946), 39–40.

82. USSBS, "Interrogations of Japanese Officials," 2:320.

83. Gian B. Gentile, *How Effective Is Strategic Bombing?* (New York: New York Univ. Press, 2001), chapter 2.

84. This is the argument of both John W. Huston (a USAF chief historian) and Sebastian Cox, and was articulated in the foreword and introduction to the British Survey Report.

14. The Emergence of a Paradigm

1. The vast majority of ships sunk by submarines in World War II were merchant ships, not warships. In other words, navies do not attack an enemy's strongest point, but rather its weakest.

2. Homer Lea, *The Valor of Ignorance* (New York: Harper and Bros., 1909), 49.

3. An authoritative source cites 8 million military deaths and 6.5 civilian. Micheal Clodfelter, *Warfare and Armed Conflicts: A Statistical Reference,* 2 vols. (Jefferson, N.C.: McFarland, 1992), 2:781–82.

4. James S. Corum, *The Roots of Blitzkrieg* (Lawrence: Univ. Press of Kansas, 1992), chapter 1.

5. Robert A. Doughty, *The Seeds of Disaster: The Development of French Army Doctrine, 1919–1939* (Harrisburg, Pa.: Stackpole, 2014), chapter 1.

6. Robert D. Heinl Jr., *Dictionary of Military and Naval Quotations* (Annapolis, Md.: Naval Institute Press, 1966), 288.

7. For the fullest discussion, see Basil H. Liddell Hart, *Strategy* (New York: Praeger, 1954).

8. James F. Schnabel, *Policy and Direction: The First Year,* Unites States Army in the Korean War (Washington, D.C.: Office of the Chief of Military History, 1972), 46–60.

9. Robert F. Futrell, *The United States Air Force in Korea, 1950–1953,* rev. ed. (Washington, D.C.: Office of Air Force History, 1983), 3.

10. Robert J. Donovan, *The Tumultuous Years: The Presidency of Harry S Truman, 1949–1953* (New York: Norton, 1982), chapter 26.

11. Doris M. Condit, *History of the Office of the Secretary of Defense,* vol. 2, *The Test of War, 1950–1953* (Washington, D.C.: Historical Office of the Secretary of Defense, 1988), chapter 4.

12. In 2011 dollars, the Korean War cost the United States $341 billion. Stephen Daggett, "Costs of Major U.S. Wars," Congressional Research Service report (Washington, D.C.: Congressional Research Service, June 29, 2010), 2. Casualty figures are not reliable, but it is estimated that 1.5 million military and civilians died during the war. Clodfelter, *Warfare,* 2:1215–16.

13. Robert M. Utley, *The Commanders: Civil War Generals Who Shaped the American West* (Norman: Univ. of Oklahoma Press, 2018), 14.

14. Colonel Harry G. Summers Jr., *On Strategy: A Critical Analysis of the Vietnam War* (Novato.: Presidio, 1982). For a more balanced account, see Gregory A. Daddis, *Westmoreland's War: Reassessing American Strategy in Vietnam* (New York: Oxford Univ. Press, 2014).

15. Lieutenant Colonel Andrew F. Krepinevich Jr., *The Army and Vietnam* (Baltimore, Md.: Johns Hopkins Univ. Press, 1986).

16. For the origins of this strategy, see Jacob Van Staaveren, *Gradual Failure: The Air War over North Vietnam, 1965–1966* (Washington, D.C.: Air Force History and Museums Program, 2002).

17. In the aftermath of the Tet Offensive in February 1968, Westmoreland called for 206,000 more US troops for Vietnam. Soon after, he was kicked upstairs to become Army chief of staff and the disengagement strategy termed "Vietnamization" began instead. Jeffrey J. Clarke, *Advice and Support: The Final Years, 1965–1973,* United States Army in Vietnam (Washington, D.C.: Center of Military History, 1988), 291.

18. This high estimate was advanced by General Edward C. "Shy" Meyer, a former US Army chief of staff. Richard P. Hallion, *Storm over Iraq: Air Power and the Gulf War* (Washington, D.C.: Smithsonian, 1992), 3.

19. Ibid., 2–4, 133.

20. General H. Norman Schwarzkopf with Peter Petre, *It Doesn't Take a Hero* (New York: Bantam, 1992), 356–60; Diane T. Putney, *Airpower Advantage: Planning the Gulf War Air Campaign, 1989–1991* (Washington, D.C.: Air Force History and Museums Program, 2004).

21. John Andreas Olsen, *John Warden and the Renaissance of American Air Power* (Washington, D.C.: Potomac Press, 2007), chapter 8.

22. Schwarzkopf, *It Doesn't Take a Hero,* 439; Thomas A. Keaney and Eliot A. Cohen, eds., *Gulf War Air Power Survey, Summary Report* (Washington, D.C.: GPO, 1993), 102–7; Michael R. Gordon and Lieutenant General Bernard E. Trainor, *The Generals' War: The Inside Story of the Conflict in the Gulf* (Boston: Little, Brown, 1995), 350.

23. Keaney and Cohen, *Gulf War Air Power Survey,* 107; Gordon and Trainor, *The Generals' War,* 351–52.

24. Hallion, *Storm over Iraq,* 252.

25. John A. Tirpak, "Legacy of the Air Blockade," *Air Force Magazine,* February 2003, 46–56. According to a Congressional Research Service report, the operations in Iraq and Afghanistan between 2001 and 2010 cost the United States over $1.1 trillion. Daggett, "Costs of Major U.S. Wars," 2.

26. Mark Bowden, *Black Hawk Down: A Story of Modern War* (New York: Atlantic Monthly, 1999), 333.

27. The simultaneous air and ground campaigns were complementary although not coordinated. Colonel Mark A. Bucknam, "Michael E. Ryan: Architect of Air Power Success," in *Air Commanders,* ed. John Andreas Olsen (Washington, D.C.: Potomac Press, 2013), 264.

28. Colonel Robert C. Owen, ed., *Deliberate Force: A Case Study in Effective Air Campaigning* (Maxwell AFB, Ala.: Air Univ. Press, 2000), 161.

29. For an excellent overview, see Benjamin S. Lambeth, *NATO's Air War for Kosovo: A Strategic and Operational Assessment* (Santa Monica, Calif.: RAND Corp., 2001).

30. Cruise missiles were also launched from US and UK ships in the Indian Ocean.

31. Benjamin S. Lambeth, *Air Power against Terror: America's Conduct of Operation Enduring Freedom* (Santa Monica, Calif.: RAND Corp., 2005), 95–103.

32. Ibid., 130–33.

33. Richard B. Andres, Craig Wills, and Thomas E. Griffith Jr., "Winning with Allies: The Strategic Value of the Afghan Model," *International Security* 30 (winter 2005/2006), 139.

34. Walter J. Boyne, *Operation Iraqi Freedom* (New York: Forge, 2003), 95–106. See also Michael R. Gordon and Lieutenant General Bernard E. Trainor, *The Endgame: The Inside Story of the Struggle for Iraq, from George W. Bush to Barack Obama* (New York: Pantheon, 2012).

35. Thomas E. Ricks, *Fiasco: The American Military Adventure in Iraq* (New York: Penguin, 2006), 125.

36. Benjamin S. Lambeth, *The Unseen War: Allied Air Power and the Takedown of Saddam Hussein* (Annapolis, Md.: Naval Institute Press, 2013), 129, 138–39.

37. Ibid., 294.

38. Carl Conetta, "Catastrophic Interdiction: Airpower and the Collapse of the Iraqi Field Army in the 2003 War," Project on Defense Alternatives Briefing Memo #30, September 26, 2003, 5–6.

39. Michael R. Gordon, and Lieutenant General Bernard E. Trainor, *Cobra II: The Inside Story of the Invasion and Occupation of Iraq* (New York: Vintage, 2007), 426–27, 488.

40. See updated casualty figures by phase of operation at http://www.icasualties.org/ and https://www.statista.com/statistics/262894/western-coalition-soldiers-killed-in-afghanistan/. The RAF lost a C-130 to ground fire in the aftermath of major combat operations. Three Coalition aircraft were also lost and three crewmen killed by friendly fire, shot down by Patriot batteries. Lambeth, *The Unseen War,* 114–17.

41. Larry Diamond, *Squandered Victory: The American Occupation and the Bungled Effort to Bring Democracy to Iraq* (New York: Times Books, 2005), 39.

42. David Fitzgerald, *Learning to Forget: US Army Counterinsurgency Doctrine and Practice from Vietnam to Iraq* (Stanford, Calif.: Stanford Security Studies, 2013), 2.

43. For an excellent discussion of how this paradigm succeeded in Afghanistan, see Andres, Wills, and Griffith, "Winning with Allies," 124–60. For how airpower plus SOF plus indigenous Kurdish forces overcame twelve Iraqi divisions in northern Iraq, see Richard Andres, "The Afghan Model in Northern Iraq," *Journal of Strategic Studies* 29 (June 2006): 395–422.

44. Diamond, *Squandered Victory,* 51.

45. "Four Years Later, Iraqis Split on Occupation," *Chicago Tribune,* March 20, 2007, 7. For a more positive view of US Army occupation, see Gordon and Trainor, *The Endgame.*

46. For the background, see Jessica Stern and J. M. Berger, *ISIS: The State of Terror* (New York: Ecco, 2015).

47. Anne Barnard and Hwaida Saad, "Raqqa, ISIS 'Capital,' Is Captured, U.S.-Backed Forces Say," *New York Times,* October 17, 2017, 1.

48. Sarah El Deer, "U.S.-Backed Forces Capture Syria Oil Field from ISIS," *Chicago Tribune,* October 23, 2017, 11.

49. Coalition airstrikes in Afghanistan had declined significantly during 2017 as ISIS targets took priority. By the end of that year the targets shifted back to Afghanistan. Brian Everstine, "US Aircraft Return to Surge-Level Operations in Afghanistan," *Air Force Magazine* website, November 21, 2017; Phillip Walter Wellman, "US Munition Drops on Afghanistan on Pace to Set Record This Year," *Stars and Stripes,* July 20, 2018, 3.

50. "In Case You Missed It: Airpower Killed ISIS," *Air Force Magazine,* March 2018, 2.

51. Allison Fedirka, "Two Perspectives on the Conflict in Afghanistan," March 30, 2018, https://geopoliticalfutures.com/two-perspectives-conflict-afghanistan/.

52. Democracies still fight a great deal, but generally not each other. The first to look seriously at the issue was Quincy Wright, *A Study of War,* 2 vols. (Chicago: Univ. of Chicago Press, 1942). See also Edward D. Mansfield and Jack L. Snyder, *Electing to Fight: Why Emerging Democracies Go to War* (Cambridge, Mass.: MIT Univ. Press, 2005); Bruce M. Russett, *Grasping the Democratic Peace: Principles for a Post–Cold War World* (Princeton, N.J.: Princeton Univ. Press, 1993); and R. J. Rummel, *Death by*

Government: Genocide and Mass Murder in the Twentieth Century (New Brunswick, N.J.: Transaction, 1994).

53. "An Interview with Richard L. Armitage," *Prism* 1 (December 2009): 107.

54. Amy Chua, *Political Tribes: Group Instinct and the Fate of Nations* (New York: Penguin, 2018), 3.

55. Harry S Truman, *Memoirs,* vol. 2, *Years of Trial and Hope, 1946–1952* (New York: Doubleday, 1956), 106.

56. For the text of Obama's speech, see: https://www.nytimes.com/2009/12/11/world/europe/11prexy.text.html.

57. Clifford H. Bernath and David C. Gompert, "The Power to Protect: Using New Military Capabilities to Stop Mass Killings," Refugees International report (Washington, D.C.: Refugees International, July 2003), 3.

58. United Nations Security Council, "Secretary-General, Briefing Security Council, Says International Community Must 'Continue to Act with Speed and Decision' for Sake of Libyan Civilians," New York, March 24, 2011, https://www.un.org/press/en/2011/sc10210.doc.htm.

59. Angeline Lewis, "Air Power in the Rules-Based Global Order," Air Power Development Centre Paper No. 44, Canberra, Australia, March 2018, 7–14.

60. Karl P. Mueller, ed., *Precision and Purpose: Airpower in the Libyan Civil War* (Santa Monica, Calif.: RAND Corp., 2015), 6.

61. "Security Council Unanimously Calls on UN Members to Fight ISIS," *The Guardian,* November 20, 2015, https://www.theguardian.com/world/2015/nov/21/un-calls-for-all-able-member-states-to-join-fight-against-isis.

62. "UN Will Start to Investigate War Crimes Committed by ISIS from Early 2019," *Al Shaid,* December 7, 2018, https://alshahidwitness.com/un-investigate-isis-war-crimes/.

63. "An Interview with Richard L. Armitage," 107.

64. Michael Howard, *War and the Liberal Conscience* (New Brunswick, N.J.: Rutgers Univ. Press, 1978), passim.

65. Alan Vick et al., *Air Power in the New Counterinsurgency Era* (Santa Monica, Calif.: RAND Corp., 2006), 127 and chapter 2.

66. One source states that the cost for the wars in the Middle East approached $6 trillion by the end of 2017. Leo Shane III, "Report: Full Cost of U.S. Wars Overseas Approaching $6 trillion," https://www.militarytimes.com/news/pentagon-congress/2017/11/08/report-full-cost-of-us-wars-overseas-approaching-6-trillion/.

67. The question of whether the American people are casualty-averse is contentious. One authority says that the "expectations of success matter most." Christopher Gelpi, Peter D. Feaver, and Jason Reiffler, *Paying the Human Costs of War: American Public Opinion and Casualties in Military Conflicts* (Princeton, N.J.: Princeton Univ. Press, 2009), 2, 13. Are there expectations of success after more than eighteen years of war in Iraq and Afghanistan?

Bibliography

Aberth, John. *Plague in World History.* Lanham, Md.: Rowman and Littlefield, 2011.

Adams, Jack. *The Doomed Expedition: The Norwegian Campaign of 1940.* London: Leo Cooper, 1989.

"Afghanistan: Protection of Civilians in Armed Conflict." United Nations Assistance Mission in Afghanistan report. New York: United Nations Assistance Mission in Afghanistan, February 15, 2018.

Air Ministry. *The Origins and Development of Operational Research in the Royal Air Force.* London: HMSO, 1963.

Alger, John I. *The Quest for Victory: The History of the Principles of War.* Westport, Conn.: Greenwood, 1982.

Allardice, Bruce S. *More Generals in Gray.* Baton Rouge: Louisiana State Univ. Press, 1995.

Anderson, Fred. *Crucible of War: The Seven Years' War and the Fate of Empire in British North America, 1754–1766.* New York: Knopf, 2000.

"An Interview with Richard L. Armitage." *Prism* 1 (December 2009): 103–12.

Andres, Richard B. "The Afghan Model in Northern Iraq." *Journal of Strategic Studies* 29 (June 2006): 395–422.

———. "Air Power and Cyber," in *Routledge Handbook of Air Power,* ed. John Andreas Olsen, 203–14. London: Routledge, 2018.

Andres, Richard B., Craig Wills, and Thomas E. Griffith Jr. "Winning with Allies: The Strategic Value of the Afghan Model." *International Security* 30 (winter 2005/2006): 124–60.

Arkush, Elizabeth N., and Mark W. Allen, eds. *The Archeology of Warfare: Prehistories of Raiding and Conquest.* Gainesville: Univ. Press of Florida, 2006.

Armitage, David. *Civil Wars: A History in Ideas.* New York: Knopf, 2017.

Aron, Raymond. *Clausewitz, Philosopher of War.* Englewood Cliffs, N.J.: Prentice-Hall, 1985.

Asada, Sadao. "The Shock of the Atomic Bomb and Japan's Decision to Surrender—A Reconsideration." *Pacific Historical Review* 67 (November 1998): 477–512.

Bacevich, A. J. "The Paradox of Professionalism: Eisenhower, Ridgway, and the Challenge to Civilian Control, 1953–1955." *Journal of Military History* 61 (April 1997): 303–34.

Baer, George W. *One Hundred Years of Sea Power: The U.S. Navy, 1890–1990.* Stanford, Calif.: Stanford Univ. Press, 1994.

Bahrani, Sainab. *Rituals of War: The Body and Violence in Mesopotamia.* New York: Zone Books, 2008.

Bamford, James. *Body of Secrets: Anatomy of the Ultra-Secret National Security Agency.* New York: Doubleday, 2001.

Banks, William C., and Stephen Dycus. *Soldiers on the Home Front: The Domestic Role of the American Military.* Cambridge, Mass.: Harvard Univ. Press, 2016.

Bartlett, Lieutenant Colonel Merrill L., ed. *Assault from the Sea: Essays on the History of Amphibious Warfare.* Annapolis, Md.: Naval Institute Press, 1983.

Bassford, Christopher. *Clausewitz in English: The Reception of Clausewitz in Britain and America, 1875–1945.* Oxford, UK: Oxford Univ. Press, 1994.

———. "John Keegan and the Grand Tradition of Trashing Clausewitz: A Polemic." *War in History* 1 (November 1994): 319–36.

Bauer, K. Jack. *Zachary Taylor: Soldier, Planter, Statesman of the Old Southwest.* Baton Rouge: Louisiana State Univ. Press, 1988.

Bell, A. C. *A History of the Blockade of Germany, 1914–1918.* London: HMSO, 1937.

Bellinger, Vanya Eftimova. *Marie von Clausewitz: The Woman behind the Making of* On War. New York: Oxford Univ. Press, 2016.

Bennett, Matthew, et al. *Fighting Techniques of the Medieval World, AD 500–AD 1500.* New York: Thomas Dunne, 2005.

Bennett, Ralph. *Ultra and Mediterranean Strategy.* New York: William Morrow, 1989.

———. *Ultra in the West: The Normandy Campaign, 1944–45.* New York: Charles Scribner, 1980.

Benson, E. F. *The Life of Alcibiades: The Idol of Athens.* New York: Appleton, 1929.

Benson, Robert. *A History of U.S. Communications Intelligence during World War II: Policy and Administration.* Fort Meade, Md.: National Security Agency, 1997.

Bernath, Clifford H., and David C. Gompert. "The Power to Protect: Using New Military Capabilities to Stop Mass Killings." Refugees International report. Washington, D.C.: Refugees International, July 2003.

Beyerchen, Alan. "Clausewitz, Nonlinearity, and the Unpredictability of War." *International Security* 17 (winter 1992/93): 59–90.

Biographical Directory of the United States Congress, 1774–1989. Bicentennial edition. Washington, D.C.: GPO, 1989.

Bland, Larry I., Sharon Ritenour, and Clarence E. Wunderlin Jr., eds. *The Papers of George Catlett Marshal.* Vol. 2, *"We Cannot Delay," July 1, 1939–December 6, 1941.* Baltimore, Md.: Johns Hopkins Univ. Press, 1986.

Blumenson, Martin. "A Deaf Ear to Clausewitz: Allied Operational Objectives in World War II." *Parameters* 23 (summer 1993): 16–27.

Bolger, Lieutenant General Daniel P. *Why We Lost: A General's Inside Account of the Iraq and Afghanistan Wars.* Boston: Houghton Mifflin, 2014.

"Bombing Germany: General Trenchard's Report of Operations of British Airmen against German Cities." *The New York Times Current History,* April 1919, 152.

Bond, Horatio, ed. *Fire and the Air War.* Philadelphia, Pa.: National Fire Protection Association, 1946.

Boog, Horst, et al. *Germany and the Second World War.* Vol. 6, *The Global War.* Oxford, UK: Clarendon, 2001.

Boog, Horst, Gerhard Krebs, and Detlef Vogel. *Germany and the Second World War.* Vol. 7, *The Strategic Air War in Europe and the War in the West and East Asia, 1943–1944/5.* Oxford, UK: Clarendon, 2006.

Bowden, Mark. *Black Hawk Down: A Story of Modern War.* New York: Atlantic Monthly, 1999.

Boyer, Peter J. "General Clark's Battles." *New Yorker,* November 17, 2003, 70–88.

Boyne, Walter J. *Operation Iraqi Freedom.* New York: Forge, 2003.

Brower, Charles F. *Defeating Japan: The Joint Chiefs of Staff and Strategy in the Pacific War, 1943–1945.* New York: Palgrave, 2012.

Bruscino, Thomas. "Naturally Clausewitzian: U.S. Army Theory and Education from Reconstruction to the Interwar Years." *Journal of Military History* 77 (October 2013): 1251–75.

Bucholz, Arden. *Hans Delbrück and the German Military Establishment: War Images in Conflict.* Iowa City: Univ. of Iowa Press, 1985.

Budiansky, Stephen. *Battle of Wits: The Complete Story of Codebreaking in World War II.* New York: Free Press, 2000.

Builder, Carl H. *The Masks of War: American Military Styles in Strategy and Analysis.* Baltimore, Md.: Johns Hopkins Univ. Press, 1989.

Butler, Amy. "Sharpening Focus." *Aviation Week and Space Technology,* February 26, 2007, 28.

Butler, J.R.M. *Grand Strategy.* Vol. 2, *September 1939–June 1941.* History of the Second World War. London: HMSO, 1957.

Byler, Charles A. *Civil-Military Relations on the Frontier and Beyond, 1865–1917.* Westport, Conn.: Praeger, 2006.

Carlton, Eric. *War and Ideology.* Savage, Md.: Barnes and Noble, 1990.

Caven, Brian. *The Punic Wars.* London: Weidenfeld and Nicolson, 1980.

Cebrowski, Vice Admiral Arthur K., and John J. Garstka. "Network-Centric Warfare: Its Origins and Future." *US Naval Institute Proceedings* 124 (January 1998): 28–35.

Chandler, David. *The Campaigns of Napoleon: The Mind and Method of History's Greatest Soldier.* New York: Macmillan, 1966.

Chernow, Ron. *Grant.* New York: Penguin, 2017.

Chua, Amy. *Political Tribes: Group Instinct and the Fate of Nations.* New York: Penguin, 2018.

Claasen, Adam A. *Hitler's Northern War: The Luftwaffe's Ill-Fated Campaign, 1940–1945.* Lawrence: Univ. Press of Kansas, 2001.

Clark, Alan. *The Donkeys.* New York: William Morrow, 1962.

———. *The Fall of Crete.* New York: William Morrow, 1962.

Clark, General Wesley K. *Waging Modern War: Bosnia, Kosovo, and the Future of Combat.* New York: PublicAffairs, 2001.

Clarke, Jeffrey J. *Advice and Support: The Final Years, 1965–1973.* United States Army in Vietnam. Washington, D.C.: Center of Military History, 1988.

Clausewitz, Carl von. *On War.* Translated and edited by Michael Howard and Peter Paret. Princeton, N.J.: Princeton Univ. Press, 1976.

———. *Principles of War.* Translated by Hans W. Gatzke. Harrisburg, Pa.: Military Service Publishing, 1942.

Clodfelter, Micheal. *Warfare and Armed Conflicts: A Statistical Reference.* 2 vols. Jefferson, N.C.: McFarland, 1992.

Coakley, Robert W. *The Role of Federal Military Forces in Domestic Disorders, 1789–1878.* Washington, D.C.: Center of Military History, 1988.

Coddington, Edwin B. *The Gettysburg Campaign: A Study in Command.* New York: Simon and Schuster, 1997.

Cohen, Eliot A., ed. *Gulf War Air Power Survey.* 5 vols. Washington, D.C.: GPO, 1993.

Collins, Joseph J. "What Civil-Military Crisis?" *Armed Forces Journal,* February 2010, 18–21.

Condit, Doris M. *History of the Office of the Secretary of Defense.* Vol. 2, *The Test of War, 1950–1953.* Washington, D.C.: Historical Office of the Secretary of Defense, 1988.

Conetta, Carl. "Catastrophic Interdiction: Airpower and the Collapse of the Iraqi Field Army in the 2003 War." Project on Defense Alternatives Briefing Memo #30, September 26, 2003.

Cooke, Ronald C., and Roy Conyers Nesbit. *Target: Hitler's Oil.* London: William Kimber, 1985.

Cooper, William J., Jr. *Jefferson Davis, American.* New York: Knopf, 2000.

Corbett, Julian S. *Some Principles of Maritime Strategy.* Annapolis, Md.: Naval Institute Press, 1988.

Corum, James S. *The Roots of Blitzkrieg.* Lawrence: Univ. Press of Kansas, 1992.

Cosmas, Graham A. *MACV: The Joint Command in the Years of Escalation, 1962–1967.* Washington, D.C.: Center of Military History, 2006.

Cox, Sebastian, ed. *The Strategic Air War against Germany, 1939–1945.* London: Frank Cass, 1998.

Craig, Gordon. *The Politics of the Prussian Army.* New York: Oxford Univ. Press, 1956.

Craven, Wesley Frank, and James Lea Cate, eds. *The Army Air Forces in World War II.* 7 vols. Chicago: Univ. of Chicago Press, 1948–58.

Cunliffe, Marcus. *Soldiers and Civilians: The Martial Spirit in America, 1775–1865.* Boston: Little, Brown, 1968.

Daddis, Gregory A. *Westmoreland's War: Reassessing American Strategy in Vietnam.* New York: Oxford Univ. Press, 2014.

Daggett, Stephen. "Costs of Major U.S. Wars." Congressional Research Service report. Washington, D.C.: Congressional Research Service, June 29, 2010.

Daniels, Gordon, ed. *A Guide to the Reports of the United States Strategic Bombing Survey.* London: Office of the Royal Historical Society, 1981.

Davies, Huw J. "Diplomats as Spymasters: A Case Study of the Peninsular War, 1809–1813." *Journal of Military History* 76 (January 2012): 37–68.

Davis, Lance E., and Stanley L. Engerman. *Naval Blockades in Peace and War: An Economic History since 1750.* New York: Cambridge Univ. Press, 2006.

Davis, Paul. *About Time: Einstein's Unfinished Revolution.* New York: Simon and Schuster, 1995.

Davis, Richard G. *Carl A. Spaatz and the Air War in Europe.* Washington, D.C.: Smithsonian, 1992.

Davis, Vernon E. "The History of the Joint Chiefs of Staff in World War II, Vol. I: Origins of the Joint and Combined Chiefs of Staff." JCS History Office study. Washington, D.C.: JCS History Office, 1972.

Daws, Gavan. *Prisoners of the Japanese: POWs of World War II in the Pacific.* New York: William Morrow, 1994.

Delbrück, Hans. *History of the Art of War: Within the Framework of Political History.* 4 vols. Westport, Conn.: Greenwood, 1975–85.

Deptula, Brigadier General David A. "Effects-Based Operations: Change in the Nature of Warfare." Aerospace Education Foundation report. Arlington, Va.: Aerospace Education Foundation, 2001.

D'Este, Carlo. *World War II in the Mediterranean, 1942–1945.* Chapel Hill, N.C.: Algonquin, 1990.

Diamond, Larry. *Squandered Victory: The American Occupation and the Bungled Effort to Bring Democracy to Iraq.* New York: Times Books, 2005.

Donovan, Robert J. *The Tumultuous Years: The Presidency of Harry S Truman, 1949–1953.* New York: Norton, 1982.

Doughty, Robert A. *The Seeds of Disaster: The Development of French Army Doctrine, 1919–1939.* Harrisburg, Pa.: Stackpole, 2014.

Douhet, Giulio. *The Command of the Air.* Translated by Dino Ferrari. New York: Coward-McCann, 1942.

Drew, Dennis M. "Rolling Thunder, 1965: Anatomy of a Failure." CADRE paper. Maxwell AFB, Alabama, 1986.

Duffy, Michael. "The Revolt of the Generals." *Time,* April 24, 2006, 41–42.

Dunlap, Major General Charles J., Jr. "Lawfare: A Decisive Element of 21st-Century Conflicts?" *Joint Force Quarterly* 54 (3rd quarter 2009): 34–39.

Earle, Edward Mead, ed. *Makers of Modern Strategy.* Princeton, N.J.: Princeton Univ. Press, 1944.

Echevarria, Antulio J., II. *Clausewitz and Contemporary War.* New York: Oxford Univ. Press, 2007.

Egerton, Douglas R. *The Wars of Reconstruction: The Brief, Violent History of America's Most Progressive Era.* New York: Bloomsbury, 2014.

Ehlers, Robert S., Jr. *Targeting the Third Reich: Air Intelligence and the Allied Bombing Campaigns.* Lawrence: Univ. Press of Kansas, 2009.

Ehrman, John. *Grand Strategy.* Vol. 6, *October 1944–August 1945.* History of the Second World War. London: HMSO, 1956.

Eisenhower, John S. D. *Agent of Destiny: The Life and Times of General Winfield Scott.* Lawrence: Univ. Press of Kansas, 1997.

"Electric Grid Cybersecurity." Congressional Research Service report. Washington, D.C.: Congressional Research Service, September 4, 2018.

Elliot, Gil. *The Twentieth Century Book of the Dead.* New York: Scribner's, 1977.

Ellis, John. *Brute Force: Allied Strategy and Tactics in the Second World War.* New York: Viking, 1990.

English, John A. *Marching through Chaos: The Descent of Armies in Theory and Practice.* New York: Praeger, 1996.

Erickson, Edward J. *Gallipoli: The Ottoman Campaign.* Barnsley, UK: Pen and Sword, 2010.

Everstine, Brian W. "Elegy for the Predator." *Air Force Magazine,* July 2018, 18–22.

"An Exchange on Civil-Military Relations." *National Interest* 36 (summer 1994): 23–31.

Feaver, Peter D. "The Civil-Military Problematique: Huntington, Janowitz, and the Question of Civilian Control." *Armed Forces and Society* 23 (winter 1996): 149–78.

Fields, Nic. *Syracuse 415–413 BC: Destruction of the Athenian Imperial Fleet.* Oxford, UK: Osprey, 2008.

Finney, Robert T. "History of the Air Corps Tactical School, 1920–1940." USAF Historical Study No. 100. Maxwell AFB, Ala.: Air Univ. Press, 1955.

Fitzgerald, David. *Learning to Forget: US Army Counterinsurgency Doctrine and Practice from Vietnam to Iraq.* Stanford, Calif.: Stanford Security Studies, 2013.

Fleming, Bruce. "Can Reading Clausewitz Save Us from Future Mistakes?" *Parameters* 32 (spring 2004): 62–76.

Forty, George. *Battle of Crete.* Surrey, UK: Ian Allen, 2001.

Fourth Freedom. "Morbidity and Mortality among Iraqi Children." Washington, D.C.: Fourth Freedom, March 1999.

Fraser, Ronald. *Napoleon's Cursed War: Popular Resistance in the Spanish Peninsular War.* London: Verso, 2008.

Fuller, J.F.C. *The Army in My Time.* London: Rich and Cowan, 1935.

———. *The Generalship of Alexander the Great.* London: Eyre and Spottiswoode, 1958.

———. *A Military History of the Western World.* 3 vols. New York: Minerva, 1954.

Futrell, Robert Frank. *Ideas, Concepts, Doctrine: Basic Thinking in the United States Air Force, 1907–1960.* 2 vols. Maxwell AFB, Ala.: Air Univ. Press, 1989.

———. *The United States Air Force in Korea, 1950–1953,* rev. ed. Washington, D.C.: Office of Air Force History, 1983.

Galambos, Louis, et al., eds. *The Papers of Dwight David Eisenhower: NATO and the Campaign of 1952,* vol. 12. Baltimore, Md.: Johns Hopkins Univ. Press, 1989.

Gall, Carlotta. *The Wrong Enemy: America in Afghanistan, 2001–2014.* Boston: Houghton, Mifflin, Harcourt, 2014.

Gartner, Scott S. *Strategic Assessment in War.* New Haven, Conn.: Yale Univ. Press, 1997.

Gat, Azar. *The Development of Military Thought in the Nineteenth Century.* Oxford, UK: Clarendon Press, 1992.

———. *The Origins of Military Thought: From the Enlightenment to Clausewitz.* Oxford, UK: Clarendon Press, 1989.

———. *War in Human Civilization.* New York: Oxford Univ. Press, 2006.

Gates, David. *The Spanish Ulcer: A History of the Peninsular War.* New York: Norton, 1986.

Gelpi, Christopher, Peter D. Feaver, and Jason Reiffler. *Paying the Human Costs of War: American Public Opinion and Casualties in Military Conflicts.* Princeton, N.J.: Princeton Univ. Press, 2009.

Gentile, Gian B. *How Effective Is Strategic Bombing?* New York: New York Univ. Press, 2001.

Giangreco, D. M. "Casualty Projections for the U.S. Invasion of Japan, 1945–1946." *Journal of Military History* 61 (July 1997): 521–82.

Gilbert, Martin. *The First World War: A Complete History.* New York: Henry Holt, 1994.

Goralski, Robert, and Russell W. Freeburg. *Oil and War: How the Deadly Struggle for Fuel in World War II Meant Victory or Defeat.* New York: Morrow, 1987.

Gordon, Michael R., and Lieutenant General Bernard E. Trainor. *Cobra II: The Inside Story of the Invasion and Occupation of Iraq.* New York: Vintage, 2007.

———. *The Endgame: The Inside Story of the Struggle for Iraq, from George W. Bush to Barack Obama.* New York: Pantheon, 2012.

———. *The Generals' War: The Inside Story of the Conflict in the Gulf.* Boston: Little, Brown, 1995.

Goss, Thomas J. *The War within the Union: Politics and Generalship during the Civil War.* Lawrence: Univ. Press of Kansas, 2003.

Goulter, Christina J. M. *A Forgotten Offensive: Royal Air Force Coastal Command's Anti-Shipping Campaign, 1940–1945.* London: Frank Cass, 1995.

Graham, Colonel J. J. *On War.* London: Cassell, 1918.

Graham, Winston. *The Spanish Armadas.* New York: Doubleday, 1972.

Grandstaff, Mark R. "Preserving the 'Habits and Usages of War': William Tecumseh Sherman, Professional Reform, and the U.S. Army Officer Corps, 1865–1881, Revisited." *Journal of Military History* 62 (July 1998): 521–46.

Grant, Rebecca. "The Cyber Menace." *Air Force Magazine,* March 2009, 24–28.

Greenfield, Kent Roberts, ed. *Command Decisions.* Washington, D.C.: Office of the Chief of Military History, 1960.

Greer, Thomas H. "The Development of Air Doctrine in the Army Air Arm, 1917–1941." USAF Historical Study No. 89. Maxwell AFB, Ala.: Air Univ. Press, 1955.

Griffith, Thomas E., Jr. *MacArthur's Airman: General George C. Kenney and the War in the Southwest Pacific.* Lawrence: Univ. Press of Kansas, 1998.

Grivas, Theodore. *Military Governments in California, 1846–1850.* Glendale, Calif.: Arthur H. Clark, 1963.

Guichard, Louis. *The Naval Blockade, 1914–1918.* New York: Appleton, 1930.

Hae-Jin Kang, Etsuko. *Diplomacy and Ideology in Japanese-Korean Relations.* New York: Macmillan, 1997.

Haffa, Robert P., Jr., and Jasper Welch. "Command and Control Arrangements for the Attack of Time-Sensitive Targets." Northrop Grumman Analysis Center paper. Roslyn, Va.: Northrop Grumman, November 2005.

Hale, John R. *Lords of the Sea: The Epic Story of the Athenian Navy and the Birth of Democracy.* New York: Viking, 2009.

Hall, Christopher D. *British Strategy in the Napoleonic War, 1803–15.* Manchester, UK: Manchester Univ. Press, 1992.

———. *Wellington's Navy: Sea Power and the Peninsular War, 1807–1814.* London: Chatham, 2004.

Hallion, Richard P. *Storm over Iraq: Air Power and the Gulf War.* Washington, D.C.: Smithsonian, 1992.

Handel, Michael I., ed. *Clausewitz and Modern Strategy.* London: Frank Cass, 1986.

Hansell, Major General Haywood S., Jr. *Strategic Air War against Japan.* Maxwell AFB, Ala.: Air Univ. Press, 1980.

Hanson, Victor Davis. *Carnage and Culture: Landmark Battles in the Rise of Western Power.* New York: Doubleday, 2001.

———. *Warfare and Agriculture in Classical Greece.* Berkeley: Univ. of California Press, 1998.

Harris, MRAF Sir Arthur T. *Dispatch on War Operations, 23rd February, 1942–8th May, 1945.* London: Frank Cass, 1995.

Harsh, J. L. "Battlesword and Rapier: Clausewitz, Jomini, and the American Civil War." *Military Affairs* 38 (October 1974): 133–38.

Hart, Peter. *Gallipoli.* New York: Oxford Univ. Press, 2011.

Hartigan, Richard S. *Lieber's Code and the Law of War.* Chicago: Precedent, 1983.

Hastings, Max. *Armageddon: The Battle for Germany, 1944–1945.* New York: Knopf, 2004.

———. *Bomber Command.* New York: Dial, 1979.

Haywood, Richard Mansfield. *The Ancient World.* New York: David McKay, 1971.

Hein, David. "Vulnerable: HMS *Prince of Wales* in 1941." *Journal of Military History* 77 (July 2013): 955–989.

Heinl, Robert D., Jr. *Dictionary of Military and Naval Quotations.* Annapolis, Md.: Naval Institute Press, 1966.

Herwig, Holger H. "1914: The Marne in the Balance." *MHQ* 22 (spring 2010): 26–33.

Higginbotham, Don. *The War of American Independence.* New York: Macmillan, 1971.

Hinsley, F. H., et al. *British Intelligence in the Second World War: Its Influence on Strategy and Operations.* 5 vols. London: HMSO, 1979–1990.

Hittle, J. D. *The Military Staff.* Harrisburg, Pa.: Military Service Publishing, 1961.

Holley, I. B. *Buying Aircraft: Materiel Procurement for the Army Air Forces.* Washington, D.C.: Office of the Chief of Military History, 1964.

Holt, Michael F. *The Rise and Fall of the American Whig Party.* New York: Oxford Univ. Press, 1999.

Holwitt, Joel Ira. *"Execute against Japan": The U.S. Decision to Conduct Unrestricted Submarine Warfare.* College Station: Texas A&M Univ. Press, 2009.

"Homeland Security: DHS's Progress and Challenges in Key Areas of Maritime, Aviation, and Cybersecurity." Government Accountability Office report GAO-10-106. Washington, D.C.: GPO, December 2, 2009.

Howard, Martin R. *Walcheren 1809: The Scandalous Destruction of a British Army.* London: Pen and Sword, 2012.

Howard, Michael. *Clausewitz.* Oxford, UK: Oxford Univ. Press, 1983.

———. *Grand Strategy.* Vol. 4, *August 1942–September 1943.* History of the Second World War. London: HMSO, 1970.

———. *The Invention of Peace: Reflections on War and International Order.* London: Profile, 2001.

———. *War and the Liberal Conscience.* New Brunswick, N.J.: Rutgers Univ. Press, 1978.

Howarth, David. *The Voyage of the Armada: The Spanish Story.* New York: Viking, 1981.

Howe, George F. *Northwest Africa: Seizing the Initiative in the West.* United States Army in World War II. Washington, D.C.: Center of Military History, 1957.

Hughes, Nathaniel Cheairs, Jr., and Roy P. Stonesifer Jr. *The Life and Wars of Gideon J. Pillow.* Chapel Hill: Univ. of North Carolina Press, 1993.

Human Rights Watch. "Off Target: The Conduct of the War and Civilian Casualties in Iraq." New York: Human Rights Watch, 2003.

Humble, Richard. *Napoleon's Peninsular Marshals.* New York: Taplinger, 1973.

Hunt, Roger D., and Jack R. Brown. *Brevet Brigadier Generals in Blue.* Gaithersburg, Md.: Old Soldier Press, 1990.

Huntington, Samuel P. *The Soldier and the State: The Theory and Politics of Civil-Military Relations.* Cambridge, Mass.: Harvard Univ. Press, 1957.

James, D. Clayton. *The Years of MacArthur.* Vol. 2, *1941–1945.* Boston: Houghton, Mifflin, 1975.

———. *The Years of MacArthur.* Vol. 3, *Triumph and Disaster, 1945–1964.* Boston: Houghton Mifflin, 1985.

Jessup, Philip C. *Elihu Root.* 2 vols. New York: Dodd, Mead, 1938.

Johnson, Timothy D. *Winfield Scott.* Lawrence: Univ. Press of Kansas, 1998.

Jolles, Otto J. *On War.* New York: Modern Library, 1943.

Jones, Vincent C. *Manhattan: The Army and the Atomic Bomb.* Washington, D.C.: Center of Military History, 1985.

Kagan, Donald. *The Fall of the Athenian Empire.* Ithaca, N.Y.: Cornell Univ. Press, 1987.

Keaney, Thomas A., and Eliot A. Cohen, eds. *Gulf War Air Power Survey, Summary Report.* Washington, D.C.: GPO, 1993.

———. *Revolution in Warfare? Air Power in the Persian Gulf.* Annapolis, Md.: Naval Institute Press, 1993.

Keegan, John. *A History of Warfare.* New York: Knopf, 1993.

———. *Six Armies in Normandy.* New York: Viking, 1982.

Keeley, Lawrence H. *War before Civilization: The Myth of the Peaceful Savage*. New York: Oxford Univ. Press, 1996.

Kennedy, Paul. *Engineers of Victory: The Problem Solvers Who Turned the Tide in the Second World War*. New York: Random House, 2013.

Kissinger, Henry. *White House Years*. Boston: Little, Brown, 1979.

Klein, Burton H. *Germany's Economic Preparations for War*. Cambridge, Mass.: Harvard Univ. Press, 1959.

Kohn, Richard H. *Eagle and Sword: The Beginnings of the Military Establishment in America*. New York: Free Press, 1975.

———. "The Erosion of Civilian Control of the Military in the United States Today." *Naval War College Review* 40 (spring 2002): 2–59.

———. "Out of Control: The Crisis in Civil-Military Relations." *National Interest* 35 (spring 1994): 3–17.

Krebs, Gerhard. "Operation Super Sunrise? Japanese-United States Peace Feelers in Switzerland, 1945." *Journal of Military History* 69 (October 2005): 1081–1120.

Kreis, John F., ed. *Piercing the Fog: Intelligence and Army Air Forces Operations in World War II*. Washington, D.C.: Air Force History and Museums Program, 1996.

Krekel, Bryan. "Capability of the People's Republic of China to Conduct Cyber Warfare and Computer Network Exploitation." US-China Economic and Security Review Commission report. Washington, D.C.: US-China Economic and Security Review Commission, October 9, 2009.

Krepinevitch, Lieutenant Colonel Andrew F., Jr. *The Army and Vietnam*. Baltimore, Md.: Johns Hopkins Univ. Press, 1986.

Kuehl, Daniel T., and Robert A. Miller. "Cyberspace and the 'First Battle' in 21st-Century War." *Defense Horizons* (September 2009): 3.

Lambeth, Benjamin S. *Air Power against Terror: America's Conduct of Operation Enduring Freedom*. Santa Monica, Calif.: RAND Corp., 2005.

———. *NATO's Air War for Kosovo: A Strategic and Operational Assessment*. Santa Monica, Calif.: RAND Corp., 2001.

———. *The Unseen War: Allied Air Power and the Takedown of Saddam Hussein*. Annapolis, Md.: Naval Institute Press, 2013.

Lane, Jack C. *Armed Progressive: General Leonard Wood*. San Rafael, Calif.: Presidio, 1978.

Larson, Edward J. *The Return of George Washington, 1783–1789*. New York: William Morrow, 2014.

Larson, Eric V., and Bogdan Savych. *Misfortunes of War: Press and Public Reactions to Civilian Deaths in Wartime*. Santa Monica, Calif.: RAND Corp., 2007.

Laurie, Clayton D., and Ronald H. Cole. *The Role of Federal Military Forces in Domestic Disorders, 1877–1945*. Washington, D.C.: Center of Military History, 1997.

Lazenby, J. F. *Hannibal's War*. Norman: Univ. of Oklahoma Press, 1978.

Lea, Homer. *The Valor of Ignorance*. New York: Harper and Bros., 1909.

Le Blanc, Steven A. *Constant Battles: The Myth of the Peaceful, Noble Savage*. New York: St. Martin's, 2003.

Leonhard, Robert R. *Fighting by Minutes: Time and the Art of War.* Westport, Conn.: Praeger, 1994.

Levy, Leonard W., ed. *Encyclopedia of the American Constitution.* New York: Macmillan, 1986.

Lewin, Ronald. *Ultra Goes to War.* New York: McGraw-Hill, 1978.

Lewis, Adrian R. *The American Culture of War.* New York: Routledge, 2007.

Lewis, Angeline. "Air Power in the Rules-Based Global Order," Air Power Development Centre Paper No. 44, Canberra, Australia, March 2018.

Lewis, Lloyd. *Sherman: Fighting Prophet.* New York: Harcourt, Brace, 1932.

Libicki, Martin C. *Cyberspace in Peace and War.* Annapolis, Md.: Naval Institute Press, 2016.

Liddell Hart, Basil H. *The Ghost of Napoleon.* London: Faber and Faber, 1933.

———. *A History of the World War.* Boston: Little, Brown, 1935.

———, ed. *The Rommel Papers.* London: Collins, 1953.

———. *Strategy.* New York: Praeger, 1954.

———. *Thoughts on War.* London: Faber and Faber, 1944.

———. *The War in Outline.* London: Faber and Faber, 1936.

———. *The Way to Win Wars: The Strategy of Indirect Approach.* London: Faber and Faber, 1929.

Linklater, Andro. *An Artist in Treason: The Extraordinary Double Life of General James Wilkinson.* New York: Walker, 2009.

Locher, James R., III. *Victory on the Potomac: The Goldwater-Nichols Act Unifies the Pentagon.* College Station: Texas A&M Univ. Press, 2004.

Lunde, Henrik O. *Hitler's Pre-Emptive War: The Battle for Norway, 1940.* Philadelphia, Pa.: Casemate, 2009.

Luttwak, Edward N. "Washington's Biggest Scandal." *Commentary,* May 1994, 29–33.

Lynn, John A. *Battle: A History of Combat and Culture.* Boulder, Colo.: Westview, 2003.

MacArthur, General of the Army Douglas. *Reminiscences.* New York: McGraw-Hill, 1964.

MacIsaac, David. *Strategic Bombing in World War Two: The Story of the United States Strategic Bombing Survey.* New York: Garland, 1976.

Machiavelli, Niccolo. *The Ruler.* London: The Bodley Head, 1954.

Maguire, A.M.E. *General von Clausewitz on War.* London: William Clowes and Sons, 1909.

Maier, Klaus A., et al., eds. *Germany and the Second World War.* Vol. 2, *Germany's Initial Conquests in Europe.* Oxford: Clarendon, 1991.

Manji, Kitajima. "The Imjin Waeran: Contrasting the First and the Second Invasions of Korea." In *The East Asian War, 1592–1598: International Relations, Violence, and Memory,* edited by James B. Lewis. New York: Routledge, 2015.

Mansfield, Edward D., and Jack L. Snyder. *Electing to Fight: Why Emerging Democracies Go to War.* Cambridge, Mass.: MIT Univ. Press, 2005.

Matloff, Maurice, and Edwin Snell. *Strategic Planning for Coalition Warfare, 1941–1942.* United States Army in World War II. Washington, D.C.: Office of the Chief of Military History, 1956.

Maurice, Major General Sir Frederic. *British Strategy: A Study of the Application of the Principles of War.* London: Constable, 1929.

McArthur, Charles W. *Operations Analysis in the U.S. Army Eighth Air Force in World War II.* Providence, R.I.: American Mathematical Society, 1990.

McFarland, Stephen L. *America's Pursuit of Precision Bombing, 1910–1945.* Washington, D.C.: Smithsonian, 1995.

McPeak, General Merrill A. *Roles and Missions.* Lake Oswego, Oreg.: Lost Wingman Press, 2017.

———. *Selected Works 1990–1994.* Maxwell AFB, Ala.: Air Univ. Press, 1995.

McPherson, James M. *Tried by War: Abraham Lincoln as Commander in Chief.* New York: Penguin, 2008.

Meilinger, Phillip S. "Between the Devil and the Deep Blue Sea: The Fleet Air Arm before World War II." *Royal United Services Institute Journal* 144 (October 1999): 73–78.

Mierzejewski, Alfred C. *The Collapse of the German War Economy, 1939–1945: Allied Air Power and the German National Railway.* Chapel Hill: Univ. of North Carolina Press, 1988.

Milward, Alan S. *War, Economy and Society, 1939–1945.* Berkeley: Univ. of California Press, 1977.

Miller, Donald L. *Masters of the Air: America's Bomber Boys Who Fought the Air War against Nazi Germany.* New York: Simon and Schuster, 2006.

Miller, Edward A., Jr. *Lincoln's Abolitionist General: The Biography of David Hunter.* Columbia: Univ. of South Carolina Press, 1997.

Millis, Walter. *Arms and Men: A Study of American Military History.* New York: Putnam, 1956.

Min'ung, Yi. "The Role of the Chosŏn Navy and Major Naval Battles during the Imjin Waeran." In *The East Asian War, 1592–1598: International Relations, Violence, and Memory,* edited by James B. Lewis. New York: Routledge, 2015.

Missall, John, and Mary Lou. *The Seminole Wars: America's Longest Indian Conflict.* Gainesville: Univ. Press of Florida, 2004.

Mitchell, Brigadier General William L. *Skyways.* Philadelphia, Pa.: J. B. Lippincott, 1930.

———. *Winged Defense: The Development and Possibilities of Modern Air Power, Economic and Military.* New York: Putnam's, 1925.

Moody, Walton S. *Building a Strategic Air Force.* Washington, D.C.: Air Force History and Museums Program, 1996.

Moon, Joshua. *Wellington's Two-Front War: The Peninsular Campaigns, at Home and Abroad, 1808–1814.* Norman: Univ. of Oklahoma Press, 2011.

Morris, John D. *Sword of the Border: Major General Jacob Jennings Brown.* Kent, Ohio: Kent State Univ. Press, 2000.

Morton, Louis. *The War in the Pacific: Strategy and Command, the First Two Years.* Washington, D.C.: Office of the Chief of Military History, 1962.

Mott, William H., and Jae Chang Kim. *The Philosophy of Chinese Military Culture: Shih vs. Li.* New York: Macmillan, 2006.

Mueller, John, and Karl Mueller. "Sanctions of Mass Destruction." *Foreign Affairs* 78 (May/June 1999): 43–53.

Mueller, Karl P., ed. *Precision and Purpose: Airpower in the Libyan Civil War.* Santa Monica, Calif.: RAND Corp., 2015.

Nielsen, Suzanne C., and Don M. Snider, eds. *American Civil-Military Relations: The Soldier and the State in a New Era.* Baltimore, Md.: Johns Hopkins Univ. Press, 2009.

Niestlé, Axel. *German U-Boat Losses during World War II.* Annapolis, Md.: Naval Institute Press, 1998.

Nolan, Dick. *Benjamin F. Butler: The Damndest Yankee.* San Rafael, Calif.: Presidio, 1991.

Olds, Robin, with Christina Olds and Ed Rasimus. *Fighter Pilot.* New York: St. Martin's, 2010.

Olsen, John Andreas, ed. *Air Commanders.* Washington, D.C.: Potomac Press, 2013.

———, ed. *Airpower Reborn: The Strategic Concepts of John Warden and John Boyd.* Annapolis, Md.: Naval Institute Press, 2015.

———. *John Warden and the Renaissance of American Air Power.* Washington, D.C.: Potomac Press, 2007.

Olson, Mancur, Jr. "The Economics of Target Selection for the Combined Bomber Offensive." *Royal United Services Institute Journal* 107 (November 1962): 308–14.

Oman, Charles. *A History of the Art of War in the Middle Ages.* 3 vols. London: Methuen, 1924.

Osinga, Frans P. B. "The Enemy as a Complex Adaptive System: John Boyd and Airpower in the Postmodern Era." In *Airpower Reborn: The Strategic Concepts of John Warden and John Boyd,* edited by John A. Olsen, 48–92. Annapolis, Md.: Naval Institute Press, 2015.

Otterbein, Keith F. *How Wars Began.* College Station: Texas A&M Univ. Press, 2004.

Overy, Richard. *The Battle.* London: Penguin, 2000.

———. *Interrogations: The Nazi Elite in Allied Hands, 1945.* New York: Penguin, 2001.

———. *Why the Allies Won.* London: Jonathan Cape, 1995.

Owen, Colonel Robert C., ed. *Deliberate Force: A Case Study in Effective Air Campaigning.* Maxwell AFB, Ala.: Air Univ. Press, 2000.

Palmer, Alan. *The Gardeners of Salonika: The Macedonian Campaign of 1915–1918.* London: Andre Deutsch, 1965.

Pape, Robert A. *Bombing to Win: Air Power and Coercion in War.* Ithaca, N.Y.: Cornell Univ. Press, 1996.

Paret, Peter. "The Function of History in Clausewitz's Understanding of War." *Journal of Military History* 82 (October 2018): 1049–66.

———, ed. *Makers of Modern Strategy: From Machiavelli to the Nuclear Age.* Princeton, N.J.: Princeton Univ. Press, 1986.

Parton, James. *"Air Force Spoken Here": General Ira Eaker and the Command of the Air.* Bethesda, Md.: Adler and Adler, 1986.

Perera, Guido. *Leaves from My Book of Life.* Vol. 2, *Washington and War Years.* Boston: Privately printed, 1975.

Perry, James M. *Touched with Fire: Five Presidents and the Civil War Battles that Made Them.* New York: PublicAffairs, 2003.

Peskin, Allan. *Winfield Scott and the Profession of Arms.* Kent, Ohio: Kent State Univ. Press, 2003.

Peters, Ralph. "In Praise of Attrition." *Parameters* 32 (summer 2004): 24–32.

Pfaff, William. "The Praetorian Guard." *National Interest* 62 (winter 2000/2001): 57–64.

Phillips, Jonathan. *The Fourth Crusade and the Sack of Constantinople.* New York: Viking, 2004.

Phillips, Thomas R., ed. *The Roots of Strategy.* Harrisburg, Pa.: Military Service Publishing, 1940.

Pickett, William B. *Eisenhower Decides to Run.* Chicago: Ivan R. Dee, 2000.

Pilcher, Major General T. D. *War According to Clausewitz.* London: Cassell, 1918.

Plaw, Avery, Matthew S. Fricker, and Carlos R. Colon. *The Drone Debate.* New York: Rowman and Littlefield, 2016.

Poole, Walter S. *The Joint Chiefs of Staff and National Policy.* Vol. 4, *1950–1952.* Washington, D.C.: Office of Joint History, 1979.

Porch, Douglas. *The Path to Victory: The Mediterranean Theater in World War II.* New York: Farrar, Straus, and Giroux, 2004.

Prados, John. *Combined Fleet Decoded: The Secret History of American Intelligence and the Japanese Navy in World War II.* New York: Random House, 1995.

Prior, Robin. *Gallipoli: The End of the Myth.* New Haven, Conn.: Yale Univ. Press, 2009.

Probert, Henry. *Bomber Harris: His Life and Times.* London: Greenhill, 2001.

Putney, Diane T. *Airpower Advantage: Planning the Gulf War Air Campaign, 1989–1991.* Washington, D.C.: Air Force History and Museums Program, 2004.

———. *ULTRA and the Army Air Forces in World War II.* Washington, D.C.: Office of Air Force History, 1987.

Rapoport, Anatol. *On War.* New York: Penguin, 1982.

Razoux, Pierre. *The Iran-Iraq War.* Cambridge, Mass.: Belknap, 2015.

Reardon, Carol. *With a Sword in One Hand and Jomini in the Other: The Problem of Military Thought in the Civil War North.* Chapel Hill: Univ. of North Carolina Press, 2012.

Reider, Colonel Bruce J. "Strategic Realignment: Ends, Ways, and Means in Iraq." *Parameters* 35 (winter 2007/2008): 46–57.

Richards, Denis. *The Fight at Odds: The Royal Air Force, 1939–1945.* 3 vols. London: HMSO, 1974.

Rhodes, P. J. *Alcibiades.* London: Pen and Sword, 2011.

Ricks, Thomas E. *Fiasco: The American Military Adventure in Iraq.* New York: Penguin, 2006.

———. *The Gamble: General David Petraeus and the American Military Adventure in Iraq, 2006–2008.* New York: Penguin, 2009.

Ritter, Gerhard. *The Schlieffen Plan.* New York: Praeger, 1958.

Roberts, David. *A Newer World: Kit Carson, John C. Frémont, and the Claiming of the American West.* New York: Simon and Schuster, 2000.

Rolf, David. *The Bloody Road to Tunis.* Harrisburg, Pa.: Stackpole, 2001.

Rollins, John, and Clay Wilson. "Terrorist Capabilities for Cyberattack: Overview and Policy Issues." Congressional Research Service report. Washington, D.C.: Congressional Research Service, January 22, 2007.

Rosen, Stephen Peter. *War and Human Nature.* Princeton, N.J.: Princeton Univ. Press, 2005.

———. *Winning the Next War: Innovation and the Modern Military.* Ithaca, N.Y.: Cornell Univ. Press, 1991.

Ross, Steven T. *American War Plans, 1941–1945.* London: Frank Cass, 1997.

———. *European Diplomatic History, 1789–1815: France against Europe.* Malabar, Fla. Krieger, 1981.

Rostow, Walt W. *Pre-Invasion Bombing Strategy.* Austin: Univ. of Texas Press, 1981.

Rummel, R. J. *Death by Government: Genocide and Mass Murder in the Twentieth Century.* New Brunswick, N.J.: Transaction, 1994.

Rumpf, Hans. *The Bombing of Germany.* New York: Holt, Rinehart and Winston, 1963.

Russett, Bruce M. *Grasping the Democratic Peace: Principles for a Post–Cold War World.* Princeton, N.J.: Princeton Univ. Press, 1993.

Sainsbury, Keith. *The North African Landings, 1942: A Strategic Decision.* Newark: Univ. of Delaware Press, 1976.

Schlight, John. *The War in South Vietnam: The Years of the Offensive, 1965–1968.* The United States Air Force in Southeast Asia. Washington, D.C.: Office of Air Force History, 1988.

Schmitt, Martin F., ed. *General George Crook: His Autobiography.* Norman: Univ. of Oklahoma Press, 1960.

Schnabel, James F. *Policy and Direction: The First Year.* United States Army in the Korean War. Washington, D.C.: Office of the Chief of Military History, 1972.

Schwab, Orrin. *A Clash of Cultures: Civil-Military Relations during the Vietnam War.* Westport, Conn.: Praeger, 2006.

Schwarzkopf, Norman H., with Peter Petre. *It Doesn't Take a Hero.* New York: Bantam, 1992.

Scullard, H. H. *Scipio Africanus: Soldier and Politician.* Ithaca, N.Y.: Cornell Univ. Press, 1970.

Sears, Stephen W., ed. *The Civil War Papers of George B. McClellan.* New York: Ticknor and Fields, 1989.

Sewall, Sarah B. *Chasing Success: Air Force Efforts to Reduce Civilian Harm.* Maxwell AFB, Ala.: Air Univ. Press, 2016.

Sefton, James E. *The United States Army and Reconstruction, 1865–1877.* Baton Rouge: Louisiana State Univ. Press, 1967.

Ségur, Count Philippe-Paul de. *Napoleon's Russian Campaign.* Boston: Houghton Mifflin, 1958.

Shy, John. *A People Numerous and Armed.* New York: Oxford Univ. Press, 1976.

Skelton, William B. *An American Profession of Arms: The Army Officer Corps, 1784–1861.* Lawrence: Univ. Press of Kansas, 1992.

Slessor, ACM John. *The Central Blue: Recollections and Reflections.* London: Cassell, 1956.

Spanier, John W. *The Truman-MacArthur Controversy and the Korean War.* Cambridge, Mass.: Belknap, 1959.

Speer, Albert. *Inside the Third Reich.* New York: Macmillan, 1970.

Stern, Jessica, and J. M. Berger. *ISIS: The State of Terror.* New York: Ecco, 2015.

Stevenson, Charles A. *Warriors and Politicians: US Civil-Military Relations under Stress.* London: Routledge, 2017.

Strauss, Barry. *The Battle of Salamis.* New York: Simon and Schuster, 2004.

Stubbington, Wing Commander John. *Kept in the Dark: The Denial to Bomber Command of Vital ULTRA and Other Intelligence Information during World War II.* Barnsley, UK: Pen and Sword, 2010.

Sullivan, General Gordon R., and Colonel James M. Dubik. "Envisioning Future War." Pamphlet. Fort Leavenworth, Kans.: US Army Command and General Staff College, 1995.

———. "War in the Information Age." Pamphlet. Carlisle Barracks, Pa.: US Army War College, Strategic Studies Institute, 1994.

Sumida, Jon Tetsuro. *Decoding Clausewitz: A New Approach to* On War. Lawrence: Univ. Press of Kansas, 2008.

Summers, Colonel Harry G., Jr. *On Strategy: A Critical Analysis of the Vietnam War.* Novato, Calif.: Presidio, 1982.

Sun Tzu. *The Art of War.* Translated by Samuel B. Griffith. London: Oxford Univ. Press, 1963.

Tedder, Lord [Arthur]. *With Prejudice.* Boston: Houghton Mifflin, 1966.

Terraine, John. *A Time for Courage: The Royal Air Force in the European War, 1939–1945.* New York: Macmillan, 1985.

Thomas, Evan, and John Barry. "Anatomy of a Revolt." *Newsweek,* April 24, 2006, 28–32.

Thompson, Wayne. *To Hanoi and Back: The USAF and North Vietnam, 1966–1973.* Washington, D.C.: Air Force History and Museums Program, 2000.

Tibbets, Paul W. *Return of the Enola Gay.* Columbus, Ohio: Mid Coast Marketing, 1998.

Till, Geoffrey. *Air Power and the Royal Navy, 1914–1945.* London: Jane's, 1979.

Thucydides. *The Landmark Thucydides: A Comprehensive Guide to the Peloponnesian War.* Edited by Robert B. Strassler. New York: Free Press, 1996.

Tocqueville, Alexis de. *Democracy in America.* 2 vols. Everyman's Library ed. New York: Knopf, 1994.

Tirpak, John A. "Legacy of the Air Blockade." *Air Force Magazine,* February 2003, 46–56.

Tooze, Adam. *The Wages of Destruction: The Making and Breaking of the Nazi Economy.* New York: Viking, 2007.

Trudeau, Noah Andre. *Gettysburg: A Testing of Courage.* New York: HarperCollins, 2002.

Truman, Harry S. *Memoirs.* Vol. 2, *Years of Trial and Hope, 1946–1952.* New York: Doubleday, 1956.

Tunner, Lieutenant General William H. *Over the Hump.* New York: Duell, Sloan, 1964.

Turnbull, Stephen. *Samurai Invasion: Japan's Korean War, 1592–1598.* London: Cassell, 2002.

UNICEF. "Child and Maternal Mortality Survey, 1999, Preliminary Report." New York: UNICEF, July 1999.

US Army Air Forces. *Mission Accomplished: Interrogations of Japanese Industrial, Military, and Civil Leaders of World War II.* Washington, D.C.: GPO, 1946.

US Army Strategic Air Forces. "ULTRA: History of US Strategic Air Force Europe vs. German Air Force." Washington, D.C., Report SRH-013, June 1945.

US State Department. *1964–1968.* Vol. 1, *Vietnam, 1964.* Foreign Relations of the United States. Washington, D.C.: GPO, 1992.

———. *The Conference at Quebec, 1944.* Foreign Relations of the United States. Washington, D.C.: GPO, 1972.

———. *The Conferences at Washington, 1941–1942, and Casablanca, 1943.* Foreign Relations of the United States. Washington, D.C.: GPO, 1968.

———. *The Conferences at Washington and Quebec, 1943.* Foreign Relations of the United States. Washington, D.C.: GPO, 1970.

Utley, Robert M. *The Commanders: Civil War Generals Who Shaped the American West.* Norman: Univ. of Oklahoma Press, 2018.

———. *Frontier Regulars: The United States Army and the Indian, 1866–1890.* New York: Macmillan, 1973.

Vagts, Alfred. *A History of Militarism, Civilian and Military,* rev. ed. London: Hollis and Carter, 1959.

Van Creveld, Martin. *The Culture of War.* New York: Ballantine, 2008.

———. *The Transformation of War.* New York: Free Press, 1991.

van der Vat, Dan. *The Dardanelles Disaster: Winston Churchill's Greatest Failure.* London: Duckworth Overlook, 2009.

Van Staaveren, Jacob. *Gradual Failure: The Air War over North Vietnam, 1965–1966.* Washington, D.C.: Air Force History and Museums Program, 2002.

Vick, Alan, et al. *Air Power in the New Counterinsurgency Era.* Santa Monica, Calif.: RAND Corp., 2006.

Wakelam, Randall T. *The Science of Bombing: Operational Research in RAF Bomber Command.* Toronto: Univ. of Toronto Press, 2009.

Warner, Ezra J. *Generals in Blue.* Baton Rouge: Louisiana State Univ. Press, 1964.

———. *Generals in Gray.* Baton Rouge: Louisiana State Univ. Press, 1959.

Wason, David. *Battlefield Detectives: Unearthing New Evidence on the World's Most Famous Battlefields.* London: Carlton, 2014.

Waterford, Van. *Prisoners of the Japanese in World War II.* Jefferson, N.C.: McFarland, 1994.

Watson, Samuel J. *Jackson's Sword: The Army Officer Corps on the American Frontier, 1810–1821.* Lawrence: Univ. Press of Kansas, 2012.

Waugh, John C. *Reelecting Lincoln: The Battle for the 1864 Presidency.* New York: Crown, 1997.

Webster, Charles, and Noble Frankland. *The Strategic Air Offensive against Germany, 1939–1945.* 4 vols. London: HMSO, 1961.

Weekman, David E. "Sanctions: The Invisible Hand of Statecraft." *Strategic Review* 26 (winter 1998): 39–45.

Weigley, Russell F. *The Age of Battles: The Quest for Decisive Warfare from Breitenfeld to Waterloo.* Bloomington: Indiana Univ. Press, 1991.

———. *The American Way of War: A History of United States Military Strategy and Policy.* New York: Macmillan, 1973.

———. *History of the United States Army.* New York: Macmillan, 1967.

Weinberg, Gerhard L. *A World at Arms: A Global History of World War II.* Cambridge, Mass.: Cambridge Univ. Press, 1994.

Werrell, Kenneth. *Blankets of Fire: U.S. Bombers over Japan during World War II.* Washington, D.C.: Smithsonian, 1996.

Westmoreland, General William C. *A Soldier Reports.* Garden City, N.Y: Doubleday, 1976.

Williams, T. Harry. *P.G.T. Beauregard: Napoleon in Gray.* Baton Rouge: Louisiana State Univ. Press, 1954.

Wilson, Colin, ed. *The Book of Time.* North Pomfret, Vt.: Westbridge, 1980.

Woodward, David R. *Trial by Friendship: Anglo-American Relations, 1917–1918.* Lexington: Univ. Press of Kentucky, 1993.

Worden, Colonel Mike. *Rise of the Fighter Generals: The Problem of Air Force Leadership, 1945–1982.* Maxwell AFB, Ala.: Air Univ. Press, 1998.

Wrangham, Richard, and Dale Peterson. *Demonic Males: Apes and the Origins of Human Violence.* Boston: Houghton Mifflin, 1996.

Wright, Donald P., and Colonel Timothy R. Reese. *On Point II: Transition to the New Campaign: The United States Army in Operation IRAQI FREEDOM, May 2003–January 2005.* Fort Leavenworth, Kans.: Combat Studies Institute, 2008.

Wright, Quincy. *A Study of War,* 2 vols. Chicago: Univ. of Chicago Press, 1942.

Yi Sun-sin, Admiral. *Nanjung Ilgi: War Diary of Admiral Yi Sun-sin.* Translated by Ha Tae-hung. Seoul: Yonsei Univ. Press, 1977.

Zuber, Terence. *Inventing the Schlieffen Plan: German War Planning, 1871–1914.* New York: Oxford Univ. Press, 2002.

Zuckerman, Solly. *From Apes to Warlords.* New York: Harper and Row, 1978.

US Strategic Bombing Survey Reports

European Theater

"Summary Report (European War)." Report 1, September 1945.

"Over-All Report." Report 2, September 1945.

"Statistical Appendix to Over-All Report." Report 2A, February 1947.

"The Effects of Strategic Bombing on the German War Economy." Report 3, October 1945.
"Aircraft Division Industry Report." Report 4, January 1947.
"Civilian Defense Division, Final Report." Report 40, January 1947.
"The German Anti-Friction Bearings Industry." Report 53, January 1947.
"The Defeat of the German Air Force." Report 59, January 1947.
"Bombing Accuracy, USAAF Heavy and Medium Bombers in the ETO." Report 63, January 1947.
"The Effects of Strategic Bombing on German Morale." 2 vols. Report 64B, May 1947.
"Oil Division Final Report." Report 109, January 1947.
"German Electric Utilities Industry Report." Report 205, January 1947.

Pacific Theater

"Summary Report (Pacific War)." Report 1, July 1946.
"Japan's Struggle to End the War." Report 2, July 1946.
"The Effects of Atomic Bombs on Hiroshima and Nagasaki." Report 3, June 1946.
"The Effects of Bombing on Health and Medical Services in Japan." Report 12, June 1947.
"The Effects of Strategic Bombing on Japanese Morale." Report 14, June 1947.
"The Japanese Aircraft Industry." Report 15, May 1947.
"Coals and Metals in Japan's War Economy." Report 36, April 1947.
"The Japanese Wartime Standard of Living and Utilization of Manpower." Report 42, January 1947.
"Japanese Merchant Shipping." Report 48, January 1947.
"The Effects of Strategic Bombing on Japan's War Economy." Report 53, December 1946.
"The War against Japanese Transportation, 1941–45." Report 54, May 1947.
"Effects of Air Attack on Japanese Urban Economy: Summary Report." Report 55, March 1947.
"Interrogations of Japanese Officials." 2 vols. Report 72, July 1946.
"The Campaigns of the Pacific War." Report 73, July 1946.
"Effects of Incendiary Bomb Attacks on Japan." Report 90, April 1947.

Index

Abizaid, John P., 231n62
Abu Ghraib prison (Iraq), 21, 63
Adams, John, 143
Adams, John Quincy, 144, 220
Afghanistan, 3, 23–24, 28, 31–32, 37–38, 40, 46–48, 51, 60, 62, 85–86, 139, 157, 217–20, 222–23
Agincourt (1415), 127
Aideed, Mohamed Farrah, 216
Air Corps Tactical School (ACTS), 105, 169, 171, 180, 187
aircraft (British): Gladiator, 117; Hurricane, 117; Spitfire, 107, 117; Lancaster, 198
aircraft (US): B-17, 197–98; B-24, 106–7, 198; B-29, 99–100, 103, 163–64, 198–206; P-38, 187; P-47, 107, 187; P-51, 187; F-4, 109–10; F-105, 109–10; F-117, 183; EP-3, 26; Predator, 46; Reaper, 46
air interdiction, 55, 123, 182, 213
airlift, 55, 61–62, 115, 117, 121, 137, 237n20
air superiority, 54–56, 79–80, 86, 106, 109, 116, 119–20, 123, 139, 177–78, 195, 204, 211–13
Alcibiades, 68–70, 83, 239n7
Alexander, Harold, 161–62
Alexander the Great, 91, 111
al Qaeda, 25, 40, 46, 59, 215–17
Arbela (331 BC), 91
Armitage, Richard L., 220, 223
Arnold, Henry "Hap," 54, 163–65, 168–69, 187–88, 199, 210
Arthur, Chester, 154
Auchinleck, Claude, 123

Bacon, Francis, 210
Ball, George, 188
Banks, Nathaniel P., 146–47, 152
Bassford, Christopher, 31
Beauregard, P.G.T., 145
Benton, Thomas Hart, 144–45
blockade/sanctions, 43–44, 73, 115, 135, 201–2, 205
Blücher, Gebhard von, 57
Blumenson, Martin, 21
Bomber Command (RAF), 163, 168–69, 176, 179–80, 186, 198
Boyd, John, 103, 183–84
Boyle, Jeremiah, 152
Bradley, Omar, 188
Bremer, L. Paul, 218
Britain, Battle of (1940), 98–99
British Bombing Survey Unit, 197–98
British Ministry of Economic Warfare (MEW), 172–73

Brook, Alan, 120
Brown, Jacob J., 144
Buckner, Simon Bolivar, 149
Burbridge, Stephen, 152
Bureau of Refugees, Freedmen, and Abandoned Lands, 153
Burnside, Ambrose E., 150, 152
Bush, George W., 24, 33, 39–40, 157, 220, 222
Butler, Benjamin, 146, 157
Butt Report, 168
Byrd, Richard, 188

Calhoun, John C., 144
Carden, Sackview, 75–79
Carlton, Eric, 26
Casablanca Directive, 174, 177
Cebrowski, Arthur, 60
center of gravity, 22, 64, 135, 230n46
Chamberlain, Joshua Lawrence, 149
Charles Martel, 92–93
Cheney, Richard, 215
China, 20, 26–27, 37, 39, 44–45, 55, 61, 131, 163, 181, 198–99, 205, 212–14, 224
Chua, Amy, 36–37
Churchill, Winston, 21, 74–80, 115, 122–23, 130, 163, 174, 197, 242n79
Clark, Wesley, 21, 156, 184, 211, 231n56, 250n79
Clausewitz, Carl von, 1–3, 6, 11–28, 30–34, 38–40, 41–44, 52–53, 102, 130–31, 134, 208–10
Clausewitz, Marie von, 13
Clay, Henry, 144
Clay, Lucius D., 158, 188
close air support (CAS), 55, 81, 123, 213
collateral damage, 21, 47–48, 50, 63, 85, 135
command and control, 24, 51, 60, 130, 162
Committee of Operations Analysts (COA), 168–69, 172–73, 187
Constantinople (1204), 93–94
Corbett, Julian, 14, 53
Cork, Admiral Lord, 116–17, 246n10
Cornwallis, Charles, 97
Cox, Sebastian, 197–98
Crete (1941), 121, 210
Cunningham, Andrew, 121
cyberwar, 44–47, 55, 60–61

D'Olier, Franklin, 188–89
Davis, Jefferson, 144–45, 156
Delbrück, Hans, 19
Dewey, George, 155
Dix, John, 146, 152
Doolittle, Jimmy, 200
Douhet, Giulio, 170
Dowding, Hugh, 99

Eaker, Ira, 168–69, 176
Earle, Edward Meade, 188
Echevarria, Antulio, 13
Eighth Air Force, 112, 163, 168–70, 178, 180–81, 187, 189, 195–96, 200, 256n10
Eisenhower, Dwight D., 19, 78–80, 83, 122–23, 130–31, 156, 161–63, 166, 174–75, 211
Enemy Objectives Unit (EOU), 172–73, 176, 180

Fairchild, Muir, 187
Farragut, David, 151
Feaver, Peter , 138
Fifteenth Air Force, 163, 195
Fillmore, Millard, 141
First Silesian War of 1740, 17
Fisher, "Jackie," 74–75, 77, 240n43
Fiske, Bradley, 155
Foch, Ferdinand, 19–20, 53
Fossey, Dian, 34
Frederick Wilhelm, 13, 54
Frederick the Great (Frederick II of Prussia), 14, 17, 111

Frémont, John C., 145, 150
Freyberg, Bernard, 121
Fuller, J.F.C., 19, 53, 160, 210
Fumimaro Konoye, Prince, 206

Gaddafi, Muammar, 36, 222
Galbraith, John Kenneth, 188
Galland, Adolf, 177
Gallipoli (1915), 74–77, 81–85, 210, 242n79
Garfield, James, 148–49, 211
Garlasco, Marc, 47
Gat, Azar, 38, 229n9
Gee, Oboe, H2X, 168, 195
George III, 142
Germany, 4–6, 33, 78–81, 106–8, 111, 114, 122–23, 128–29, 131, 165–66, 170, 172–80, 186–98, 200, 204, 206, 209, 211, 220
Ghormley, Robert, 188
Göering, Hermann, 99, 114, 260n44
Goodall, Jane, 34
Gordon, John B., 149, 253n31
Gorrell, Edgar S., 170
Grant, Ulysses "U. S.," 88, 129–30, 147, 149–54, 211, 254n50
Greene, Nathaniel, 97
Gylippus, 69–70

Haditha massacre (Iraq), 21
Haig, Alexander, 156, 211
Hamas, 40
Hamilton, Ian, 74–77
Hampton, Wade, 150
Hancock, Winfield Scott, 149, 211
Hannibal, 87, 91–92, 111
Hansando (1592), 95–96
Hanson, Victor Davis, 41
Harris, Arthur, 163, 169, 174, 178, 261n56
Harrison, William Henry, 141, 144, 148
Harrison, Benjamin, 148, 152
Hayes, Rutherford B., 145, 148, 211
Hezbollah, 40
Hiroshima/Nagasaki (1945), 99–100, 103, 200, 206, 211
Hisatsune Sakomizu, 206
Hitler, Adolf, 33, 36, 98–99, 106, 115, 178, 206
Ho Chi Minh, 37
Hooker, Joseph, 150–51
Horner, Chuck, 58
Horton, Max, 161
Howard, Michael, 13, 17, 20–21, 122, 223–24
Howard, Oliver O., 153
Hunter, David, 150
Huntington, Samuel P., 128, 156
Hussein, Saddam, 24, 36, 43, 50, 112, 136, 214–15, 217–19

Iberian Campaign (1807-1814), 24, 34, 71–73, 81, 208, 210
indigenous ground troops, 2, 24, 219, 225, 231n61
insurgency, 20, 24–25, 34, 71, 83, 95–96, 208, 213, 220, 224, 233n18
Iran, 44–45, 50, 55, 59–60, 135, 218, 220
Iraq, 3, 21, 23–24, 28, 31–33, 35–37, 39–40, 43–44, 47–50, 57–58, 60, 62, 85–86, 89, 112, 136, 139, 157, 183–84, 217–20, 222–23
Islamic State of Iraq and Syria (ISIS), 25, 40, 48, 59, 64, 219–20, 222–23, 225
Ismay, Hastings, 118

Jackson, Andrew, 143–44, 211
Japan, 5–6, 27, 29, 33, 36, 39, 99–100, 122, 129, 134, 159–66, 188–90, 198–206, 211–12
Jefferson, Thomas, 143
Johnson, Leon, 106
Johnson, Lyndon, 20, 23, 31, 131–32, 213–14
Johnson, Andrew, 152–54, 156
Joint Strategic Target Planning Staff, 180

Joint warfare, 4–5, 58–59, 114, 117–23, 135, 140, 160, 164, 210, 219
Jomini, Antoine-Henri, 19, 52

Kant, Immanuel, 233n21
Kantarō Suzuki, 206
Keegan, John, 19, 25–26, 38
Keeley, Lawrence, 38
Kennedy, Paul, 123
Kenney, George C., 156, 164, 257n18
Khafji, Iraq, 50
Ki-moon, Ban, 222
Kindleberger, Charles, 176
King, Ernest, 159, 162, 164
Kitchener, Horatio, 75–76
Kluck, Alexander von, 98
Kohn, Richard H., 142
Korean War, 1, 20, 23, 27, 32, 54, 85, 105, 111, 131, 134, 157, 181–82, 212–13
Kosovo, 23, 47, 51, 86, 136, 216, 219
Krepinevich, Andrew, 23

Lamachus, 68–70
leadership, 22, 72, 76, 80, 83, 118, 183
LeBlanc, Steven, 38
Lee, Robert E., 88, 104, 111, 130, 153, 245n9
LeMay, Curtis E., 108, 156, 199–200, 202
Lewis, Adrian, 42
Lewis, Meriwether, 143
Lewis, Angeline, 222
Libya, 24, 51, 62, 78, 81, 85–86, 106, 139, 222–25
Liddell Hart, Basil H., 14, 19–20, 42, 59, 77, 85, 210
Lieber, Francis, 129
Lincoln, Abraham, 145–47, 149–54
Logan, John B., 146–47, 152
Longstreet, James, 104, 245n9
Ludendorff, Erich, 19–20, 229n29
Luftwaffe, 81, 99, 106–07, 114–23, 173, 177–79, 187, 191, 195
Lynn, John, 41

MacArthur, Douglas, 5, 19, 105, 122, 131, 134, 156–58, 159–62, 164–65, 212
Machiavelli, Niccolo, 24, 52
Mackesy, P. J., 116–18, 123
Maginot Line, 114, 209
Mahan, Alfred Thayer, 53, 119
Marne (1914), 97–98, 104
Marshall, George, 78
Masakuzu Kawabe, 201
McCain, John, 156
McClellan, George B., 149, 151–52, 211, 253n37
McClernand, John, 146–47
McKinley, William, 32, 149, 154–55
McNamee, Frank, 188
measures of effectiveness, 174, 177, 182–83
Miles, Nelson A., 155, 254n57
military doctrine, 1, 5, 7, 23, 42, 54, 118, 120, 134, 160, 167–71, 183, 186–87, 200, 219
military intelligence, 6, 14, 29, 50, 59–60, 73, 77, 80, 83, 86, 120, 136, 178–81, 185, 200, 215, 219, 225
Milosovic, Slobodan, 216
Mitchell, "Billy," 54, 134, 170, 210
Moltke, Helmuth von, 104
Montgomery, Bernard, 53, 78, 80, 165
Moore, John, 71
Mountbatten, Louis, 163
Mussolini, Benito, 33, 36

Napoleon, 1, 4, 11–12, 14, 21, 24–25, 32, 54, 57, 71–73, 82, 88, 102–04, 111, 120, 208–12
National Guard/Reserves/Militia, 127–28, 137, 145
Netcentricity, 60–61, 136
Nicias, 68–70, 83
Nimitz, Chester, 5, 122, 159 162–65
Nitze, Paul, 188, 262n9

Northern Alliance (in Afghanistan), 38, 51, 217
Norwegian Campaign (1940), 4, 114–23, 210

Obama, Barack, 138, 221, 223
Olds, Robin, 109–10, 246n23
Operations: ANACONDA, 21; BOLO, 109; CHROMITE, 105; DESERT STORM, 22–23, 46–47, 50–51, 62, 112, 136, 214–16, 219; LINEBACKER II, 182; MARKET GARDEN, 166; NORTHERN WATCH (over Iraq), 62, 215; OVERLORD, 163, 174, 177; ROLLING THUNDER, 109, 215; SATURATE, 182; SEA LION, 98; SOUTHERN WATCH (over Iraq), 62, 215; STRANGLE, 182; TORCH, 78–81, 162, 164, 187
Operations Research (OR), 6, 167–70, 174, 178
Osami Nagano, 206
Otterbein, Keith, 38

Palmer, John McCauley, 147–49
Pape, Robert, 184
Paret, Peter, 13, 17, 19
Patton, George, 80, 111
Peloponnesian War, 67–70, 82, 84
Pershing, John, 130, 134
Pfaff, William, 157
Philip II, 94–95, 242n10
Phillips, Tom, 122
Pierce, Franklin, 141
Pillow, Gideon J., 144
Ploesti, 106–07, 111
Polk, James K., 144
Pope, John A., 150–51, 154
precision guided munitions (PGMs), 24, 50–51, 54, 62–63, 112, 135–36, 185, 188, 236nn5–6, 238nn37–38
Priest, Dana, 157
Punic Wars, 17, 91–92, 103

Reconstruction, 152–54, 157–58
Ricks, Thomas, 36, 219
Ridgway, Matthew, 131
Rommel, Erwin, 78, 111, 123
Roosevelt, Franklin, 6, 78–80, 160, 174
Roosevelt, Theodore, 155
Root, Elihu, 155
Rosecrans, William S., 150
Rosen, Stephen Peter, 35–36, 39
Rostow, Walt, 176
Royal Air Force (RAF), 99, 116–20, 122, 163, 167, 170–71, 187–89, 197–98
Royal Navy, 14, 73, 77, 82–84, 115, 118, 120–22, 162–63, 186
Rumsfeld, Donald, 57, 157
Russell, Robert, 188
Russia/Soviet Union, 34, 44, 51, 55–57, 61, 72, 74, 76, 78–79, 82, 98, 103–04, 161, 166, 180–81, 189, 191, 200, 206, 208, 224, 236n32

Salamis/Platea (480–79 BC), 90
Schlieffen, Alfred von 97–98, 104, 111, 244n20
Schofield, John M., 154, 254n50
Schurz, Carl, 147, 149, 152
Schwarzkopf, Norman, 50, 58, 214–15
Schweinfurt/Regensburg, 107–08, 111, 174, 187, 196
Scott, Winfield, 133, 141, 144, 150, 156, 158, 211
Sea control, 14, 55, 70, 73, 77, 80, 84–86, 120, 210
Serbia, 21, 47, 216
Sewall, Sarah B., 47
Sheridan, Philip, 154
Sherman, William T., 151–52, 155, 255n72
Shinseki, Eric, 24

ships, British: HMS *Ark Royal,* 117; HMS *Formidable,* 121; HMS *Glorious,* 117; HMS *Prince of Wales,* 122; HMS *Repulse,* 122; HMS *Rodney,* 120; HMS *Suffolk,* 116
Sickles, Daniel E., 148, 252n29
Slocum, Henry W., 154
Smith, W. J., 180–81
Soemu Toyoda, 206
Spaatz, Carl, 80, 163–64, 169, 174, 187–88
Spanish Armada (1588), 94–95
special operations forces (SOF), 2, 24, 51, 217, 219–20, 225, 231n61
Speer, Albert, 178
Stilwell, Joseph, 163, 257n17
Stockdale, James, 156
Strategic Air Command (SAC), 180–81
strategic bombing, 6, 105, 135, 164–65, 167–68, 171–81, 183, 186–206, 209–11, 213
Stueben, William von, 129
Stuxnet, 44, 48
Sullivan, Gordon, 184
Summers, Harry, 20
Sun Tzu, 51, 102, 160
Syria, 24, 51, 60, 62, 85, 139, 219–20, 223

Taliban, 25, 38, 40, 59, 217
Taylor, Zachary, 141, 144, 211
Tedder, Arthur, 80, 175–77, 184, 198
Terraine, John, 116
Terry, Alfred H., 154, 254n51
Themistocles, 90
Thomas, George H., 154
Thucydides, 68, 239n3
Tocqueville, Alexis de, 127–28, 136, 138
Tours (732), 92–93
Trenchard, Hugh, 112, 210
Truman, Harry S, 100, 131, 157, 212, 220–21
Trump, Donald, 138, 157, 212, 223
Twentieth Air Force, 163–64, 200

Ultra intelligence/Enigma, 120, 176–77, 179–80, 261n56
unity of command, 4–5, 56–57, 61, 116, 118, 159–66
US Strategic Bombing Survey (USSBS), 6, 186–207, 211

Vagts, Alfred, 128
Van Creveld, Martin, 19, 42
Van Voorhis, Daniel, 160
Viet Cong, 25, 133, 183
Vietnam War, 2, 5, 20, 23, 27, 29, 31, 37–40, 46, 50, 55, 59, 62–63, 85, 89, 109–10, 112–13, 131–32, 135, 137, 181–83, 213–15, 219

Wallace, Lew, 148
Warden, John, 183–84
Washington, George, 96–97, 129, 137, 141, 143–44, 211
Weigley, Russell, 19, 89
Wellesley, Arthur, 57, 71–73, 83–84, 111
Westmoreland, William, 19–20, 23, 132
Wiart, Carton de, 116
Wilkinson, James, 255n71
Williams, Robert, 108
Wilson, Woodrow, 129, 155
Wood, Leonard, 155–56
Wright, Theodore, 188

XX Bomber Command, 163–64, 199
XXI Bomber Command, 163–64, 199

Yorktown (1781), 96–97

Zama (205 BC), 91–92
Zuckerman, Solly, 175–76, 198